Constitutional Civil Liberties

C. Herman Pritchett

University of California
Santa Barbara

470310

Prentice-Hall, Inc., Englewood Cliffs, New Jersey 07632

Library of Congress Cataloging in Publication Data

Pritchett, C. Herman (Charles Herman). (date)
  Constitutional civil liberties.

  Includes index.
  1. Civil rights—United States. I. Title.
KF4749.P74 1984   342.73′085   83-15940
ISBN 0-13-167858-2   347.30285

Editorial/production supervision
  and interior design: Dee Amir Josephson
Cover design: Wanda Lubelska
Manufacturing buyer: Ron Chapman

Printed in the United States of America

10 9 8 7 6 5 4 3 2 1

ISBN 0-13-167858-2

Prentice-Hall International, Inc., *London*
Prentice-Hall of Australia Pty. Limited, *Sydney*
Editora Prentice-Hall do Brasil, Ltda., *Rio de Janeiro*
Prentice-Hall Canada Inc., *Toronto*
Prentice-Hall of India Private Limited, *New Delhi*
Prentice-Hall of Japan, Inc., *Tokyo*
Prentice-Hall of Southeast Asia Pte. Ltd., *Singapore*
Whitehall Books Limited, *Wellington, New Zealand*

Contents

Preface

When the delegates to the Constitutional Convention concluded their summer's labors on September 17, 1787, the document they had drafted did not include a Bill of Rights. The reason for this omission has never been completely understood. Several explanations were given. Some thought a bill of rights was not necessary. After all, the new national government created by the Constitution was a government of delegated powers, which meant that it could exercise no power not granted by the Constitution. Because that document gave the government no authority to infringe on people's liberties, it could not be done and there was no problem. Besides, there were some protective provisions in the body of the Constitution, such as the right to jury trial.

But it soon became evident that the framers had made a mistake. In the state ratifying conventions, the absence of a Bill of Rights was a major concern, and several states threatened to withhold ratification unless a bill of rights was added. The First Congress promptly assumed this responsibility, under the leadership of James Madison, and ten amendments were ratified in 1791, which soon became recognized as a major Bill of Rights. Along with certain other provisions in the original Constitution, and as supplemented by later amendments, particularly the due process and equal protection clauses of the Fourteenth Amendment, the American Constitution provides a remarkable statement of fundamental libertarian principles.

Although many factors determine whether a regime will live up to its principles, a major responsibility in the United States has fallen on the

Supreme Court, as the ultimate interpreter of the constitutional language. The purpose of this book is to present the record of the Supreme Court's dealings with the civil liberties provisions of the Constitution. Two introductory chapters explain the various provisions bearing on civil liberties, and analyze the theoretical devices the Court has develped to guide its interpretation of this language. There follows a group of five chapters dealing with the four great freedoms of the First Amendment—speech, press, assembly and association, and religion. Two specialized speech and press issues, obscenity and libel, have distinctive problems entitling them to a separate chapter.

From this concentration on the First Amendment, Chapters 8 and 9 move on to the guarantees of due process of law in the Fifth and the Fourteenth Amendments. Due process is treated first in its guise as a general obligation for all governmental action, and then in the form of the quite specific restraints on criminal procedure found in the Fourth through the Eighth Amendments. The length of Chapter 9 testifies to the constantly escalating responsibility of the Supreme Court in setting and enforcing standards of due procedure in the conduct of criminal trials by federal and state courts.

Chapters 10, 11, and 12 deal with separate yet closely related constitutional protections. The equal protection clause of the Fourteenth Amendment, which for almost a century after its adoption in 1868 did little more than protect corporations from taxation, came alive in 1954 with the Supreme Court decision in *Brown v. Board of Education,* declaring racial segregation in the public schools unconstitutional. For thirty years since that ruling the Court has been at the center of the revolution in racial attitudes, assuming unprecedented responsibility for maneuvering in areas of highly volatile public attitudes.

Chapter 11 moves on to what may seem a quite different issue, the protection of property rights by the due process concept. But it was in dealing with property that the Court developed one of its most innovative ideas, turning a protection on procedure into a guarantee of substantive rights. The resulting doctrine, termed substantive due process, was employed by the Court to strike down protective social and economic legislation in the first third of the twentieth century. Widely condemned by the liberal thought of that era, substantive due process as a bar to economic legislation disappeared with the coming of the Roosevelt New Deal.

But, as Chapter 12 explains, racial equal protection and a revived substantive due process provided the justification for an activist Court at mid-century to bring a variety of other inequalities and restrictions and long-established discriminations under judicial review. The resulting controversies over issues of privacy, abortion, sex and age discrimination, inequalities in educational support, and the like, continue to embroil the

Court, and with changes in membership, it has recently withdrawn from some of its advanced positions.

A final chapter concerns constitutional protections for the exercise of the franchise, a basic instrument for the protection of civil liberties and constitutional rights.

In dealing with the development of judicial definitions of civil liberties, this book necessarily attempts breadth of coverage rather than detailed analysis. Only the major judicial decisions are discussed in depth. For the remainder, the holdings are summarized, and citations to additional cases are provided for scholars who wish to go further into the constitutional issues raised. The most recent decisions of the Supreme Court have been favored, but with due recognition of earlier cases in which formative principles were established.

Although the author has generally endeavored to let the cases and the rulings speak for themselves, there has been no hesitation to criticize judicial reasoning. The author's position on constitutional interpretation is close to that of Justice Oliver Wendell Holmes, who wrote:

> The life of the law has not been logic; it has been experience. The felt necessities of the time, the prevalent moral and political theories, intuitions of public policy, avowed or unconscious, even the prejudices which judges share with their fellow-men, have had a good deal more to do than the syllogism in determining the rules by which men should be governed.

As an aid to understanding the judicial mode of operation and the relation of the courts to the other two branches, the reader of this volume would profit from prior knowledge about the American constitutional system such as is provided by the author's companion volume, *Constitutional Law of the Federal System*.

C. Herman Pritchett

1

Constitutional Basis for Protection of Civil Liberties

The one essential quality of constitutionalism, says Charles H. McIlwain, is as a legal limitation on government. Tom Paine wrote that a constitution is "to liberty, what a grammar is to language." Of course, a written constitution is not necessary to the protection of civil liberties, as English experience so well demonstrates. And the most elaborate safeguards in a written constitution will be meaningless unless the country to which they apply has a tradition that makes freedom a value of the highest order, and unless there are the resources, the opportunities, and the will to protect the principles of an open society from attack or frustration.

The American tradition of civil liberty is composed of many strands. Basic is the Christian-Hebraic belief in the worth of the individual, and acceptance of a moral obligation to shape the institutions of society so that they will promote the unfolding and the enrichment of human character. Centuries of struggle in England to achieve political institutions that would aim toward equality before the law and equalization of political power, resulting in such documents as Magna Carta (1215), the Petition of Right (1628), and the Bill of Rights (1689), were a living part of the early American tradition. The writings of the seventeenth- and eighteenth-century political philosophers, particularly John Locke, with their notions about natural law and the origins of government in a compact freely entered into by its citizens, were an essential element in American Revolutionary thought. The Declaration of Independence put these ideas about liberty and equality into classic phraseology.

1

All this was the heritage of the new nation, the "common law" of American liberties. If it had never been spelled out in a written constitution, it would nonetheless have continued to be effective in guiding the political decisions of the developing commonwealth.

THE BILL OF RIGHTS

As a matter of fact, the theory of the Constitutional Convention in 1787 was that the traditional liberties did not need much in the way of specific constitutional protection. The basic concept of limited national government was to be achieved by division of functions, separation of powers, and checks and balances, calculated to frustrate any drive toward dictatorial power. The drafters of the Constitution relied on the open spaces of the American continent to guarantee escape from confining situations. They saw the boundless resources of the country as insurance of economic opportunity. They believed the broad expanse of the Republic would encompass such a variety of interests as to make combination into a domineering majority difficult. Said Madison in No. 10 of *The Federalist:*

> The smaller the society, the fewer probably will be the distinct parties and interests composing it . . . and . . . the more easily will they concert and execute their plans of oppression. Extend the sphere, and you take in a greater variety of parties and interests; you make it less probable that a majority of the whole will have a common motive to invade the rights of other citizens.

Thus individual liberty did not need to be planned for. It would come automatically as the by-product of a system of economic opportunity, social mobility, and political responsibility.

Although this seems to have been the dominant theory of the Convention, it was departed from in a few instances. There are in fact several provisions that bear more or less closely on issues of civil liberty: protection against suspension of the writ of habeas corpus; prohibition of the passage of bills of attainder or ex post facto laws by either Congress or the state legislatures; the ban on religious tests as a qualification for public office; the requirement of trial by jury; the restrictions on conviction for treason; and the guarantee to citizens of each state of all privileges and immunities of citizens in the several states.

When the proposed Constitution went to the states for ratification, it quickly became apparent that the framers' view of civil liberties as needing no special protection in the new charter was not widely shared. In several of the important states, ratification was secured only on the understanding that amendments protecting individual rights would be immediately added to the Constitution. In his first inaugural address, Washington urged Congress to give careful attention to the demand for these amendments.

Madison took the lead in bringing together the various suggestions for amendments, which he presented to the House on June 8, 1789. His original idea was that they should be incorporated into the body of the Constitution at the places where they would appropriately belong. Most of the proposals had to do with limiting the power of Congress over citizens, and these were to follow the clause in Article I, section 9, prohibiting congressional adoption of bills of attainder and ex post facto laws. The new language to be inserted at this point would have prohibited Congress from abridging the freedom of religion, of speech, press, or assembly, and of bearing arms. There were also restrictions on quartering troops, prosecuting citizens for crime, and inflicting punishment. Changes aiming at a fuller guarantee to citizens of a fair trial by a jury in their own district and the benefits of the common law were to be worked into the jury trial provision of Article III.

When the House took up consideration of the amendments, Roger Sherman of Connecticut objected to the insertion of new material into, and the deletion of superseded material from, the original Constitution; and he was eventually able to convince the House that the amendments should be appended to the Constitution, each complete, independent, and understandable in itself. The House proposals went to the Senate on August 24. Twelve amendments were approved by the Senate; and after concurrence by the House, they were sent to the states on September 25, 1789.

Two of these proposed amendments ultimately failed of ratification. The first had to do with the ratio between population and the number of representatives in the House, and the second would have postponed the effect of any alteration in the compensation of congressmen until an election had intervened. The remaining ten amendments were ratified by the necessary eleven states (there being fourteen states in the Union by that time) on December 15, 1791.

The ten amendments can be thought of as falling into four categories. The First, and justly the most famous of the amendments, covers freedom of speech, press, assembly, and religion. The Second and Third, which are of little contemporary significance, deal with the right of the people to keep and bear arms,[1] and the quartering of soldiers in private

---

[1] The Second Amendment has been widely but mistakenly interpreted to guarantee the ownership and possession of guns. In fact, it ties "the right of the people to keep and bear arms" to the need to maintain a "well-regulated militia." Consequently, the Supreme Court in *United States v. Cruikshank* (1875) held that the amendment protected only the right of the states to maintain and equip a militia and did not guarantee to individuals the right to bear arms. In *United States v. Miller* (1939) the Court ruled that unless defendants could show that their possession of firearms in violation of federal statutes had "some reasonable relationship to the preservation or efficiency of a well-regulated militia," they could not challenge a gun control statute on Second Amendment grounds.

The Court cited *Miller* with approval in *Lewis v. United States* (1980), along with three court of appeals decisions upholding gun control legislation. In *Lewis* the Court noted: "These legislative restrictions on the use of firearms are neither based upon constitutionally suspect criteria, nor do they trench upon any constitutionally protected liberties."

homes. The Fourth through the Eighth are concerned primarily with procedural protections in criminal trials, but other matters are also covered, such as the prohibition on taking of private property for public use without just compensation. Finally, the Ninth and Tenth Amendments are simply declaratory of the existing constitutional situation. The Ninth Amendment provides that the enumeration of certain rights in the Constitution shall not be construed to deny or disparage others retained by the people. The Tenth concerns primarily state powers rather than individual rights, and thus has little bearing on the discussion of this volume.

Only gradually did the conception grow that these ten amendments constituted a great Bill of Rights.[2] About half the state constitutions at the time did not include a bill of rights in their provisions, and it could be argued that these ten amendments accomplished no substantial changes in the constitutional pattern. They took away from Congress few powers which it could reasonably have been thought to have had before the amendments were ratified, and the procedural limitations on criminal trials would no doubt have been carried over from the common law in any event. Unquestionably, however, these provisions have had a tremendous value in the development of American constitutional thinking and practice.

CIVIL RIGHTS PROBLEMS TO THE CIVIL WAR

Three-quarters of a century elapsed after the Bill of Rights was added to the Constitution before any more amendments dealing with civil liberties were adopted. No detailed account of the application of constitutional guarantees during that period can or need be attempted. The ex post facto clause was early given a definitive and restricted interpretation in *Calder v. Bull* (1798). The Alien and Sedition Acts of 1798 raised some constitutional questions, but they never got to the Supreme Court. As the nineteenth century wore on, all other issues paled into obscurity in the fierce light of the slavery controversy, until that issue was excised by the brutal surgery of the Civil War. The Supreme Court's involvement in civil liberties issues during the first half of the nineteenth century was infrequent, but the little that did happen was inextricably involved in subsequent constitutional thought, and it is impossible to understand the post-Civil War amendments without some grasp of the Court's prior actions in four major respects.

---

[2] See Zechariah Chafee, Jr., *How Human Rights Got into the Constitution* (Boston: Boston University Press, 1952); Irving Brant, *The Bill of Rights: Its Origin and Meaning* (Indianapolis: Bobbs-Merrill, 1965); Stephen C. Halpern, ed., *The Future of Our Liberties: Perspectives on the Bill of Rights* (Westport, Conn.: Greenwood Press, 1982).

The Bill of Rights and the States

First we may look at the differences of opinion that arose as to whether the provisions of the Bill of Rights, and more particularly the first eight amendments, were applicable to the federal government alone, or whether they also affected the states. It may seem surprising that doubt on such a fundamental point could have been left in the drafting of the amendments, but the fact is that only two of the amendments are specifically stated as restraints upon the United States. They are the First Amendment, which is by its terms made applicable only to Congress, and one clause of the Seventh, which provides that "no fact tried by jury, shall be otherwise reexamined in any court of the United States, than according to the rules of the common law." All the other amendments, from the Second through the Eighth, state general libertarian principles, with no indication that their protective effect is only against federal action.

Nevertheless, the Supreme Court as early as 1833, in a unanimous opinion written by Chief Justice Marshall, ruled that these amendments were inapplicable to the states. This was the famous case of *Barron v. Baltimore,* and the specific issue was whether the city of Baltimore, by street grading that had diverted streams from their natural courses and rendered Barron's wharf unusable, had deprived him of property without due process of law, contrary to the Fifth Amendment. Obviously his claim could not stand unless the Fifth Amendment applied to state and local governments.

The issue, said Marshall, was of great importance but not of much difficulty.

> The constitution was ordained and established by the people of the United States for themselves, for their own government, and not for the government of the individual states. . . . The powers they conferred on this government were to be exercised by itself; and the limitations on power, if expressed in general terms, are naturally, and, we think, necessarily applicable to the government created by the instrument.

Following this appeal to logic, Marshall turned to history. It was well known that the ratification of the Constitution was not secured without immense opposition. "In almost every convention by which the constitution was adopted, amendments to guard against the abuse of power were recommended. These amendments demanded security against the apprehended encroachments of the general government—not against those of the local governments."

Finally, Marshall's appeal was to the textual provisions of the original Constitution. He called attention to sections 9 and 10 of Article I, both containing a series of prohibitions on legislative action. But in section 9 the language is general, whereas in section 10 all the prohibitions are imposed specifically on the states. Thus section 9 forbids ex post facto laws and bills of attainder generally, while in section 10 the ban is repeated for the states. Whenever a constitutional provision was meant to affect the states, Marshall concluded, "words are employed which directly express that intent. . . . These amendments contain no expression indicating an intention to apply them to the state governments. This court cannot so apply them."

These are powerful arguments, and they have been fully incorporated into American constitutional development. Nevertheless, *Barron v. Baltimore* did not represent a universally accepted view.[3] When it came time to draft the post-Civil War amendments, one of the leading motives of some members of Congress was precisely to liquidate the effects of this decision.

The Meaning of Privileges and Immunities

The second dilemma of the pre-Civil War period concerned the meaning of Article IV, section 2—the privileges and immunities clause. The provision that "the citizens of each state shall be entitled to all privileges and immunities of citizens in the several states" was perhaps the vaguest of all civil rights language in either the original Constitution or the amendments, and a difficult problem was thereby created for reviewing courts. By all odds the best-known of the early judicial efforts along this line was that of Justice Bushrod Washington, sitting in federal circuit court in *Corfield v. Coryell* (1825). This case involved a New Jersey statute that prohibited any person not a resident of New Jersey from gathering oysters in the state. Washington held that this act was not a violation of Article IV, section 2, because the privileges and immunities that the Constitution protects are those "which are, in their nature, fundamental; which belong, of right, to the citizens of all free governments." He went on to suggest quite a list of rights that met this test: protection by the government; enjoyment of life and liberty; the right to acquire and possess property; the right of a citizen of one state to pass through, or reside in, other states for purposes of trade or profession; protection by the writ of habeas corpus; the right to institute and maintain court actions; exemption from higher taxes than are paid by other citizens of the state; and the elective franchise, as regulated by the laws of the particular state in which it is exercised. "These, and many others which might be mentioned, are, strictly speaking, privileges and immunities."

This language of Washington's, which was well known and widely quoted, sounds, as Fairman says, like "pure natural law."[4] It does not seek to discover the nature of these privileges and immunities by reference to the Bill

[3] See William W. Crosskey, *Politics and the Constitution in the History of the United States* (Chicago: University of Chicago Press, 1953), pp. 1056–1082.

[4] Charles Fairman, "Does the Fourteenth Amendment Incorporate the Bill of Rights?" 2 STANFORD LAW REVIEW 5, 12 (1949).

of Rights or any other part of the Constitution. Rather Washington speaks simply of "fundamental" rights, belonging to "the citizens of all free governments," and then throws in a hodgepodge of activities, some of which, such as the practice of a profession or exercise of the elective franchise, obviously are subject to a wide variety of state regulations. According to Washington, the provision established a uniform, nationwide set of standards, applicable to all states. In effect he revised the sentence to read: "The citizens of each state shall be entitled to all privileges and immunities of citizens of the United States in the several states." This position, as developed and applied into the Civil War period and beyond, Crosskey calls the "old Republican view" of the privileges and immunities clause, a part of the "common faith" of that party.[5] As such it had great importance in the drafting and adoption of the Fourteenth Amendment.

Opposed to the "Washington–old Republican" interpretation of the privileges and immunities clause was another, which was in fact probably the one intended by the framers. The language can be read as meaning simply that a citizen of one state going into another state is not discriminated against because of out-of-state origin. As a matter of fact, Washington's opinion in *Corfield v. Coryell* was so broad that it may seem to support this interpretation also. On this basis there is no need to search for any natural law or fundamental standards; the privileges and immunities to which an individual is entitled are those that are standard in that state, applied without discrimination. Under this view the clause is read as though it said: "The citizens of each state shall be entitled in each of the other states to all privileges and immunities of the citizens of the state in which they shall happen to be."

Under this second interpretation the clause does not bulk so large in its import for civil liberties. It is more of an instrument for interstate adjustment and comity. As the preamble of the corresponding provision in the Articles of Confederation put it, the intent was "the better to secure and perpetuate mutual friendship and intercourse among the people of the different states in this Union." But it seems clear that Representative Bingham, the "old Republican" who subsequently carried the privileges and immunities clause over from the Article IV into the Fourteenth Amendment saw in it a much more potent instrument, a guarantee of certain basic rights, variously defined as those specified elsewhere in the Constitution or, more broadly, as those belonging of right to the citizens of all free governments.

Constitutional Issues of Slavery

The most important and notorious of the Supreme Court's decisions on the slavery issue, the case of *Dred Scott v. Sandford* (1857), has a bearing on the

---

[5] William W. Crosskey, "Charles Fairman, 'Legislative History,' and the Constitutional Limitations on State Authority," 22 UNIVERSITY OF CHICAGO LAW REVIEW 1, 11 (1954).

matter just dealt with, and on the drafting of the Fourteenth Amendment.[6] A Negro named Dred Scott, a slave in Missouri, had been taken by his owner into the state of Illinois, where slavery had been forbidden by the Northwest Ordinance of 1787, and also into the territory of Upper Louisiana (Minnesota), where slavery was forbidden by the Missouri Compromise. Having then been returned to Missouri, Scott brought suit for his freedom in a Missouri court, on the ground of his periods of residence in free territory. His claim was denied by the state supreme court, which held that Scott's legal status was determined by the law of the state in which he resided.

Taking advantage of the fact that a citizen of New York had become Scott's owner, Scott's friends then brought a similar suit in the federal courts based on diversity of citizenship. The issue of Scott's citizenship, which could have been crucial to the case, was minimized by the judge. He held that citizenship, for purposes of federal court jurisdiction, meant only residence and the power to own property. Consequently he permitted the case to be tried, and ruled against Scott on the merits of his claim to freedom.

The Supreme Court's decision was delayed until just after Buchanan's inauguration in 1857. Ignoring the complex whirl of events in which the case had its setting, we need note only two of the Court's main holdings, as announced by Chief Justice Taney. First, no Negro slave could be a citizen with power to sue in the federal courts. Scott had not become a free man by reason of the Missouri Compromise, because it was unconstitutional. Unless he had some other claim to freed status, he was still a slave and so without right to bring suit in the federal courts.

Second, and more fundamental, Taney contended that Negroes had been regarded as persons of an inferior order when the Constitution was adopted, and that it had not considered them as "citizens." Consequently, all persons of African descent, whether slaves or not, were barred from access to the federal courts under the diversity of citizenship clause and, indeed, from the enjoyment of any rights or protections under the Constitution. Specifically, Taney wrote that "persons" of Dred Scott's "class" were not "a portion of this people" or "constituent members of this sovereignty." They were "not included, and were not intended to be included, under the word 'citizens' in the Constitution, and can therefore claim none of the rights and privileges which that instrument provides for and secures to citizens of the United States."

What were the rights and privileges of citizens of the United States that Taney thus foreclosed to all persons of African descent? In addition to the right to sue in the federal courts, there was eligibility to the Congress or the Presidency, which is limited to citizens of the United States. But what about

---

[6] See Carl B. Swisher, *History of the Supreme Court of the United States: The Taney Period, 1836–1864* (New York: Macmillan, 1974), V: Chapter 24; Don E. Fehrenbacher, *The Dred Scott Case: Its Significance in American Law and Politics* (New York: Oxford University Press, 1978).

rights guaranteed by the Constitution to "the people" or to "persons" generally? Taney's use throughout his opinion of "the people" of the American Union as synonymous with "citizens of the United States" certainly suggests that these broader guarantees were no more effective than the narrower ones.

But what about Article IV, section 2? If a state gives its free Negro residents the status of state citizens, would they not be able to claim protection in other states for the privileges and immunities of state citizenship? Taney said no. In his view Article IV, section 2, protected only the rights of citizens of the United States. Each state, he said, might confer "the character of citizen" upon anyone it thought proper, but such a citizen would not be entitled to "the privileges and immunities of a citizen in the other states." To put a "citizen" of any given state on a plane of "perfect equality" with the citizens of every other state as to rights of person and property would be, in effect, to make him a citizen of the United States. And since the Court had started out by saying that persons of Dred Scott's class could not be citizens of the United States, obviously the privileges and immunities clause had to be interpreted so as not to open a loophole in that doctrine.

So the privileges and immunities clause, under the pressure of the slavery issue, was given a very restricted interpretation indeed. Its protections were available only to those citizens of the states who were also citizens of the United States. This prevented the clause from protecting blacks. But Taney then went on to remove its protection further by holding that it covered only citizens of the United States who were temporarily in other states. There they were entitled to the minimum privileges and immunities generally prevailing in that state. But a state was left perfectly free to create inequalities in rights among its *own* citizens.

The Meaning of Due Process

The due process clause of the Fifth Amendment closely approaches the privileges and immunities clause in vagueness. The Supreme Court has confessed that "few phrases of the law are so elusive of exact apprehension as this."[7] But "due process" did have something in the way of an ascertainable history. It was generally thought to be descended from the Latin phrase "per legem terrae" in the Magna Carta of 1215. In chapter 39 of that document the king promised: "No freeman shall be arrested, or imprisoned, or disseized, or outlawed, or exiled, or in any way molested; nor will we proceed against him, unless by the lawful judgment of his peers or by the law of the land."

The Petition of Right of 1628 prayed that "freemen be imprisoned or detained only by the law of the land, or by due process of law, and not by the King's special command without any charge." In 1819 Daniel Webster tried

---

[7] *Twining v. New Jersey* (1908).

his hand at defining due process in his argument in the *Dartmouth College* case, describing it as "the general law; a law, which hears before it condemns, which proceeds upon inquiry, and renders judgment only after trial," so that "every citizen shall hold his life, liberty, property, and immunities, under the protection of the general rules which govern society."

The *Dartmouth College* decision did not turn on the due process clause, however, and actually it was not until 1856 that the Supreme Court first interpreted it, in the case of *Murray's Lessee v. Hoboken Land & Improvement Company*. An act of Congress had authorized the Treasury Department, without recourse to judicial process, to issue warrants against and make a levy on the property of federal revenue collectors found to be indebted to the United States. The complaint was made that this was a taking of property without due process of law. The Supreme Court upheld the statute, on the ground that the procedure prescribed was not in conflict with any specific provisions of the Constitution, nor with the settled usages under English common and statute law which had been carried over into the practice of this country.

These, then, are the most important pre-Civil War contributions (both positive and negative) made by the Supreme Court to the understanding of civil liberties under the Constitution. The lines of judicial interpretation thus opened up were of great significance when Congress undertook those postwar modifications in the Constitution that John Frank has referred to as constituting "the second American Revolution."

DRAFTING OF THE FOURTEENTH AMENDMENT

Of the three post-Civil War amendments, only the Fourteenth need concern us here. The Thirteenth Amendment, abolishing slavery and involuntary servitude, became effective in December, 1865. While achieving its immediate purpose, it was quickly seen to be inadequate to the task of making the freedmen into free people. The principal application of the Thirteenth Amendment has been to invalidate state "peonage" legislation.[8]

---

[8] Peonage usually involves an employer giving an employee an advance of wages and then compelling the worker to stay on the job until the debt is worked off. A number of state statutes have allowed or fostered such a system of indentured labor. See *Bailey v. Alabama* (1911) and *Pollock v. Williams* (1944).

There are exceptional circumstances in which compulsory labor is permissible. A state may require able-bodied persons to devote a reasonable amount of their time to such public duties as jury service or repair of the roads [*Butler v. Perry* (1916)]. Forced service for military purposes is not interpreted as involuntary servitude [*Selective Draft Law Cases* (1918)]. Nor does the Thirteenth Amendment cover special professions that operate under conditions requiring continued service for a specified time, such as seamanship [*Robertson v. Baldwin* (1897)]. In *Heart of Atlanta Motel v. United States* (1964) the Court found "no merit" in the contention that, by requiring appellant to rent rooms to blacks against its will, Congress was subjecting the motel to involuntary servitude.

But in *Jones v. Alfred H. Meyer Co.* (1968), the Supreme Court adopted an interpretation of the amendment under which it applies to all racial discrimination stemming from former slave status.[9] The Fifteenth Amendment, forbidding abridgement of the right to vote because of race, color, or previous condition of servitude, took effect in March, 1870, and will be discussed in Chapter 13.

The formative period of the Fourteenth Amendment was between January 12, 1866, when the first drafts were considered by the Joint Committee on Reconstruction, and June 13 of the same year, when the House concurred in the Senate version. What was it that the Congress, under control of Republican Reconstructionists, was trying to do? Its basic motivation was undoubtedly to protect the rights of the newly freed blacks, to establish constitutional guarantees that would be effective when, as ultimately would happen, military control was withdrawn from the Southern states. The "Black Codes" of those states had been grossly discriminatory, forbidding blacks to own property, to have access to the courts, and so on. Since *Barron v. Baltimore* had limited the effect of the Bill of Rights to the federal government, the only provision in the Constitution as it then existed that might cover blacks was the privileges and immunities clause. However, the *Dred Scott* decision, as just noted, eliminated this possibility. Thus new guarantees were needed.

The first move of the Thirty-ninth Congress was toward statutory protection. A civil rights bill was introduced by Senator Trumbull of Illinois on January 5, 1866, and became law on April 9 by passage over President Johnson's veto, two months before the Fourteenth Amendment was adopted by Congress. The Civil Rights Act provided that persons born in the United States were citizens of the United States, and that such citizens, without regard to color, were entitled in every state and territory to the same rights to contract, sue, give evidence, and hold property as were enjoyed by white citizens, and to the equal benefit of all laws for the security of person and property. Any person who under color of law caused any such civil right to be denied would be guilty of a federal offense.

By the Civil Rights Act the federal government asserted its power to control civil rights *within* the several states for the purpose of preventing discrimination against the newly freed blacks. Where did it get this power? Senator Trumbull cited three sources: the Thirteenth Amendment, the privileges and immunities clause, and the Declaration of Independence. "Liberty and slavery," he said, "are opposite terms." Consequently an unjust encroachment upon liberty was "a badge of servitude which, by the Constitution, is prohibited." As for privileges and immunities, he was relying upon the *Corfield v. Coryell* interpretation, which saw them as

---

[9] See discussion in Chapter 11.

"such fundamental rights as belong to every free person . . . the great fundamental rights of life, liberty, and the pursuit of happiness, and the right to travel, to go where he pleases. This is the right which belongs to the citizen of each State." The Declaration of Independence he threw in for good measure.

However, Trumbull's arguments failed to convince some in Congress who were wholly in favor of the bill. Particularly, Representative John A. Bingham of Ohio, an important member of the Joint Committee on Reconstruction, challenged reliance on the privileges and immunities clause because it gave no enforcement authority to Congress. The Thirteenth Amendment argument was not accepted. Consequently there was a strong feeling among the Republican Reconstructionists that the civil rights of the freedmen must be put on a firmer constitutional footing, and one that would not be subject to repeal by a later Congress. Thus discussion of the Fourteenth Amendment proceeded concurrently with the action on the Civil Rights Act.

It is not possible to examine in detail the evolution of the amendment from the first drafts submitted in the Joint Committee on January 12 to its final passage.[10] But we can get a sense of the developmental process by noting the successive versions of the first section proposed by Bingham, whose role entitled him to rate as "father" of the amendment. His first draft said simply: "The Congress shall have power to make all laws necessary and proper to secure to all persons in every State within this Union equal protection in their rights of life, liberty and property."

We note two things about this language. First, it would supply the constitutional authority for legislation that Bingham felt to be lacking for the Civil Rights Act. Second, it was concerned with giving Congress power to protect civil rights, rather than with stating standards of protection that would be enforceable directly by the courts. This latter point deserves underlining, for it is essential to understanding the spirit of the times. The Presidency under Johnson was in eclipse. The Supreme Court, in the aftermath of the *Dred Scott* decision, was at very nearly the lowest point in its history. Congress was in the saddle, and the first thing that occurred to its members was that Congress should undertake the protection of civil liberties by legislation and by securing whatever authority was necessary for such legislation.

---

[10] See Horace E. Flack, *The Adoption of the Fourteenth Amendment* (Baltimore: Johns Hopkins Press, 1908); Joseph B. James, *The Framing of the Fourteenth Amendment* (Urbana: University of Illinois Press, 1956); Charles Fairman, "Does the Fourteenth Amendment Incorporate the Bill of Rights? The Original Understanding," STANFORD LAW REVIEW 5–139 (1949) and "The Supreme Court and the Constitutional Limitations on State Governmental Authority," 21 UNIVERSITY OF CHICAGO LAW REVIEW 40–78 (1953).

On January 27 a revised Bingham draft proposed to give Congress legislative power "to secure all persons in every State full protection in the enjoyment of life, liberty and property; and to all citizens of the United States in every State the same immunities and equal political rights and privileges." This was poor drafting. How much protection is "full" protection? Did the "same immunities" mean the same throughout the nation, or merely the same for white and black in each state? Bringing "political" rights into the amendment added a whole new field of concern.

The Joint Committee rejected this draft by a tie vote, so Bingham tried again. This time his proposal ran: "Congress shall have power to make all laws which shall be necessary and proper to secure to citizens of each State all privileges and immunities of citizens in the several States; and to all persons in the several States equal protection in the rights of life, liberty and property."

The text was reported to the two houses on February 13. In the House Bingham explained that both parts of his proposal were already in the Constitution and binding on the states, and that he was merely adding the power of Congress to enforce them. Since this contention is in flat contradiction to the holdings of *Barron* and *Dred Scott,* it must be assumed that Bingham was intending to repeal those decisions.

If this was Bingham's view and purpose, then one essential element was missing from his formulation. He had failed to do anything about repealing another of the doctrines of the *Dred Scott* case, namely, that persons of African descent, whether slaves or not, could not be citizens of the United States under the Constitution. The Civil Rights Act did have a provision guaranteeing the status of blacks as citizens of the United States, but the draft of the Fourteenth Amendment did not, and during the House discussion no one suggested that it was needed.

After a three-day House debate at the end of February, further consideration of Bingham's draft was postponed. In April the Joint Committee undertook further revisions, and on April 28 the first section of the Fourteenth Amendment, in what was to be its final form save only for the first sentence defining citizenship, was adopted. It was again the work of Bingham. In contrast to the draft that the House had debated, this version was not merely a grant of power to Congress. It was a direct obligation on the states. Moreover, the long debate as to whether the amendment should leave the states free to set their own standards on civil rights and merely seek to prevent unequal application of those standards, or whether it should set up general standards of treatment to which the practices in each state must conform, was finally settled. It would do both. So there was an equal protection clause that guaranteed no discrimination, though without the "life, liberty and property" language of the earlier draft. But there was also the privileges and immunities clause carried over from Article IV, section 2, and made applicable to "citizens of the United States." And to this was now added the due process clause from the Fifth Amendment.

The House passed this version on May 10. The Senate took it up on May 23, and there it was handled by Jacob M. Howard of Michigan. It was in fact Howard who, seeing the need for a definition of citizenship, subsequently added the first sentence of the present amendment to fill that gap. Howard devoted more attention to explaining the privileges and immunities clause to the Senate than to the other parts of the first section. He agreed that the privileges and immunities guaranteed by Article IV were somewhat vague, and thought it would be "a somewhat barren discussion" to determine what they were. "But it is certain," he added, "the clause was inserted in the Constitution for some good purpose."

Whatever these privileges and immunities were—and Howard quoted from Justice Washington in *Corfield v. Coryell*—they "are secured to the citizen solely as a citizen of the United States and as a party in their courts. They do not operate in the slightest degree as a restraint or prohibition upon State legislation." The Supreme Court, as we have just seen, had ruled to this effect in the *Dred Scott* case. Moreover, the first eight amendments were in the same situation, because of *Barron v. Baltimore.* Howard specifically recited the provisions of these amendments and said that the privileges and immunities clause of the Fourteenth Amendment would make this "mass of privileges, immunities, and rights, some of them secured by the second section of the fourth article . . . some by the first eight amendments of the Constitution," effective on the states. "The great object of the first section of this amendment is . . . to restrain the power of the States and compel them at all times to respect these great fundamental guarantees."

With regard to the equal protection and due process clauses, he pointed out that they would "disable a State from depriving not merely a citizen of the United States, but any person, whoever he may be, of life, liberty, or property without due process of law, or from denying to him the equal protection of the laws of the State." Similarly in the House Bingham had stressed the difference between the protection of "citizens" in the first clause and "persons" in the second and third clauses, and had said that the amendment would protect the "inborn rights of every person," both "citizen and stranger."

It is not feasible to report the additional debate in detail. The Senate approved the resolution, as amended, on June 8, and the House accepted the revised version on June 13. Thus, with the concurrence of the necessary states, were added to the Constitution three important new standards for the protection of civil liberties against state action. Equal protection, a general guarantee against discrimination, was the most specific of the new provisions. The other two—due process, and privileges and immunities—were concepts without precise contours that would have such meaning as they might be given by Congress and, more importantly, by the Supreme Court.[11] To this process of spelling out the implications for individual liberties of the Bill of Rights and the Fourteenth Amendment, we now turn, giving attention first to freedom of speech and press.

[11] A very useful source on the legislative history of the Thirteenth, Fourteenth, and Fifteenth Amendments is Alfred Avins, ed., *The Reconstruction Amendments' Debates* (Richmond, Va.: Virginia Commission on Constitutional Government, 1967). See also Charles Fairman, *Reconstruction and Reunion, 1864–88* (New York: Macmillan, 1971), chaps 19-21.

2

The Judicial Approach
to the First Amendment

"Congress shall make no law . . . abridging the freedom of speech, or of the press." This great principle of an open society was incorporated into the Constitution when the First Amendment was ratified on December 15, 1791. No one who has even the faintest understanding of how democratic self-government functions can harbor any doubt as to the fundamental importance of freedom of ideas. The case against suppression of opinion was put in perhaps its most perfect literary form for modern times by Justice Oliver Wendell Holmes's dissent in the case of *Abrams v. United States* (1919):

> Persecution for the expression of opinions seems to me perfectly logical. If you have no doubt of your premises or your power and want a certain result with all your heart you naturally express your wishes in law and sweep away all opposition. To allow opposition by speech seems to indicate that you think the speech impotent, as when a man says that he has squared the circle, or that you do not care whole-heartedly for the result, or that you doubt either your power or your premises. But when men have realized that time has upset many fighting faiths, they may come to believe even more than they believe the very foundations of their own conduct that the ultimate good desired is better reached by free trade in ideas—that the best test of truth is the power of the thought to get itself accepted in the competition of the market, and that truth is the only ground upon which their wishes safely can be carried out. That at any rate is the theory of our Constitution.

Holmes is here making a "utilitarian" defense of free speech, basing its justification on its value to society. But freedom to speak may also be defended as a natural right that individuals must enjoy if they are to achieve the full potentialities of their intellectual and moral endowments. Interference with such rights would on this basis be objectionable, not because society was deprived of truths it might otherwise have discovered, but because individuals were thwarted in the development and expression of their rational faculties.

Our task, however, is not to discuss generally the philosophical or moral or social case for freedom of expression but rather to examine more specifically the meaning and effect that the libertarian principles of the First Amendment have achieved in American experience through judicial interpretation and enforcement.[1]

THE ENGLISH HERITAGE
AND THE INTENTION OF THE FRAMERS

In *Robertson v. Baldwin* (1897) the Supreme Court said: "The law is perfectly well settled that the first ten amendments to the Constitution, commonly known as the Bill of Rights, were not intended to lay down any novel principles of government, but simply to embody certain guaranties and immunities which we had inherited from our English ancestors."

If the First Amendment was in fact intended to be limited to principles inherited from our English ancestors, then Blackstone's famous definition of the liberty of the press would be a principal guide to its meaning:

> The liberty of the press is indeed essential to the nature of a free state; but this consists in laying no previous restraints upon publications, and not in freedom from censure for criminal matter when published. Every freeman has an undoubted right to lay what sentiments he pleases before the public; to forbid this, is to destroy the freedom of the press; but if he publishes what is improper, mischievous or illegal, he must take the consequence of his own temerity.[2]

If the First Amendment ratifies Blackstone's understanding of freedom of the press and of speech, then it is a protection only against previous restraint, or censorship. This is of course an important guarantee and one that has been fully incorporated into American reasoning. Banning of books, preventing newspapers from being published, forbidding or breaking up peaceful assemblies—such actions are associated with dictatorships; they are not permissible under the First Amendment.

[1] For a broad consideration of the libertarian philosophy, see Thomas I. Emerson, *The System of Freedom of Expression* (New York: Random House, 1970).

[2] Blackstone, *Commentaries*, 1765 IV; 151, 152.

But Blackstone offered no principle that would protect speakers or publishers from punishment for what they had said or written. He would permit punishment, not only for speech or publication that is illegal or criminal, but also for matter that is "improper" or "mischievous." His rules would allow broad scope for governmental prosecutions against those who had exercised the right of free speech or free press. English practice, in fact, permitted wide latitude for severe action against the crime of "seditious libel"—that is, defaming or criticizing the government or its officers. If the First Amendment carried over the English law of seditious libel, then freedom of speech and press in America were subject to serious limits.

That this English legacy had in fact persisted was evident when Congress adopted the Sedition Act of 1798. This statute provided punishment for making false, scandalous, and malicious statements against the government of the United States, either house of Congress, or the President, with intent to defame them or bring them into contempt or disrepute, or to stir up the hatred of the people against them, or bring about sedition in any of its various forms. The act was broad enough to make criminal virtually any criticism of the government.

The Federalist members of Congress who passed this legislation as a device for punishing their Jeffersonian critics obviously did not regard it as barred by the First Amendment. However, the violent public reaction against the numerous prosecutions instituted under the act indicated that the Federalists were in error. The act expired by its own terms in 1801 without ever reaching the Supreme Court for a constitutional test. Many convictions were secured under it, but the fines levied were subsequently repaid by act of Congress, and President Jefferson pardoned all those who had been found guilty under the act. Eventually the Sedition Act was formally declared to have been unconstitutional by the Supreme Court in *New York Times v. Sullivan* (1964).[3]

EARLY AVOIDANCE OF THE FIRST AMENDMENT

Supreme Court interpretation and enforcement of the First Amendment is generally regarded as beginning with the Sedition and Espionage Act cases after World War I; but there had been earlier attempts to invoke the protection of the First Amendment that the Supreme Court had rebuffed by various tactics. As David M. Rabban summarizes the pre-1919 period:

[3] For historical analyses see Walter Berns, "Freedom of the Press and the Alien and Sedition Laws: A Reappraisal," in Philip B. Kurland, ed., *The Supreme Court Review: 1970* (Chicago: University of Chicago Press, 1970), pp. 109–160; Leonard W. Levy, *Legacy of Suppression: Freedom of Speech and Press in Early American History* (Cambridge, Mass.: Harvard University Press, 1960).

Supreme Court decisions in the generation before World War One reflected a tradition of hostility to the value of free speech. The Court rejected First Amendment claims whenever it confronted them directly. But confrontation, even in rejection, at least lent these claims some status. More frequently, in rendering decisions that today would be based on an analysis of the First Amendment, the Court did not address free speech issues at all. The Court repeatedly denied that cases implicated freedom of expression, and often made no reference to the First Amendment.[4]

Many of these cases involved congressional restrictions on access to the mails; they will be discussed in Chapter 4. At the state level, where infringements on speech and press freedom were more likely to occur, a literal interpretation of the First Amendment, which refers only to Congress, would make it inapplicable. But in fact the earlier speech and press claims against state restrictions that did find their way to the Supreme Court were rejected on other grounds. *Davis v. Massachusetts* (1897) upheld a Boston ordinance that required a permit from the mayor for any public address in a public park. An injunction against labor picketing was justified in *Gompers v. Bucks Stove & Range Co.* (1911) on the ground that speech as a means for accomplishing an unlawful purpose was conduct, not speech. Motion picture censorship was upheld in *Mutual Film Corp. v. Industrial Commission of Ohio* (1915) because film exhibition was simply a profit-making business and not "part of the press of the country."

Justice Holmes wrote two early opinions holding that speech could be penalized if it had a "bad tendency" on public welfare. In *Patterson v. Colorado* (1907) he upheld a contempt conviction for criticizing judicial behavior as subsequent punishment for obstructing the administration of justice. In *Fox v. Washington* (1915) an article protesting enforcement of a ban on nude bathing was regarded as having encouraged a breach of the law. Finally, in *Prudential Insurance Co. v. Cheek* (1922) the Court flatly held that "the Constitution of the United States imposes upon the States no obligation to confer upon those within their jurisdiction . . . the right of free speech.

While this ruling might have seemed to foreclose any role for the First Amendment in the states, a constitutional alternative was available. As we will see in Chapter 11, since the 1870s the Court had been interpreting the due process clause of the Fourteenth Amendment to protect economic freedoms and property rights against state action, and it had shown no hesitation to strike down state legislation on what came to be known as "substantive due process" grounds. In the 1923 case of *Meyer v. Nebraska*, the Court was confronted with a situation where a property right and a censorship issue were closely allied. Wartime hysteria had

---

[4] "The First Amendment in Its Forgotten Years," 90 YALE LAW JOURNAL 514, 542 (1981).

caused the Nebraska legislature to forbid the teaching of German even in private schools, but the Supreme Court saw this as an attack on the livelihood of German language teachers and ruled that the "liberty" to teach a foreign language was protected by the Fourteenth Amendment due process clause. Then in 1925 the Court, in *Pierce v. Society of Sisters,* invalidated a Ku Klux Klan-backed Oregon constitutional amendment, aimed at parochial schools, that denied parents the "liberty" of sending their children to private schools. Again the Court pointed out that this law would destroy the property rights of religious schools.

It was by this property-oriented, substantive due process route that the Supreme Court came to its precedent-shattering decision in *Gitlow v. New York* (1925), only one week after the *Pierce* decision. In the course of upholding the conviction of a prominent Communist under the New York criminal anarchy statute, Justice Sanford for the conservative Court made this astounding concession: "We may and do assume that freedom of speech and of the press . . . are among the fundamental rights and 'liberties' protected . . . from impairment by the States." This issue had not been argued before the Court, and the holding was unnecessary to the decision of the *Gitlow* case. It was in this offhand manner that the historic decision was made enormously enlarging the coverage of the First Amendment and the jurisdiction of the Supreme Court to guarantee the freedom of speech and press against state or local action as well as against Congress.

THE CLEAR AND PRESENT DANGER TEST

The usual reason for seeking to control or punish speech is that the speech threatens to result in dangerous or illegal acts. Ideas do have consequences. "Words," as Judge Learned Hand said in the *Masses* case, "are not only the keys of persuasion, but the triggers of action."[5] The shout of "Fire" in a crowded theater can directly cause the most deadly panic. A person may be persuaded by speech or writing to commit murder. Words may lead to the development of a plan for overthrowing the government.

It is clear that words which directly incite to illegal acts are themselves tainted with illegality. The common law recognized the crime of incitement to violence, and the First Amendment has never been understood as extending its sanctuary to speech criminal in purpose and intent. But it immediately becomes apparent there are questions of degree involved here. How closely related must the speech be to the crime in order to taint the speech with illegality? How clear must the purpose be to

[5] *Masses Publishing Co. v. Patten* (1917).

incite to crime? What degree of immediacy must there be in the situation? And, since these questions are going to be determined in legal prosecutions, who will be responsible for doing so—the trial judge, or the jurors?

At one extreme, the theory can be adopted that words do not become criminal until they have a tendency to produce immediate breach of the peace. But if this is the rule to be applied, then no new legislation or judicial standards are needed, for the common-law rules on criminal solicitation or incitement cover the case.

But the lawmakers and the public are often unwilling to confine restrictive powers over speech within such narrow limits, particularly in crisis situations. They may begin to move against speech merely because it is unpopular. They may say, as Justice Sanford did in *Gitlow v. New York* (1925): "The State cannot reasonably be required to measure the danger from every . . . utterance in the nice balance of a jeweler's scale. A single revolutionary spark *may* kindle a fire that, smouldering for a time, *may* burst into a sweeping and destructive conflagration."

This "remote and indirect tendency" test was in fact operative prior to the adoption of the First Amendment. The English common law of sedition made words criminal if they cast blame on the government or its officials, on the ground that bringing them into disrepute would *tend* to overthrow the state. The American Sedition Act of 1798 adopted this same standard, but in other respects the act was an advance on the common law of criminal sedition in that it entrusted criminality to the jury rather than the judge, and admitted truth as a defense. This act was rejectd by the political process, and the authority of the "remote and indirect tendency" test which it embodied was at least somewhat impaired. But no other standard was stated, nor was there judicial need for one in the federal courts until World War I, when enforcement of the Espionage Act of 1917 and the Sedition Act of 1918 forced the issue onto the Supreme Court's calendar.

Justice Holmes, who had been so distinctly unfriendly to earlier free speech claims, was the Court's spokesman in its postwar encounters with the Espionage Act. This statute, which prohibited the making of false statements intended to interfere with the successful prosecution of the war, as well as acts obstructing recruiting or causing insubordination in the Armed Forces, was at issue in *Schenck v. United States* (1919). The defendants had mailed circulars to men eligible for the draft, declaring conscription to be unconstitutional despotism and urging them to assert their rights. Holmes spoke for a unanimous Court in finding that such speech was not protected by the First Amendment because of the "clear and present danger" that it would result in illegal action:

> The character of every act depends upon the circumstances in which it is done.... The most stringent protection of free speech would not protect a man in falsely shouting fire in a theatre and causing a panic.... The question in every

case is whether the words used are used in circumstances and are of such a nature as to create a clear and present danger that they will bring about the substantive evils that Congress has a right to prevent. It is a question of proximity and degree.

Then he added, with particular reference to the problems of the *Schenck* case: "When a nation is at war many things that might be said in time of peace are such a hindrance to its effort that their utterance will not be endured so long as men fight and that no Court could regard them as protected by any constitutional right."[6]

Thus the clear and present danger test proved a rather illusory protection to freedom of speech in wartime. It was, in effect, a rationalization for sending persons to jail because of their speech, though it did insist that the relationship between speech and illegal acts must be proximate, not remote and indirect. Professor Zechariah Chafee, Jr., praised the *Schenck* ruling as supplying "for the first time an authoritative judicial interpretation in accord with the purpose of the framers of the Constitution."[7]

By the fall of 1919, however, Holmes was manifesting a surprisingly increased concern about freedom of speech, perhaps due to criticism of his *Schenck* opinion by Learned Hand.[8] In *Abrams v. United States* (1919) Holmes and Justice Louis D. Brandeis voted to strike down a conviction on clear and present danger grounds, but they were unable to carry the Court majority with them. The crime in *Abrams* was printing and circulating pamphlets attacking the government's action in sending American troops to Vladivostok and Murmansk in the summer of 1918 and calling for a general strike of munitions workers. Holmes's dissent is probably his most famous piece of rhetoric; but here we need note only the effort he made to sharpen up and strengthen the clear and present danger test by these words:

> We should be eternally vigilant against attempts to check the expression of opinions that we loathe and believe to be fraught with death, unless they so imminently threaten immediate interference with the lawful and pressing purposes of the law that an immediate check is required to save the country. . . . Only the emergency that makes it immediately dangerous to leave the correction of evil counsels to time warrants making any exception to the sweeping command, "Congress shall make no law . . . abridging the freedom of speech."

Holmes was again unsuccessful in *Gitlow v. New York* (1925). Justice Sanford for the majority denied that the clear and present danger

---

[6] In the same month, March, 1919, Holmes wrote two more unanimous opinions for the Court upholding convictions in Espionage Act cases: *Frohwerk v. United States* (1919) and *Debs v. United States* (1919).

[7] Zechariah Chafee, Jr., *Free Speech in the United States* (Cambridge, Mass.: Harvard University Press, 1941), p. 82.

[8] See Gerald Gunther, "Learned Hand and the Origins of Modern First Amendment Doctrine," 27 STANFORD LAW REVIEW 719 (1975).

test was even applicable as a test of the New York criminal anarchy act. Brandeis made a final effort to restate the test in *Whitney v. California* (1927), involving conviction of a Communist under the California syndicalism act. A legislative declaration that a danger exists which justifies restrictions on speech and assembly creates, he said, merely a "rebuttable presumption." If the conditions alleged by the legislature do not, in fact, exist, then the courts, guided by the clear and present danger test, must refuse to enforce the statute. Brandeis admitted that the standards for the test had not yet been clearly fixed, and he undertook once more the task of formulation:

> To courageous, self-reliant men, with confidence in the power of free and fearless reasoning applied through the processes of popular government, no danger flowing from speech can be deemed clear and present, unless the incidence of the evil apprehended is so imminent that it may befall before there is opportunity for full discussion. If there be time to expose through discussion the falsehood and fallacies, to avert the evil by the processes of education, the remedy to be applied is more speech, not enforced silence. Only an emergency can justify repression. . . . Moreoever, even imminent danger cannot justify resort to prohibition of these functions essential to effective democracy, unless the evil apprehended is relatively serious. Prohibition of free speech and assembly is a measure so stringent that it would be inappropriate as the means for averting a relatively trivial harm to society. . . . The fact that speech is likely to result in some violence or in destruction of property is not enough to justify its suppression. . . . Among free men, the deterrents ordinarily to be applied to prevent crime are education and punishment for violations of the law, not abridgment of the rights of free speech and assembly.

The subsequent history of the clear and present danger test—its development in the 1930s and 1940s and its subsequent decline—will be found in later chapters. But at this point it may be noted that from 1919 to 1927, its successive statements were eloquent but it kept no one out of jail.

LEGISLATIVE REASONABLENESS

Looking back, we see that the clear and present danger test was, at first, not a test for the validity of legislation—the Espionage Act was admittedly constitutional—but only a test for determining how closely words had to be related to illegal acts in order to be infected with their illegality. Even in *Gitlow*, Holmes did not appear to challenge the New York statute. He merely doubted whether Gitlow's "redundant discourse" was included in the statutory prohibition. It was not until *Whitney* that clear and present danger was definitely set forth as a basis on which courts, and indeed, all Americans, could "challenge a law abridging free speech and assembly by showing that there was no emergency justifying it."

This development brought the clear and present danger test into direct conflict with an earlier standard of judicial review—namely, that legislative conclusions embodied in statutes must be upheld by courts if there is any basis on which a "reasonable man" could have reached the same conclusion as the legislature. The reasonable man theory was embraced by the majority in *Gitlow* and *Whitney*. Those decisions held that the function of the Court, when confronted with a statute alleged to infringe basic civil liberties, was limited to judging whether a reasonable man could have reached the legislature's conclusion as to the existence of a danger demanding that protective action be taken. As Sanford said in *Gitlow:* "Every presumption is to be indulged in favor of the validity of the statute." Legislatures should be rebuked only if they act "arbitrarily or unreasonably."

Now there is sound authority for the reasonable man theory of judicial review. Holmes himself was ordinarily one of the most ardent exponents of this test. As he said in his famous dissent to *Lochner v. New York* (1905), he would not invalidate any statute "unless it can be said that a rational and fair man necessarily would admit that the statute proposed would infringe fundamental principles as they have been understood by the traditions of our people and our law." Of course, *Lochner* was not a civil liberties case; the issue was whether New York could limit the hours of employment in bakeries. But in 1923 Holmes did apply the reasonable man test in what came very close to being a civil liberty case, *Meyer v. Nebraska*. The Court majority here, as previously noted, held invalid a state law that sought to prevent the teaching of the German language in the primary schools. Holmes refused to go along with this judgment, because be believed that whether children in their early years should hear and speak only English at school was "a question upon which men reasonably might differ and therefore I am unable to say that the Constitution of the United States prevents the experiment being tried."

This quotation epitomizes the doctrine upon which Holmes's reputation for liberalism was based. The reasonable man theory was a method of letting the legislatures have their own way. A conservative Supreme Court, from 1880 on, had insisted on the right to substitute its judgment for that of Congress or the state legislatures as to the constitutionality of laws which changed the rules respecting rights and uses of property. Holmes thought that the Court had no such license from the Constitution to override the views of popularly elected legislatures, except to veto statutes for which no case could possibly be made that would satisfy a reasonable man. This was the core of his liberalism.

Why, then, did Holmes appear to abandon the reasonable man test in the civil liberties field? And could it be liberalism to advocate a doctrine of narrow judicial review in dealing with economic regulation and broad judicial review over regulations limiting freedom of speech and press? This apparent paradox was explained in two different ways on the Roosevelt Court, and the divergence was the basis for some of its classic arguments.

PREFERRED POSITION

One explanation, adopted on numerous occasions and associated with the judicial quartet of Black, Douglas, Murphy, and Rutledge, was that the reasonable man test, although appropriate in all other fields, did not apply where the basic freedoms of the First Amendment were at issue. There, it was contended, the judiciary had to hold itself and legislatures to higher standards because of the "preferred position" that the Constitution gives to First Amendment freedoms. Stated in an extreme form, the argument is that any law touching communication is infected with presumptive invalidity. A more moderate statement is that, because First Amendment values are so essential to a free society, legislative action infringing those values must be shown to be not only "reasonably" adapted to the attaining of valid social goals but justified by overwhelmingly conclusive considerations.

The development of the preferred position view must be indicated rather summarily. Holmes himself never made this argument. Its origin might be found in Justice Cardozo's statement in a 1937 decision that First Amendment liberties were on "a different plane of social and moral values." Freedom of thought and speech, he said, is "the matrix, the indispensable condition, of nearly every other form of freedom. . . . Neither liberty nor justice would exist if they were sacrificed."[9] A somewhat similar position was taken a little earlier in the same year, in the case of *Herndon v. Lowry*. But the credit for the invention is usually given to Justice Stone, in a footnote that he appended to a 1938 decision.[10]

The case in question concerned application of a congressional act prohibiting transportation of certain types of compounded milk products in interstate commerce, and Stone was rehearsing the familiar arguments for the reasonable man theory of judicial review:

> The existence of facts supporting the legislative judgment is to be presumed, for regulatory legislation affecting ordinary commercial transactions is not to be pronounced unconstitutional unless in the light of the facts made

[9] *Palko v. Connecticut* (1937).

[10] *United States v. Carolene Products Co.* (1938). For the interesting history of this footnote, see Alpheus T. Mason, *Harlan Fiske Stone: Pillar of the Law* (New York: Viking, 1956), pp. 512–516.

known or generally assumed it is of such a character as to preclude the assumption that it rests upon some rational basis within the knowledge and experience of the legislators.

At this point occurred the footnote:

> There may be narrower scope for operation of the presumption of constitutionality when legislation appears on its face to be within a specific prohibition of the Constitution, such as those of the first ten amendments, which are deemed equally specific when held to be embraced within the Fourteenth. . . . It is unnecessary to consider now whether legislation which restricts those political processes which can ordinarly be expected to bring about repeal of undesirable legislation, is to be subjected to more exacting judicial scrutiny under the general prohibitions of the Fourteenth Amendment than are most other types of legislation. . . . Nor need we enquire . . . whether prejudice against discrete and insular minorities may be a special condition, which tends seriously to curtail the operation of those political processes ordinarily to be relied upon to protect minorities, and which may call for a correspondingly more searching judicial inquiry.

This is admittedly a tentative and qualified pronouncement; Frankfurter, who vigorously challenged the whole preferred position argument as "mischievous," was justified in concluding that it "did not purport to announce any new doctrine" and that, if it had, a footnote would hardly have been an "appropriate way" of doing so.[11] But within a year and a half the idea that Stone had at least suggested leaped from the footnotes to become the doctrine of an almost unanimous Court, Justice Frankfurter included, in the 1939 handbill casses.[12] Speaking through none other than Justice Roberts, the Court said:

> In every case, therefore, where legislative abridgement of the rights [to freedom of speech and press] is asserted, the courts should be astute to examine the effect of the challenged legislation. Mere legislative preferences or beliefs respecting matters of public convenience may well support regulation directed at other personal activities, but be insufficient to justify such as diminishes the exercise of rights so vital to the maintenance of democratic institutions. And so, as cases arise, the delicate and difficult task falls upon the courts to weigh the circumstances and to appraise the substantiality of the reasons advanced in support of the regulation of the free enjoyment of the rights.

McReynolds was the only dissenter.

The "preferred position" phrase was apparently not actually employed until Stone, by then Chief Justice, used it in 1942 in his dissent from *Jones v. Opelika*, where the Court majority upheld municipal

---

[11] *Kovacs v. Cooper* (1949).

[12] *Schneider v. Irvington* (1939).

license taxes on booksellers as applied to Jehovah's Witnesses and cited the fact that these were general tax ordinances, not levies aimed at this particular group. In reply Stone observed:

> The First Amendment is not confined to safeguarding freedom of speech and freedom of religion against discriminatory attempts to wipe them out. On the contrary, the Constitution, by virtue of the First and Fourteenth Amendments, has put those freedoms in a preferred position. Their commands are not restricted to cases where the protected privilege is sought out for attack. They extend at least to every form of taxation which, because it is a condition of the exercise of the privilege, is capable of being used to control or suppress it.

One year later Justice Douglas restated his thought, but now for the Court majority, in *Murdock v. Pennsylvania* (1943), which overruled *Jones v. Opelika:* "Freedom of press, freedom of speech, freedom of religion are in a preferred position." The phrase reappeared in several subsequent decisions. Even Justice Jackson, whose subsequent thoughts were most antagonistic to the preferred position argument, lent it support in his 1943 holding in the second flag-salute case.[13] Perhaps the strongest of all the statements along this line was that by Justice Rutledge in *Thomas v. Collins* (1945):

> Any attempt to restrict those liberties must be justified by clear public interest, threatened not doubtfully or remotely, but by clear and present danger. The rational connection between the remedy provided and the evil to be curbed, which in other contexts might support legislation against attack on due process grounds, will not suffice. These rights rest on firmer foundation. Accordingly, whatever occasion would restrain orderly discussion and persuasion, at appropriate time and place, must have clear support in public danger, actual or impending. Only the gravest abuses, endangering paramount interests, give occasion for permissible limitation.

The task of rebutting the preferred position doctrine was principally assumed by Justice Frankfurter. It was his contention that Holmes by the clear and present danger test had not really challenged the reasonable man theory or intended to develop an alternative to it as a test for the validity of legislation. He was dismayed by the uses to which the Roosevelt Court began to put the clear and present danger test. He contended that it was being used for a purpose other than Holmes had intended— namely, to determine the constitutionality of legislation; that it was being applied in much different areas than Holmes had contemplated, including contempt of court proceedings and violation of petty police regulations; and that the spirit of its use was much different from what Holmes would have approved. In dissenting from the Court's decision in *Bridges*

---

[13] *West Virginia State Board of Education v. Barnette* (1943).

v. California (1941), he charged that Justice Black's employment of the clear and present danger test with preferred position embellishment was an unthinking "recitation of phrases that are the shorthand of a complicated historic process." In *Pennekamp v. Florida* (1946) he came close to denying any meaning at all to the doctrine, saying: "'Clear and present danger' was never used by Mr. Justice Holmes to express a technical legal doctrine or to convey a formula for adjudicating cases. It was a literary phrase not to be distorted by being taken from its context."

In *Kovacs v. Cooper* (1949) Justice Frankfurter, reacting against Justice Reed's acceptance of the "preferred position" phrase in the Court's opinion, made the clearly mistaken claim that this doctrine had "never commended itself to a majority of this Court." But in the same opinion he gave evidence of the persuasiveness of the preferred position idea when he agreed that "those liberties of the individual which history has attested as the indispensable conditions of an open as against a closed society come to this Court with a momentum of respect lacking when appeal is made to liberties which derive from shifting economic arrangements."

THE ABSOLUTIST-LITERALIST POSITION

Beyond the preferred position argument stands the contention that the First Amendment gives *absolute* protection to the freedoms it names. This approach asserts that the First Amendment means literally what it says— that Congress shall *make no law* that has the effect of limiting, or reducing in compass, freedom of speech and press. On this reasoning any law passed by Congress that abridges the freedom of speech or press is unconstitutional on its face, and the circumstances alleged to justify it need not even be considered.

The principal proponent of the absolutist position on the Supreme Court was Justice Black, who summarized this argument in *Smith v. California* (1959) as follows:

> ✓I read "no law abridging" to mean *no law abridging*. The First Amendment, which is the supreme law of the land, has thus fixed its own value on freedom of speech and press by putting these freedoms wholly "beyond the reach" of *federal* power to abridge. No other provision of the Constitution purports to dilute the scope of these unequivocal commands of the First Amendment. Consequently, I do not believe that any federal agencies, including Congress and this Court, have power or authority to subordinate speech and press to what they think are "more important interests."

The tenets of the absolutist doctrine, however, were developed most completely by Alexander Meiklejohn. He writes:

No one who reads with care the text of the First Amendment can fail to be startled by its absoluteness. The phrase, "Congress shall make no law . . . abridging the freedom of speech," is unqualified. It admits of no exceptions. To say that no laws of a given type shall be made means that no laws of that type shall, under any circumstances, be made. That prohibition holds good in war as in peace, in danger as in security.[14]

Meiklejohn distinguished between public and private speech. It is public speech, concerned with public issues, for which absolute protection is essential, because in a self-governing system the citizens are the rulers and must be free to examine and discuss all ideas relating to the public issues they must decide:

Just so far as, at any point, the citizens who are to decide an issue are denied acquaintance with information or opinion or doubt or disbelief or criticism which is relevant to that issue, just so far the result must be ill-considered, ill-balanced planning for the general good. . . . When a question of policy is "before the house," free men choose to meet it not with their eyes shut, but with their eyes open. To be afraid of ideas, any idea, is to be unfit for self-government. Any such suppression of ideas about the common good, the First Amendment condemns with its absolute disapproval. The freedom of ideas shall not be abridged.

Meiklejohn sought support for his view from another protection of speech found in the Constitution that has unquestioningly been treated as an absolute right. That is the provision in Article I, section 6, to the effect that members of Congress "shall not be questioned in any other place" for "any speech or debate in either house."

The parallel is an interesting one: Congress "shall make no law," and congressmen "shall not be questioned." The congressional right of free speech is taken at its face value. Members of Congress are absolutely protected from prosecution because of what they have said in Congress or its committees or its official publications. The Constitution makes a similar judgment, say the absolutists, concerning freedom of speech, because of the importance of freedom of discussion to democratic self-government. The Constitution knows how to grant qualified rights, if that is its purpose and intent. Take the due process clause of the Fifth Amendment. It does not state an absolute prohibition. It does not say that persons shall not be deprived of life, liberty, or property. It says that persons *may* be so deprived, provided due process of law is followed. Life,

---

[14] Alexander Meiklejohn, *Free Speech and Its Relation to Self-government* (New York: Harper & Row, Pub., 1948), pp. 17, 26–27. An expanded version of his views is contained in *Political Freedom: The Constitutional Powers of the People* (New York: Harper & Row, Pub., 1960). See also his "The First Amendment is an Absolute," in Philip B. Kurland, ed., *The Supreme Court Review, 1961* (Chicago: University of Chicago Press, 1961), pp. 245–266.

liberty, and property are qualified rights under the Fifth Amendment. But freedom of speech under the First Amendment is limited by no such qualifications.

Literalism-absolutism does create some problems for its advocates. A purely literal reading of the First Amendment, which applies by its terms only to Congress, would have prevented the Court from extending the amendment's coverage to the states as was done in the *Gitlow* case. Chafee denies that Meiklejohn's supposed boundary between public and private speech actually exists: "There are public aspects to practically every subject."[15] To Meiklejohn's charge that Holmes subverted the First Amendment by permitting it to be breached whenever there was a clear and present danger, Chafee responds that the only practicable alternative to Holmes's limited immunity for speech was not absolute immunity but no immunity at all. Black's absolutism led him into a quixotic attack on the validity of the entire law of libel.[16] It is significant that Justice Murphy, as devoted a civil libertarian as ever sat on the Court, admitted in *Chaplinksy v. New Hampshire* (1942): "It is well understood that the right of free speech is not absolute at all times and under all circumstances."

BALANCING

The converse of the absolutist position that the government has *no* power to limit expression in constitutionally protected areas is that the government has *some* power to limit expression in all areas. The extent of this power must be determined in every case by balancing the case for freedom against the case for order or security.

The clear and present danger test was, of course, a form of balancing, but the scales were definitely tipped in favor of freedom; as Justice Brandeis said, the apprehended evil must be not only clear and present but also "relatively serious" and so "imminent" that it could not be averted by the processes of education. Advocates of the preferred position for civil liberties also allowed for balancing, but freedom's thumb on the scales was even heavier here.

The more recent proponents of balancing on the Supreme Court, principally Justice Harlan, have weighed freedom against order with no preferences. The basic notion of the balancers, as Emerson has expressed it, is "that the court must, in each case, balance the individual and social interest in freedom of expression against the social interest sought by the regulation which restricts expression."[17]

---

[15] Book review, 62 HARVARD LAW REVIEW 891 (1949).

[16] See Chapter 5; also Edmond Cahn, "Mr. Justice Black and the First Amendment 'Absolutes': A Public Interview," 37 NEW YORK UNIVERSITY LAW REVIEW 37 (1962).

[17] Thomas I. Emerson, "Toward a General Theory of the First Amendment," 72 YALE LAW JOURNAL 877 (1963); *Toward a General Theory of the First Amendment* (New York: Random House, 1966), pp. 53–54.

The balancing formula was applied in the 1950s in cases where the Court was passing on the validity of congressional action against Communists. Initially utilized by Chief Justice Vinson in *American Communications Association v. Douds* (1950), it was perhaps most clearly stated by Justice Harlan in *Barenblatt v. United States* (1959) for the Court majority in upholding the power of congressional investigation. In some circumstances, Harlan said, the First Amendment would protect an individual from disclosing his associational relationships to a congressional committee. But a witness does not have the right to resist inquiry in all circumstances. Consequently there must be "a balancing by the courts of the competing private and public interests at stake in the particular circumstances shown." Harlan then proceeded to review the individual and the governmental interests at stake, and concluded that "the balance . . . must be struck in favor of the latter."

Justice Black, dissenting in *Barenblatt*, agreed that balancing might be employed by courts to test the validity of a law which "primarily regulates conduct" but which has a minor effect on speech or "indirectly" affects ideas. But he vigorously denied that laws directly abridging First Amendment freedoms could be justified by a balancing process. Such action was a direct challenge to his absolutist interpretation of First Amendment protections. He also protested that Harlan had misused the balancing test because he had balanced "the right of the Government to preserve itself, against Barenblatt's right to refrain from revealing Communist affiliations." The real interest in Barenblatt's silence, Black felt, was not a mere personal one. It was "the interest of the people as a whole in being able to join organizations, advocate causes and make political 'mistakes' without later being subjected to governmental penalties for having dared to think for themselves. . . . It is these interests of society, rather than Barenblatt's own right to silence, which I think the Court should put on the balance against the demands of the Government, if any balancing process is to be tolerated."

Emerson criticizes balancing because it "frames the issues in such a broad and undefined way, is in effect so unstructured, that it can hardly be described as a rule of law at all." It provides "no hard core of doctrine to guide a court," but rather casts it loose "in a vast space . . . to strike a general balance in the light of its own best judgment. . . . If a court takes the test seriously, the factual determinations involved are enormously difficult and time-consuming, and quite unsuitable for the judicial process." But in fact the test does not allow courts to exercise any real degree of independent judgment, because it gives "almost conclusive weight to the legislative judgment."[18]

On the other hand, Dean Alfange, Jr., feels that the balancing doctrine

---

[18] See also criticisms of balancing in Laurent B. Frantz, "The First Amendment in the Balance," 71 YALE LAW JOURNAL 1424–50 (1962); Martin Shapiro, *Freedom of Speech: The Supreme Court and Judicial Review* (Englewood Cliffs, N.J.: Prentice-Hall, 1966), Chapter 3.

has been unfairly abused by liberals because it has been unfairly used by its proponents. He defends balancing of interests as a central feature of sociological jurisprudence; it is an activist technique, well adapted to the settlement of First Amendment cases; it is essential to "an accurate appraisal of reality." He concludes: "The alternative to balancing is to prepackage decisions by setting up objective standards in advance, which, because of their unavoidable abstractness, cannot be made adequate to deal with the constantly varying factual situations which each case presents."[19]

OVERBREADTH

Balancing may be aborted by a more rigorous judicial doctrine, the test of overbreadth.[20] A statute is challenged for overbreadth "on its face," not as applied. The parties and the facts in the case become almost irrelevant. The statute itself is on trial. If a statute's language is so general, if it reaches dangerously close to forbidden restrictions on expression or can be so interpreted, it may have a "chillng effect" that goes far beyond the immediate parties to the litigation. The very existence of such an overbroad law may cause others not before the court to refrain from constitutionally protected expression. An example is *Aptheker v. Secretary of State* (1964) where a statute forbidding the issuance of a passport to any member of the Communist party was held to assume overbroadly and unconstitutionally that all members of the party were a danger to the United States if they engaged in foreign travel.

Related to the overbreadth concept are the tests of "less drastic means" and "void for vagueness." Like overbreadth, they judge legislation on its face, and require courts to forecast the probable effects of restrictive language on speech and action. The less drastic means test accepts the legitimacy of a legislative purpose, but insists that it can be achieved by less threatening language or sanctions.[21] The objection to statutory vagueness is that it fails to give adequate notice of the legislative purpose or intention.

THE TWO-LEVEL THEORY

Finally, the Supreme Court has on occasion sought to solve some of its First Amendment problems by dividing expression into two levels—one level to which the First Amendment applies and a second level of expression that does not deserve constitutional protection. The Court first spelled out this theory in the case of *Chaplinsky v. New Hampshire* (1942). Chaplinsky, threatened with arrest after creating a public disturbance by his open denunciations of all religion as a "racket," had told a city marshal of Rochester, New

[19] "The Balancing of Interests in Free Speech Cases: In Defense of an Abused Doctrine," 2 LAW IN TRANSITION QUARTERLY 1, 22 (1965).

[20] "The First Amendment Overbreadth Doctrine," 83 HARVARD LAW REVIEW 844 (1970).

[21] "Less Drastic Means and the First Amendment," 78 YALE LAW REVIEW 464 (1969).

Hampshire, that "you are a goddamned racketeer" and "a damned fascist and the whole government of Rochester are fascists or agents of fascists." The Court upheld Chaplinsky's conviction for violating a state statute against calling anyone "offensive or derisive" names in public. Justice Murphy, writing for a unanimous Court, said:

✓ There are certain well-defined and narrowly limited classes of speech, the prevention and punishment of which has never been thought to raise any Constitutional problem. These include the lewd and the obscene, the profane, the libelous, and the insulting or "fighting" words—those which by their very utterance inflict injury or tend to incite an immediate breach of the peace. It has been well observed that such utterances are no essential part of any exposition of ideas, and are of such slight social value as a step to truth that any benefit that may be derived from them is clearly outweighed by the social interest in order and morality.

This conception that only speech with "social value" is protected by the First Amendment solved the Court's immediate problem in the *Chaplinksy* case, but it has difficult and serious implications that have made the two-level theory of dubious value.

APPRAISAL

The various doctrines just reviewed are obviously related to the results that their judicial practitioners wished to achieve and the conceptions they had of their judicial responsibilities. In fact, Martin Shapiro, referring to the "polemical origins" of these doctrines, goes so far as to say that it is a "grave error to take them seriously instead of viewing them in their true light as the superficial ploys of the deeper struggle between activist and modest [self-restraint] tendencies on the Court." [22] Without going this far, one can point up the relations between these doctrines and their consequences for judicial review.

The absolutist position involves a maximum of judicial challenge to legislatures with a minimum exercise of judicial judgment, because the absolutist automatically strikes down any legislation that abridges protected liberties. The two-level theory is another manifestation of absolutism, but at the other end of the scale; expressions on the lower level are absolutely unprotected, so the judge need neither challenge legislative infringements on expression at that level nor exercise judicial judgment.

The reasonable man test and the balancing technique as employed on the Court may be paired. Both are doctrines of judicial self-restraint and rationalizations for letting legislatures have their own way. The test of reasonableness, as Felix S. Cohen wrote, "makes of our courts lunacy

[22] Op. cit., p. 87.

commissions sitting in judgment upon the mental capacity of legislators."[23] Since legislators are seldom lunatics, their actions are seldom without some justification in reason.

The clear and present danger test and the preferred position doctrine are also closely related. Both require judges to take at least a moderately activist stance and to exercise responsible judgment in determining whether the First Amendment has been breached. These tests do not give the automatic answers of the absolutists, but, in contrast to the pseudo-standards of the reasonableness and balancing doctrines, they do supply positive and workable standards to guide judicial judgment.[24]

With this introduction to the principal standards developed by or available to the Supreme Court for interpreting First Amendment freedoms, we now turn to an examination of their application in specific fields of protected expression.

---

[23] L. K. Cohen, ed., *The Legal Conscience: Selected Papers of Felix S. Cohen* (New Haven: Yale University Press, 1960), p. 44.

[24] See Shapiro, op. cit., Chapter 4, for a strong defense of the clear and present danger and preferred position tests.

3
Freedom of Speech

The First Amendment provides that "the freedom of speech" shall not be abridged by law. Communication by speech is by definition a social experience that must involve the interaction of at least two persons. Here is the beginning of a community interest in the speech process. Suppose two persons are discussing politics in a private home. Certainly there is no case for governmental restraint here. But wait! What if the discussion becomes an argument and voices are raised, to the annoyance of neighbors? Or suppose one of the discussants applies offensive language to the other, who resents it and starts a brawl? Suppose a weapon is drawn? At some point along the way a speech situation in which the government could have no interest has turned into a matter justifying public intervention, and all this with only two participants.

As we increase the number of discussants and move them from a private to a public location, the opportunities for public intervention are multiplied. Suppose an unpopular group wants to meet in a public school auditorium. Suppose demonstrators convene in a public park or parade on a public street, thereby creating traffic problems and making it likely that persons unsympathetic to the demonstrators will happen by and be tempted to display their opposition. Suppose that loudspeakers being used at an outdoor meeting annoy by their noise, regardless of the words used, other members of the public rightfully in the area.

Obviously there is no end to the complications that can arise in a speech situation as we move out from a constitutionally protected core into areas where preservation of speech rights must compete with other allowable public interests. Because, as Justice Jackson said in *Kunz v. New York* (1951), "the vulnerability of various forms of communication to community control must be proportioned to their impact upon other community interests," it will be helpful to distinguish three different communication situations: pure speech (speech without conduct), speech plus conduct, and symbolic speech (conduct without speech).

PURE SPEECH

"Pure speech" is a concept created by the Supreme Court. It was first developed in the Court's labor picketing decisions to take account of the fact that picketing is more than speech. In the 1940 case of *Thornhill v. Alabama* the Court broadly assimilated peaceful picketing to freedom of speech, and so protected it by the First Amendment against abridgement. But very soon the Court concluded that this was a partially incorrect conception of picketing, and began to qualify its position. As Justice Douglas said in a 1942 decision: "Picketing by an organized group is more than free speech, since it involves patrol of a particular locality and since the very presence of a picket line may induce action of one kind or another, quite irrespective of the nature of the ideas which are being disseminated."[1] In *Cox v. Louisiana* (1965) Justice Goldberg speaks of those "who communicate ideas by pure speech," as contrasted with those "who would communicate ideas by conduct such as patrolling, marching, and picketing on streets and highways." Again in the same opinion he refers to "speech in its pristine form." Pure speech would include, we can assume, communication taking place by the spoken word in face-to-face contacts, addresses or remarks at meetings, speech amplified by mechanical means or on the channels of the various communications media. Pure speech can range from dull expositions to the most emotional harangues. The distinctive qualities of pure speech are that it relies for its effect only on the power of the ideas or emotions that are communicated by speech and that usually the audience is a voluntary one which chooses to listen to the speaker's message.

Because pure speech situations generally cause no interference with or inconvenience to those not involved in the communication process, justification for community control is at an absolute minimum. In fact, legislation permitting the restriction or punishment of pure speech is generally regarded as invalid on its face. For example, in *Street v. New York* (1969), the Court dealt with a New York statute making it a misdemeanor to mutilate or cast contempt on the American flag "by

[1] *Bakery and Pastry Drivers Local v. Wohl* (1942).

words or act," and it held that punishment "merely for speaking defiant or contemptuous words" was unconstitutional.

There are, however, many borderline situations where exception may be taken to the general rule. In Chapter 2 we noted that *Chaplinsky v. New Hampshire* (1942) held "fighting words" to be unprotected by the First Amendment, since they were so likely to cause a breach of the peace. The "fighting words" holding, though never overruled, has been narrowly interpreted.[2] In *Gooding v. Wilson* (1972) a Georgia statute punishing "opprobrious words or abusive language, tending to cause a breach of the peace," was invoked to convict a black man who had called a white police officer a "son of a bitch" and had threatened to kill him, choke him, or cut him to pieces. The Supreme Court reversed the conviction because the Georgia courts had not narrowed this statutory language to apply only to "fighting words."

The federal statute punishing threats to kill the President was involved in the case of *Watts v. United States* (1969). A speaker at a public rally on the Washington Monument grounds said that if he was drafted for the Vietnam War and given a rifle, "the first man I want to get in my sights is L. B. J." The Supreme Court reversed his conviction on the ground that any statute making criminal "a form of pure speech" must be strictly interpreted, and this "political hyperbole" was not regarded as a true threat but only as "a very crude offensive method of stating a political opposition to the President."

Statutes punishing public use of "offensive" language or public swearing have likewise been held to strict standards.[3] *Cohen v. California* (1971) concerned a young man who had expressed his opinion of the Vietnam War by wearing in public a jacket bearing the words "Fuck the Draft." He was convicted of disturbing the peace by "offensive conduct." Justice Harlan for the Court held that he had engaged in pure speech, not conduct, and reversed on the ground that use of this four-letter word was unlikely to cause "violent reaction" and that the state lacked authority as a guardian of public morality to try to remove the word from the public vocabulary. In this latter connection Harlan took issue with Murphy's assumption in the *Chaplinsky* case that only speech which is an essential part of an "exposition of ideas" and of "social value

[2] As John Hart Ely says, the category of "fighting words" is "no longer to be understood as a euphemism for either controversial or dirty talk but requires instead an unambiguous invitation to a brawl." See "Flag Desecration," 88 HARVARD LAW REVIEW 1482, 1493 (1975).

[3] In *Eaton v. City of Tulsa* (1974), a witness in court referred to an alleged assailant as "chicken shit." His conviction for contempt of court was reversed by the Supreme Court, which held that this "single isolated use of street vernacular, not directed at the judge or any officer of the court," did not constitute contempt. See also *In re Little* (1972), *Papish v. University of Missouri* (1973), and *Lewis v. New Orleans* (1974).

as a step to truth" is entitled to constitutional protection. In a very perceptive passage Harlan wrote:

> . . . much linguistic expression serves a dual communicative function; it conveys not only ideas capable of relatively precise, detached explication, but otherwise inexpressible emotions as well. In fact, words are often chosen as much for their emotive as their cognitive force. We cannot sanction the view that the Court, while solicitous of the cognitive intent of individual speech, has little or no regard for that emotive function which practically speaking, may often be the more important element of the overall message sought to be communicated.

Of course, "shouting fire in a theater" has been regarded as a classic type of punishable speech ever since Justice Holmes used this example in *Schenck v. United States* (1919). A more up-to-date version of this offense would be saying that there is a bomb on a plane. *Kovacs v. Cooper* (1949) ruled that limits can be set for sound amplification of speech in public places.[4]

Serious limitations on the political speech of government employees were imposed by the Hatch Act, which forbade civil servants to take an active part in political management or campaigns. The Supreme Court upheld the law by a four to three vote in *United Public Workers v. Mitchell* (1947) as an acceptable method of redressing "the present supposed evils of political activity."[5]

The Supreme Court itself undertook a somewhat quixotic campaign against political appointments in *Elrod v. Burns* (1976) and *Branti v. Finkel* (1980). In *Elrod* the incoming county sheriff had fired non-civil-service bailiffs, security guards, and process servers of the opposite party, while in *Branti* it was assistant public defenders who belonged to the wrong party. Justice Brennan wrote both opinions, holding that the dismissals penalized political beliefs and infringed First Amendment freedoms. In *Elrod* he made an exception for employees in policy-making or confidential positions, which the sheriff's aides clearly were not. But assistant public defenders arguably had policy-making duties, so in *Branti* Brennan revised the test to "whether the hiring authority can demonstrate that party affiliation is an appropriate requirement for the effective performance of the public office involved." Justice Powell, dissenting in both cases, charged that the Court had declared "unconstitutional a practice as old as the Republic, a practice which has contributed significantly to the democratization of American politics."

Following the profligate use of funds in the 1972 Nixon campaign,

---

[4] Compare *Saia v. New York* (1948).

[5] The Hatch Act was again upheld in *U.S. Civil Service Commission v. National Association of Letter Carriers* (1973). Nonpolitical speech rights of public employees were limited in *Arnett v. Kennedy* (1974) and *Connick v. Myers* (1983).

Congress adopted a campaign finance law in 1974 that limited both contributions and expenditures, required disclosure of campaign contributions, and provided for public financing of presidential elections. This effort to regulate excessive use of money in elections was a substantial failure, due partly to the incredible complications of enforcement and partly to the Supreme Court's interpretation of the statute.[6] In *Buckley v. Valeo* (1976) the act was attacked on the ground that limitations on contributions and expenditures curbed the First Amendment freedom of contributors and candidates to express themselves in the political marketplace. The Court upheld the limitations on direct contributions to political candidates as representing "only a marginal restriction upon the contributor's ability to engage in free communication." However, the Court did conclude that expenditure limitations would seriously limit access to the expensive mass media which are "indispensable instruments of effective political speech," and so were unconstitutional. The statute also violated the First Amendment by forbidding individuals or groups to make expenditures "relative to particular candidates," such as buying newspaper or television advertising, so long as such expenditures were made independently of the candidate or his agents.

This ruling struck down all the spending ceilings: on independent expenditures on behalf of a candidate, on personal funds spent by a candidate in his own campaign, and on total outlays by the candidate. To be sure, presidential candidates who accept public financing (amounting to $29,440,000 for each major candidate in 1980) are forbidden to raise or spend any additional funds. But the Court's ruling left volunteer political action committees free to spend unlimited amounts, so long as they act independently of the official campaign organizations.[7] The result has been to weaken party organizations and to turn the financing of congressional elections over largely to political action committees representing special interest groups. There were over 3,600 PACs in 1982, and they spent approximately $80 million in that year's elections.

SPEECH PLUS CONDUCT

"Speech plus," as the Court sometimes refers to speech plus conduct, involves the communication of ideas by patrolling, marching, and pick-

---

[6] J. Skelly Wright, "Politics and the Constitution: Is Money Speech?" 85 YALE LAW JOURNAL 1001 (1976).

[7] In *Common Cause v. Schmitt* (1982) the Court, evenly divided, let stand a lower court decision upholding the right of political action committees and other independent groups to spend unlimited amounts in support of presidential candidates. Nor may governments limit campaign contributions by individuals to organizations formed to support or oppose referendums and other ballot measures; *Citizens Against Rent Control v. Berkeley* (1981). But the $5,000 annual limit on contributions to a political action committee is constitutional; *California Medical Association v. Federal Election Commission* (1981).

eting on sidewalks, streets, or other public areas. "Speech plus" is a constitutional hybrid. Insofar as it is speech, it is protected. Insofar as it is conduct, it is subject to regulation where good cause is shown. Picketing and demonstrating involve physical movement of the participants, who rely less upon the persuasive influence of speech to achieve their purposes and more upon the public impact of assembling, marching, and patrolling. Their purpose is to bring a point of view—by signs, slogans, singing, or their mere presence—to the attention of the widest possible public, including those uninterested or even hostile. Demonstrators are likely to seek maximum exposure by going where they will be seen and heard by the most people, which increases the possibility of traffic problems, inconvenience to the public, and breach of the peace.

Communication by use of the streets or other public areas is guaranteed by the concept of the "public forum."[8] It is interesting to note that Holmes, while a member of the Massachusetts supreme court, upheld a Boston ordinance that required a permit from the mayor for persons to "make any public address" on Boston Common. A legislature, he said,

> as representative of the public . . . may and does exercise control over the use the public may make of such places. . . . For the Legislature absolutely or conditionally to forbid public speaking in a highway or public park is no more an infringement of the rights of a member of the public than for the owner of a private house to forbid it in his house.[9]

This early Holmes ruling had to be distinguished or disregarded as dictum when the Supreme Court in the 1930s and 1940s began seriously to consider the constitutional status of meetings in public places. *Hague v. C.I.O.* (1939), the first such encounter, grew out of a Jersey City ordinance that prohibited assemblies "in or upon the public streets, highways, public parks or public buildings" without a permit from the director of public safety. Under Mayor Hague, who became famous for his boast, "I am the law," the CIO was denied use of public halls in Jersey City on the ground that it was a Communist organization. Members of the CIO were searched when coming into the city, were threatened with arrest if they discussed the Wagner Act, were arrested for distributing printed matter, and were forcibly ejected from the city and put on the boat for New York.

The Supreme Court by a five to two vote held that these invasions

---

[8] See Harry Kalven, Jr., "The Concept of the Public Forum," in Philip B. Kurland, ed., *The Supreme Court Review: 1965* (Chicago: University of Chicago Press, 1965), p. 23; Geoffrey R. Stone, "Fora Americana: Speech in Public Places," in Philip B. Kurland, ed., *The Supreme Court Review: 1974* (Chicago: University of Chicago Press, 1974), p. 233.

[9] *Commonwealth v. Davis* (1895); upheld by the U.S. Supreme Court, *Davis v. Massachusetts* (1897).

of liberty could not be defended as valid police regulations. "Wherever the title of street and parks may rest," wrote Justice Roberts, "they have immemorially been held in trust for the use of the public and time out of mind have been used for the purpose of assembly, communicating thoughts between citizens and discussing public questions." Their use for communication of views on national questions may be regulated in the interests of all, but may not in the guise of regulations, be abridged or denied.

So it was established that individuals and groups have a right of access to the public forum for discussion of public issues. This means that speakers can mount soapboxes on street corners, or address groups in public parks. But it does not follow that their access to the public forum is an absolute right beyond restraint or regulation in the public interest.[10] After all, sidewalks, streets, and parks serve other purposes in addition to communication. In an effort to accommodate and reconcile these conflicting interests, legislatures and city councils have rather generally provided for some form of restraint on access to the public forum, thereby creating potential First Amendment problems.

Permit Systems

The duty and responsibility of governmental authorities to keep the streets open obviously justifies them in requiring that persons desiring to parade on the streets secure permits. The Court so held in *Cox v. New Hampshire* (1941), where it unanimously approved the conviction of a group of Jehovah's Witnesses who had marched single file along a downtown city street, carrying placards to advertise a meeting, without securing the special license required by state statute for "parades or processions" on a public street. The statute was held to be a reasonable police regulation, administered under proper safeguards. The Court made clear that it was treating the license requirement as merely a traffic regulation and that the conviction was not for conveying information or holding a meeting. As Justice Reed said in a later case, *Poulos v. New Hampshire* (1953), involving the same statute: "Regulation and suppression are not the same, and courts of justice can tell the difference."

The constitutionality of a permit system can be challenged in two ways. First, the ordinance or statute may be so restrictive, or give such discretionary power to public officials to deny permits, as to be unconstitutional on its face. For example, a city ordinance of Birmingham,

---

[10]In *Lehman v. City of Shaker Heights* (1974), the Supreme Court held that buses on a municipally owned transit system were not a "public forum" and that a candidate for political office could be refused advertising space on the buses without violating his free speech rights. In *People for Free Speech at SAC v. U.S. Air Force* (1982) the Court let stand a lower court ruling that an annual "open house" at an Air Force base was not a "public forum" and exclusion of anti-war protesters did not violate their rights to free speech.

Alabama, authorized a city commission to refuse a parade permit if "in its judgment the public welfare, peace, safety, health, decency, good order, morals or convenience require that it be refused." In *Walker v. Birmingham* (1967) the Supreme Court intimated that this ordinance was unconstitutional on its face, and it specifically so held in *Shuttlesworth v. Birmingham* (1969).

Kunz v. New York (1951) invalidated a New York City ordinance that made it unlawful to hold public worship meetings on the street without first obtaining a permit from the police commissioner. The Court majority regarded the ordinance as giving to "an administrative official discretionary power to control in advance the right of citizens to speak on religious matters on the streets of New York . . . with no appropriate standards to guide his action."

Second, the permit regulations, though phrased with due regard for constitutional requirements, may be administered in a discriminatory or repressive fashion. The authorities may deny permits to some groups, or seek to confine parades to remote areas of the city, or find that demonstrations are never compatible with traffic requirements. In *Niemotko v. Maryland* (1951) a group of Jehovah's Witnesses requesting use of a city park for religious services was denied a permit by the city council, after a hearing where the Witnesses were queried about their alleged refusal to salute the flag and their interpretation of the Bible. The Supreme Court concluded that the permit was denied because of dislike for the group's views and unanimously held such action not only an infringement on freedom of speech but also a denial of equal protection of the law.

Injunctions

In addition, or as an alternative, to control by permits, demonstrations may be limited by court injunctions, which can be fashioned by the judge to specify the form and area of demonstration and even the number of participants. Injunctions may also protect the right to demonstrate. The famous Selma march led by Martin Luther King, Jr., in 1965 took place under the protection of an injunction forbidding interference by Governor George Wallace. Judge Frank Johnson, in issuing the injunction, said: "[The] extent of the right to assemble, demonstrate and march peaceably along the highways and streets in an orderly manner should be commensurate with the enormity of the wrongs that are being protested and petitioned against." Judge Johnson regarded the wrongs here as "enormous."[11]

When a permit for a demonstration has been refused or an injunction has been issued against it, the demonstrators have two choices. They can go ahead with their demonstration and risk arrest, or they can bring

[11] *Williams v. Wallace* (1965).

court action to secure review of the ban. Martin Luther King, Jr., took the first course in 1963 when he and some of his followers, having been denied a Birmingham parade permit, defied a state court injunction against racial demonstrations while tensions were high. He contended that the injunction denied his constitutional rights, and he feared that his protest movement would lose its momentum if he paused to litigate the injunction. For the majority in *Walker v. Birmingham,* Justice Stewart admitted that the injunction raised substantial constitutional issues, but held that it should have been challenged in court, not disobeyed. He sympathized with the "impatient commitment" of the civil rights leaders to their cause, but said, "Respect for judicial process is a small price to pay for the civilizing hand of law, which alone can give abiding meaning to constitutional freedom." Justice Brennan for the minority charged that the Court was ignoring the doctrine of constitutional supremacy and raising Alabama's judicial ruling "above the right of free expression guaranteed by the Federal Constitution." [12]

The 1977 plan of an American Nazi group to stage a march through Skokie, Illinois, a community with a large Jewish population, many of whom had come through the Holocaust, generated a textbook array of countermeasures and litigation. Initially a state court issued a broad injunction against parading in party uniforms, displaying the swastika, or distributing pamphlets that incite hatred. The state supreme court refused to stay the injunction or expedite the appeal, but the U.S. Supreme Court reversed in *National Socialist Party v. Skokie* (1977). An Illinois court then modified the injunction, leaving in effect only the swastika ban, but the state supreme court held the entire injunction unconstitutional, relying on the Supreme Court's decisions protecting "fighting words" and "offensive speech." [13]

Skokie responded with three ordinances, one requiring a massive permit fee, another prohibiting political parades in military style uniforms, and a third invoking the Illinois group libel law. [14] A federal district court held the ordinances unconstitutional, and the Supreme Court denied a stay. With this legal victory, the Nazis cancelled the Skokie march and twenty-five members held a rally in a Chicago park with no serious violence. [15]

Restricted Areas

There are certain types of public areas or buildings where the right to demonstrate may be forbidden because of serious conflict with other

[12] But *Carroll v. President and Commissioners of Princess Anne* (1968) held that an *ex parte* injunction was incompatible with the First Amendment.

[13] *Collin v. Smith* (1978); *Smith v. Collin* (1978).

[14] See the discussion of that law in *Beauharnais v. Illinois* (1942) in Chapter 5.

[15] See David Hamlin, *The Nazi-Skokie Conflict* (Boston: Beacon Press, 1980).

public interests. Traffic considerations may foreclose demonstrations in highly congested areas. Thus Justice Goldberg said in *Cox v. Louisiana* (1965) that no one could "insist upon a street meeting in the middle of Times Square at the rush hour as a form of freedom of speech or assembly." Justice Black would have gone further. In the same case he denied that "speech plus" is speech at all, and would have given the state "general power . . . to bar all picketing on its streets and highways." But this was a minority view, directly in conflict with the *Hague* principle that the use of streets and public places "for purposes of assembly, communicating thoughts between citizens, and discussing public questions [is] a part of the privileges, rights, and liberties of citizens."

Statutes prohibiting the obstruction of "public passages" (i.e., streets and sidewalks) are clearly constitutional if applied in a nondiscriminatory fashion.[16] However, such a statute was invalidated in the *Cox* case because it made a specific exemption for labor picketing. A school antipicketing ordinance was declared invalid in *Police Department of Chicago v. Mosley* (1972), but *Grayned v. Rockford* (1972) upheld an ordinance forbidding noisy and disruptive picketing outside public schools.

A civil rights demonstration on the grounds of the South Carolina state capitol by some two hundred black students was upheld by the Court in *Edwards v. South Carolina* (1963) as the exercise of "basic constitutional rights in their most pristine and classic form." Meetings and demonstrations on the grounds of the United States Capitol have been forbidden since 1882, but this ban was declared unconstitutional by the Court of Appeals for the District of Columbia in a judgment upheld by the Supreme Court in 1972.[17]

Demonstrations in the vicinity of the White House were governed until 1967 by an informal agreement that the District of Columbia police would be given prior notice. But a gathering of 30,000 pro-Israeli demonstrators in Lafayette Park across from the White House in June, 1967, led the National Park Service to issue regulations requiring permits for demonstrations. In 1983 the Park Service permitted a group demonstrating over the plight of the homeless to pitch tents in Lafayette Park, but refused them permission to sleep there over night. The Court of Appeals for the District of Columbia voted, six to five, that for this group sleeping was a form of expression.[18]

In *Greer v. Spock* (1976) the Court upheld the authority of the armed services to bar political candidates and demonstrators from military bases, saying that the business of a military installation is "to train soldiers, not to provide a public forum." The case arose at Fort Dix, New

[16] See *Cameron v. Johnson* (1968).

[17] *Chief of the Capitol Police v. Jeanette Rankin Brigade* (1972).

[18] See "Regulation of White House Demonstrations," 119 UNIVERSITY OF PENNSYL-VANIA LAW REVIEW 688 (1971); *The New York Times*, March 18, 1983.

Jersey, which is crossed by ten paved roads with no entrance barriers or sentries.[19]

In 1949 Congress passed a statute making it illegal to picket or parade in or near a building housing a federal court with the intention of interfering with the administration of justice or influencing judges or jurors in the discharge of their duties. This statute resulted from the picketing of federal courthouses by partisans of the defendants during trials involving leaders of the Communist party, and was adopted by Congress at the urging of the organized bar and the federal judiciary. Several states, including Louisiana, enacted statutes on the same model. In the case of *Cox v. Louisiana,* this statute was invoked against Cox, whose demonstrators had taken up positions 125 feet from the courthouse.

Justice Goldberg for the Court found this law to be "a statute narrowly drawn to punish specific conduct that infringes a substantial state interest in protecting the judicial process." It was "on its face a valid law dealing with conduct subject to regulation so as to vindicate interests of society ... the fact that free speech is intermingled with such conduct does not bring with it constitutional protection." Justice Black was even stronger in his support for the statute, saying: "The streets are not now and never have been the proper place to administer justice."

Whether the Supreme Court itself can be picketed was at issue in *United States v. Grace* (1983). A federal statute bars picketing, distributing leaflets, and demonstrating on the Supreme Court grounds, including the sidewalk that encircles the block-square site of the Court. The Court upheld the ban on protests within the Court building or on Court grounds, but allowed carrying flags, banners, or signs on the perimeter sidewalks.

A public library was the scene of a peaceful sit-in by five blacks protesting its racially discriminatory policies in *Brown v. Louisiana* (1966). In spite of Justice Black's argument that "order and tranquility" are essential to the operation of libraries and that they are not permissible places for demonstrations, Justice Fortas for the five-judge majority held that by their "silent and reproachful presence" where they had a right to be, the protesters were exercising their constitutional right to petition the government for the redress of grievances. But later that year, in *Adderly v. Florida* (1966), the Court took a different view of a demonstration on the grounds of a county jail, protesting segregation in the jail. Now speaking for the majority, Black held that jail grounds, where security is essential, are not open to the public and cannot be the site of demonstrations.

Whether demonstrators have a right of access to the grounds of shopping centers, which are technically private property, has been trou-

[19] Similarly, *Brown v. Glines* (1980) upheld regulations requiring members of the air force to obtain approval from their commanders before circulating petitions on air force bases. See also *Secretary of the Navy v. Huff* (1980). Brennan charged that these decisions were based on "a series of platitudes about the special nature and overwhelming importance of military necessity."

blesome. In *Amalgamated Food Employees Union v. Logan Valley Plaza* (1968) the Court upheld the right of a labor union to picket a store in a shopping center where there was no other feasible way to convey the facts of a labor dispute to the public. The Court relied on *Marsh v. Alabama* (1946), which had approved the right to distribute religious literature in the business district of a company-owned town. But in *Lloyd Corp. v. Tanner* (1972) it was distribution of handbills that was involved, which the Court refused to protect because there were "adequate alternative avenues of communication" that would not infringe on private property rights. *Hudgens v. NLRB* (1976) was another labor picketing situation, but the Court now not only declined to follow *Logan Valley;* Stewart's opinion contended that the guarantee of free expression was completely inapplicable to shopping centers, and that *Lloyd* had overruled *Logan Valley.*

Just as it appeared that the matter of access to shopping centers had been settled in the negative, it was unsettled again by *PruneYard Shopping Center v. Robins* (1980). The case involved students who had set up tables in a shopping center for distributing pamphlets and securing signatures on petitions. The California supreme court upheld the students on the ground that the state constitution protected speech and petitioning, even in shopping centers. Justice Rehnquist for a unanimous Court then avoided reversal by ruling that California could provide in its own constitution for individual liberties more expansive than those conferred by the federal Constitution, so long as there was no taking without just compensation or violation of any other federal constitutional provision.[20]

Privacy Problems

Picketing or demonstrating in residential areas raises privacy issues but was upheld by dictum in *Gregory v. Chicago* (1969). There, some one hundred predominantly black activists had marched on the sidewalks around the home of Mayor Daley to protest policies of the Chicago superintendent of schools. Residents of the wholly white area, resenting the intrusion, threatened the marchers with violence; the police, fearing a riot, arrested some of the demonstrators, five of whom were found guilty of disorderly conduct. The Supreme Court reversed the convictions as unsupported by evidence and also expressed the opinion that such a march, "if peaceful and orderly, falls well within the sphere of conduct protected by the First Amendment.[21]

[20] See "Private Abridgement of Speech and the State Constitution," 90 YALE LAW JOURNAL 165 (1980).

[21] See "Picketers at the Doorstep," 9 HARVARD CIVIL RIGHTS–CIVIL LIBERTIES LAW REVIEW 95 (1974). *Carey v. Brown* (1980) held the Illinois law against residential picketing unconstitutional because the act exempted from its prohibitions picketing of a place of employment involved in a labor dispute.

May the state protect individuals in their homes from unwanted communications? *Martin v. City of Struthers* (1943) tested an ordinance that made it unlawful for a person distributing "handbills, circulars or other advertisements" to ring the doorbell or otherwise summon the occupant of a residence to the door for the purpose of receiving such material. The ordinance was applied against a member of Jehovah's Witnesses who was distributing a dodger announcing a meeting and lecture. The motivation for the ordinance was to protect the daytime sleep of residents of this industrial town, since many of them were employed on night shifts in factories.

By a six to three vote, the Supreme Court invalidated the ordinance. Justice Black noted that "for centuries it has been a common practice in this and other countries for persons not specifically invited to go from home to home and knock on doors or ring doorbells to communicate ideas to the occupants or to invite them to political, religious, or other kinds of public meetings." To be sure, door-to-door visitation might be a nuisance or a blind for criminal activities. But it was also a customary part of the techniques of many political, religious, and labor groups, and "is essential to the poorly financed causes of little people."

Breard v. Alexandria (1951) appeared to reverse the balance struck between householders and canvassers in *Martin*. Here an ordinance barring house-to-house canvassing was applied successfully against solicitation for magazine subscriptions. But the commercial element in the solicitation was regarded by the Court as distinguishing *Breard* from *Martin*.

Subsequent rulings have upheld the rights of noncommercial canvassers. *Hynes v. Mayor of Oradell* (1976) invalidated an ordinance requiring house-to-house canvassers in political campaigns to give advance written notice to the local police department, though on grounds of vagueness of the ordinance rather than on violation of privacy or First Amendment grounds. But *Village of Schaumberg v. Citizens for a Better Environment* (1980) relied firmly on First Amendment interests in striking down an ordinance that barred door-to-door solicitation of contributions by charitable organizations that did not use at least 75 percent of their receipts for charitable purposes.

Outside the home a person runs the risks of all the annoyances, distractions, and dangers of modern urban life. Some of these the law may attempt to alleviate, but if speech is an element in the alleged offense there may be constitutional issues, as the sound truck decisions illustrate. In *Saia v. New York* (1948) the Court upheld the right of a minister to engage regularly in preaching over a loudspeaker in a public park, over Frankfurter's protest that uncontrolled noise disturbs "the refreshment of mere silence." But the following year *Kovacs v. Cooper* undermined *Saia* by approving an ordinance making it unlawful for sound trucks emitting "loud and raucous" noises to operate on public streets.[22]

The right to approach persons peacefully in public places to engage them in conversation is a protected interest, provided the other party does not object. A classic case was *Cantwell v. Connecticut* (1940). Cantwell, a Jehovah's Witness seeking converts, stopped two pedestrians and asked that they listen to a record on the phonograph he was carrying. They agreed. The record was a violent attack on Catholics, and they were Catholics. They reacted, but nonviolently, and no blows were struck; nevertheless, Cantwell was convicted of breach of the peace. The Supreme Court reversed, holding that there had been "no intentional discourtesy, no personal abuse."

But solicitation by the Hare Krishna sect has tended to be more persistent and annoying, concentrating particularly in airports and other centers where people congregate. Local legislatures have responded with a variety of restraints. In *Heffron v. International Society for Krishna Consciousness* (1981) the Minnesota state fair had limited all organizations to fixed locations, which restricted the sect's usual peripatetic solicitation for funds. The Court rejected the Krishna protest and upheld the restrictions as a legitimate measure of crowd control.

Picketing and Boycotts

Picketing in labor disputes has a long history and presents special problems. Initially all labor picketing was regarded by the courts as tortious conduct and illegal. Gradually the view developed that peaceful picketing by strikers who had a direct economic interest to serve might be permitted by the state, but "stranger picketing" remained outside the law. In 1921 the Supreme Court cautiously admitted that "strikers and their sympathizers" might maintain one picket "for each point of ingress and egress" at a plant or place of business. Unless severely limited in this way, the Court concluded, picketing "indicated a militant purpose, inconsistent with peaceable persuasion."[23]

It is a long jump from 1921 to 1940, when in the case of *Thornhill v. Alabama* Justice Murphy put peaceful picketing of all kinds under the protection of the free speech clause, saying: "in the circumstances of our times the dissemination of information concerning the facts of a labor dispute must be regarded as within that area of free discussion that is guaranteed by the Constitution."[24]

---

[22]A similar claim of "aural aggression" was rejected in *Public Utilities Commission v. Pollak* (1952), where the District of Columbia public transportation system had installed radio receivers in its streetcars broadcasting news, music, and advertisements. Douglas and Black, dissenting, protested that the rights of a "captive audience" were being violated.

[23]*American Steel Foundries v. Tri-City Central Trades Council* (1921).

[24]The way had been prepared for *Thornhill* by Justice Brandeis's holding in *Senn v. Tile Layers' Protective Union* (1937).

But picketing is more than a form of communication. It is likely that many people respect picket lines simply to avoid trouble or charges of being antiunion, not because they are intellectually persuaded by the signs pickets carry. On many picket lines the purpose is not so much publicity as it is economic coercion. Moreover, picketing in labor disputes often results in violence. Almost immediately after *Thornhill,* the Court had to begin qualifying the right to picket. In *Milk Wagon Drivers Union v. Meadowmoor Dairies* (1941), the Court held that the Illinois courts were justified in enjoining all picketing in a labor dispute which had been so marred by past violence that it was believed impossible for future picketing to be maintained on a peaceful basis. But the likelihood of violence was not the only ground on which the Court proved willing to support restrictions on picketing. In *Carpenters and Joiners Union v. Ritter's Cafe* (1942), Ritter was having a residence built by nonunion labor, but the pickets were operating around his cafe, a mile away, where the pressure would hurt him more. By a five to four vote the Court ruled that Texas had the right to restrict picketing to the area within which a labor dispute arises.

More important as illustrating the conflict between rights of communication and other lawful social interests was a series of cases beginning in 1949. *Giboney v. Empire Storage & Ice Co.* (1949) upheld an injunction against a union that was picketing to force an employer to agree to a restraint of trade that was illegal under state law. *Hughes v. Superior Court of California* (1950) approved an injunction against a citizen group that was demanding that a store's employees be in proportion to the racial origin of its customers. In *International Brotherhood of Teamsters v. Hanke* (1950), the injunction, which the Court approved, had been issued simply to prevent a union from dictating business policy to self-employed used-car dealers. An effort by pickets to force an employer to coerce his employees into joining the union was successfully enjoined in *International Brotherhood of Teamsters, Local 695 v. Vogt* (1957). Thus it appears that legislatures and judges are largely free to define public purposes and protect public interests that may override picketing rights. As Justice Frankfurter said in the *Hughes* case: "Picketing, not being the equivalent of speech as a matter of fact, is not its inevitable legal equivalent. Picketing is not beyond the control of a State if the manner in which picketing is conducted or the purpose which it seeks to effectuate gives ground for its disallowance."

Civil rights organizations conducted a seven-year boycott of white merchants in Port Gibson, Mississippi, in which some violence occurred. The state courts held the boycott unlawful and assessed damages of $1.2 million against the organizers and participants, including the national NAACP. The Supreme Court in *NAACP v. Claiborne Hardware Co.* (1982) ruled that a nonviolent, politically motivated boycott designed to force governmental or economic change enjoyed First Amendment protection. While violence and fighting words that provoke immediate violence are not protected, in this case the "emotionally charged rhetoric" of the boycott organizer encouraging unity of black citizens and participation in the boycott was protected speech. With no evidence that the NAACP had knowledge of or ratified any acts of violence, damages against the organization were stricken.

SYMBOLIC SPEECH AND EXPRESSION

Symbolic speech involves the communicating of ideas or protests by conduct, such as burning a draft card or pouring blood over draft files to express opposition to the Vietnam War. Such action serves as a surrogate for speech and conveys an ideational message perhaps more effectively than speech would do. But is symbolic speech for that reason entitled to the full constitutional protection of normal speech?

The Supreme Court had an early encounter with this question in *Stromberg v. California* (1931), involving a state law that made it a felony to display a red flag as an "emblem of opposition to organized government." Conviction of the director of a children's summer camp for raising a red flag every morning was reversed by the Supreme Court on the ground that the statutory language was so loose as to threaten free political discussion.

A much more significant form of symbolic speech was the sit-in movement that developed in the early 1960s to protest racial discrimination, primarily in Southern eating places. As a protest, blacks would take seats at lunch counters and, if refused service, continue to sit there until arrested or ousted by force. They were customarily charged either with breach of the peace resulting from trespass, or criminal trespass (that is, remaining on private property after being requested to leave).

Ordinarily, trespass on private property is clearly illegal and subject to punishment. Does it gain a protected status when it is employed as a form of expression, as a social protest? A sit-in, Justice Harlan readily conceded in *Garner v. Louisiana* (1961), "was a form of expression within the range of protections afforded by the Fourteenth Amendment." It was

> . . . as much a part of the "free trade in ideas" . . . as in verbal expression, more commonly thought of as "speech." It, like speech, appeals to good sense and to "the power of reason as applied through public discussion" . . . just as much as, if not more than, a public oration delivered from a soapbox at a street corner. This Court has never limited the right to speak, a protected "liberty" under the Fourteenth Amendment . . . to mere verbal expression.

However, Harlan went on to deny that the Fourteenth Amendment would protect "demonstrations conducted on private property over the objection of the owner," which of course was the issue in the sit-in cases. Black put the same view even more forcibly in *Bell v. Maryland* (1964): "Unquestionably petitioners had a constitutional right to express these views [against refusal of service] wherever they had an unquestioned legal right to be." But they had no legal right to be on the premises of the restaurant against the owner's will. "The right to freedom of expression is a right to express views—not a right to force other people to supply a platform or a pulpit."

The Court as a whole, however, never endorsed the view that sit-ins involving trespass were illegal. Though it decided a dozen sit-in cases between 1960 and 1964, it never found one that would require it to pass squarely on the constitutional situation of sit-in trespassers. Eventually the federal Civil Rights Act of 1964, plus similar state statutes, terminated the constitutional issue by making racial discrimination in public accommodations unlawful.[25]

The clearest instance of Court approval for symbolic speech came in *Tinker v. Des Moines School District* (1969). School officials had forbidden pupils to wear black armbands as a protest against Vietnam on the ground that this gesture might cause controversy in the school. The Court, however, upheld the students, saying that "apprehension of disturbance is not enough to overcome the right to freedom of expression." By contrast, the Court refused in *United States v. O'Brien* (1968) to grant the legitimacy of symbolic draft card burning. Chief Justice Warren wrote: "We cannot accept the view that an apparently limitless variety of conduct can be labeled 'speech' whenever the person engaging in the conduct intends thereby to express an idea."[26]

Another, and rather common, form of protest against the Vietnam War involved mutilation or unconventional treatment of the American flag. Various federal and state statutes make such conduct punishable. The Supreme Court has appeared to assume that abuse of the flag can be made illegal, but it has nevertheless usually found grounds for reversing convictions by strict interpretation of the statutes involved. *Street v. New York* (1968) has already been noted. In *Smith v. Goguen* (1974), where a youth had worn a small flag on the seat of his pants, a statute punishing "contemptuous" treatment of the flag was held unconstitutionally vague and overbroad. At the time of the Cambodian invasion, a college student hung a flag upside down with a peace symbol attached outside his window. The Court in *Spence v. Washington* (1974) reversed

---

[25] For decisions subsequent to the 1964 act, see *Bell v. Maryland* (1964) and *Hamm v. City of Rock Hill* (1964).

[26] For a critique of this decision, see Dean Alfange, Jr., "Free Speech and Symbolic Conduct," in Philip B. Kurland, ed., *The Supreme Court Review: 1968* (Chicago: University of Chicago Press, 1968), pp. 1–52.

his conviction for improper use of the flag, holding that he was engaged in a form of communication.[27]

While public nudity has in some instances been regarded as a form of expression entitled to constitutional protection, in *California v. LaRue* (1972) regulations of the state Alcoholic Beverage Control Department forbidding nude entertainment in bars and other licensed establishments were upheld, Justice Rehnquist concluding that the activity in question partook "more of gross sexuality than of communication."

SPEECH AND BREACH OF THE PEACE

In all states there are statutes defining and punishing such misdemeanors and crimes as breach of the peace, disorderly conduct, inciting to riot, and the like. Speech can be, and often is, the direct cause of incitement to breach of the peace. A group assembled to hear speakers or to communicate ideas by demonstrating or picketing can easily develop into a disturbance of the public tranquillity. Law-enforcement officers and courts are continually required to balance the claims of free speech against those of law and order.

Reviewing the Supreme Court's experience with these difficult problems, we find that three stages in the judicial analysis can be distinguished. First, the Court must determine whether the speech involved in the prosecution for breach of the peace is of a type that enjoys constitutional protection. Normally there is no difficulty in deciding this issue favorably. The assertion in *Chaplinsky v. New Hampshire* (1942) that certain types of speech—"the lewd and obscene, the profane, the libelous, and the insulting or 'fighting' words"—are so lacking in social utility as to forfeit any claim to First Amendment protection has been largely reconsidered by the Court. In the overwhelming majority of speech prosecutions, there can be no doubt that the First Amendment is applicable. The principal problem, as we have seen, comes in connection with symbolic speech.

The second question is whether the ordinance or statute under which the speaker is being prosecuted, both on its face and as judicially applied in the instant case, validly states or recognizes the constitutional status which protected speech enjoys under the First Amendment. The best case to illustrate this requirement is *Terminiello v. Chicago* (1949). The controversy there arose out of a fascist-type speech made under riotous conditions in a Chicago auditorium in 1946. Following the affair, Terminiello was found guilty of disorderly conduct under an ordinance covering "all persons who shall make, aid, countenance, or assist in

---

[27]But in *Kime v. United States* (1982) the Court refused to hear a constitutional challenge to a law making deliberate mutilation of the American flag a federal crime.

making any improper noise, riot, disturbance, breach of the peace, or diversion tending to a breach of the peace."

This case seemed to offer the Supreme Court an opportunity and an obligation to consider the facts of this disturbance against a background of free speech theory that would give due weight to the right of a speaker to address willing listeners in a private hall, and the nature of the community's obligation to defend that right against violent interruptions from outsiders. But a five-judge majority, speaking through Justice Douglas, never reached this issue. It appeared from an examination of the record that the trial judge had charged the jury that "breach of the peace" consists of any "misbehavior which violates the public peace and decorum" and that the "misbehavior may constitute a breach of the peace if it stirs the public to anger, invites dispute, brings about a condition of unrest, or creates a disturbance, or if it molests the inhabitants in the enjoyment of peace and quiet by arousing alarm."

The Court majority held that this construction of the ordinance was as relevant and as binding as though the "precise words had been written into the ordinance." Consequently, the issue was whether an ordinance which penalized speech that might "invite dispute" or "bring about a condition of unrest" was constitutional. Justice Douglas's brief opinion, almost without argument and completely without reference to the facts of the riotous meeting, concluded that speech could not be censored or punished on such grounds but only where it was shown likely "to produce a clear and present danger of a serious substantive evil that rises far above public inconvenience, annoyance, or unrest." Consequently, the conviction was reversed.

If the Court had not invalidated the ordinance by this construction, it would have had to proceed to the third stage of the analysis and determine whether the danger of breach of the peace resulting from the speech was so real that it overrode the claims of constitutional protection. This is precisely what the dissenters in *Terminiello,* who found no fault with the ordinance, did. Justice Jackson supplied a detailed summary of the factual situation on which the prosecution was based and which was in the trial judge's mind as he charged the jury. He conveyed some sense of the inflammatory situation at the meeting by quoting at length from the stenographic record of Terminiello's speech and his testimony at the trial. For Jackson, who had been Allied prosecutor in the Nazi war crimes trials at Nuremberg, this exhibition of political, racial, and ideological conflict was not an isolated or unintended collision of forces. "It was a local manifestation of a worldwide and standing conflict between two groups of revolutionary fanatics, each of which had imported to this country the strong-arm technique developed in the struggle by which their kind has devastated Europe."[28]

---

[28] Other breach of the peace cases already discussed are *Cantwell v. Connecticut* (1940) and *Cohen v. California* (1971).

A federal breach of the peace statute that presents serious questions of constitutionality is the Anti-Riot Act of 1968. Reacting to the violent demonstrations of that period and believing that they were caused by certain activists moving through the country, Congress attached a rider to the 1968 Civil Rights Act making it a crime to travel in interstate commerce for the purpose of inciting riots. Violation of the statute was charged against the Chicago Seven in connection with the violence at the 1968 Democratic convention. Five of the defendants were convicted, but the court of appeals reversed for errors in the trial.[29] However, by a vote of two to one, the appeals court upheld the constitutionality of the act.[30]

THE EXPECTATION OF VIOLENCE

To secure a conviction for breach of the peace involving speech, we have seen that the peace need not be actually broken. It may be enough that the speech tended with sufficient directness toward a breach of the peace. But who is to make this determination, and on what grounds?

Initially, of course, the chances of violence must be appraised by the police or other law-enforcement officers present at the scene of the potential disturbance, in deciding whether to arrest the speaker. Then the prosecuting attorney must prove to a trial judge and jury, using primarily evidence supplied by the police, that a breach of the peace had been committed or incited. Finally, the record of the trial-court proceedings will be reviewed by one or more appellate courts to determine whether the conviction can be supported on the facts and the law. Each stage of judicial review moves further away from the immediacy of the events, and relies more and more on a cold written record. On what basis can judges thus remote from the controversy challenge the judgment of the police who were on the scene?

A policeman's lot in a trouble spot is not a happy one. He must appraise the chances of violence, and determine how long he can let the speech or demonstration go on without interfering, in the hope that violence will not actually break out. If he determines that he must intervene, he must decide which of the participating parties offers the greater threat to the peace. Should he arrest the speaker or those who are threatening the speaker? And how will he later prove in court that his judgment was the one called for by his obligation to preserve the peace?

---

[29] *United States v. Dellinger* (1972). During the Indian occupation of Wounded Knee, South Dakota, in 1973, at least fifty persons were arrested in various states under the Anti-Riot Act when they crossed state lines in autos with food and clothing for the "rioters" at Wounded Knee.

[30] See Lionel H. Frankel, *Law, Power, and Personal Freedom* (St. Paul, Minn.: West Publishing Company, 1975), pp. 695–728.

Only a comparatively few Supreme Court decisions speak to these issues. *Feiner v. New York* (1951) involved a university student who made a rather inflammatory speech on a Syracuse streetcorner to some seventy-five listeners. Two policemen, aware of a certain "restlessness" in the crowd, demanded that Feiner stop and, when he refused, arrested him. Feiner's conviction for disorderly conduct was upheld by the Supreme Court. The evidence as to whether "a clear danger of disorder" threatened as a result of the speech, Chief Justice Vinson said, had been weighed by the trial court, and the conclusion had been affirmed by two higher state courts. Feiner had a right to speak, but he did not have a right to "incite to riot." But Justice Douglas, dissenting, thought that the record indicated no likelihood of riot. "It shows an unsympathetic audience and the threat of one man to haul the speaker from the stage. It is against that kind of threat that speakers need police protection. If they do not receive it and instead the police throw their weight on the side of those who would break up the meetings, the police become the new censors of speech."

The *Feiner* case did indeed approve a formula, the so-called "heckler's veto," which can make police suppression of speech quite simple. Any group that wishes to silence a speaker can cause a disturbance in the audience that will justify the police in requesting the speaker to stop, backed up by the threat of a disorderly conduct charge.

By 1963, when *Edwards v. South Carolina* was decided, the civil rights revolution was in full swing and the Court had had more time to think about police obligations in handling speakers and demonstrators. In the *Edwards* situation, a peaceful demonstration on the South Carolina state capitol grounds was ordered to disperse, and when the demonstrators refused, they were arrested and subsequently convicted of the common-law crime of breach of the peace.

With only one dissent, the Supreme Court reversed the conviction. The reasoning followed the three stages already described. First, the students were exercising "basic constitutional rights in their most pristine and classic form." Second, the offense had not been defined in "a precise and narrowly drawn regulatory statute" aimed at "certain specific conduct." Rather, they were convicted of an offense "so generalized" that it was admittedly "not susceptible of exact definition." As in the *Terminiello* case, South Carolina law as interpreted and applied here had sought "to make criminal the peaceful expression of unpopular views," which the Fourteenth Amendment does not permit.

Although this holding would have been sufficient to decide the case, the Court, perhaps mindful of the criticism it had received in *Terminiello* for ignoring the factual situation, went on to the third stage. On the basis of its own "independent examination of the whole record," the Court denied that there had been sufficient danger of breach of the peace to

justify the police demand to disperse. The students had "peaceably assembled" and "peaceably expressed their grievances." Not until they were
warned to "disperse on pain of arrest did they do more." Even then, there
was only a "religious harangue" and the signing of songs. "There was no
violence or threat of violence on their part, or on the part of any member
of the crowd watching them. Police protection was 'ample.'"

In *Cox v. Louisiana* (1965) there was, in addition to the charges
noted earlier, also a breach of the peace conviction. The Court found *Cox*
strikingly similar to *Edwards* and reversed the conviction, Goldberg
holding the speech and assembly involved here constitutionally protected
and the law applied "unconstitutionally broad." The Court's independent
examination of the record, supported by a television news film of the
events which the Court viewed, indicated that the meeting was "orderly
and not riotous." The fear of violence was based on the presence of a
group of 100 to 300 tense and agitated white citizens who were looking
on from across the street. But they were separated from the students by
seventy-five armed policemen, a fire truck, and the fire department, and
the evidence indicated that they could have handled the crowd. Only after
this finding of an absence of danger did Justice Goldberg note, as an
additional reason for reversing the conviction, that the breach of the
peace statute involved here was "unconstitutionally vague in its overly
broad scope."

REDRESS FOR VIOLATION
OF SPEECH RIGHTS

Protection of free speech rights has been almost entirely in the hands of
courts as they develop and apply constitutional standards in trying
prosecutions for alleged speech offenses of the type discussed in this
chapter. There has been no recent congressional legislation to protect
speech rights; the civil rights acts of 1957, 1960, 1964, 1965, and 1968 dealt
primarily with public accommodations, racial segregation, voting, and
housing. In fact, Congress was more likely to limit speech rights, as by
the Anti-Riot Act of 1968 and the investigations conducted by Senator
Joseph McCarthy and the House Committee on Un-American Activities.
The principal administrative agencies in the civil rights field are the
Commission on Civil Rights, created by the 1957 act, and the Civil
Rights Division in the Department of Justice, but neither has been much
concerned with speech rights.

This means that positive action to enforce speech rights and to
secure redress for abuse of those rights must depend primarily on the
initiative of individuals or civil rights groups. Their recourse to the
courts may be to seek injunctive protection, as we have seen. Also, redress
in the form of money damages may be sought under the Civil Rights Act
of 1871, which provides that:

Every person who, under color of any statute, ordinance, regulation, custom, or usage, of any State or Territory, subjects, or causes to be subjected, any citizen of the United States or other person within the jurisdiction thereof to the deprivation of any rights, privileges, or immunities secured by the Constitution and laws, shall be liable to the party injured in an action at law, suit in equity, or other proper proceeding for redress [42 U.S.C., sec. 1983].[31]

Only recently have suits under section 1983 been successful, whether for deprivation of speech or any other civil rights. In *Tenney v. Brandhove* (1951) damages were sought against a California legislative investigating committee by a man who contended that a hearing had been held to intimidate him and prevent him from exercising his free speech rights. The Supreme Court ruled that the committee members had legislative immunity from suit. *Pierson v. Ray* (1967) arose out of a demonstration by a group of white and black clergymen against segregated interstate bus terminal facilities. Convictions in police court of breach of the peace were subsequently reversed on appeal, and the clergymen then sued the police judge under section 1983. But the Supreme Court ruled that the statute had not abolished the traditional immunity of judges for acts within their judicial role.

The first substantial awards for violations of rights of speech and assembly came in 1975, when a Washington, D.C., jury in a class action suit brought by the American Civil Liberties Union awarded some $12 million in varying amounts to 1,200 persons who were arrested during the 1971 Mayday antiwar demonstrations as they listened to speeches on the steps of the United States Capitol.

ACADEMIC FREEDOM

Involvement of the courts in constitutional claims of academic freedom sharply increased during the troubled times on American campuses in the late 1960s and 1970s. So far as students are concerned, the issues were generally free speech claims for student newspapers and campus assemblies and due process in disciplinary actions taken by authorities against students. On the free expression issue, the principal Supreme Court decisions were *West Virginia State Board of Education v. Barnette* (1943), holding that students cannot be required to salute the flag as a part of school exercises, and *Tinker v. Des Moines School District* (1969), where Fortas, upholding the right of students to wear black armbands in protest against the Vietnam War, said: "In our system, state-operated schools may not be enclaves of totalitarianism."

[31]See "Developments in the Law—Section 1983 and Federalism," 90 HARVARD LAW REVIEW 1133 (1977).

The principal due process ruling was *Goss v. Lopez* (1975), which held that before students could be suspended from public schools, they be given notice of charges and an opportunity to defend themselves. *Wood v. Strickland* (1975) added that in a student suit against school officials for violation of civil rights, the officials were not entitled to good faith immunity if they reasonably should have known that their acts violated the students' constitutional rights. But *Ingraham v. Wright* (1977) upheld corporal punishment in the public schools.

So far as teachers are concerned, academic freedom issues usually arise out of dismissal or discipline because of views or associations. The association problem will be discussed in Chapter 6. In one of those cases, *Keyishian v. Board of Regents* (1967), Brennan said:

> Our Nation is deeply committed to safeguarding academic freedom, which is of transcendent value to all of us and not merely to the teachers concerned. That freedom is therefore a special concern of the First Amendment, which does not tolerate laws that cast a pall of orthodoxy over the classroom.

Teacher tenure has been rather effectively protected by the American Association of University Professors. The Supreme Court's entry into the field came in *Pickering v. Board of Education* (1968), where it ruled that a high school teacher could not be dismissed because he had written a letter to the local newspaper critical of the handling of funds by the school board. In *Perry v. Sinderman* (1972), a junior college professor was discharged after ten years, allegedly because of his public criticism of the college administration. The Court held that he had an "expectancy" of tenure, that he was entitled to a hearing, and that if his removal was because of his views, his free speech rights had been violated. In *Givhan v. Western Line Consolidated School District* (1979), the teacher had been ousted because of private complaints to the principal. The Court held that the First Amendment forbids the abridgement of private as well as public speech.[32]

But *Board of Regents v. Roth* (1972) ruled that a professor not rehired after one year had no constitutional right to a statement of reasons or a hearing. *Nortonville Joint School District v. Nortonville Education Assn.* (1976) upheld the firing of teachers who had engaged in an illegal strike. A woman professor who had been denied tenure at the University of Georgia brought a suit alleging sex discrimination. When the judge ordered members of the promotion committee to reveal how they had voted, one professor refused and was jailed for three months for contempt. The Supreme Court denied review.[33]

[32] See also *Mt. Healthy School District V. Doyle* (1977).
[33] *In re Dinnan* (1980); cert. denied, *Dinnan v. Blaubergs* (1982).

4

Freedom of the Press

When Blackstone wrote that "the liberty of the press consists in laying no *previous* restraints upon publications," he was stating a principle that had become established in England by 1695 and in the colonies by 1725. The issue had thus been closed for decades by the time the First Amendment was adopted. Whatever other doubts there might have been about its intent, there could be no question that it was meant to restate the ban on previous restraints of the press.

The tradition of press freedom is firmly established in the United States.[1] There has of course been censorship in wartime. In the heat of political controversy, as for example over the abolition of slavery, presses have been destroyed, and newspapers have been burned or refused delivery through the mails. Newspapers can be shut down by strikes of their employees. They may fail because of economic pressures, a fate that has left so many American cities as one-newspaper towns. Access to the news can be "managed" by public officials. The Nixon administration carried on an orchestrated attack against the press. The lot of the publisher or distributor of unpopular doctrine can be made difficult in various ways. But the fact remains that *legal* efforts to restrain the freedom of the press have been comparatively few.

[1] But see Leonard W. Levy, *Legacy of Suppression: Freedom of Speech and Press in Early American History* (Cambridge, Mass.: Harvard University Press, 1960).

FREEDOM FROM OVERT PRIOR RESTRAINT

The basic free press right is that publishers shall not be required to have government permission to publish or be subjected to a governmental ban on publication. When Blackstone was defining freedom of the press, licensing of publishers was the typical means of government control, and that is obviously unconstitutional under the First Amendment. But in the Supreme Court's first great anticensorship decision, *Near v. Minnesota* (1931), control took the form of a statute providing for the abating, as a public nuisance, of "malicious, scandalous and defamatory" newspapers or periodicals and the enjoining of anyone maintaining such a nuisance. The paper involved was a Minneapolis weekly devoted to attacks on the law-enforcement officers of the city, who were charged with permitting "Jewish gangsters" to control illegal operations in the area and with deriving graft from those activities.[2]

The statute as applied against this paper was declared unconstitutional by a five to four vote. The minority of Butler, Van Devanter, McReynolds, and Sutherland defended the statute on the ground that it did not constitute prior restraint as that idea had been historically understood. "It does not authorize administrative control in advance such as was formerly exercised by the licensers and censors but prescribes a remedy to be enforced by a suit in equity." Instead of arbitrary administrative action this statute guaranteed the due process of the law courts. Moreover, since the injunction could be issued only *after* a malicious or defamatory publication had appeared and been adjudged a nuisance, it was not a *previous* restraint but the abating of a nuisance already committed. But Chief Justice Hughes replied for the majority that the object of the statute was not punishment but suppression, and concluded: "This is of the essence of censorship."

The second major point of the dissenters was that the reasonable man rule should be applied here. "The Act was passed in the exertion of the State's power of police, and this court is by well-established rule required to assume, until the contrary is clearly made to appear, that there exists in Minnesota a state of affairs that justifies this measure for the preservation of the peace and good order of the State." Butler went on: "It is of the greatest importance that the States shall be untrammeled and free to employ all just and appropriate measures to prevent abuses of the liberty of the press."

Hughes in reply did not assert that the protection against previous restraint was "absolutely unlimited." He did, however, deny that it was normally within the legislative range of choice to pass previous restraint legislation, or that there was any obligation on courts to presume the validity of such legislation. The legitimacy of prior restraints could be

[2] For an interesting account of this decision, see Fred W. Friendly, *Minnesota Rag* (New York: Random House, 1981).

recognized only in "exceptional cases." He specified four such exceptional situations. One was where the success of the nation's armed forces was at stake in time of war, and here he quoted from Holmes in the *Schenck* case, though he did not directly invoke the clear and present danger test. Another was when the "primary requirements of decency" were enforced against obscene publications. The third arose where the security of community life had to be protected "against incitements to acts of violence and the overthrow by force of orderly government." Fourth, it might be necessary for equity courts "to prevent publications in order to protect private rights." Only the last two could conceivably be relevant in the *Near* case, but Hughes held them inapplicable. The purpose of the statute was not to redress individual or private wrongs. As for the chance that the circulation of scandal might tend to disturb the public peace, "the theory of the constitutional guaranty is that even a more serious public evil would be caused by authority to prevent publication."

Near v. Minnesota was followed in 1936 by a decision invalidating an effort to discourage publications by discriminatory taxation, a type of restraint that had been common in English and early American history. In 1934 the Louisiana legislature, under the control of Huey Long, enacted a 2 percent tax on gross receipts from advertising on all firms publishing newspapers or periodicals having a circulation of more than 20,000 copies per week. It was denominated as a license tax on the privilege of engaging in the business of selling advertising but was clearly aimed at city newspapers, which on the whole were opposed to the Long regime, whereas the country press was favorable to Long.

In *Grosjean v. American Press Co.* (1936), the Supreme Court unanimously held the tax unconstitutional. Newspapers were of course not immune from any of the ordinary forms of taxation:

> But this is not an ordinary form of tax, but one single in kind, with a long history of hostile misuse against the freedom of the press. . . . The tax here involved is bad not because it takes money from the pockets of the appellees. . . . It is bad because, in the light of its history and of its present setting, it is seen to be a deliberate and calculated device in the guise of a tax to limit the circulation of information to which the public is entitled in virtue of the constitutional guaranties.

In *Minneapolis Star and Tribune v. Minnesota* (1983) a tax on newsprint and ink was likewise declared unconstitutional. Unlike *Grosjean*, here there was no punitive motive, but the Court held, eight to one, that singling out the press for taxation burdened the interests protected by the First Amendment and could be justified only by counterbalancing interests of compelling importance, and not simply as a revenue measure.

The First Amendment does not, however, entitle publishers to any special exemption from governmental regulation of business practices that may be constitutionally applied to businesses generally. The Wagner Act regulating labor relations was held applicable to the press by a five to four vote in *Associated Press v. National Labor Relations Board* (1937). Similarly the antitrust provisions of the Sherman Act and the wage and hour requirements of the Fair Labor Standards Act have been held applicable to the publishing industry.[3]

Occasionally a legislature concludes that some "worthy" purpose can be served by an outright prohibition on publication. Any such law is of course unconstitutional on its face. For example, in *Mills v. Alabama* (1966) a state law, applied to the editor of a Birmingham newspaper, made it a crime to electioneer or solicit votes on election day in support of, or in opposition to, any proposition being voted on. The editor had published on election day an editorial urging voters to approve a change to the mayor-council form of city government for Birmingham, a change that was generally understood to be aimed at establishing a more moderate racial policy in the city by eliminating its two most prominent segregationist officials. The state supreme court sustained the criminal conviction of the editor, on the ground that the law was a reasonable election regulation and served the salutary purpose of protecting the public from confusing last-minute charges when, because of lack of time, they could not be answered or their truth determined. Justice Black said it was "difficult to conceive of a more obvious and flagrant abridgement of the constitutionally guaranteed freedom of the press."[4]

Motivated by an anti-CIA newsletter that published the names of CIA agents abroad, Congress in 1982 passed a statute making it a crime to publish the names of U.S. agents, even if the information came from public sources. The law was immediately challenged as unconstitutional.

Handbills

Anyone with a hand printing press is a publisher for purposes of the First Amendment, with full rights not to be hampered by government restrictions in the publishing and circulation of the printed product. This has been established by a series of Supreme Court decisions on handbills.

The first was *Lovell v. Griffin* (1938), in which the Supreme Court unanimously condemned as unconstitutional a municipal ordinance re-

---

[3] *Associated Press v. United States* (1945), *Lorain Journal v. United States* (1957), *Citizen Publishing Co. v. United States* (1969), *Oklahoma Press Publishing Co. v. Walling* (1946).

[4] Again, a law imposing criminal sanctions for publication of confidential proceedings before a state commission investigating judicial conduct was struck down in *Landmark Communications v. Virginia* (1978). Statutory efforts to protect the anonymity of juvenile offenders by forbidding publication of their names were declared unconstitutional in *Oklahoma Publishing Co. v. District Court* (1977) and *Smith v. Daily Mail Publishing Co.* (1979).

quiring official permission to distribute publications. The ordinance covered distribution "by hand or otherwise" of "literature of any kind," which was made a nuisance unless written permission in advance was obtained from the city manager. Counsel for the city argued that the ordinance was justified because of the "sanitary problem in removing from . . . streets papers, circulars and the other like materials." Moreover, it was contended that the petitioner in this case, a member of Jehovah's Witnesses selling their literature from door to door, was not a member of the press, and so not "in the class of persons who are entitled to invoke the constitutional provisions touching the freedom of the press."

The Supreme Court held the ordinance "invalid on its face." It was an absolute prohibition of distribution without permit, "not limited to ways which might be regarded as inconsistent with the maintenance of public order or as involving disorderly conduct, the molestation of the inhabitants, or the misuse or littering of the streets." The First Amendment was appropriately invoked, because liberty of the press necessarily embraced the distribution of pamphlets and leaflets. "These indeed have been historic weapons in the defense of liberty, as the pamphlets of Thomas Paine and others in our own history abundantly attest. The press in its historic connotation comprehends every sort of publication which affords a vehicle of information and opinion."

Subsequent decisions widened the protection afforded distribution of handbills.[5] In *Talley v. California* (1960) the Court declared unconstitutional a state law that required all handbills to have printed on them the names and addresses of the persons who prepared, distributed, or sponsored them, though three dissenting justices were not convinced that the First Amendment protects the "freedom of anonymous speech." *Organization for a Better Austin v. Keefe* (1971) upheld the action of a racially integrated citizen organization in distributing leaflets critical of a real estate broker's "blockbusting" activities, even though the leaflets were circulated in the suburb where the broker lived rather than in the area under attack.[6]

The Pentagon Papers Case

The most significant challenge to press freedom in American history occurred in 1971 when the Nixon administration secured injunctions against the *New York Times* and the *Washington Post* to prevent them from continuing their publication of the so-called Pentagon papers. These papers came from a many-volumed study, made at the direction of the Defense Department, of the circumstances leading to United States

[5] See *Schneider v. Irvington* (1939) and *Jamison v. Texas* (1943).

[6] *Valentine v. Chrestensen* (1942) held that First Amendment protection does not extend to commercial handbills.

involvement in the Vietnam War. The study was classified as secret, but Daniel Ellsberg, who had access to the volumes through his employment by a private research agency, violated government security rules and furnished copies to the press. After considering the matter for several months, the *New York Times* began publication of the papers on June 13, 1971, and several other newspapers followed shortly thereafter.[7]

Judicial action proceeded with incredible speed. The government went into court in New York on June 15, asking for an injunction against further publication, and in Washington against the *Washington Post* on June 18. The Courts of Appeals for the Second Circuit and for the District of Columbia acted on June 19. The Supreme Court agreed to accept the cases on June 25, heard argument on June 26, and handed down a six to three decision quashing the injunctions on June 30.

The Supreme Court, badly divided, gave its ruling in *New York Times v. United States* in a three-paragraph per curiam opinion, simply holding that the government had not met the "heavy burden" of justifying any system of prior restraint. All nine justices then proceeded to state their own views. For Black and Douglas, the issue was clear and plain: "every moment's continuance of the injunctions against these newspapers amounts to a flagrant, indefensible, and continuing violation of the First Amendment." Brennan's position differed only in that he seemed to accept the possibility that in extreme cases the government might present proof of great danger to national interests justifying an injunction, which it had not done here. Marshall, drawing on the holding in the *Steel Seizure Case*, particularly stressed the fact that Congress had on two occasions declined to pass legislation that would have given the President the power he was now seeking to have the courts exercise. "When Congress specifically declines to make conduct unlawful it is not for this Court to redecide those issues—to overrule Congress," he concluded.

Stewart and White completed the six-judge majority. White, like Marshall, stressed the absence of any congressional authorization for prior restraints in these circumstances and could find no inherent power in the executive or the courts "to authorize remedies having such sweeping potential for inhibiting publications by the press." Stewart thought that the Constitution had made the President responsible for protecting the confidentiality necessary to carry out responsibilities in the fields of international relations and national defense and that the courts could not be asked, in the absence of specific laws or regulations, to take over this function. Both Stewart and White, however, expressed concern that the

[7] See Martin Shapiro, *The Pentagon Papers and the Courts* (San Francisco: Chandler Publishing Company, 1972; Sanford J. Ungar, *The Papers and the Papers* (New York: Dutton, 1972); *The Pentagon Papers* (New York: Bantam, 1971).

national interest had been damaged by the publications and inferred that they believed criminal proceedings could be brought against the publishers.

The dissenters were Chief Justice Burger and Justices Harlan and Blackmun. All protested the speed with which the cases had been heard. Burger heatedly castigated the newspapers for accepting "stolen property." Blackmun warned that if publication of the papers prolonged the war or further delayed the freeing of United States prisoners, "then the Nation's people will know where the responsibility for these sad consequences rests."

While the result in *New York Times* was clear enough, the Court's opinions do not add up to a sound defense of freedom of the press. It would appear that at least four members of the Court, and possibly five, believed that the newspapers could be criminally punished for their action. This view was particularly spelled out by White, who said that "failure by the Government to justify prior restraint does not measure its constitutional entitlement to a conviction for criminal publication." He cited various provisions of the criminal code as possibly relevant and added: "I would have no difficulty in sustaining convictions under these sections. . . ."

The Department of Justice appeared to be less certain than White that statutorily defined crimes had been committed in the Pentagon Papers case. The indictments secured against Daniel Ellsberg had to fall back on generalized charges of espionage, theft, and conspiracy. The case was a weak one. The "theft" was of information, not of documents. The documents were copied by Ellsberg and returned. Can "information" be stolen? Was the espionage law violated when the information "stolen" was not given to a foreign power? Moreover, there is no law, only executive orders, setting up the classification system and pertaining to the disclosure of classified information. The collapse of the Ellsberg prosecution due to illegal action by the government prevented any definitive answer to these questions.

But the experience did call attention to the absence of any Official Secrets Act in the United States. A massive revision of the federal criminal code presented to Congress in 1975 would have filled this gap by making it a crime to pass national defense information or any classified information to unauthorized persons, but the bill did not pass, and subsequent revisions were substantially modified.

The H-Bomb and the CIA

In 1979 a national storm blew up over the proposal of *Progressive* magazine to publish an article entitled "The H-Bomb Secret." The article, which was popularly thought to explain how to make the bomb, was written by a man with no special training or access to secret data; but the government contended that the publication would do immediate and irreparable harm, and applied to a Wisconsin federal judge for an injunction against publication. Recognizing that he had to bear a heavy burden of proof to justify an injunction and that the article really did not tell how to make a bomb, the judge nevertheless granted a preliminary injunction on the ground that the article could possibly provide information enabling smaller nations to avoid scientific blind alleys and permit them to move faster toward a practical bomb. But before appellate proceedings could be completed, similar information on nuclear weapons was published in other sources, and the government then abandoned the injunction effort.

Another serious conflict between press freedom and national security arose out of the Central Intelligence Agency's practice of requiring its agents, as a condition of employment, to promise not to publish anything about the activities of the agency without CIA clearance. Because of this obligation, one agent's book about his 14 years in the CIA was published with 168 blank spaces where the agency had demanded deletions. The agent, Victor Marchetti, was also permanently enjoined from speaking or writing about classified material he obtained while he was a CIA employee without agency clearance.[8]

More distressing was the case of Frank Snepp, another former CIA employee who wrote a book containing no classified information, but presenting a very unfavorable picture of the last days of the American presence in Vietnam. Because he failed to secure CIA clearance, the Supreme Court held in *Snepp v. United States* (1980) that he had breached a position of trust, causing the United States irreparable harm, and must surrender all present and future profits from the book to the government.[9] Anything he might write in the future on any subject had to be submitted to the CIA for clearance.

In 1983 President Reagan issued an executive order, enforceable by the Department of Justice, extending the secrecy and prepublication review requirements approved in *Snepp* to all government employees with access to classified data. The order requires review of any information relating to intelligence, including letters to the editor, book reviews, and scholarly papers. Employees must submit to a polygraph (lie detector) test if asked to do so by federal agents investigating a leak of information.

---

[8] Victor Marchetti and John D. Marks, *The CIA and the Cult of Intelligence* (New York: Knopf, 1974).

[9] The actual language of the astoundingly vindictive per curiam opinion was that Snepp must "disgorge the benefits of his faithlessness." The book was *Decent Interval* (New York: Random House, 1978).

INDIRECT PRIOR RESTRAINT

The Post Office

In *Ex parte Jackson* (1878), Justice Field observed: "Liberty of circulating is as essential to that freedom [of the press] as liberty of publishing; indeed, without the circulation, the publication would be of little value." By this test access to the Post Office should be a constitutional right, but this has not been the case. Exclusion of lottery tickets from the mails was upheld in *Jackson* and also in *In re Rapier* (1892). Field reconciled his approval of this ban with his views on freedom of circulation by saying, "In excluding various articles from the mail, the object of Congress has not been to interfere with the freedom of the press ... but to refuse its facilities for the distribution of matter deemed injurious to the public morals." The same rationale was used to justify exclusion of obscene matter from the mails, which will be discussed in Chapter 5.

About 1940 the Post Office, without any statutory authority and with the cooperation of the Bureau of Customs, progressed from obscenity to "foreign political propaganda," confiscating periodicals and books regarded as politically questionable that were mailed to residents of the United States. The Russian newspapers *Pravda* and *Izvestia* were typical of the materials intercepted. This practice was stopped by President Kennedy's Executive Order in 1961. The next year Congress retaliated by passing a statute specifically authorizing the postmaster general to detain "communist political propaganda" and to deliver it only upon the addressee's request. In *Lamont v. Postmaster General* (1965), the Supreme Court unanimously declared this statute unconstitutional, holding that to force an addressee to request in writing that mail be delivered was an abridgement of First Amendment rights.

The power of the Post Office over second-class mailing privileges was one of two weapons used during World War I, with Supreme Court approval, to effect a blatant censorship of the press. The second was the Espionage Act of 1917, one entire title of which was devoted to use of the mails. It provided that any newspaper published in violation of any provisions of the act would be nonmailable. The law was promptly applied to *The Masses*, a revolutionary antiwar monthly journal.[10] When the same action was taken against a socialist paper, and upheld by the Court in *Milwaukee Publishing Co. v. Burleson* (1921), Justice Brandeis protested that the postmaster general had become "the universal censor of publications," and Justice Holmes added: "The United States may give up the Post Office when it sees fit, but while it carries it on the use of the

---

[10]*Masses Publishing Co. v. Patten* (1917).

mails is almost as much a part of free speech as the right to use our tongues, and it would take very strong language to convince me that Congress ever intended to give such a practically despotic power to any one man."

These protests proved ineffective, and again in World War II precisely the same technique was employed. In fields unrelated to national security, however, some support for the Holmes-Brandeis position on the powers of the postmaster general with respect to second-class mail was given by the Supreme Court's 1946 decision in *Hannegan v. Esquire.* Postmaster General Walker sought to withdraw second-class privileges from *Esquire,* on the ground that the magazine did not meet the statutory test of being "published for the dissemination of information of a public character, or devoted to literature, the sciences, arts, or some special industry." He argued that the material in *Esquire,* although not obscene in a technical sense, was so close to it that it was "morally improper and not for the public welfare and the public good."

A unanimous Supreme Court held that Congress had not meant to grant the postmaster general rights of censorship when it attached these conditions to the second-class privilege. Under the statute he was limited to determining whether a publication "contains information of a public character, literature or art"; he was not granted "the further power to determine whether the contents meet some standard of the public good or welfare." The Holmes-Brandeis dissent in *Milwaukee Publishing Co.* was noted, with the comment: "Grave constitutional questions are immediately raised once it is said that the use of the mails is a privilege which may be extended or withheld on any grounds whatsoever."[11]

Reporters' Privilege

By common law or statute, certain relationships, such as lawyer-client, priest-penitent, doctor-patient, and husband-wife are privileged— that is, those involved cannot be forced in court proceedings to reveal what passed between them.[12] Newspeople argue that they should have a similar privilege with respect to their confidential informants, on the ground that often information will be given to them only if they can promise not to reveal their sources. Accepting this premise, many states

[11] A federal statute prohibiting the placing of unstamped material in postal boxes was protested by civic associations and other nonprofit organizations that customarily put notices of their meetings in mail boxes. But the Supreme Court in *U. S. Postal Service v. Council of Greenburgh* (1981) upheld the statute, saying a mail box is not a public forum with guaranteed access to all comers.

[12] In *Upjohn Co. v. United States* (1981) the Court held that communications between corporate employees and corporations' counsel are covered by the attorney-client privilege.

have adopted "shield laws," which do guarantee the confidentiality of reporters' news sources.[13]

The Supreme Court, however, rejected the claim of confidentiality by a vote of five to four in *Branzburg v. Hayes* (1972). A reporter who had developed contacts in the Black Panther organization in San Francisco, and another who had published stories about drug activities in Kentucky, were subpoenaed to appear before grand juries to be questioned about their knowledge of illegal activities. Both refused, claiming that requiring them to give testimony to a grand jury would deny press freedom by making them in effect government agents, destroying their credibility as newsmen, and drying up their news sources.

Justice White for the Court dismissed these claims rather brusquely. His main theme, repeated time and again in the opinion, was that reporters have the same obligation "as other citizens . . . to answer questions relevant to an investigation into the commission of crime." He was uncertain how much burden would be imposed on news gathering by refusing to grant the privilege, but in any event the public interest in pursuing and prosecuting crimes must take precedence. None of the traditional types of infringement on press freedom was involved here, White noted—no prior restraint, no command to publish, no tax, no penalty for publishing, no denial of access to confidential sources. If grand juries should abuse their powers (as some clearly had[14]), White promised that the courts would intervene. His final "pragmatic" point, that the press was powerful and "far from helpless to protect itself from harassment or substantial harm," rather overlooked the fact that it is not "the press" but individual reporters who must weigh the prospect of going to jail for defying a grand jury subpoena, as a considerable number have done.

Justice Stewart, dissenting in *Branzburg*, attacked White's "simplistic and stultifying absolutism," which was insensitive to "the critical role of an independent press" and willing to approve annexing "the journalistic profession as an investigative arm of the government." As Stewart saw it, "a corollary of the right to publish must be the right to gather news," and "the right to gather news implies, in turn, a right to a confidential relationship between a reporter and his source." He was convinced that the absence of this right would "either deter sources from divulging information or deter reporters from gathering and publishing information."

---

[13] See "Reporters and Their Sources: The Constitutional Right to a Confidential Relationship," 80 YALE LAW JOURNAL 317 (1970); Maurice Van Gerpen, *Privileged Communication and the Press* (Westport, Conn.: Greenwood Press, 1979).

[14] See David J. Fine, "Federal Grand Jury Investigation of Political Dissidents," 7 HARVARD CIVIL RIGHTS–CIVIL LIBERTIES LAW REVIEW 432 (1972).

The *Branzburg* decision led Senator Sam Ervin to make a gallant but unsuccessful effort to draft a federal shield law. Actually there was considerable disagreement within the publishing fraternity as to whether a shield law was desirable. Some feared that any law on this subject would seem to grant the legitimacy of statutory regulation of the press, and they would prefer to rely simply on the First Amendment, which they contend the Court wrongly interpreted in *Branzburg*.[15]

Many states do have shield laws, but they are not necessarily effective. The most notable example concerned a *New York Times* reporter, Myron A. Farber, who spent 39 days in a New Jersey jail, while his paper was fined a total of $325,000 for civil and criminal contempt, for his refusal to submit his notes to the judge upon demand by the defense in a murder case. Although New Jersey had a shield law, the state supreme court ruled that the law must yield when it conflicted with the fair trial guarantee of the Sixth Amendment. The Supreme Court refused to review the case.[16]

The "Special Position" of the Press

After *Branzburg* the contention that the press occupied a "special position" that guarantees not only the right to print but also access to news sources continued to be rejected by the Court. In *Saxbe v. Washington Post* (1974) the Court upheld, five to four, a federal prison regulation under which media representatives, while given general permission to interview inmates, were forbidden to request interviews with particular prisoners.[17] In spite of his *Branzburg* dissent Stewart rejected the "special access" claim of the press and the contention "that the Constitution imposes upon government the affirmative duty to make available to journalists sources of information not available to members of the public generally." But Powell, dissenting, contended that the Court was carrying the *Branzburg* doctrine too far. Because the people must depend on the press for information concerning public institutions, "absolute prohibition of prisoner-press interviews negates the ability of the press to discharge that function and thereby substantially impairs the right of the people to a free flow of information and ideas on the conduct of their Government."[18]

The issue was raised again in *Houchins v. KQED, Inc.* (1978), and

---

[15] Robert G. Dixon, "The Constitution Is Shield Enough for Newsmen," 60 AMERICAN BAR ASSOCIATION JOURNAL 707 (1974).

[16] *New York Times v. Jascalevich* (1978), *New York Times v. New Jersey* (1978). See Myron Farber, "Somebody Is Lying," The Story of Dr. X (New York: Doubleday, 1982).

[17] Similar California prison regulations were upheld in *Pell v. Procunier* (1974).

[18] See the broad discussion of this issue in David M. O'Brien, *The Public's Right to Know* (New York: Praeger, 1981).

the right of access and special position for the press were rejected even more bluntly. Here television station representatives were refused permission to inspect and photograph a portion of a county jail where a prisoner's suicide had reportedly occurred. The sheriff did allow monthly tours of the jail, open to the public and media representatives, but no tape recordings or cameras were permitted or interviews with inmates. Chief Justice Burger ruled that the Court had never "implied a special privilege of access to information as distinguished from a right to public information which has been obtained." But Stewart, though concurring, did assert that journalists had greater rights of access than the general public.

The Court's antimedia attitude continued. In *First National Bank of Boston v. Bellotti* (1978) Burger referred to the press as "media conglomerates" entitled to no special or "institutional" privileges. In 1979 the Court refused to review a lower court holding that reporters have no right to advance notice when government agents subpoena their long-distance telephone records.[19]

The most severe blow, however, came in *Zurcher v. Stanford Daily* (1978), where the Court upheld the action of Palo Alto police who, with a general warrant, searched the files and premises of the Stanford University student newspaper for photographs that might permit identification of participants in a campus riot. Critics of the search contended that the constitutional method of securing information needed in a criminal case from third parties not suspected of participation in the crime was by issuance of a subpoena rather than by an unannounced search. As Stewart said, in this case there was no need to protect life or property, and the evidence sought was not contraband. Such an incursion into a newsroom was bound to have "a deterrent effect on the availability of confidential news sources" and result in "physical disruption." But White for the five-judge majority held there was no "constitutional difference" between search warrants and subpoenas.

The case brought out a sharp conflict between Powell and Stewart as to the constitutional status of the press. Powell wrote:

> If the Framers had believed that the press was entitled to a special procedure, not available to others, when government authorities required evidence in its possession, one would have expected the terms of the Fourth Amendment to reflect that belief.

[19] *Reporters Committee v. American Telephone & Telegraph Co.* (1979). In 1980 the Justice Department issued new regulations defining the procedures to be followed in subpoenaing telephone toll records of reporters which recognized for the first time that reporters have a qualified, but not absolute, right to safeguard the privacy of their long-distance telephone records (*New York Times,* November 13, 1980).

Stewart rebutted:

> Perhaps as a matter of abstract policy a newspaper office should receive no
> more protection from unannounced police searches than, say, the office of a
> doctor or the office of a bank. But we are here to uphold a Constitution.
> And our Constitution does not explicitly protect the practice of medicine or
> the business of banking from all abridgement by government. It does
> explicitly protect the freedom of the press.

In *Zurcher* the Court had finally gone too far. The type of "third
party" search approved there appeared to permit incursions into any
home or office if the police believed evidence of crime could thereby be
obtained. In an unusual reversal of roles, the Department of Justice asked
Congress to forbid general warrant police searches of news offices of the
type the Supreme Court had approved. Congress responded by adoption
of the Privacy Protection Act of 1980. Its main protections apply to
persons engaged in the preparation of newspapers, books, broadcasts, or
other similar forms of public communication. Federal agents may not
seize their work-product materials unless the reporter or writer is suspected of committing a crime or there is some life-threatening situation.
Justice Department guidelines specify that subpoenas are preferable to
search warrants unless the use of subpoenas might seriously delay an
investigation or lead to the destruction of evidence.

FREE PRESS AND FAIR TRIAL

A free press problem of increasing importance and difficulty relates to the
right of newspapers to publish information and comment about current
criminal proceedings. The right to a fair trial, as will be discussed in
more detail in Chapter 9, includes among other features the right to trial
by an unbiased jury. A fair trial requires that the judge and jury make
their judgments solely on the basis of the evidence introduced in the
courtroom, and of course they must be subjected to no outside pressures
in reaching their decisions.

The American tradition of press freedom has given newspapers
complete freedom to report the facts of criminal investigations and
prosecutions. From the time a crime is committed, newspapers undertake
to publish every bit of information they can secure concerning the crime
and the criminal, usually with the cooperation of the police and prosecutors. They recount the evidence and the previous criminal record, if any,
of the suspect. In particularly gruesome crimes, the press may whip up
feeling against the person charged. "Trial by newspaper" may be so
complete and effective that the task of securing a jury that has not
prejudged the case becomes very difficult. Occasionally a newspaper will

go so far as to attempt to exert editorial pressure on the judge or jury while the case is still being tried.

In such a situation there is a fundamental conflict between two constitutional rights—a fair trial and a free press. The basic justification for freedom of the press is that untrammeled public discussion and expression of all conceivable views offers the best chance of achieving truth and wisdom. Public policy making must be subjected to the influence of popular pressures. But in a trial at law the purpose is to safeguard the proceedings as fully as possible *from* popular pressures. The whole judicial apparatus is aimed at limiting a jury or judge to consideration of relevant and probative facts bearing on the controversy. Admittedly there is and must be popular interest in and discussion of the way the judicial function is performed. But while a case is pending in court the public interest in the evenhanded administration of justice requires that the judge and jury be subject to no dictates or pressures but those of their own judgment and consciences.

The Contempt Power

The power of judges to punish for contempt is the principal instrument by which a judge can protect proceedings in court from newspaper pressure. However, American judges are seriously limited in their use of the contempt power to restrain out-of-court comments about current court proceedings. The English practice is much more restrictive in this connection than the American. Only the barest facts may be published in England concerning a pending prosecution, and anything remotely smacking of comment on the case would lay the offender open to contempt charges. The American tradition, with its great reliance upon elected judges at the state and local level, its rough-and-ready standards of justice on the frontier, and its general hostility toward restraints, has been much less willing to concede the immunity of judicial proceedings from outside comment. In addition, summary punishment procedures tend to arouse greater resentment when applied to contempts occurring out of court than when committed in the presence of the court.[20]

These attitudes were reflected in a federal statute adopted in 1831 that forbade summary punishments except in the case of misbehavior in the presence of the court, "or so near thereto as to obstruct the administration of justice." This act effected a substantial limitation on the contempt power, but near the turn of the century some federal district courts again undertook summary punishment for publications. The Supreme Court

---

[20] See Ronald L. Goldfarb, *The Contempt Power* (New York: Columbia University Press, 1963).

gave approval to this trend in *Toledo Newspaper Co. v. United States* (1918), holding that a newspaper publishing objectionable comments about a judge and his conduct of pending litigation was "so near thereto" as to justify summary punishment. Justice Holmes, dissenting with Brandeis, denied that there had been any obstruction of justice, saying: "I think that 'so near as to obstruct' means so near as actually to obstruct—and not merely near enough to threaten a possible obstruction." He added that "a judge of the United States is expected to be a man of ordinary firmness of character."

The *Toledo* decision was overruled in 1941 by *Nye v. United States* as the Court adopted the Holmes position that "so near thereto" means physical proximity. Consequently newspapers are protected by statute from summary punishment for comments on federal judicial decisions.

So far as state courts are concerned, the freedom of newspapers from contempt prosecutions derives from the Fourteenth Amendment and the Supreme Court's decision in *Bridges v. California* (1941). A radical labor leader, Harry Bridges, and a conservative, labor-baiting newspaper, the *Los Angeles Times,* had with unique impartiality been brought to book for contempt. The newspaper was cited by a California judge who was trying a case involving assault by labor union members on nonunion truck drivers. At a time when the defendants had been found guilty, but not yet sentenced, the *Times* said editorially: "Judge A. A. Scott will make a serious mistake if he grants probation to Matthew Shannon and Kennan Holmes. This community needs the example of their assignment to the jute-mill." As for Harry Bridges, while a motion for a new trial was pending in a case involving a dispute between an AFL and a CIO union, he sent a telegram to the United States secretary of labor calling the judge's decision "outrageous," threatened that an attempt to enforce it would tie up the entire Pacific Coast, and warned that his union did "not intend to allow state courts to override the majority vote" in NLRB elections.

The Supreme Court reversed both contempt citations by a narrow five to four margin. Justice Black for the majority held there would have to be "a clear and present danger" that such comments would obstruct justice in order for the contempt citations to be justified, and he saw no such threat. To accept the possibility that such publications would in themselves have a "substantial influence upon the course of justice would be to impute to judges a lack of firmness, wisdom, or honor,—which we cannot accept as a major premise."

Justice Frankfurter made a strong attack on the application of the clear and present danger test in these circumstances. Holmes had no thought of using it for such a purpose, he contended.

A trial is not a "free trade in ideas," nor is the best test of truth in a courtroom "the power of the thought to get itself accepted in the competition of the market." A court is a forum with strictly defined limits for discussion. . . . We cannot read into the Fourteenth Amendment the freedom of speech and of the press protected by the First Amendment and at the same time read out age-old means employed by states for securing the calm course of justice. . . . To assure the impartial accomplishment of justice is not an abridgement of freedom of speech or freedom of the press. . . . In fact, these liberties themselves depend upon an untrammeled judiciary whose passions are not even unconsciously aroused and whose minds are not distorted by extrajudicial considerations.

This argument was continued in two subsequent cases, *Pennekamp v. Florida* (1946) and *Craig v. Harney* (1947), both of which freed newspapers from contempt charges. By this line of decisions, Justices Jackson and Frankfurter charged in *Shepherd v. Florida* (1951), the Supreme Court had "gone a long way to disable a trial judge from dealing with press interference with the trial process."

Pretrial Publicity

The Court was also reluctant to attempt control of pretrial publicity.[21] Not until 1961, in *Irvin v. Dowd*, did the Court reverse a state conviction because of pretrial publicity. Here the defendant was a man accused of six murders, whose confession had been issued by the police in press releases that were intensively publicized. Because of the popular indignation generated by the publicity, one change of venue to an adjoining county was granted, but feeling was high there also, and a second change was refused. Convincing evidence of prejudice against the defendant was demonstrated when it took four weeks to select the jury from a panel of 430, of whom 268 had to be excused because of fixed opinions of guilt. Eight of the twelve jurors selected, though claiming not to have fixed opinions, thought the defendant was guilty. The Supreme Court unanimously concluded: "With his life at stake, it is not requiring too much that petitioner be tried in an atmosphere undisturbed by so huge a wave of public passion and by a jury other than one in which two thirds of the members admit, before hearing any testimony, to possessing a belief in his guilt."

In *Rideau v. Louisiana* (1963) the pretrial publicity was compounded by television. A man accused of murder made a confession, which he subsequently repeated in a filmed television "interview" with the sheriff. The film was shown three times on the local television station; three of

---

[21] See *Maryland v. Baltimore Radio Show* (1950) and *Stroble v. California* (1952).

the members of the jury that tried him two months later had seen the film. The Supreme Court reversed the conviction on the ground that a change of venue should have been granted so that the jury could have been drawn "from a community of people who had not seen and heard Rideau's televised 'interview.'"

Closed Trials

The Sixth Amendment guarantees an accused "the right to a speedy and public trial." In *Craig v. Harney* (1947) the Supreme Court said:

> A trial is a public event. What transpires in the courtroom is public property. . . . There is no special perquisite of the judiciary which enables it, as distinguished from other institutions of democratic government, to suppress, edit or censor events which transpire in proceedings before it.

Nevertheless, judges have ordered closure of various stages in criminal proceedings with considerable frequency, at the request of both prosecutors and defendants.

Gannett Co., Inc. v. DePasquale (1979) gave what proved to be temporary support to trial closure. The proceeding involved was actually a pretrial hearing on a motion to suppress allegedly involuntary confessions and certain physical evidence in a second-degree murder case. Though the event had aroused comparatively little public or press attention, defendants requested closure to prevent the buildup of adverse publicity, and the district attorney did not oppose. The trial judge granted the motion, and when a reporter protested, ruled that the interest of press and public was outweighed by defendants' right to a fair trial.

In a five to four ruling, the Supreme Court admitted that the Sixth Amendment presumed "open trials" as the norm, but concluded that members of the public had no constitutional right under the Sixth Amendment to attend criminal trials. Stewart asserted that the public trial guarantee was "created for the benefit of the defendant" and that history failed to show any intention on the part of the framers of the Sixth Amendment "to create a constitutional right in strangers to attend a pretrial proceeding. . . ." Burger, concurring, sought to limit the reach of the ruling by emphasizing that the proceeding was a *pretrial* hearing, not a trial. But Rehnquist's understanding of *Gannett* was that "If the parties agree on a closed proceeding, the trial court is not required by the Sixth Amendment to advance any reason whatever for declining to open a pretrial hearing or trial to the public."

Judges across the country were encouraged by *Gannett* to grant closure motions, to the apparent embarrassment of the Court. The Chief Justice issued an unusual public statement suggesting that judges were "misreading" the Court's decision. But obviously it was the decision itself that was at fault, and the Court quickly sought to repair the damage. In *Gannett* the First Amendment issue had been ignored, except for Powell's concurring opinion, where it was not determinative. But in *Richmond Newspapers, Inc. v. Virginia* (1980), decided one year to the day after *Gannett*, and involving a trial rather than a pretrial hearing, the Court, without disturbing the views it had expressed on the Sixth Amendment in *Gannett*, held that the right of public and press to attend criminal trials was granted by the First and Fourteenth Amendments, unless there was some "overriding interest articulated in the findings." Blackmun was gratified "to see the Court wash away at least some of the graffiti that marred the prevailing opinions in Gannett." Only Rehnquist dissented, protesting that it was "unhealthy" for this "small group of lawyers who have been appointed to the Supreme Court and enjoying virtual life tenure" to be dictating the trial procedures in state courts.[22]

Problems in Conduct of the Trial

The televising of a trial was held in *Estes v. Texas* (1965) to be inherently prejudicial to a fair trial. But the decision was based in part on the courtroom disturbance which the bulky cameras and bright lights then required would create. The issue returned in *Chandler v. Florida* (1981), by which time television technology had much improved. On this ground the Court distinguished *Estes* and ruled unanimously that there was no constitutional barrier to state court experimentation with radio, television, or still photographic coverage of criminal trials, even if the accused objected.

There are many other problems with press coverage of trials. National attention was focused on the fair trial issue by the scandalous press involvement in the nationally famous trial of Dr. Sam Sheppard for the murder of his wife in 1964. One Cleveland newspaper in particular conducted a campaign to cast suspicion on Sheppard, to get him indicted, and to convict him in the eyes of the public. Every action in the case took place in a carnival of publicity. The coroner's inquest was held in a school gymnasium with live broadcasting. When Sheppard was brought in to the city hall under arrest, scores of newscasters, photographers, and reporters were awaiting his arrival. In the courtroom three of the four rows of benches were assigned to the communications media, and a press table was even erected inside the bar of the court, so close to Sheppard that he could not consult with his lawyers without being overheard. The

---

[22] In *Globe Newspaper Co. v. Superior Court* (1982) the Court declared unconstitutional a Massachusetts law mandating closure of a court to press and public during the testimony of a minor who was a rape victim. The decision left judges free to decide on a case-by-case basis whether to close the courtroom during such testimony.

jurors were subjected to constant publicity; their pictures appeared in Cleveland newspapers more than forty times.

The Supreme Court, appalled by this travesty of justice, reversed the conviction in *Sheppard v. Maxwell* (1966); in the course of the opinion, Justice Clark suggested what the judge should have done to control the trial. First, he should have adopted stricter rules governing the use of the courtroom by newsmen. Their number should have been limited, and their conduct more closely regulated. (They even handled exhibits lying on the counsel table during recesses.) Second, the judge should have "insulated" the witnesses; instead, they were interviewed at will by newsmen. Third, "the court should have made some effort to control the release of leads, information, and gossip to the press by police officers, witnesses, and the counsel for both sides." The prosecution repeatedly made alleged "evidence" available to the news media that was never offered in the trial. As for the highly distorted reports of the trial in the papers, Clark thought the judge "should have at least warned the newspapers to check the accuracy of their accounts."

The American Bar Association responded to this challenge with the Reardon report proposing rules that would limit statements for dissemination to the public on pending criminal cases by lawyers, court attachés, and law-enforcement officers. From the time of arrest or filing of a charge until the end of the trial, information could not be released outside of court on such matters as prior criminal record, existence or contents of any confession, performance of examinations, identity of prospective witnesses, or possible guilt or innocence. These rules would be made effective as to lawyers through the ABA Canons of Professional Ethics, enforceable by disciplinary proceedings, and as to law-enforcement agencies by internal regulations. On the touchy question of enforcement against the press, the ABA committee recommended use of the contempt power in limited instances while cases were actually on trial.

The American Newspaper Publishers Association sharply attacked these proposals. They contended that any interference with news sources concerning criminal investigations and prosecutions would be censorship and that a free press requires not only freedom to print without prior restraint but also free and uninhibited access to information. They denied that pretrial and intrial reporting had any real bearing on the outcome of criminal cases, and contended that the press was actually a positive influence in assuring a fair trial.[23]

The net result of this heightened concern about prejudicial publicity was to encourage judges all over the country to issue "gag orders" when

---

[23] See Alfred Friendly and Ronald L. Goldfarb, *Crime and Publicity: The Impact of News on the Administration of Justice* (New York: Twentieth Century Fund, 1967).

dealing with sensational prosecutions.[24] In *Nebraska Press Assn. v. Stuart* (1976) the press was barred for eleven weeks from reporting the fact of a confession in a gruesome murder case, even though it was testified to in a preliminary hearing open to the public. The Supreme Court unanimously struck this order down as unconstitutional prior restraint. Burger's opinion did not absolutely forbid all gag orders, and he seemed to leave open the possibility that judges might achieve the same purposes by closed court hearings, but they would bear a "heavy burden of demonstrating, in advance of trial, that without prior restraint a fair trial will be denied." Brennan would have held all gag orders "constitutionally impermissible."[25]

It is good that police and prosecutors have been warned to avoid prejudicial publicity, and the press could well practice some self-limitation. But there are other protections for the integrity of the criminal trial process than gag orders. The voir dire examination of potential jurors, and the availability of challenges of jurors, offer substantial guarantees against prejudice. Change of venue must be granted on a showing of local feeling against the defendant.[26] The jury can be protected from publicity during the trial by sequestration. Motions for mistrial can be granted, and convictions can be voided on appeal. These alternatives offer substantial protection against trials unfair because of prejudicial publicity and are perferable to judicial control by prior restraints on the news media.

ACCESS TO THE PRESS

The basic concept of press freedom has been that of John Stuart Mill and Oliver Wendell Holmes—a marketplace of ideas in which free competition will result in the truth winning out. Insofar as American newspapers are concerned, the situation is quite different. Economic realities have killed hundreds of newspapers. Earlier efforts by the government to enforce competition between newspapers by bringing Sherman Act prosecutions have now been succeeded by legislation seeking to save failing newspapers by authorizing competitors to pool operations and facilities.[27]

[24] Andrew M. Schatz, "Gagging the Press in Criminal Trials," 10 HARVARD CIVIL RIGHTS-CIVIL LIBERTIES LAW REVIEW 608 (1975); Robert T. Roper, "The Gag Order: Asphyxiating the First Amendment," 34 WESTERN POLITICAL QUARTERLY 372 (1981).

[25] On the same day that *Nebraska Press* was decided, the Court refused to review the contempt conviction of William Farr, a Los Angeles newsman, for refusing to reveal the name of an attorney who had given Farr information concerning the Manson murder case in violation of the judge's gag order (*Farr v. Pitchess* [1976]).

[26] *Groppi v. Wisconsin* (1971), *Murphy v. Florida* (1975).

[27] See Keith Roberts, "Antitrust Problems in the Newspaper Industry," 82 HARVARD LAW REVIEW 319 (1968).

Popular access to the "free marketplace of ideas" is of course subject to the decisions of the editors and publishers. While all papers welcome letters and news items, decisions on what to publish are controlled by available space and editorial policy. A newspaper is not a public utility. It is the essence of First Amendment rights that a paper's contents or policies in selecting news may not be dictated by government. The press cannot be forced to be "fair," at least in its news or editorial columns.

This issue was clarified by the Supreme Court's decision in *Miami Herald Publishing Co. v. Tornillo* (1974). A Florida "right to reply" law provided that if a newspaper attacked the personal character or official record of any political candidate, the paper was obligated to print, without charge, any reply the candidate might make to the attack. While the case for compulsory access to news columns had been ably argued by Jerome A. Barron in a widely noted article,[28] the Court unanimously viewed the statute as a clear attempt at government control over the exercise of editorial judgment. Even Justice White, who had not been too friendly to the press in the *Branzburg* case, here said, "this law runs afoul of the elementary First Amendment proposition that government may not force a newspaper to print copy which, in its journalistic discretion, it chooses to leave on the newsroom floor."

COMMERCIAL SPEECH

In *Valentine v. Chrestensen* (1942), a clever attempt by the exhibitor of a submarine to bring a commercial handbill under the protection of the *Lovell* and *Schneider* decisions failed.[29] The *Chrestensen* decision gave rise to the concept that the First Amendment did not apply to "commercial speech," which was furthered by the Court's decision in *Pittsburgh Press Co. v. Pittsburgh Commission on Human Relations* (1973). A "human relations" ordinance was construed in this case to forbid local newspapers from carrying help-wanted advertisements in sex-designated columns. Such advertisements, the Court said, are "classic examples of commercial speech." But Stewart, one of four dissenters, was alarmed; he thought that if "a government agency can force a newspaper publisher to print his classified advertising pages in a certain way in order to carry out governmental policy . . . I see no reason why Government cannot force a

[28] "Access to the Press—A New First Amendment Right," 80 HARVARD LAW REVIEW 1641 (1967).

[29] See "Freedom of Expression in a Commercial Context," 78 HARVARD LAW REVIEW 1191 (1965).

newspaper publisher to conform in the same way in order to achieve other goals thought socially desirable."

It soon appeared, however, that the Court intended to define "commercial speech" very narrowly. In *New York Times v. Sullivan* (1964), a major decision to be discussed more fully in Chapter 5, a Birmingham police commissioner who sued the newspaper for libel contended that the allegedly libelous statements were not protected by the First Amendment because they appeared in a paid advertisement. The Court's reply was that this "was not a 'commercial' advertisement in the sense in which the word was used in *Chrestensen.*" This ad, which had been submitted by persons active in the civil rights movement, "communicated information, expressed opinion, recited grievances, protested claimed abuses, and sought financial support on behalf of a movement whose existence and objectives are matters of the highest public interest and concern."

The *New York Times* precedent was followed in *Bigelow v. Virginia* (1975), where a newspaper had published, contrary to Virginia law, an advertisement for a legal abortion service in New York. Justice Blackmun, upholding the paper, distinguished the *Pittsburgh* case. Here the ad "conveyed information of potential interest and value to a diverse audience—not only to readers possibly in need of the services offered, but also to those with a general curiosity about, or genuine interest in, the subject matter or the law of another State . . . and to readers seeking reform in Virginia."

The concept of commercial speech was carried significantly further in *Virginia State Board of Pharmacy v. Virginia Citizens Consumer Council* (1976). Here the state had forbidden pharmacists to advertise the price of prescription drugs, but the Court ruled that even "purely commercial" advertising was entitled to some First Amendment protection in a "free enterprise economy." Stewart, concurring, emphasized that the Court was not questioning the government's right to regulate false or deceptive advertising. Rehnquist, the sole dissenter, thought there was a strong "societal interest against the promotion of drug use for every ill, real or imaginary," and warned that this ruling could not be confined to pharmacists and prices, but would extend to "lawyers, doctors, and all other professions."

His forecast was correct. In *Bates v. State Bar of Arizona* (1977), a law firm that had run newspaper ads specifying the price of routine legal services had run afoul of the state bar's ban on advertising. The Court in *Bates* repeated its conclusion that significant social interests were served by such commercial speech, and rejected fears that professionalism of the bar would suffer. But Powell and Stewart now joined Rehnquist in dissent, arguing that advertising of professional services had much more potential for deception than advertising prepackaged prescription drugs, and Rehnquist protested the "demeaning" of the First Amendment.[30]

Moving beyond the advertising of goods and services, the Court in *First National Bank of Boston v. Bellotti* (1978) encountered the problem of corporate expenditure of funds to influence votes on election issues not materially related to the property, business, or assets of the corporation. The Court majority concluded that a corporation had First Amendment interests apart from its property rights. But four justices dissented, pointing to the long-standing "fear of corporate domination of the electoral process." Again Rehnquist was the most vocal, asserting that "the Fourteenth Amendment does not require a State to endow a business corporation with the power of political speech."[31]

In *Metromedia, Inc. v. San Diego* (1981) the Court struck down a complicated ordinance regulating billboard advertising. In the interests of traffic safety and aesthetics, it banned commercial billboards except for on-site advertising of goods and services. Noncommercial billboards were also banned, but with twelve specified exceptions (political campaigns, for example). Justice White for the Court held that this ordinance reached "too far into the realm of protected speech," but the five opinions written were long and confusing, providing almost no guidance on the First Amendment status of billboards.

SPECIAL PROBLEMS OF RADIO AND TELEVISION

In spite of the importance of the electronic media as channels of news and discussion, they have been fatally handicapped in their claims for

[30] *Bates* was followed in *In re R.M.J.* (1982), where the Court ruled that states and bar associations can prohibit only advertising that is inherently misleading. But the Court did agree with a New York court's discipline of a lawyer who mailed flyers to local real estate brokers asking them to recommend him to their clients; *Greene v. Grievance Committee* (1982). See also *American Medical Assn. v. Federal Trade Commission* (1982).

[31] Free speech for corporations was again upheld in two 1980 cases. In *Consolidated Edison Co. v. Public Service Commission of New York,* an electric utility had violated state regulations by inserting in monthly bills discussion of controversial public policies. In *Central Hudson Gas v. Public Service Commission of New York,* the utility was engaging in promotional advertising, which the state had banned in the interest of energy conservation.

But *Friedman v. Rogers* (1979) held that a state law did not violate the commercial speech rights of optometrists or other professionals when it prohibited them from practicing under trade or corporate names. A trade name is a form of commercial speech that has no "intrinsic meaning," and the Court regarded such regulation as protecting the public from deceptive or misleading use of optometrical trade names.

In *Linmark Associates v. Willingboro* (1977), a township seeking to stem "white flight" from a racially integrated neighborhood adopted an ordinance prohibiting the posting of real estate "For Sale" signs on front lawns. Such suppression of information that was neither false nor misleading the Court found completely unacceptable.

full First Amendment protection by the fact that their existence depends upon government licenses. Licenses are granted by the Federal Communications Commission in its discretion on a showing of "public interest, convenience and necessity," and are subject to renewal every three years.[32] They can be revoked or suspended for violation of statutory standards or FCC rules. While these sanctions are rarely used, FCC control, guidance, or criticism is expressed in many other ways.[33]

The FCC is forbidden by its statute to exercise powers of censorship over the media, yet broadcast programming is one of the factors likely to be taken into account in deciding whether the "public interest" is being served by a station. Section 315(a) of the Federal Communications Act, the "equal time" provision, requires that if one political candidate receives time on the air, any opponents must be granted equal amounts of broadcast time. The broadcasting of obscene or profane language is forbidden by statute, and the industry is subject to the antitrust laws.[34]

But it is an FCC policy, the "fairness doctrine," which in application has provided the clearest insight into the constitutional status of broadcasters.[35] From the beginning the FCC stressed the obligation of licensees to devote a reasonable amount of time to coverage of public issues and to provide an opportunity for presentation of contrasting points of view. In 1967 the FCC issued rules making more specific its requirement that when personal attacks or political editorials were broadcast, the station must notify the persons involved and give them a reasonable opportunity to respond over the station's facilities.

In *Red Lion Broadcasting Co. v. Federal Communications Commission* (1969), the Supreme Court upheld the fairness regulations by a three-step reasoning process. First, because the limited number of broadcast

---

[32] Renewal is usually granted as a matter of course, but in 1969 the Court of Appeals for the District of Columbia reversed the FCC and denied renewal of a television station in Jackson, Mississippi, on grounds of racial discrimination in programming (*United Church of Christ v. FCC*). In 1980 the FCC in its most drastic disciplinary move stripped RKO General, Inc., of licenses for three major television stations on charges of business misconduct. In *FCC v. National Citizens Committee* (1978) the Supreme Court upheld an FCC ban on the future acquisition of radio or television stations by newspapers, but allowed existing combinations of newspapers and broadcasting outlets to continue.

[33] For example, an FCC policy statement that appeared to prohibit stations from playing "drug related" songs on the air was upheld in *Yale Broadcasting Co. v. FCC* (1973). See "Morality and the Broadcast Media: A Constitutional Analysis of FCC Regulatory Standards," 84 HARVARD LAW REVIEW 664 (1971). The FCC imposed on the networks the "family hour" concept, an early evening period during which the level of sex and violence would be reduced, and also required that a half hour of prime evening time be reserved for local station programming.

[34] In *FCC v. Pacifica* (1978) the Court upheld an FCC finding that the language in a broadcast monologue was "indecent"; the Court held that the FCC ruling to this effect was not censorship and did not violate the station's First Amendment rights.

[35] See the valuable study by Richard E. Labunski, *The First Amendment Under Siege: The Politics of Broadcast Regulation* (Westport, Conn.: Greenwood Press, 1981).

channels requires government allocation and licensing, a First Amendment right in this field "comparable to the right of every individual to speak, write, or publish," is simply impossible. Second, since licensees must be selected and given monopoly rights, they must be subject to further regulation to prevent the abuses of private censorship. But, third, the government's power does have constitutional limits, and Congress intended the regulatory schemes to give broadcasting "the widest journalistic freedom consistent with its public obligations." Only the minimal regulation necessary to ensure the individual's right to receive information and society's need for an informed electorate is permitted.

Applying these principles, Justice White in *Red Lion* held for the Court that the FCC fairness doctrine had struck a fair balance. The FCC had not refused to permit a station to express its own views; it had not censored a program. All it had done was to say that, once a station's facilities were used for a personal attack on an individual, he or she must be permitted to reply. The contrast with the *Tornillo* decision, striking down a right-to-reply law affecting newspapers, is obvious.[36]

While the result achieved by the fairness doctrine in *Red Lion* seems proper, its extension would have serious potentialities. For example, in 1972 NBC broadcast a documentary stressing abuses in the nation's private pension systems. After a complaint of biased presentation had been filed, the FCC ruled that the program had in fact been unfair and ordered NBC to balance the broadcast by another program. NBC refused and appealed to the Court of Appeals for the District of Columbia, which in *Accuracy in Media v. NBC* (1974) reversed the FCC and cautioned the agency "not to intervene or burden or second-guess the journalist" except in the clearest cases of abuse by broadcasters.[37]

CBS has had a policy of refusing to accept paid editorial advertisements. The case of *CBS v. Democratic National Committee* (1973) involved refusal to sell time to a group that wished to express its views on the Vietnam War. The Supreme Court ruled that Congress had intended "private broadcasting to develop with the widest journalistic freedom

---

[36] See Louis L. Jaffe, "The Editorial Responsibility of the Broadcaster: Reflections on Fairness and Access," 85 HARVARD LAW REVIEW 768 (1972); Richard A. Kurnit, "Enforcing the Obligation to Present Controversial Issues: The Forgotten Half of the Fairness Doctrine," 10 HARVARD CIVIL RIGHTS–CIVIL LIBERTIES LAW REVIEW 137 (1975).

[37] The Supreme Court declined review. The Court also let stand an appeals court ruling that the FCC has no authority to require the Corporation for Public Broadcasting to provide "objectivity and balance" in the programs it funds and supplies to noncommercial broadcasting stations (*Accuracy in Media, Inc. v. FCC* [1967]). Under the fairness doctrine the Polish-American Congress requested television time to rebut some "Polish jokes" on the Dick Cavett show, but the FCC refusal to intervene was upheld by the Supreme Court in *Polish-American Congress v. FCC* (1976).

consistent with its public obligations," and did not require the FCC "to mandate a private right of access to the broadcast media."[38]

The First Amendment was successfully invoked by a television station in *Cox Broadcasting Corp. v. Cohn* (1975), where a station that identified a deceased rape victim during trial of the alleged rapists was sued by the father of the victim for invasion of his right of privacy. The Court held that the First Amendment forbade imposing sanctions for an accurate publication obtained from official court documents open to public inspection.[39]

In conclusion, two factors have operated to reduce public regulation of the electronic media and to strengthen their claim to full First Amendment rights. One is the general reaction against government regulation manifested in both the Carter and Reagan administrations. For example, in 1981 the FCC, having concluded that the radio marketplace had become so large and diverse that competition among stations had supplanted the need for strict federal regulation, freed the nation's 8,500 radio stations from such regulation as maximum limits on commercials and minimum percentage requirements for news and public affairs programming.

Second, with cable television and direct satellite-to-home transmission, increasingly programmers can bypass the conventional broadcast spectrum. The resulting multiplicity of channels undercuts the historic case for public regulation and limits on First Amendment rights. The number of competing images may make the fairness doctrine unnecessary and promote balance in public affairs coverage.

[38] But in *CBS, Inc. v. FCC* (1981) the Court held that the networks should not have refused to sell time in 1979 for a Democratic campaign presentation featuring President Carter. The networks had contended that it was too early for the presidential campaign of 1980 to begin.

[39] For a further discussion of invasion of privacy by publication, see Chapter 5.

5

Obscenity and Libel

Historically two types of expression have been denied the protection of the First Amendment—the obscene and the libelous. Punishment for such publications was long thought to require no constitutional justification. In *Near v. Minnesota* (1931), Chief Justice Hughes simply assumed that one of the exceptions to the rule of no prior restraint was enforcement of "the primary requirements of decency . . . against obscene publications," and he likewise took it for granted that the law of criminal libel rested upon a "secure foundation." The same view was reflected in Justice Murphy's acceptance in *Chaplinsky v. New Hampshire* (1942) of "the lewd and obscene" and "the libelous" as classes of speech "the prevention and punishment of which has never been thought to raise any Constitutional problem." In both fields the Supreme Court has more recently found it necessary to reconsider these earlier views.[1]

[1] Among the many serious discussions of obscenity, see Harry M. Clor, *Obscenity and Public Morality* (Chicago: University of Chicago Press, 1969); Charles Rembar, *The End of Obscenity* (New York: Random House, 1968); Richard H. Kuh, *Foolish Figleaves? Pornography in—and out of—Court* (New York: Macmillan, 1967); Harry Kalven, Jr., "The Metaphysics of the Law of Obscenity," in Philip B. Kurland, ed. *The Supreme Court Review, 1960* (Chicago: University of Chicago Press, 1960), pp. 1–45; Louis Henkin, "Morals and the Constitution: The Sin of Obscenity," 63 COLUMBIA LAW REVIEW 391 (1963); Harry M. Clor, ed., *Censorship and Freedom of Expression* (Chicago: Rand McNally, 1971); *The Report of the Commission on Obscenity and Pornography* (New York: Random House, 1970).

OBSCENITY

Legal restraints on obscenity and legal standards governing the degree of frankness in discussion of sexual matters date in England from the passage of Lord Campbell's Act in 1857. A few years later, in the United States, the crusading zeal of Anthony Comstock led to the passage of regulatory legislation in many states. Congress enacted a statute in 1872 making unmailable obscene or indecent publications or devices.

Why did legislatures act against obscenity, and why did American judges for so long assume the constitutionality of such legislation? In general, there seem to have been two kinds of concerns. First, obscenity has been regarded as bad in and of itself. It is indecent. It is a violation of good moral standards. It appeals to "prurient interest" and "stimulates impure sexual thoughts." It arouses feelings of disgust and revulsion or, alternatively, it induces unhealthy psychological excitement. In the words of the federal postal law, the obscene is the "lewd," the "lascivious," the "filthy."

Second, obscenity may be regarded as criminally punishable because of its evil effects on individuals and society. Obscene material, it is alleged, will have a tendency to deprave the minds or characters of persons exposed to it. It will corrupt the public morals. It will lead to immoral or antisocial sexual conduct. It will result in the advocacy of improper sexual values.

It was this second approach that was embodied in the first widely accepted legal definition of obscenity, that framed in 1868 by Justice Cockburn in the English case of *Queen v. Hicklin.* He said: "I think the test of obscenity is this, whether the tendency of the matter charged as obscenity is to deprave and corrupt those whose minds are open to such immoral influences, and into whose hands a publication of this sort may fall."

Under the pressure of this "effects" test, Justice Cockburn had to specify *who* was being depraved and corrupted, and his answer was, "those whose minds are open to such immoral influences." It was this feature of the *Hicklin* test that rendered it ultimately unacceptable, for, as Judge Learned Hand said in *United States v. Kennerly* (1913), it "would forbid all which might corrupt the most corruptible." Hand did not think that "society is prepared to accept for its own limitations those which may perhaps be necessary to the weakest of its members. . . . To put thought in leash to the average conscience of the time is perhaps tolerable, but to filter it by the necessities of the lowest and least capable seems a fatal policy."

The *Hicklin* test ignored literary and other social values, judged a whole book by passages taken out of context, and tested for obscenity by the tendency of the passages alone to deprave the minds of those open to such influence and into whose hands the book might come. Nevertheless, this test became so thoroughly established in the United States that in 1913 Judge Hand felt compelled to give it effect in the *Kennerly* decision, even though he personally rejected it in the following memorable language:

I hope it is not improper for me to say that the rule as laid down, however consonant it may be with mid-Victorian morals, does not seem to me to answer to the understanding and morality of the present time. . . . I question whether in the end men will regard that as obscene which is honestly relevant to the adequate expression of innocent ideas, and whether they will not believe that truth and beauty are too precious to society at large to be mutilated in the interests of those most likely to pervert them to base uses.

It was not until the 1930s that this remarkably sage counsel began to be effective in judicial decisions.[2] In the celebrated *Ulysses* case of 1934, Judge Augustus N. Hand in the court of appeals explicitly repudiated the *Hicklin* rule and replaced it with this new standard:

While any construction of the statute that will fit all cases is difficult, we believe that the proper test of whether a given book is obscene is its dominant effect. In applying this test, relevancy of the objectionable parts to the theme, the established reputation of the work in the estimation of approved critics, if the book is modern, and the verdict of the past, if it is ancient, are persuasive pieces of evidence; for works of art are not likely to sustain a high position with no better warrant for their existence than their obscene content.[3]

The abandonment of the *Hicklin* test permitted more civilized judgments on literary works, but it left the legal tests for obscenity vague, and it did nothing toward reconciling obscenity prosecutions with free speech theory. The Supreme Court finally undertook this task in the *Roth* case.

The Two-Level Theory

Roth v. United States (1957) and its companion case, *Alberts v. California,* required the Court to rule on the constitutionality of both federal and state obscenity laws. The task, so long avoided, turned out to be surprisingly easy. Justice Brennan, writing for the majority, held there was no First Amendment problem because obscenity was "not within the area of constitutionally protected speech." The First Amendment extends to "all ideas having even the slightest redeeming social importance—unorthodox ideas, controversial ideas, even ideas hateful to the prevailing climate of opinion. . . . But implicit in the history of the First Amendment is the rejection of obscenity as utterly without redeeming social importance." Since obscenity is not "protected speech," there is no necessity to show any connection with unlawful action in order to justify criminal punishment. Rather, "convictions may be had without proof either that obscene material will perceptibly create a clear present danger of antisocial conduct, or will probably induce its recipients to such conduct." It is sufficient to allege, as had been done in these cases, that the materials circulated had incited "impure sexual thoughts."

[2] See *United States v. Dennett* (1930), *United States v. One Obscene Book Entitled "Married Love"* (1931), *United States v. One Book Entitled "Contraception"* (1931).

[3] *United States v. One Book Entitled "Ulysses"* (1934).

So the obscene is not constitutionally protected. But what is obscene? That was the question which the Court now had to answer, and it was not so easy. Brennan made clear that he did not mean to say all discussions of sex were obscene; indeed, sex is "a great and mysterious motive force in human life . . . one of the vital problems of human interest and public concern." Consequently it was necessary to find a legal test for obscenity to supplant the *Hicklin* test that would fully protect the right to deal with sexual subjects. This is the test he proposed: "whether to the average person, applying contemporary community standards, the dominant theme of the material taken as a whole appeals to prurient interest."

The improvements in this standard over *Hicklin* are obvious. It is the average person, not the most susceptible person, whose morals are to be protected. The dominant theme of the material taken as a whole is the basis for judgment, not isolated passages from a book. Applying contemporary community standards recognizes that obscenity is a relative concept. Since the trial courts in both *Roth* and *Alberts* had defined obscenity consistently with this standard, Justice Brennan concluded that the convictions should be upheld.

Justices Douglas and Black, dissenting, denied Brennan's basic constitutional premise that obscenity can be punished because of the thoughts it provokes, with no proof that it has incited overt acts or antisocial conduct. "The test of obscenity the Court endorses today gives the censor free range over a vast domain. To allow the State to step in and punish mere speech or publication that the judge or the jury thinks has an *undesirable* impact on thoughts but that is not shown to be a part of unlawful action is drastically to curtail the First Amendment."

Justice Harlan also dissented so far as enforcing the federal statute was concerned. The charge against Roth was selling a book that tended to "stir sexual impulses and lead to sexually impure thoughts." He suggested that much of the great literature of the world could be stigmatized under such a view of the statute, and he believed that the federal government had no power "to bar the sale of books because they might lead to any kind of 'thoughts.'" But so far as the constitutionality of the state law was concerned, he felt obliged to accept as not irrational the legislature's conclusion that distribution of certain types of literature might induce criminal or immoral sexual conduct. He approved application of the state law in the *Alberts* case because his own "independent perusal" of the material convinced him that its suppression would not unconstitutionally "interfere with the communication of 'ideas' in any proper sense of that term."

Because the *Roth* decision upheld the constitutionality of obscenity laws, and because it flatly denied that obscenity was entitled to any constitutional protection under the First Amendment, the opinion when it was first handed down was widely considered to be a forecast of strong judicial support for further obscenity prosecutions. Certainly the four dissenters regarded the *Roth* reasoning as dangerously broad. Harlan, for example, found "lurking beneath its disarming generalizations" a number of problems that left him with "serious misgivings" as to the future effect of the decision.

Limiting the Obscenity Concept

However, it soon appeared that the Court recognized the dangers of the two-level theory and intended to define the concept of obscenity very strictly. In *Kingsley International Pictures Corp. v. Regents* (1959), a film version of *Lady Chatterly's Lover* had been banned because it portrayed approvingly an adulterous relationship. Justice Stewart for a unanimous Court reversed this action. What New York had done was to censor a motion picture "because that picture advocates an idea"—the idea "that adultery under certain circumstances may be proper behavior." This idea might well be contrary to moral standards, religious precepts, and legal codes. But, said Stewart, the Constitution does not protect only those ideas "that are conventional or shared by a majority. It protects advocacy of the opinion that adultery may sometimes be proper, no less than advocacy of socialism or the single tax." There can be no prosecution, then, for "thematic obscenity." Ideas cannot be obscene.

The next important step in limiting the obscenity concept was taken in *Manual Enterprises, Inc. v. Day* (1962), where Justice Harlan wrote the opinion. As already noted, he had been concerned over the breadth of the "prurient interest" test announced in *Roth,* and in *Manual* he was able to narrow it by adding a second test. In his view, "prurient interest" was only another way of stating the *Hicklin* "effect" test of depraving and corrupting. He believed that conviction for obscenity should require proof of *both* the elements analyzed earlier in this chapter; there must be prurient interest effect *and* "patent offensiveness." He pointed out that some acknowledged masterpieces of art or literature might have a dominant theme appealing to prurient interest, but he would rank such works as obscene only if their "indecency" was self-demonstrating. On the basis of the patent offensiveness test, Harlan absolved of obscenity the material involved in *Manual*— magazines with photographs intended to appeal to male homosexuals. He found the magazines to be "dismally unpleasant, uncouth, and tawdry," but not "beyond the pale of contemporary notions of rudimentary decency."

A third test, likewise restrictive of the scope of the obscenity concept, was put forward by Justice Brennan in *Jacobellis v. Ohio* (1964). Its foundation was his statement in the *Roth* case that obscenity is "utterly without redeeming social importance." At that time he had simply been defending the two-level theory and justifying the constitutionality of laws against obscenity. But his statement was also relevant as a test *for* obscenity. If it is true that obscenity is "utterly without redeeming social importance," then it must be equally true that anything *with* redeeming social importance cannot be obscene. This was what Brennan spelled out in the *Jacobellis* case, which dealt with censorship of the film "The Lovers." He wrote that

> . . . material dealing with sex in a manner . . . that has literary or scientific or artistic value or any other form of social importance, may not be branded as obscenity and denied the constitutional protection. Nor may the constitutional status of the material be made to turn on a "weighing" of its social importance against prurient appeal, for a work cannot be prescribed unless it is "utterly" without social importance.

Thus the Court had by 1964 set up three tests for obscenity—prurient interest appeal, patent offensiveness, and utterly without redeeming social value. In the famous *Fanny Hill* case of 1966 *(A Book Named "John Cleland's Memoirs of a Woman of Pleasure" v. Attorney General of Massachusetts)* the Court made it clear that the three tests were independent and that a book had to fail all three before it could be adjudged obscene. The supreme court of Massachusetts had granted that the book might have "some minimal literary value," but did not think that gave it any social importance. Since it appealed to prurient interest and was patently offensive, the state court held it obscene. Justice Brennan for the Supreme Court ruled that this was a misinterpretation of the social value criterion. "Each of the three federal constitutional criteria is to be applied independently; the social value of the book can neither be weighed against nor canceled by its prurient appeal or patent offensiveness." Since the state court admitted the book had a "modicum of social value," that was enough to rescue it from the charge of obscenity.

Though the justices encountered some difficulties in applying these standards, there did emerge a clear majority view that there was a class of materials, called "hard-core pornography," which was not protected by the First Amendment. Some members of the Court believed that nothing else would meet the Court's three tests for obscenity. Justice Harlan said in *Manual Enterprises*: "At least one important state court and some authoritative commentators have considered *Roth* and subsequent cases to indicate that only 'hard-core' pornography can constitutionally be reached under this or similar state obscenity statutes. But, as Chief Justice Warren asked in *Jacobellis*: "Who can define 'hard-core pornography' with any greater clarity than 'obscenity'?" Justice Stewart in the same case confessed: "I shall not attempt . . . to define the kinds of material I understand to be embraced within [hard-core pornography]; and perhaps I could never succeed in intelligibly doing so. But I know it when I see it, and the motion picture involved in this case is not that."

The Pandering Test

The Supreme Court's obscenity decisions undoubtedly contributed toward an increase in the openness with which sexually stimulating materials were published and advertised. When the magazine *Eros,* announced as a quarterly "devoted to the subjects of Love and Sex," was founded in 1962 by Ralph Ginzburg, he said in an advertisement that it was "the result of recent court decisions that have realistically interpreted America's obscenity laws and that have given to this country a new breath of freedom of expression. . . . *Eros* takes full advantage of this new freedon of expression. It is *the* magazine of sexual candor."

Ginzburg had misinterpreted the extent of the new freedom. He was prosecuted and convicted under the federal obscenity statute for the publication of *Eros* and certain other materials and sentenced to five years in prison. The Supreme Court, some members of which had apparently become concerned over the commercial exploitation of sex resulting from its earlier decisions, unexpectedly affirmed the conviction by a vote of five to four in *Ginzburg v. United States* (1966).

In justification of this ruling, Justice Brennan for the majority announced a new, fourth test for obscenity—the setting or context in which the publications claimed to be obscene were presented to the public. The Court conceded that Ginzburg's publications "standing alone . . . might not be obscene." But when viewed "against a background of commercial exploitation of erotica solely for the sake of their prurient appeal," a different conclusion was justified.

Each of the accused publications, the Court found, had been "originated or sold as stock in trade of the sordid business of pandering." The "leer of the sensualist" permeated the advertising. The publisher "deliberately emphasized the sexually provocative aspects of the work, in order to catch the salaciously disposed." He engaged in the "exploitation of interests in titillation by pornography." The magazine was even mailed from Middlesex, New Jersey, after arrangements to mail it from Intercourse, Pennsylvania, had proved unsuccessful.

Justice Brennan did not state the new "context" test very precisely. He simply affirmed for the Court that "the question of obscenity may include consideration of the setting in which the publications were presented as an aid to determining the question of obscenity." He did not discuss the relationship of the context test to the other three tests, except to say that "in close cases evidence of pandering may be probative with respect to the nature of the material in question and thus satisfy the *Roth* test." But surely the holding is that the setting test can override the other three, since materials otherwise not clearly obscene can become "illicit merchandise" because of the way in which they are presented.[4]

In *Mishkin v. New York* (1966), decided the same day as *Ginzburg,* the Court by a vote of six to three upheld the criminal conviction of a man who published and arranged for the writing of books concerned largely with deviant sexual practices. The New York courts applied hard-core pornography as their obscenity standard, which of course met the Supreme Court's constitutional requirements. The principal feature of interest in *Mishkin* was its treatment of the "average person" aspect of the *Roth* test. Counsel for Mishkin argued that books emphasizing flagellation, fetishism, lesbianism, and masochism such as were here at issue were so deviant that they would not appeal to the prurient interest of an "average" person, but instead would "disgust and sicken." Justice Brennan countered this legalism by adjusting "the prurient-appeal requirement to social realities," saying: "where the material is designed for and primarily disseminated to a clearly defined deviant sexual group, rather than the public at large, the prurient-appeal requirement of the *Roth* test is satisfied if the dominant theme of the material taken as a whole appeals to the prurient interest in sex of the members of that group."

The Warren Court Reconsiders

Appearing to recognize that its confusing obscenity decisions had created what C. Peter Magrath called a "disaster area," in 1967 the Court took a new tack.[5] A brief and uncomplicated per curiam opinion in *Redrup v. New York* recapitulated the Court's past problems in reaching a consensus and suggested that in the future it would uphold obscenity convictions only (1) where the statute "reflected a specific and limited state concern for juveniles," or (2) where "individual privacy" had been assaulted by obscene material "in a manner so obtrusive as to make it impossible for an unwilling individual to avoid exposure to it," or (3) where there was "pandering" of the *Ginzburg* type.

Pursuant to this new and promising line, the Court in *Ginsberg v. New York* (1968) upheld a state statute prohibiting the sale of obscene materials to minors under seventeen years of age. Congress picked up the point about imposing obscenity on captive audiences and in 1967 passed a law providing that persons receiving in the mail material that they regarded

[4] In *Splawn v. California* (1977) Justice Stevens argued that *Ginzburg* had been overruled by *Virginia State Board of Pharmacy,* which extended First Amendment protection to commercial speech. But the *Splawn* majority did not agree and upheld a conviction where a film was "sexually provocative" but not obscene, on the ground that it had been commercially exploited for the sake of its prurient appeal. A pandering charge was also upheld as properly brought in *Pinkus v. United States* (1978).

[5] "The Obscenity Cases: Grapes of Roth," in Philip B. Kurland, ed., *The Supreme Court Review, 1966* (Chicago; University of Chicago Press, 1966), pp. 7–78.

as obscene could demand the removal of their names from the firm's mailing list, after which a second mailing would be basis for prosecution. This law was upheld in *Rowan v. Post Office Department* (1970).

In *Stanley v. Georgia* (1969), however, none of the three *Redrup* justifications was present. In fact, this was an egregious case where federal and state agents equipped with a warrant to search a private home for gambling evidence found instead some obscene films which they proceeded to view and then confiscate, charging the resident with possession of obscene matter. Justice Marshall's opinion was a ringing defense of every person's right to "satisfy his intellectual and emotional needs in the privacy of his own home" and a denial of the state's right "to control the moral content of a person's thoughts." The decision was unanimous, but three justices would have preferred to rest the case on a finding of unconstitutional search and seizure.

The Burger Court Takes Over

If, as *Stanley* held, private possession of obscene materials is constitutionally privileged, it might seem to follow that there is a constitutional right to receive such materials through any modes of distribution as long as adequate precautions are taken to prevent their dissemination to unconsenting adults and minors. In *United States v. Reidel* (1971), a prosecution for mailing allegedly obscene material, the trial court did in fact hold that "if a person has the right to receive and possess this material, then someone must have the right to deliver it to him." But the Supreme Court declined to accept this logic. *Stanley* did not overrule *Roth*, White held. Obscenity was still unprotected by the First Amendment, and the government could exclude it from the mails.[6] *United States v. Thirty-seven Photographs* (1971), decided at the same time, upheld seizure of obscene photographs taken from the luggage of a returning foreign traveler as he went through customs. White's opinion upheld the power of Congress "to exclude noxious articles from commerce," even if the photos were for private use, but two of the six-judge majority concurred only on the understanding that commercial use of the photographs was intended in this case.[7]

Black, Douglas, and Marshall dissented. Black wryly suggested that the right of private possession of obscenity recognized by *Stanley* was now effective "only when a man writes salacious books in his attic, prints them in his basement, and reads them in his living room."

By 1973, with four Nixon appointees, the Court was ready for a new

---

[6] In *United States v. Orito* (1973), the Court upheld the federal law forbidding the knowing transportation of obscene material by common carrier in interstate commerce. See also *Hamling v. United States* (1974).

[7] However, in *United States v. 12 200-Ft. Reels of Super 8 MM. Film* (1973), a later Court held that Congress had the constitutional power to proscribe the importation of obscene matter even though the material was for the importer's private, personal use and possession.

effort to clear up the obscenity mess. In *Miller v. California* (1973) Chief Justice Burger set out to "formulate standards more concrete than those in the past." First, he accepted the *Roth* "prurient interest" and "contemporary community standards" test. However, he rejected the Warren Court's notion that "community" meant the "national community." It would be an "exercise in futility" to seek such a national consensus, he said; the nation is too big and diverse. "It is neither realistic nor constitutionally sound to read the First Amendment as requiring that the people of Maine or Mississippi accept public depiction of conduct found tolerable in Las Vegas, or New York City." In *Miller* the jury had been instructed to evaluate the materials with reference to contemporary standards in California, and this was held to be constitutionally adequate.[8]

Second, Burger revised the *Manual* "patent offensiveness" test to read, "whether the work depicts or describes, in a patently offensive way, sexual conduct specifically defined by the applicable state law." To aid state legislatures, Burger gave some examples of what he had in mind: "representations or depictions of intimate sexual acts, normal or perverted, actual or simulated," and "representations or depictions of masturbation, excretory functions, and lewd exhibition of the genitals."

Finally, Burger rejected the "utterly without redeeming social value" test which, he said, placed on prosecutors the impossible task of proving a negative. He substituted for it this test: "whether the work, taken as a whole, lacks serious literary, artistic, political, or scientific value."

With these new or revised tests, Burger proudly announced that for the first time since *Roth* a Court majority had agreed on "concrete guidelines to isolate 'hard core' pornography from expression protected by the First Amendment." Abandoning the "casual" standards announced in *Redrup*, he asserted that the Court was now providing "positive guidance to the federal and state courts alike."

Several other obscenity cases were decided the same day. *Paris Adult Theatre I v. Slaton* (1973) held that "adult" theaters were not protected by the First Amendment merely because they exhibited for consenting adults only. Specifically rejected was the *Redrup* position that the state's concern was only with protecting children and unconsenting adults. There are, Burger said, "legitimate state interests at stake in stemming the tide of commercialized obscenity . . . in the quality of life and the total community environment . . . [and] the public safety itself." Answering the argument that there is no conclusive proof of a connection between antisocial behavior and obscenity, Burger replied: "From the beginning of civilized societies, legislators and judges have acted on various unprovable assumptions."

---

[8]*Pinkus v. United States* (1978) held that children are not to be included as part of the "community" by whose standards obscenity is to be judged, but "sensitive persons" can be included, and the materials' prurient appeal to "deviant groups" can be considered by the jury. *New York v. Ferber* (1982) allowed states to ban the production, sale, or distribution of child pornography, whether it meets the legal definition of obscenity or not.

Miller and its four companion cases were all decided by a five to four vote, with Stewart joining Douglas, Brennan, and Marshall in dissent. Principal interest attaches to Brennan's agonizing reappraisal of his position. Having been a principal formulator of the Court's obscenity views since *Roth*, he now concluded that all their efforts had failed to "bring stability to this area of the law without jeopardizing fundamental First Amendment values." None of the available formulas had reduced the Court's vagueness to a tolerable level, nor would Burger's new formulations help. Parenthetically, Brennan expressed some distaste at being charged with deciding "whether a description of human genitals is sufficiently 'lewd' to deprive it of constitutional protection." And why should it be thought that the First Amendment protects only expressions of *"serious literary or political value"*?

The only solution, Brennan concluded, was to abandon the idea he himself had authored in *Roth*—namely, "that there exists a definable class of sexually oriented expression that may be totally suppressed." Save only for the juvenile and unconsenting adult exceptions, he would hold that "the First and Fourteenth Amendments prohibit the state and federal governments from attempting wholly to suppress sexually oriented materials on the basis of their allegedly 'obscene' contents."

Rather embarrassingly for Burger's claims that a new day had dawned and that the Court had returned to local communities the right to decide what was obscene, a Georgia jury promptly held *Carnal Knowledge*, a widely acclaimed and nationally distributed film, obscene. The Court in *Jenkins v. Georgia* (1974), having viewed the film, felt compelled to reverse the finding. Cautioning that *Miller* did not mean to give local juries unbridled discretion, Justice Rehnquist said that this movie did not depict sexual conduct in a patently offensive way and so could not be held obscene under the *Miller* tests.

There is little reason to agree with Burger that *Miller* has solved the Court's obscenity problems. Rather, the prospect of applying local community standards presents a serious threat to national distribution of books, magazines, and films. Because mailing of pornographic material can be proceeded against either in the area where it was mailed or received, prosecutors can shop for forums where they anticipate jury attitudes will be most favorable for conviction.[9] In *Battista v. United States* (1981) the Court

[9] In 1975 postal authorities sent to Los Angeles for advertised "adult material" and had it delivered to a pseudonym in New Hampshire, where they brought prosecution, on the assumption that a New Hampshire jury would be more likely to convict than one in Los Angeles. The federal court in New Hampshire, however, granted a defense motion to transfer the case to Los Angeles. In a similar case transferred from Iowa to Los Angeles, the government contended that Iowa community standards should nevertheless be used. The federal judge in Los Angeles agreed and then dismissed the charges on grounds that a Los Angeles jury could not determine what Iowa standards were (*New York Times,* July 11, 1975). But in *Novick, Haim and Unique Specialties Inc. v. U.S. District Court* (1975) the Supreme Court refused to hear a request from two Los Angeles men, charged with sending obscene materials through the mails, that they be tried in Los Angeles rather than Louisiana. See also *Marks v. United States* (1976).

let stand obscenity convictions, fines, and prison sentences imposed in Memphis, Tennessee, on two distributors and the producer of the movie *Deep Throat*, rejecting contentions that it should determine whether the movie was legally obscene and whether it should have been judged by the community standards of Memphis.[10]

Combat Zones

The concentration of adult theaters, book shops, massage parlors, and similar establishments in a small area can turn local communities into deteriorated and high-crime areas. Some cities have resorted to zoning laws to restrict the number or concentration of these operations, and this type of zone defense was upheld in *Young v. American Mini Theatres, Inc.* (1976). The Detroit ordinance prohibited operation of any adult movie theater or bookstore within 1,000 feet of any other such establishment or within 500 feet of a residential area. Though the ordinance differentiated between establishments on the basis of the content of their communications, prevention of which is a prime concern of the First Amendment, the Court majority concluded that here content was a legitimate basis for classification of theaters. Justice Powell regarded the ordinance as "an example of innovative land-use regulation, implicating First Amendment concerns only incidentally."

The Techniques of Morals Censorship

Legislative limitations on the circulation of allegedly obscene literature usually employ the technique of subsequent punishment. In addition to the normal protection of criminal punishment procedures thus provided, *Smith v. California* (1959) held that a bookseller must be proved to be aware of the obscene contents of a book to justify a conviction. If sellers were absolutely liable for having obscene books in their possession, the Court believed that they would tend to restrict the books sold to those personally inspected, which would be a serious bar to the free flow of communications.

Prior restraint cannot be employed against allegedly obscene books because obscene literature does not lose the protection of the First Amendment until its status under *Roth* has been determined in court. In *Bantam*

---

[10] *Ward v. Illinois* (1977) upheld an obscenity conviction under an Illinois statute, even though the language did not meet the "specific prerequisites" for conviction mandated by *Miller*. Justice Stevens, dissenting, predicted the "ultimate downfall" of the "Miller structure." In *Smith v. United States* (1977) he charged that the absence of uniform national standards for obscenity made criminal prosecutions "an unacceptable method of abating a public nuisance which is entitled to at least a modicum of First Amendment protection." However, as already noted, the Burger Court in *Cohen v. California* (1971) did hold that wearing the expression "Fuck the Draft" on a T-shirt in public is not obscene. To be obscene, Justice Harlan wrote, an "expression must be, in some significant way. erotic," and he did not think that "this vulgar allusion . . . would conjure up such psychic stimulation."

In 1983 President Reagan suggested appointment of an anti-pornography coordinator to tighten enforcement of obscenity laws.

Books, Inc. v. Sullivan (1963) a statute creating a public commission which threatened book distributors with prosecution if they handled objectionable literature was held unconstitutional as prior restraint. But a procedure under which an injunction was secured, followed by prompt trial, after which the offending material could be seized by the sheriff and destroyed, was upheld in *Kingsley Books v. Brown* (1957). Chief Justice Warren, dissenting, charged that book seizure "savors too much of book burning," and the Court subsequently struck down search and seizure statutes that provided slightly less procedural protection.[11]

State censorship of motion pictures was approved by the Court in the 1915 case of *Mutual Film Corp. v. Industrial Commission of Ohio.* The motion picture of that era was of course only an entertaining novelty rather completely devoid of any ideational content, and it was readily assimilated to burlesque or other theatrical spectacles that were customarily subjected to control on moral grounds. Moreover, the 1915 decision antedated the Court's concern with civil liberties problems.

Over the years both motion pictures and the Court changed. The movies came somewhat closer to being commentaries on the social scene, and in documentary films and newsreels they rivaled the newspapers in reporting current events, yet censorship continued to be practiced. It was not until 1952, in *Burstyn v. Wilson,* that the 1915 censorship opinion was finally reversed and motion pictures were recognized as coming at least partly under the protection of the First Amendment.[12] However, *Burstyn* did not ban all prior restraints on motion pictures; it merely held that the charge in this case, which was "sacrilege," was not an acceptable ground. Subsequent rulings took the same line.[13] Consequently, movie censorship is not unconstitutional on its face, as book censorship would be; but the Court imposed such strict procedural limitations on state and local censorship boards in *Freedman v. Maryland* (1965) that they have been abandoned.[14]

In *Southeastern Promotions, Ltd. v. Conrad* (1975), city officials in Chattanooga had refused to rent a city auditorium for performance of the rock musical *Hair* on the ground that it was obscene. The Court reversed, holding that prior restraint of a theatrical production in a public forum,

---

[11] *Marcus v. Search Warrant* (1961) and *A Quantity of Copies of Books v. Kansas* (1964). In *Blount v. Rizzi* (1971), a statute allowing the post office to stop the mail of businesses found in administrative hearings to sell pornographic matter was held unconstitutional because it did not provide sufficient procedural protections.

[12] See Ira H. Carmen, *Movies, Censorship, and the Law* (Ann Arbor: University of Michigan Press, 1966).

[13] *Times Film Corp. v. Chicago* (1961).

[14] The *Freedman* requirements are as follows: (1) the burden of proving that the film is obscene rests on the censor; (2) the censor must either pass the film within a brief period or go to court to restrain its showing; (3) the procedure must assure a prompt judicial decision. In 1981 the Maryland motion picture board of censors, the last one in the nation, was allowed to die under the state's "sunset" law (*New York Times,* June 28, 1981).

though not necessarily unconstitutional per se, could be imposed only under the procedural safeguards set forth in *Freedman*.

Roaden v. Kentucky (1973) held that seizure of a film by a sheriff without a constitutionally sufficient warrant was essentially the same restraint on expression as seizure of all books in a bookstore and was unreasonable prior restraint under the Fourth and Fourteenth Amendments. But *Heller v. New York* (1973) upheld a film seizure where the judge issuing the warrant saw the entire film before signing the seizure warrant; an adversary hearing prior to seizure was not required.[15]

Nudity as Obscenity

Nudity may be an element in obscenity, and of course nudity in public places can be punished as breach of the peace, indecent exposure, or the like. But nudity can under some circumstances be considered a form of expression with a claim to First Amendment protection. In *Erznoznik v. Jacksonville* (1975) an ordinance prohibiting the showing of films containing nudity at drive-in theaters with screens visible from the public streets was struck down as a restraint based solely on the content of communication. The First Amendment right was to be preferred over the privacy rights of persons passing by who might be offended by nudity.

As already noted, a ban on topless entertainers in bars was upheld in *California v. LaRue* (1972).[16] But in *Schad v. Borough of Mount Ephraim* (1981), the nude dancing was in connection with an adult bookstore, not a bar, and the Court held that "nude dancing is not without its First Amendment protection from official regulation."

LIBEL

First some definitions and distinctions are in order. *Libel* is the defamation of character by print or other visual presentation such as television. *Slander* is defamation by oral presentation. Defamation itself needs definition. The Sedition Act of 1798 spelled out the concept as "false, scandalous and malicious writing ... with the intent . . . to bring into contempt or disrepute; or to excite ... the hatred of the good people of the United States."

Prosecutions for libel can be *civil* or *criminal*. The theory of a criminal prosecution is that libel is an offense against the peace and good order of the

---

[15] *U.S. Marketing v. Idaho* (1982) struck down a nuisance abatement law that permitted the state to order a one-year closing of establishments selling obscene books or showing obscene films. But states can prove that movies are obscene on the preponderance of the evidence. not by the stricter standard of "beyond a reasonable doubt" (*Cooper v. Mitchell Brothers* [1981]).

[16] See also *Doran v. Salem Inn, Inc.* (1975) and *New York State Liquor Authority v. Bellanca* (1981).

community, likely to incite acts of physical retaliation. In earlier times when there were no laws punishing defamation, dueling developed as a method by which wounded feelings of honor could be avenged. Criminal punishment for libel provides a lawful means of redress and is designed to avert the possibility that libelous utterances will provoke an enraged victim to breach of the peace. Libels of the government or public officials may be made criminally punishable, as by the Sedition Act of 1798. Criminal libel statutes provided for fines and sentences of imprisonment within defined limits. The act of 1798 specified maximum sentences of a $5,000 fine and five years in prison.

A civil prosecution for libel is a suit for monetary damages brought by the victim against the publisher of the libel. The civil suit has generally tended to supplant criminal prosecutions for libel in the area of private defamation. As Justice Brennan said in *Garrison v. Louisiana* (1964), the civil remedy "enabled the frustrated victim to trade chivalrous satisfaction for damages [and] substantially eroded the breach of the peace justification for criminal libel laws."

Damages in a civil suit may be of two types—*compensatory* and *punitive*. Compensatory damages are intended to reimburse the individual for actual financial loss resulting, for example, from loss of employment or earning power or reputation occasioned by the libel. The amount of such losses can be reasonably well established by evidence. Punitive damages are exemplary in character, intended to compensate the victim for his suffering and to punish the libeler for malicious intent. There is no objective standard for determining the amount of punitive damages, and they have tended to escalate in recent years. When Theodore Roosevelt won a libel suit after he had left the Presidency against a newspaper that had charged he cursed and was intoxicated while campaigning, he was awarded damages of six cents. But more recently awards sought, and occasionally received, have escalated dramatically. A beauty contest winner who sued *Penthouse* magazine was awarded $1.5 million in compensatory damages and $12.5 million in punitive damages. A newspaper in Alton, Illinois, lost a $9.2 million libel judgment that threatened to bankrupt the paper. A suit by a drug rehabilitation organization against the American Broadcasting Company for $21 million was settled out of court. General William C. Westmoreland sued CBS Inc. for $120 million for its portrayal of him in a Vietnam documentary.

Seditious Libel

Seditious libel is defamation of the government and its officials and is punished criminally. American experience with seditious libel was strongly influenced by English practice. The English law of seditious libel permitted punishment for publications tending to bring into hatred or contempt, or to excite disaffection against, the king, the government, Parliament, or the administration of justice. The English law of libel was initially developed by the Star Chamber, which made no use of a jury. After the Star Chamber was abolished in 1641, the King's Bench was influenced by its tradition and permitted juries only a limited role, such as finding facts as to authorship or publication, reserving for the bench the question of whether these facts constituted a libel. A long line of oppressive libel prosecutions finally led to Fox's Libel Act in 1792, which allowed the jury to find a general verdict in cases of criminal libel. The American Sedition Act of 1798 also entrusted the determination of criminality to the jury, and in addition admitted truth as a defense.

It was the contention of Zechariah Chafee in his influential book, *Free Speech in the United States,* that the First Amendment was intended to abolish the law of seditious libel, a position also accepted by Justice Holmes. This view has been questioned by Leonard Levy, who argues that it was not until after adoption of the act of 1798 that opinion crystallized against seditious libel.[17] He points out that Jefferson, although he attacked the act of 1798 and its use against his partisans, was willing to see his Federalist opponents prosecuted for seditious libel in the states after he became President.

Over a century later, in *United States v. Press Publishing Co.* (1911), a New York newspaper was indicted for publishing criminal libels against the President and secretary of war in articles dealing with the acquisition of the Panama Canal. The Supreme Court avoided a decision on the merits, but seemed to leave open the possibility that criminal libel prosecutions were permissible under the Constitution. It was not until 1964 in the case of *New York Times Co. v. Sullivan* that the Court flatly declared seditious libel suits unconstitutional, in the process expressing the belated opinion that the Sedition Act of 1798 had violated the First Amendment. Justice Brennan, who wrote the Court's opinion, said that the right to criticize official conduct was "the central meaning of the First Amendment."[18] In *Rosenblatt v. Baer* (1966) he added that the Constitution does not tolerate prosecution for libel of government "in any form."

The *New York Times* Case and Libel
of Public Officials

The modern constitutional law of libel begins with the case of *New York Times Co. v. Sullivan.* That newspaper had printed as a paid advertisement a criticism of the treatment of blacks in Montgomery,

---

[17] Leonard W. Levy, *Legacy of Suppression* (Cambridge, Mass.: Harvard University Press, 1960), and *Jefferson and Civil Liberties: The Darker Side* (Cambridge, Mass.: Harvard University Press, 1963).

[18] See Harry Kalven, Jr., "The *New York Times* Case: A Note on 'The Central Meaning of the First Amendment,'" in Philip B. Kurland, ed., *The Supreme Court Review: 1964* (Chicago: University of Chicago Press, 1964), pp. 191–222.

Alabama. The ad was submitted by reputable persons, but it was later discovered that it contained some factual errors. The police commissioner of Montgomery, though not mentioned in the ad either by name or specific reference to his office, contended that criticism of the Montgomery "police" constituted a libel of him. The case was tried in Alabama.

The trial judge ruled that the statements in the ad were "libelous per se." He instructed the jury that legal injury was implied from the bare fact of publication, that compensatory (or general) damages did not need to be alleged or proved but were presumed, and also that "falsity and malice" were presumed, thus justifying punitive damages as well. The judge refused to require that the verdict differentiate between compensatory and punitive damages.

The Alabama jury awarded damages of $500,000, an amount one thousand times greater than the maximum fine provided by the Alabama criminal defamation statute. Another commissioner who sued on the basis of the same ad also got a $500,000 judgment, eleven additional libel suits were filed against the *Times* seeking a total of $5.6 million, while five suits asking $1.7 million were brought at the same time against the Columbia Broadcasting System based on its coverage of Alabama civil rights controversies. This indicates the magnitude of the threat to the solvency of major communications media which these libel proceedings had raised.

The Supreme Court unanimously reversed the *Sullivan* libel judgment on the ground that the Alabama libel law, as applied against the *New York Times*, failed to provide safeguards for freedom of speech and press required by the Constitution. The earlier statements in such cases as *Near* and *Chaplinsky* that the Constitution does not protect libelous publications were now qualified. A libel law, like any other, must meet constitutional standards; "libel can claim no talismanic immunity from constitutional limitations."

The *New York Times* case, Justice Brennan said for the Court, had to be considered "against the background of a profound national commitment to the principle that debate on public issues should be uninhibited, robust, and wide-open, and that it may well include vehement, caustic, and sometimes unpleasantly sharp attacks on government and public officials." This advertisement, as an expression of grievance and protest on a major public issue, clearly qualified for constitutional protection.

Had it forfeited that standing by the falsity of some of the statements and the alleged defamation of the police commissioner? The Court did not think so. Erroneous statement is inevitable in free debate. "A rule compelling the critic of official conduct to guarantee the truth of all his factual assertions—and to do so on pain of libel judgments virtually unlimited in amount" would be fatal to robust debate on public issues. It would impose a "pall of fear and timidity . . . upon those who would give voice to public criticism." A defense for "erroneous statements honestly made" is essential to the survival of First Amendment freedoms.

The Court did, however, attach one important reservation to this broad constitutional protection for freedom of comment. Defamatory false-hood relating to official conduct would be actionable if made with "actual malice"—that is, "with knowledge that it was false or with reckless disregard of whether it was false or not." But actual malice would have to be proved. Recognizing that this particular case might be tried again, the Court thought it wise to warn that the facts presented in the Alabama trial would not sustain a finding of actual malice on the part of the *New York Times.* Nor did the Court find any sufficient evidence in the record to transmute the general, "impersonal" criticisms of Alabama government into personal criticism, and hence potential libel, of the officials of that government.[19]

Justices Black, Douglas, and Goldberg would have gone further than the Court. They argued for "absolute, unconditional" freedom of publications from libel suits. Black contended that the press must have "an absolute immunity for criticism of the way public officials do their public duty." He charged that "state libel laws threaten the very existence of an American press virile enough to publish unpopular views on public affairs and bold enough to criticize the conduct of public officials." The "actual malice" test, he thought, was "an elusive, abstract concept, hard to prove and hard to disprove." It would be an uncertain, "evanescent protection for the right critically to discuss public officers."

Though the Court did not give criticism of public officials the complete protection for which Black argued, *New York Times* did leave public officials very largely defenseless against any except the most vicious attacks, thus adopting the Harry Truman maxim that "If you can't stand the heat, stay out of the kitchen." Some members of the Court were disturbed by this prospect. In *Rosenblatt v. Baer* (1966), Stewart expressed fear that the Court, in protecting the right of free discussion under the First Amendment, was neglecting "the right of a man to the protection of his own reputation from unjustified invasion and wrongful hurt. . . . The protection of private personality . . . is left primarily to the individual States under the Ninth and Tenth Amendments." He would not permit the First Amendment to undermine the right of the states to safeguard the "rights and value of private personality [which] far transcend mere personal interests. Surely if the 1950s taught us anything, they taught us that the poisonous atmosphere of the easy lie can infect and degrade a whole society." He would prevent a state from converting its law of defamation into a law of seditious libel, but that was as far as he would go. The same concern was evinced by Fortas in

---

[19] The Court applied the principles of the *New York Times* civil suit to a prosecution for criminal defamation in *Garrison v. Louisiana* (1964). The "actual malice" rule was interpreted in *Time Inc. v. Pape* (1971).

St. Amant v. Thompson (1968) in these words: "The First Amendment does not require that we license shotgun attacks on public officials in virtually unlimited open-season. The occupation of public officeholder does not forfeit one's membership in the human race."[20]

Libel of "Public Figures"

Following the *New York Times* decision, the Supreme Court was not long in extending constitutional safeguards against libel suits beyond public officials to "public figures"—that is, private citizens who had thrust themselves into public controversies or who had a status in life that commanded wide interest and legitimate public attention.

Associated Press v. Walker (1967) concerned a well-known right-wing general who filed suits totalling more than $20 million against the Associated Press and television companies for statements they had made about his activities on the University of Mississippi campus during the rioting occasioned by the admission of a black student in 1962. He was reported as having "assumed command of the crowd" and having "led a charge of students against federal marshals." He won one jury award of $3 million, reduced by the judge to $2.25 million, and another of $800,000, reduced by the judge to $500,000.

This latter award was unanimously set aside by the Supreme Court in *Associated Press v. Walker* (1967), though there was disagreement on the reasoning. Five justices thought the *New York Times* rule limiting libel to "malicious falsehoods" should apply equally to public officials and "public figures," whereas the other four justices, led by Harlan, would allow damages to "public figures" on a showing of "highly" unreasonable conduct constituting an extreme departure from the standards of investigation and reporting ordinarily adhered to by responsible publishers." On neither standard was Walker held entitled to damages. Harlan noted that Walker's appearance on the campus during the rioting was "hot news" that had to be handled quickly and, though there might have been errors in the dispatch, there was not "the slightest hint of a severe departure from accepted publishing standards."

However, in a second case, *Curtis Publishing Co. v. Butts* (1967), Chief Justice Warren switched sides and a five-judge majority upheld the libel judgment of $460,000 won by the former athletic director of the University of Georgia against the *Saturday Evening Post* for an article charging him with giving his team's plays to an opponent. Writing for the majority, Harlan pointed out that, unlike the *Walker* case, the *Saturday Evening Post*

---

[20] In a message to Congress on campaign reform, on March 8, 1974, President Nixon proposed that a federal libel law be considered to give political candidates and public officials greater protection from attacks in the press and by opponents. He wanted to encourage "good and decent people" to run for office without "fear of slanderous attacks."

story was not "hot news," and charged that the magazine had ignored "elementary precautions" and conducted an inadequate investigation in preparing the article.

The "public figure" rule has been a major reliance in subsequent libel reasoning. In *Greenbelt Cooperative Publishing Assn. v. Bresler* (1970) the "public figure" was a real estate developer who had applied for zoning variances. In *Monitor Patriot Co. v. Roy* (1971) a newspaper article had characterized a candidate for the state legislature as a "former small-time bootlegger." The Court held that candidates for public office must be treated the same as public officials and that a publication charging criminal conduct, no matter how remote in time or place, against a candidate would have the full protection of the *New York Times* rule.[21]

Defamation of Private Individuals

Compared with public officials and public figures, Justice Powell asserted in *Gertz v. Robert Welch, Inc.* (1974), private individuals have less opportunity to counteract false statements about themselves, and are, therefore, more vulnerable to injury; so "the state interest in protecting them is correspondingly greater." The Court majority, however, was slow to accept this rationale. In fact, *Rosenbloom v. Metromedia* (1971) had practically rejected the "private individual" distinction as a guide to decision in libel cases.

A news distributor had been arrested and charged with distribution of obscene magazines. A radio newscast repeated the charge and used the term "smut distributors." Subsequently, a jury acquitted Rosenbloom on instructions of the judge that the nudist magazines were not obscene. Rosenbloom then sued the station for defamation and got a substantial award (which was reversed on appeal).

The Court's opinion was a confusing one, with eight justices announcing their views in five separate opinions, none of them commanding more than three votes. Brennan's judgment for the Court held that Rosenbloom's status as a private individual who had not voluntarily chosen to become involved in the public arena was irrelevant. The controlling consideration was that the issue raised by his arrest was "a subject of public or general interest" in which the community had a vital concern—namely, proper enforcement of the criminal laws on obscenity. Brennan consequently would apply the *New York Times* rule "to all discussion and communication involving matters of public or general concern, without regard to whether the persons involved are famous or anonymous."

[21] But during Barry Goldwater's candidacy for President in 1964, Ralph Ginzburg's magazine *Fact* pictured him as mentally unstable on the basis of opinions solicited from a large number of psychiatrists. A jury found a "reckless disregard of truth" in the preparation of the article and awarded Goldwater a judgment of $75,000. The Supreme Court declined review in *Ginzburg v. Goldwater* (1970), over the protest of Black and Douglas.

The Court continued this erosion of the private individual distinction in *Old Dominion Branch No. 496 v. Austin* (1974), where a letter carrier who refused to join the union, and who had been listed as a "scab" in the union publication, lost his $45,000 defamation judgment when the Supreme Court held that the *New York Times* rule covered all participants in labor disputes.[22]

In *Gertz v. Robert Welch, Inc.*, however, the Court finally found a bona fide "private individual" who was constitutionally entitled to sue a traducer for defamation, and in the process it overruled *Rosenbloom*. Gertz was a Chicago lawyer who had been retained to sue a policeman by a family whose son the policeman had killed. The John Birch Society magazine published an article saying that the suit was part of a communist campaign against the police, that Gertz was a "Leninist," a "Communist-fronter," and, by implication, that he had an extensive criminal record. Justice Powell's opinion asserted that Gertz was a private individual, no matter how much attention he might receive as counsel in a newsworthy lawsuit, and that he was entitled to defend his reputation by a libel suit. However, under the *Gertz* ruling, publishers continued to be protected by the negligence rule: private individuals must prove failure of the publisher to exercise normal care.

Time Inc. v. Firestone (1976) involved a Florida court decision upholding a jury verdict of $100,000 against *Time* magazine for referring to a divorcee as an "adulteress" when the decree had not specifically found the woman guilty of adultery. Applying the *Gertz* rule, the Court limited "public figures" to those who thrust themselves "into the forefront of particular public controversies in order to influence the resolution of the issues involved." Participants in divorce proceedings, even if sensational, do not meet this test. Though the divorce decree was very loosely drawn and "full of talk about adultery," the Court held that publishers could be held liable for a reporter's negligent misreading of a court decision, even if the news story was "a rational interpretation of an ambiguous document." The case was returned to the Florida courts for a finding on the issue of negligence.[23]

In *Wolston v. Reader's Digest Association* (1979) the nephew of an admitted Russian spy, who had been held in contempt for failure to respond to a grand jury subpoena, was erroneously named in a book as a convicted Russian agent. The Court held that his contempt conviction did not make him a public figure; as a private individual he needed to prove only negligence, not malice.

Again, *ABC v. Vegod* (1980) held that corporations cannot be regarded

---

[22] See also *Linn v. United Plant Guard Workers* (1966).

[23] *Phillips v. Evening Star Newspaper Co.* (1981) held that a newspaper could be sued for libel if it relied on oral statements of police officers later shown to be erroneous.

as public figures even when they advertise widely for the public's business. *Moss v. Lawrence* (1981) ruled that a professional political adviser for former Vice-President Agnew was not a public figure, nor was a government contractor.[24] The founders of a California resort, alleged by *Penthouse* magazine to be run by "mobsters," were held not to be public figures and could proceed with their $630 million suit.[25]

Additional encouragement to libel suit plaintiffs was provided by *Herbert v. Lando* (1979). Here the Court ruled that a Vietnam veteran, admittedly a public figure, who contended that he had been libeled on a television program, must be allowed to query the broadcasters about their thoughts, motivations, and internal editorial processes to facilitate proof of malice.

Invasion of Privacy by Publication

In dealing with cases charging invasion of privacy by publication, the Supreme Court has tended to employ the same standards used in its libel decisions. The leading case is *Time Inc. v. Hill* (1967). In 1952 a Pennsylvania family named Hill had been held hostage in their home for nineteen hours by three escaped convicts. A novel portraying a similar incident was published in 1953, and was made into a play that appeared on Broadway in 1955. *Life* magazine made a feature story of the play, which it linked directly to the experience of the Hills, even taking pictures of the actors in the house where the Hills lived when the incident occurred. In fact, both the book and play were highly fictionalized accounts, differing in many respects from the family's experience.

The Hills sued for damages under a state law protecting privacy and were awarded $30,000. The Supreme Court by a vote of five to four set the judgment aside. Justice Brennan stressed that the risk of exposure to publicity is "an essential incident of life in a society which places a primary value on freedom of speech and of press." The press cannot be saddled with "the impossible burden of verifying to a certainty the facts associated in news articles with a person's name, picture or portrait, particularly as related to non-defamatory matter." However, Brennan thought the press could be held to the same standard he had previously developed for libel suits in *New York Times v. Sullivan* (1964)—namely, that "knowing or reckless falsehood" could not be protected. Since it was not clear that the trial judge had charged the jury in these terms, the Court reversed the

---

[24] *Loudon Times-Mirror v. Arctic Co.* (1981).

[25] *Penthouse International v. Rancho La Costa* (1981). In spite of her fame, Carol Burnett was considered a private figure for purposes of her libel suit against the *National Enquirer;* the jury awarded her $1.6 million in general and punitive damages, reduced by the judge to $800,000. In *Valley News v. McCusker* (1981) the Court refused to review a ruling that the jury, not the judge, should decide whether a libel plaintiff is a public figure.

judgment, though leaving the way open for a new trial. Justice Fortas regarded the article as a "reckless and irresponsible assault" upon the Hill family, and did not believe that the Court was adequately protecting the constitutional right of privacy.

As we have just seen, by 1974 the Court had come closer to sharing Fortas's concern about privacy, and this new attitude found expression in *Cantrell v. Forest City Publishing Co.* (1974). The *Cleveland Plain Dealer* published a feature story discussing the impact upon a local family of the father's death in a bridge collapse. The story contained a number of inaccuracies and false statements. In fact, it described and attributed various quotations to the widow, though she was not at home when the reporter made his visit. The Supreme Court upheld an award for invasion of privacy. While there was some confusion as to whether the trial court had applied the common law or the *New York Times* definition of malice, in any event the story contained "knowing falsehoods."[26]

Libel by Public Officials

A word should be said about libelous utterances *by* public officials. In *Barr v. Matteo* (1959) the Supreme Court established the rule of immunity from legal liability for all federal administrative officials for statements made within the "outer perimeter" of their official duty. This case had arisen when the director of a government agency had issued a press release announcing the suspension of two employees along with allegedly defamatory and malicious comments about them.

Members of Congress, under the "speech or debate" clause of Article I, also enjoy absolute immunity for any statements they may make in their official capacity. However, *Hutchinson v. Proxmire* (1979) imposed some limits on congressional immunity. It was Senator William Proxmire's practice to make a "Golden Fleece of the Month Award" for government expenditures he regarded as particularly wasteful or ridiculous. One such award, with attendant press releases, was made to a federal agency that had funded a behavioral scientist's research into aggressive behavior in animals. The Supreme Court ruled that issuing press releases was not an essential part of the Senate's business; consequently Proxmire's alleged defamatory

---

[26] The risk that authors who create fictional characters closely resembling actual persons may engender lawsuits for libel or invasion of privacy was demonstrated by *Mitchell v. Bindrim* (1979). Author Mitchell secured permission to attend nude encounter sessions run by psychologist Bindrim on the assurance that she would not write about the activity. Subsequently she did publish a book about nude encounters that unfavorably portrayed a character allegedly recognizable as Bindrim. He sued Mitchell and her publisher and secured an award of $75,000. However, in 1982 a New York court dismissed a libel suit against a novelist accused of basing one of his characters in part on a former girl friend; *New York Times*, December 16, 1982.

The Court ruled against claims for invasion of privacy in *Cox Broadcasting Corp. v. Cohn* (1975) and *Paul v. Davis* (1976).

comments about the scientist and his research were not immunized by the speech or debate clause.[27]

Group Libel

The case of *Beauharnais v. Illinois* (1942) raised the interesting question whether groups, as well as individuals, can be libeled. Is it possible, or desirable, to offer legal protection to groups against defamatory statements? There is of course general acceptance of the importance of groups in a democratic society, and it is likewise clear that defamatory statements about a group can have serious adverse effects upon members of that group. Nevertheless, groups are not persons, and they are legitimate subjects of public discussion. Any conception that comments about groups are limited by laws against criminal defamation is bound to impose substantial barriers to uninhibited discussion of public issues.

The problem of group defamation was presented in its most horrifying form by Hitler's success in calculated exploitation of anti-Semitism. This represented a kind of evil that can destroy the fabric of civilized communities, and it is not suprising that, in the United States, efforts to control what the Indiana Legislature called "hate racketeering" were adopted. Actually, the Illinois law involved in *Beauharnais* had been passed in 1917, reflecting the state's reaction to earlier racial problems. The statute made it unlawful to publish or exhibit any writing, picture, drama, or moving picture that portrays "depravity, criminality, unchastity, or lack of virtue of a class of citizens, of any race, color, creed or religion . . . [or] exposes the citizens of any race, color, creed or religion to contempt, derision, or obloquy or which is productive of breach of the peace or riots."

Joseph Beauharnais, head of an organization called the White Circle League, circulated on Chicago street corners racist leaflets which were in the form of petitions to the mayor and city council. The leaflets made defamatory and derogatory comments about blacks and asked the use of the police power to protect the white race from their "rapes, robberies, knives, guns and marijuana." The leaflets also appealed for persons to join the White Circle League and asked for financial contributions. Beauharnais was convicted of violating the statute and was fined $200.

The Supreme Court upheld the conviction and statute by a five to four vote, Justice Frankfurter writing the opinion. Every state, he noted, provides for the punishment of libels directed at individuals. Clearly, it is libelous falsely to charge a person "with being a rapist, robber, carrier of knives and guns, and user of marijuana." The question, then, is whether the Fourteenth Amendment prevents states from punishing libels "directed at designated

---

[27] In *Doe v. McMillan* (1973) officials of the Government Printing Office were held immune from prosecution for printing the report of a congressional committee that constituted an invasion of privacy, where the report served a legitimate legislative function.

collectivities and flagrantly disseminated." His answer was that the Illinois Legislature might reasonably have decided to seek ways "to curb false or malicious defamation of racial and religious groups, made in public places and by means calculated to have a powerful emotional impact on those to whom it was presented." Where the individual is "inextricably involved" in the group, speech that could be libelous if directed to the individual may also be treated as libelous when directed at the group.

Justices Black, Douglas, Reed, and Jackson dissented, though Jackson's position differed from that of the other three. To Black, this decision manifested the shocking results of the reasonable man test in the civil liberties field. By treating the Illinois statute as a libel law, Frankfurter had taken the case out of the context of all the Court's free speech decisions on "the bland assumption that the First Amendment is wholly irrelevant. It is not even accorded the respect of a passing mention." Such a law, Black was sure, would present "a constant overhanging threat to freedom of speech, press and religion."

Justice Jackson agreed with the majority on the constitutionality of the group libel law, but thought that convictions would have to meet the clear and present danger test by taking into account the "actual or probable consequences" of the libel. In this case there should have been an appraisal of the particular form, time, place, and manner of the communications. Is a leaflet inherently less dangerous than the spoken word, because less "emotionally exciting?" Is the publication "so foul and extreme" as to defeat its own ends? Perhaps its appeal for money, "which has a cooling effect on many persons," would negate its inflammatory tendencies. Perhaps it would impress the passer-by "as the work of an irresponsible who needed mental examination." By failing to insist on such an inquiry into the circumstances, Jackson thought the majority had failed to achieve a constitutional balance between state power and individual rights.

Subsequent developments have tended to undermine the authority of the *Beauharnais* decision. The attempt of American Nazis to march in Skokie, already discussed, presented a substantially greater prospect of racial violence that did Beauharnais' pamphlets. But most of the judges who ruled on the Skokie incident found *Beauharnias* no longer persuasive. The appellate court in *Collin v. Smith* (1978) said: "It may be questioned . . . whether the 'tendency to induce violence' approach sanctioned implicitly in *Beauharnais* would pass constitutional muster today." However, at the Supreme Court level Blackmun insisted that *"Beauharnais* has never been overruled or formally limited in any way."[28]

---

[28] The *Beauharnais* decision is thoughtfully defended by Hadley Arkes, *The Philosopher in the City* (Princeton, N.J.: Princeton University Press, 1981), Chapter 2. Great Britain adopted the group libel formula in the Race Relations Act of 1965, which makes it unlawful to stir up in a public place "hatred against any section of the public in Great Britain distinguished by color, race, or ethnic or national origins." See Anthony Lester and Geoffrey Bindman, *Race and Law in Great Britain* (Cambridge, Mass.: Harvard University Press, 1972).

Recent Supreme Court decisions making it easier for plaintiffs, even public officials and public figures, to win libel awards, sometimes in startling amounts, may discourage reckless personal assaults or invasions of privacy. But at the same time the threat of prosecution for libel tends to suppress criticism or legitimate complaints in the field of public affairs.[29] The specter of virtually unlimited damage awards can have a substantial effect on the media's performance of its vital role. Even if damages are not awarded, the costs of prolonged litigation are bound to discourage journalistic initiative. The American Civil Liberties Union has taken a position against libel suits arising out of public discussion, on the ground that they tend to suppress free speech and free press.[30]

[29] In a sample of 54 defamation and invasion of privacy cases brought against the media between 1978 and 1982, the defendants were ordered to pay damages in 47, in 9 cases amounting to more than $1 million. Punitive damages were assessed in 30 of these cases, with 7 awards exceeding $1 million (*New York Times*, November 4, 1982).

[30] In 1982 the ACLU adopted the following position: "The ACLU regards the existence of the right of action for defamation to be violative of the First Amendment . . . when the speech relates to . . . a subject of public concern. For this purpose, public concern can be deemed to relate to anything having an impact on the social or political system or climate." ACLU, *Civil Liberties* (February, 1983). In a widely publicized 1983 libel suit against the popular "60 Minutes" CBS television program by a doctor who was not a public figure, the jury decided for CBS on the ground that, whether charges made by Dan Rather on the broadcast were true, they were made in a good faith belief that they were true.

6

Freedom of Association

There is no provision in the Constitution specifically protecting freedom of association, yet the right of individuals to organize into groups for political, economic, religious, and social purposes is universally recognized. The constitutional basis for this freedom must be derived from the right of assembly and the freedoms of speech, press, and religion. The Supreme Court has remarked upon "the close nexus between the freedoms of speech and assembly," and noted how "effective advocacy of both public and private points of view, particularly controversial ones, is undeniably enhanced by group association."[1]

Because it is so closely linked with these First Amendment freedoms, discussion of associational freedom in this volume is partly subsumed under other headings—for example, in dealing with political parties, labor unions,[2] and religious groups. In this chapter our concern is primarily with

---

[1] *National Association for the Advancement of Colored People v. Alabama* (1958). See Reena Raggi, "An Independent Right to Freedom of Association," 12 HARVARD CIVIL RIGHTS-CIVIL LIBERTIES LAW REVIEW 1 (1977).

[2] Recognition of the right of workers to associate in labor unions of course involved a long and bloody struggle. Unions were originally regarded as illegal conspiracies under the common law, and their legal right to exist was primarily the result of state court decisions. Early efforts by Congress to aid organization were frustrated by the Supreme Court in *Adair v. United States* (1908) and *Coppage v. Kansas* (1915), but the Norris-LaGuardia Act outlawing the labor injunction was upheld in *Lauf v. E. G. Shinner & Co.* (1938), as was the Wagner Act in *National Labor Relations Board v. Jones & Laughlin Corp.* (1937). See Charles O. Gregory, *Labor and the Law* (New York: W. W. Norton, & Co., Inc., 1961); Harry H. Wellington, *Labor and the Legal Process* (New Haven, Conn.: Yale University Press, 1968).

unpopular organizations whose rights of association have been under the most pressure.

Associative freedom, of course, is not absolute for any group, any more than are the freedoms of speech, press, and assembly. The freedom of group life is always subject to some degree of regulation in the public interest. Totalitarians carry this regulation to the point of completely subjecting all groups to the purposes of the state. Anarchists go to the other extreme in proposing that the state abdicate its functions to groups. The liberal state seeks to encourage the maximum of group freedom compatible with general public welfare.[3]

In recent American experience, the organization whose associational rights have been under greatest pressure is the Communist party. To meet the threat that communism appeared to present to American security after the Russian Revolution established a basis for the party's worldwide operations, much restrictive and punitive legislation was passed both by Congress and the state legislatures, and reviewing courts have had to struggle with very difficult problems in reconciling traditional and basic associative freedoms with society's right to counter organized efforts conceived to threaten its way of life and undermine national security.

THE COMMUNIST PARTY AND GUILT BY ASSOCIATION

The Supreme Court's introduction to the interpretation of statutory restrictions on radicals came during and immediately after World War I, involving the Espionage Act of 1917 and the Sedition Act of 1918. Both enactments had to be construed in a wartime setting, which hardly encouraged the Court to be venturesome in protecting the speech rights of the assorted socialists, pacifists, pro-Germans, communists, and anarchists who were prosecuted under those statutes. The more significant of the decisions—particularly the *Abrams, Schenck,* and *Debs* cases—have already been commented on, and the ineffectiveness of the clear and present danger test, first developed in these cases, has been noted.

The "Red scare" stirred up by the Bolshevik revolution persisted for some time after the war, particularly in the form of the raids conducted by Attorney General A. Mitchell Palmer and his efforts toward the deportation of alien radicals. But the national return to normalcy largely took the federal government out of the anticommunist field, and the Sedition Act was repealed in 1921. There remained the states, many of which had legislation

---

[3] See generally "Developments in the Law—Judicial Control of Actions of Private Associations," 76 HARVARD LAW REVIEW 983-1100 (1963); Robert A. Horn, *Groups and the Constitution* (Stanford, Calif.: Stanford University Press, 1956).

on the books aimed at radicals of various sorts. Some of these laws had been passed after the assassination of President McKinley in 1901 by an anarchist, and were directed at "criminal anarchy" or "criminal syndicalism." It was a New York statute of this sort that was involved in *Gitlow v. New York* (1925).

The Supreme Court's unanticipated concession in the *Gitlow* case— that the First Amendment applied to the states by way of the Fourteenth— opened the way for Supreme Court review of all state laws under which political radicals were convicted; and in *Whitney v. California* (1927) the Court appeared to adopt the rule of guilt by association. Miss Whitney's crime, under the California Syndicalism Act, was that she participated, without protest, in the convention that set up the Communist Labor party of California and was elected an alternate member of its state executive committee. She testified that it was not her purpose that this party should be an instrument of terrorism or violence, or violate any law, but the party was found to have been formed to teach criminal syndicalism, and as a member of the party she participated in the crime.

The Supreme Court upheld this conviction on the ground that "united and joint action involves . . . greater danger to the public peace and security than the isolated utterances and acts of individuals," but Justices Brandeis and Holmes did not agree. Brandeis said:

> The felony which the statute created is a crime very unlike the old felony of conspiracy or the old misdemeanor of unlawful assembly. The mere act of assisting in forming a society for teaching syndicalism, of becoming a member of it, or of assembling with others for that purpose is given the dynamic quality of crime. There is guilt although the society may not contemplate immediate promulgation of the doctrine. Thus the accused is to be punished, not for contempt, incitement or conspiracy, but for a step in preparation, which, if it threatens the public order at all, does so only remotely. The novelty in the prohibition introduced is that the statute aims, not at the practice of criminal syndicalism, nor even directly at the preaching of it, but at association with those who propose to preach it.

The Hughes Court of the 1930s, however, refused to accept the *Whitney* rule of guilt by association. In three important decisions— *Stromberg v. California* (1931), *DeJonge v. Oregon* (1937), and *Herndon v. Lowry* (1937)—the convictions of admitted communists were reversed because they had not personally been guilty of violating any criminal law. For example, DeJonge had addressed a Communist party meeting, and that party might have illegal objectives. But, said Hughes, "Notwithstanding those objectives, the defendant still enjoyed his personal right of free speech and to take part in a peaceable assembly having a lawful purpose, although called by that Party."

The Smith Act

What was destined to become the most famous of the anticommunist measures was the Alien Registration Act of 1940, better known as the Smith Act. Actually, alien registration was only one of the five purposes of the act. Its major importance was as a peacetime sedition act, the first federal peacetime restrictions on speaking and writing by American citizens since the ill-fated Sedition Act of 1798. Section 2 of the statute made it unlawful knowingly to advocate or teach the overthrow of any government in the United States by force or violence, to print or distribute written matter so advocating, or organize or knowingly become a member of any group that so advocates. Section 3 made punishable conspiracy to accomplish any of these ends.

The language of the Smith Act was less drastic than the Sedition Act of 1798 in that it forbade only the advocacy of force, and not mere political criticism of government officials. But it was more restrictive in at least one respect. The law made it a crime to belong to an organization that was subsequently found to advocate the overthrow of the government by force, regardless of what the individual said or did. The act did not mention the Communist party by name, but there can be no doubt that the framers of the statute believed the party advocated force and violence and intended the act to apply to it and its members.

In 1948 the Truman administration, apparently goaded by Republican charges of being "soft on communism," began a dramatic prosecution in New York of eleven leaders of the American Communist party under the Smith Act. The indictment made two charges against them: (1) willfully and knowingly conspiring to organize as the United States Communist party a society, group, and assembly of persons who teach and advocate the overthrow and destruction of the government of the United States by force and violence, and (2) knowingly and willfully advocating and teaching the duty and necessity of overthrowing and destroying the government by force and violence. No overt revolutionary acts other than teaching, advocating, and conspiring were alleged.

The trial before Judge Harold R. Medina was full of sensation and lasted for nine months. The ultimate conviction was upheld by the court of appeals, Chief Judge Learned Hand writing the opinion. The Supreme Court then granted certiorari limited to questions of the constitutionality of the Smith Act, "inherently or as construed and applied in the instant case." By vote of six to two, with Chief Justice Vinson writing the opinion, the Court confirmed the convictions in *Dennis v. United States* (1951).

The major issue confronting the Court was how to reconcile with the free speech guarantee of the Constitution convictions that treated speaking and teaching as criminal offenses. For, admittedly, the eleven had taken no action with the immediate intention of initiating a revolution. Vinson sought to validate the statute by construing it as being "directed at advocacy, not discussion." But that did not solve the problem completely. For advocacy has two aspects. It is action against which, when aimed toward unlawful ends, the government had the undoubted power to protect itself. But it also "contains an element of speech," as Vinson agreed; and consequently his opinion for the Court majority had inevitably to return to the clear and present danger test.

Vinson's argument amounted to a substantial reinterpretation of the Holmes-Brandeis doctrine, which he purported to follow. The actual formula he adopted was that used by Learned Hand in the court of appeals: "whether the gravity of the 'evil,' discounted by its improbability, justifies such invasion of free speech as is necessary to avoid the danger." Obviously, said Vinson, the clear and present danger test "cannot mean that before the Government may act, it must wait until the *putsch* is about to be executed, the plans have been laid and the signal is awaited. . . . We must therefore reject the contention that success or probability of success is the criterion."

Jackson and Frankfurter each added their own interpretations of clear and present danger. For Jackson, the problem was easy. Holmes and Brandeis had developed this test in cases that presented only "technical or trivial violations . . . arising before the era of World War II revealed the subtlety and efficacy of modernized revolutionary techniques used by totalitarian parties." Jackson would save the test, "unmodified, for application as a 'rule of reason' in the kind of case for which it was devised"— namely, hot-headed speeches on street corners or circulation of a few incendiary pamphlets. But when the issue is the probable success of a worldwide revolutionary conspiracy, it is futile for the courts to attempt prophecy in the guise of a legal decision. "The judicial process simply is not adequate to a trial of such far-flung issues."

Justice Black, dissenting, charged that the Court's decision repudiated "directly or indirectly" the clear and present danger rule: "I cannot agree that the First Amendment permits us to sustain laws suppressing freedom of speech and press on the basis of Congress' or our own notions of mere 'reasonableness.' Such a doctrine waters down the First Amendment so that it amounts to little more than an admonition to Congress." He would hold Section 3 of the Smith Act "a virulent form of prior censorship of speech and press," and "unconstitutional on its face."

Douglas's dissent wanted to know how clear and present danger could have been determined when the record contained no evidence on the "strength and tactical position" of the Communist party in the United States. In the absence of such evidence, he himself could see no danger from these "miserable merchants of unwanted ideas." "Free speech—the glory of our system of government—should not be sacrificed on anything less than plain and objective proof of danger that the evil advocated is imminent."

The Court, however, had cut itself off from consideration of the evidence relied on to prove the alleged conspiracy by its questionable action in granting certiorari limited only to the constitutionality of the statute. Actually the government's case was a most peculiar one. The evidence presented at the trial was primarily concerned with what was in the basic texts of Marxism-Leninism extending all the way back to 1848, as distributed by the Communist party and discussed at their meetings. The guilt of the Communist leaders was established by connecting them with the organization of the party and the teaching of these texts. By allowing the validity of convictions based on such textual analyses to be established by default, the Supreme Court permitted the assumption that it had accepted the principle of guilt by association; illegal conspiracy could be established by demonstrating activities—any kind of activities—in furtherance of the organizational work of the Communist party.

The *Dennis* decision encouraged the government to bring similar prosecutions, based on similar evidence, against the lesser party leaders throughout the country. The government was almost uniformly successful in these subsidiary suits, in none of which did the Supreme Court grant certiorari until October, 1955, when it agreed to review the conviction of fourteen California Communists. This time no limitation was imposed on the grant of certiorari, and the result was the shattering decision in *Yates v. United States* (1957). By a vote of six to one the Court, while not challenging the constitutionality of the Smith Act as established by the *Dennis* decision, reversed the convictions of five of the fourteen defendants and laid down conditions for Smith Act trials that made it much more difficult to secure any future convictions.

Justice Harlan, writing the majority opinion, completely abandoned the clear and present danger test, contending that *Dennis* had actually been based on the distinction between "advocacy of abstract doctrine," which is protected, and "advocacy directed at promoting unlawful action," which is not protected. He continued:

> The essence of the *Dennis* holding was that indoctrination of a group in preparation for future violent action, as well as exhortation to immediate action, by advocacy found to be directed to "action for the accomplishment" of forcible overthrow, to violence "as a rule or principle of action," and employing "language of incitement" . . . is not constitutionally protected when the group is of sufficient size and cohesiveness, is sufficiently oriented towards action, and other circumstances are such as reasonably to justify apprehension that action will occur.

Evidence in the *Yates* record sufficient to support convictions for this second type of advocacy was, Harlan said, "strikingly deficient":

> At best this voluminous record shows but a half dozen or so scattered incidents which, even under the loosest standards, could be deemed to show such

advocacy. Most of these were not connected with any of the petitioners, or occurred many years before the period covered by the indictment. We are unable to regard this sporadic showing as sufficient to justify viewing the Communist Party as the nexus between these petitioners and the conspiracy charged.

What the Court was saying was that evidence of activity in the Communist party would not meet the requirements in this case. Some of the party's activities might be wholly lawful. The defendants could be convicted only on the basis of their individual acts other than their mere relations with the party. On this basis five of the defendants were completely cleared. There was no evidence in the record to connect them with the conspiracy charged except that they had long been members and officers of the Communist party of California.

As for the other nine defendants, the Court was not prepared to go so far. There was evidence involving them—party classes, an "underground apparatus," board meetings held in a devious and conspiratorial manner— which might meet the Court's tests. "We are not prepared to say, at this stage of the case, that it would be impossible for a jury, resolving all conflicts in favor of the Government and giving the evidence . . . its utmost sweep, to find that advocacy of action was also engaged in when the group involved was thought particularly trustworthy, dedicated, and suited for violent tasks."

The Black-Douglas dissents in the *Dennis* case were partially vindicated by the *Yates* decision, though again in *Yates* Black and Douglas found themselves in disagreement with the majority opinion. While concurring in the result, they would have held the Smith Act completely unconstitutional and directed the acquittal of all defendants. In fact, this latter result was achieved six months later when the Department of Justice "reluctantly" requested the trial court to dismiss the indictments against the remaining nine defendants on the ground that "the evidentiary requirements laid down by the Supreme Court" could not be satisfied. Also on the basis of the *Yates* ruling, indictments were dismissed against six Communists in Pittsburgh and eleven in Puerto Rico; courts of appeals reversed convictions of seven who had been tried in Hawaii, four in Seattle, five in New Haven, and four in Philadelphia. It appeared that the Smith Act had been rendered virtually useless as an instrument for jailing Communists and that the more than one hundred convictions under the act had been probably illegal.

Thus the Court, which had appeared to accept guilt by association in *Dennis,* in *Yates* moved back toward its traditional insistence on proof of individual wrongdoing. But section 2 of the Smith Act, which makes unlawful mere membership in a group advocating forcible overthrow of the government, remained to be construed by the Court. When it came up for review in the case of *Scales v. United States* (1961), the Court was asked to hold it unconstitutional because it imputed guilt on the basis of associations and sympathies rather than because of concrete personal involvement in criminal conduct.

The Court, however, upheld the constitutionality of section 2 by interpreting it as applying only to "knowing," "active," members who had a "specific intent to bring about violent overthrow." Specific intent could be established by evidence showing "the teaching of forceful overthrow, accompanied by a contemporary, though legal, course of conduct clearly undertaken for the specific purpose of rendering effective the later illegal activity which is advocated."

The Court majority found that Scales was linked to illegal advocacy by this kind of evidence. Douglas, dissenting along with Warren, Black, and Brennan, contended that Scales was charged with no unlawful acts and therefore that the Court had legalized guilt by association. The majority sought to refute this charge by reversing another section 2 conviction on the same day in *Noto v. United States* (1961). In *Noto*'s trial, Justice Harlan ruled, the kind of evidence that had convicted Scales was lacking. Justice Black interpreted the *Noto* decision as telling the government that it had not had sufficient up-to-date information on the present policies of the Communist party, and he added: "I cannot join an opinion which implies that the existence of liberty is dependent upon the efficiency of the Government's informers."

The government's success in the *Scales* case was not followed up, and Smith Act prosecutions were largely abandoned. In *Brandenburg v. Ohio* (1969) the Court pronounced an obituary on the entire line of cases criminalizing association, beginning with *Whitney*, which was specifically overruled. Striking down the Ohio criminal syndicalism act in *Brandenburg*, the Court stressed *Yates*, not *Dennis*, and *Noto*, not *Scales*. Under *Brandenburg* any advocacy that falls short of a call for illegal action is wholly protected. Moreover, speech that does call for illegal action can still be protected so long as the illegal action is not being sought immediately, or there is reason to believe that the listeners will not actually commit the illegal action.[4]

---

[4] Black and Douglas used the occasion to read their own personal obsequies over the clear and present danger test, which Douglas said had been distorted beyond recognition in *Dennis* and which in any event was "not reconcilable with the First Amendment." See Hans A. Linde, "Clear and Present Danger Reexamined: Dissonance in the Brandenburg Concerto," 22 STAN-FORD LAW REVIEW 1163 (1970); Staughton Lynd, *"Brandenburg v. Ohio:* A Speech Test for All Seasons," 43 UNIVERSITY OF CHICAGO LAW REVIEW 151 (1975).

Brown v. Socialist Workers '74 Campaign Committee (1982) held that an Ohio law requiring reporting the names of campaign contributors could not constitutionally be applied to a minor political party that historically had been the subject of harassment by government officials and private persons.

THE INTERNAL SECURITY ACT OF 1950

The Internal Security Act of 1950, which got its start as the Mundt-Nixon bill in 1948 and was passed over President Truman's veto, sought to cripple the Communist party by the device of registration. The statute ordered Communist organizations to register with the attorney general, and the Subversive Activities Control Board (SACB) was established to determine which organizations should be required to register. Upon issuance of such an order by the board, the organization was required to register, disclose names and addresses of its officers, and give an accounting of sources of money and expenditures. Among the sanctions incurred by a registered organization were the following: its mail and radio broadcasts had to be identified as Communist propaganda; members could not hold nonelective federal positions; they committed a crime if they applied for or used a United States passport; and their right to work in defense plants was limited.[5]

The SACB was organized in November, 1950. The attorney general almost immediately filed a petition to compel the Communist party of the United States to register as a Communist-action organization. After many misadventures, the board finally got a favorable ruling from the Supreme Court eleven years later in *Communist Party v. Subversive Activities Control Board* (1961). The party had contended that the registration provisions were fraudulent and that the real purpose of the statute was to impose impossible requirements in order to lay a foundation for criminal prosecution of the party and its officers and members—in effect "outlawing" the party. There is much evidence that this was in fact the intention of Congress, but the Court accepted the statute as a bona fide registration law and upheld it on that basis. The Court majority declined to consider the constitutionality of any of the sanctions that the act applied to registered organizations on the ground that, since the party had not yet registered, they had not come into effect. Justice Frankfurter wrote:

> Although they become operative as soon as a registration order is made final, their application remains in a very real sense problematical. We cannot now foresee what effect, if any, upon the Party the denial of tax exemption will have. . . . We do not know that, after such an order is in effect, the Party will wish to utilize the mails. . . . It is wholly speculative now to foreshadow whether, or under what conditions, a member of the party may in the future apply for a passport, or seek government or defense-facility or labor-union

[5] Title II of the Internal Security Act, designated the Emergency Detention Act, gave the government power, in the event of war, invasion, or insurrection, to seize and hold persons who could be expected to attempt acts of espionage or sabotage even though they had as yet committed no crime. This authority was repealed in 1971, with a provision prohibiting such detention without specific congressional authorization. See Richard Longaker, "Emergency Detention: The Generation Gap, 1950–1971," 27 WESTERN POLITICAL QUARTERLY 395 (1974).

employment, or, being an alien, become a party to a naturalization or a denaturalization proceeding. None of these things may happen.

Naturally, these things did happen. The registration order having been upheld by the Supreme Court, prosecutions were brought against two leaders of the Communist party to revoke their passports. In *Aptheker v. Secretary of State* (1964) the Court declared the passport provisions of the 1950 statute unconstitutional because they too broadly and indiscriminately restricted the right to travel.

The government had no more success in compelling enforcement of the registration requirement. The party's officials refused to register after the 1961 decision and were upheld by a federal appeals court, which ruled that no one could be forced by a registration proceeding to declare his association with a party that had been labeled criminal. The Supreme Court denied certiorari.[6] The SACB, persevering, then brought action to require individual party members to register. In *Albertson v. SACB* (1965) the Supreme Court unanimously held that this would constitute compulsory self-incrimination.

Following the failure of two more SACB efforts to compel alleged "Communist-front" organizations to register,[7] this record of futility was completed in *United States v. Robel* (1967), where the Court declared unconstitutional by a vote of six to two the provision of the McCarran Act making it a crime for any member of a Communist-action organization "to engage in any employment in any defense facility." The Court was not prepared to rescue this provision, as it had done with section 2 of the Smith Act in *Scales v. United States* (1961), by interpreting it as applying only to active members with the specific intent to overthrow the government. Rather the precedent applied was *Aptheker,* and the statute was invalid because its language swept "indiscriminately across all types of associations with Communist-action groups, without regard to the quality or degree of membership. . . . The statute quite literally establishes guilt by association alone, without any need to establish that an individual's association poses the threat feared by the Government in proscribing it."

POLITICAL TRIALS
AND THE CONSPIRACY CHARGE

The prosecutions of Communist party members can be regarded as "political trials" in the sense that they were charged with opposition to the

---

[6] *Communist Party v. United States* (1963).

[7] *American Committee for Protection of Foreign Born v. SACB* (1965) and *Veterans of the Abraham Lincoln Brigade v. SACB* (1965). After a concerted effort by the Nixon administration in 1971 and 1972 to find something for the SACB to do, it was finally allowed to die in 1973 by failure to appropriate funds for it.

established political regime and threatening the safety of the state.[8] In the late 1960s and early 1970s, old-line communists were largely replaced by opponents of the war in Vietnam, the New Left, "black power" radicals, and various violent underground movements as the principal perceived threat to the political order. The two most significant prosecutions in this period were those of Dr. Benjamin Spock and four others in 1968 for encouraging resistance to the draft and the Chicago Seven in 1970 for violation of the federal Anti-Riot Act at the 1968 Democratic convention.[9]

These two cases highlighted the special constitutional issues in securing a fair "political trial." One is the unusual degree of government discretion in determining whom to prosecute. In the Spock case, the five defendants scarcely knew each other before they were indicted, and they were selected almost at random to stand trial as surrogates for and warning to the entire peace movement. Again, the selection of the eight original Chicago defendants from among the thousands who participated in the convention riots was pure prosecutorial discretion. Other characteristics of political trials are related to the public tension and near-hysteria that may be generated by such occasions and the disruptive courtroom behavior that the defendants may engage in to demonstrate their contempt for the regime.

A special constitutional problem in such trials is the common reliance on charges of conspiracy. An indictment for criminal conspiracy offers peculiar advantages for the government because it is easier to prove and more difficult to defend against than other criminal charges. A criminal conspiracy at common law occurs when two or more persons enter into an agreement to commit an unlawful act or to achieve a lawful object by unlawful means. The essence of the offense is making the agreement; under common law nothing more in the way of carrying out the conspiracy is required to justify conviction.[10]

Other features of the law of conspiracy make it attractive to prosecutors. Two individuals can be convicted for agreeing to perform an act that, if accomplished by one person, would not even be indictable. Individuals may be charged with conspiracy to commit an illegal act as well as with the illegal act itself,[11] and the statutory penalty for conspiring may be greater than for the substantive crime. Furthermore, because conspiratorial agree-

---

[8] See Otto Kirchheimer, *Political Justice: The Use of Legal Procedures for Political Ends* (Princeton, N.J.: Princeton University Press, 1961).

[9] See Jessica Mitford, *The Trial of Dr. Spock* (New York: Knopf, 1969); Jason Epstein, *The Great Conspiracy Trial* (New York: Random House, 1970); Jack Nelson and Ronald J. Ostrow, *The FBI and the Berrigans: The Making of a Conspiracy* (New York: Coward, McCann & Geoghegan, 1972).

[10] See "Conspiracy and the First Amendment," 79 YALE LAW JOURNAL 872 (1970); "Developments in the Law—Criminal Conspiracy," 72 HARVARD LAW REVIEW 920 (1959).

[11] *Iannelli v. United States* (1975) held that it is not double jeopardy to be convicted of conspiracy to violate a statute as well as the substantive offense of violating it.

ments are typically secret and thus difficult to prove, courts relax the normal rules of evidence in conspiracy cases.

Because of these characteristics, Jackson said in *Dennis v. United States* that he considered "criminal conspiracy a dragnet device capable of perversion into an instrument of injustice in the hands of a partisan or complacent judiciary." Nevertheless, since the law of conspiracy had "an established place in our system," he saw no reason not to apply it against concerted action claimed to undermine the government. Vinson's opinion for the Court in *Dennis* ignored the conspiracy issue, but Douglas, dissenting, did not. He wrote:

> Never until today has anyone seriously thought that the ancient law of conspiracy could constitutionally be used to turn speech into seditious conduct. . . . To make lawful speech unlawful because two men conceive it is to raise the law of conspiracy to appalling proportions.

The case against criminal charges for crimes of expression was also considered by the Court of Appeals for the First Circuit in reviewing the conviction of Dr. Spock and his codefendants. All three judges were disturbed by the conspiracy convictions and in fact reversed the jury findings of guilt for two of the four appellants. However, only one judge, Frank M. Coffin, rejected the punishment of political speech on the conspiracy theory as a violation of the First Amendment.[12]

THE PUBLIC SERVICE AND SUBVERSION

An important motive of legislation or administrative action aimed at the Communist party has been to keep its members out of public employment or other posts where they would be in a position to undertake subversive activities.

Loyalty Oaths

Both federal and state laws customarily require public employees to take some kind of oath of loyalty to the government. An oath denying membership in the Communist party was first upheld by the Supreme Court in *Garner v. Board of Public Works* (1951), Justice Frankfurter saying: "In the context of our time, such membership is sufficiently relevant to effective and dependable government, and to the confidence of the electorate in its government."

---

[12] See *United States v. Spock* (1969); Thomas Church, Jr., "Conspiracy Doctrine and Speech Offenses: A Reexamination of *Yates v. United States* from the Perspective of *United States v. Spock*," 60 CORNELL LAW REVIEW 569 (1975).

However, the Court quickly imposed some limits on such oaths. In *Wieman v. Updegraff* (1952), the Court unanimously insisted that the mere fact of membership was not sufficient grounds for exclusion from the public service; it must be a "knowing" association.

By 1966 a majority of the Court was ready to go further, and *Elfbrandt v. Russell* apparently reversed the *Garner* decision, by striking down an Arizona loyalty-oath law that provided punishment for anyone taking the oath who was or later became a knowing member of an organization having for one of its purposes the overthrow of the government. Justice Douglas for a five-judge majority relied on the principle of the *Aptheker* case. To punish mere knowing membership was to adopt the rule of guilt by association; beyond knowing membership there also had to be a "specific intent" to further the illegal aims of the organization before punishment was justified.

Loyalty-oath statutes have also been invalidated on other grounds. In *Cramp v. Board of Public Instruction* (1961), a Florida act requiring state employees to swear that they had never lent their "aid, support, advice, counsel, or influence to the Communist party" was held lacking in "terms susceptible to objective measurement" and so failed to inform what the state commanded or forbade. *Baggett v. Bullitt* (1964) involved two Washington provisions that required teachers to swear that they were not "subversive persons" and that they would "by precept and example promote respect for the flag . . . reverence for law and order and undivided allegiance to the government of the United States." The Court held these provisions "invalid on their face because their language is unduly vague, uncertain and broad."

In *Whitehall v. Elkins* (1967), the Court declared unconstitutional the Maryland law requiring state employees to swear they were not subversive persons that it earlier upheld per curiam in *Gerende v. Board of Supervisors* (1951). The *Gerende* decision was now distinguished on the ground that at that time the attorney general of the state had interpreted the law to apply only to persons attempting to alter the form of government by force or violence.

The net result of these decisions was to limit loyalty oaths to little more than pledges of support for the federal and state constitutions and to deflate the oath fad, which had been carried to ridiculous extremes. For example, a California constitutional provision required all individuals and organizations claiming exemption from state property taxes to file loyalty oaths; the Court voided it in *Speiser v. Randall* (1958).[13] *Cole v. Richardson* (1972) did uphold an oath that, in addition to support for the Constitution, required a pledge to "oppose the overthrow of the government . . . by force,

---

[13] *Communist Party of Indiana v. Whitcomb* (1974) invalidated a loyalty oath for political parties to get on the ballot. For state action on state security statutes, see Carol E. Jenson, *The Network of Control: State Supreme Courts and State Security Statutes, 1920–1970* (Westport, Ct.: Greenwood Press, 1982).

violence or by any illegal or unconstitutional method." But Burger's opinion implied that no one took these oaths seriously or literally. They imposed no obligation of "specific, positive action," but merely committed officials "to live by the constitutional processes of our system."

A very famous non-Communist oath, applying not to public officials but to labor union officers, was that required by the Labor Management Relations Act of 1947, better known as the Taft-Hartley Act. Section 9(h) of this act denied the protections and services of the act to any labor organization unless each of its officers filed an affidavit with the National Labor Relations Board "that he is not a member of the Communist party or affiliated with such party, and that he does not believe in, and is not a member of or support any organization that believes in or teaches, the overthrow of the United States Government by force or by any illegal or unconstitutional methods." Here for the first time in this series of measures the Communist party was definitely named.

In *American Communications Association v. Douds* (1950), the Supreme Court upheld the validity of the oath. The congressional purpose, according to Chief Justice Vinson, was to remove political strikes as an obstruction to interstate commerce. Congress had such power under the commerce clause unless results were achieved that were forbidden by other provisions of the Constitution. He agreed that political freedoms were limited by the statute because its effect was to exert "pressures upon labor unions to deny positions of leadership to certain persons who are identified by particular beliefs and political affiliations." Normally, beliefs and affiliations are "irrelevant to permissible subjects of government action," but that does not mean they are "never relevant." Here the Court conceived that beliefs and affiliations bore a reasonable relation to the apprehended evil. The persons identified by the statute did not cause damage by speech, and it was not their speech that the statute sought to restrain, but rather their use of force through the political strike. "Speech may be fought with speech. . . . But force may and must be met with force."

The Taft-Hartley oath was repealed in 1959. It had proved ineffective, since Communists were willing to take the oath, which meant that the only sanction was a perjury prosecution presenting serious difficulties of proof. Congress substituted a provision making it a crime for a member of the Communist party to serve as an officer or employee of a labor union (73 Stat. 519, 536). In *United States v. Brown* (1965) the Court by a five to four vote held this provision unconstitutional as a bill of attainder.

Removal of Public Employees

The loyalty oath was supplemented in many jurisdictions by statutory programs for the removal of public employees on loyalty grounds. The New York law was upheld by the Court in *Adler v. Board of Education* (1952).

This law required the Board of Regents to make, after notice and hearing, a listing of organizations which it found to advocate, advise, teach, or embrace the doctrine that the government should be overthrown by force or violence or any unlawful means. Membership of a schoolteacher in any such listed organization was "prima facie evidence for disqualification for appointment to or retention in" any school position, but before an individual was severed from or denied employment, there was to be a full hearing and the right of judicial review.

The Court upheld the law by a six to two vote. For the majority, Minton contended that the "guilt by association" point had been disposed of by the *Garner* opinion, and he added:

> We adhere to that case. A teacher works in a sensitive area in a schoolroom. There he shapes the attitude of young minds towards the society in which they live. In this, the state has a vital concern. . . . That the school authorities have the right and the duty to screen the officials, teachers, and employees as to their fitness to maintain the integrity of the schools as a part of ordered society, cannot be doubted. One's associates, past and present, as well as one's conduct, may properly be considered in determining fitness and loyalty. From time immemorial one's reputation has been determined in part by the company he keeps.

The *Adler* decision was eventually overruled by a five to four vote in *Keyishian v. Board of Regents* (1967), a case brought by professors in the New York State university system. Brennan for the majority disposed of *Adler* on the ground that the Court there had not considered charges that the statutory standards were too vague and uncertain in their application, and also because of intervening decisions holding that "mere membership" in the Communist party could not be constitutionally penalized.

Another rather common state action was the removal of public employees who refused to give information about alleged subversive connections, whether by taking the Fifth Amendment before a legislative committee or by some other method. In three important cases the Court divided five to four on the constitutional aspects of such action. In the first, *Slochower v. Board of Higher Education of New York City* (1956), a Brooklyn College professor had taken the Fifth Amendment before a Senate committee on all questions covering his political associations before 1941. He was discharged under a provision of the New York charter that whenever an employee utilized the privilege against self-incrimination to avoid answering a question relating to his official conduct his employment tenure "shall terminate" and the office "shall be vacant." The Court majority, speaking through Justice Clark, held that the charter provision as interpreted here had converted the employee's claim of privilege "into a conclusive persumption of guilt. Since no inference of guilt was possible from the claim before the federal committee, the discharge falls of its own weight as wholly without support."

Justice Clark went on to express the view that Slochower had no "constitutional right" to his job, and that it would be perfectly proper for "the city authorities themselves to inquire into Slochower's fitness." This was precisely what happened in *Lerner v. Casey* (1958) and *Beilan v. Board of Public Education, School District of Philadelphia* (1958). Lerner was a New York subway conductor, Beilan a public school teacher. Lerner refused to tell New York City authorities whether he was a member of the Communist party, and was dismissed as a person of "doubtful trust and reliability" because of his "lack of candor." Beilan refused to tell his superintendent whether he had held a certain position in the Communist party in 1944, and later took the Fifth Amendment before a House committee; he was dismissed for "incompetency." The Court majority upheld the official action in both cases. Again, in *Nelson v. County of Los Angeles* (1960), the majority upheld a discharge for insubordination based on refusal to answer questions before the House Un-American Activities Committee, a decision that came very close to overruling *Slochower*.

A different type of removal action was held unconstitutional by the Court in *Shelton v. Tucker* (1960). An Arkansas statute required all teachers in the public schools and state colleges, as a condition of employment, to file annually a list of every organization to which they had belonged or contributed in the preceding five years. Justice Stewart for the majority agreed that the state had a right to investigate the competence and fitness of persons hired as teachers, but considered such an "unlimited and indiscriminate" inquiry a threat to associational freedom going "far beyond what might be justified in the exercise of the State's legitimate inquiry into the fitness and competency of its teachers."

The Federal Loyalty-Security Program

President Truman set up a loyalty program for federal employees in 1947, and President Eisenhower continued it in somewhat revised form in 1953. All employees and applicants for employment were required to undergo a loyalty check, in which the FBI assisted in an investigative role. The Department of Justice prepared a list of subversive organizations to help guide the decisions of agency loyalty boards. Hearings were held by these boards when damaging information was received concerning an employee or applicant, but some of the customary protections of the hearing procedure—particularly the right to be informed of the source of the charges and the right to confront the persons making the accusations—were not guaranteed in these proceedings.

The loyalty-security program was widely attacked as denying procedural due process. In *Joint Anti-Fascist Refugee Committee v. McGrath* (1951), the Court majority held that the attorney general had not accorded necessary procedural protections to the organizations he labeled as subversive, the listing being made, as Justice Frankfurter said, "without notice, without disclosure of any reasons justifying it, without opportunity to meet the undisclosed evidence or suspicion on which designation may have been based, and without opportunity to establish affirmatively that the aims and acts of the organization are innocent."

On the more serious question whether the hearings accorded individual civil servants met due process standards, the Court divided four to four in *Bailey v. Richardson* (1951). No one would contend that, in order to discharge a federal employee for inefficiency, a quasi-judicial hearing and judicial review of the action should be required. But removals under the loyalty-security program were not ordinary removals. Loyalty charges put employees on trial not only for their jobs but for their reputations and professional standing. Removal on loyalty grounds might make it impossible to secure any other employment for which they were fitted. They were condemned as unworthy of trust and confidence. These considerations convinced four members of the Court that loyalty hearings must meet full due process standards.

In several subsequent cases the Supreme Court considered aspects of the loyalty-security system, but largely avoided the constitutional issues.[14] However, in *Greene v. McElroy* (1959), which dealt with the industrial security program in effect for private plants doing work for the government that involved access to secret information, the Court did object strongly to loyalty hearings that "failed to comport with our traditional ideas of fair procedure."

As a consequence of the *Greene* decision President Eisenhower issued an executive order that significantly enlarged the right of accused security risks in industrial establishments to confront and cross-examine their accusers. Procedural protections in the loyalty hearings of government employees were also generally improved by the agencies involved.[15]

Admission to the Bar

The Supreme Court upheld the Illinois supreme court in denying admission to the bar to a conscientious objector in *In re Summers* (1945), but in *Konigsberg v. State Bar of California* (1957) it reversed a denial of admission on character grounds involving alleged connections with the Communist party.[16] The California bar then gave the applicant another

---

[14] *Peters v. Hobby* (1955), *Cole v. Young* (1956), *Service v. Dulles* (1957), *Taylor v. McElroy* (1959), *Vitarelli v. Seaton* (1959). See also *Harmon v. Brucker* (1958).

[15] But see *Cafeteria & Restaurant Workers Union v. McElroy* (1961). A useful general study is Ralph S. Brown, Jr., *Loyalty and Security: Employment Tests in the United States* (New Haven, Conn.: Yale University Press, 1958).

[16] The same position was taken in *Schware v. New Mexico Board of Bar Examiners* (1957).

hearing and again refused him admission, this time specifically on the ground that his refusal to answer questions concerning possible Communist party membership had obstructed a full investigation into his qualifications. The Court upheld this action in 1961 by a five to four vote, concluding that a committee can require a bar applicant "to provide unprivileged answers to questions having a substantial relevance to his qualifications."[17]

The Court again reversed itself by a five to four vote in two 1971 cases, *Baird v. State Bar of Arizona* and *In re Stolar*, both involving bar applicants who declined to answer questions concerning their beliefs about government and their possible affiliations with subversive organizations. Referring to such inquiries as "relics" of the McCarthy era, Justice Black held that "views and beliefs are immune from bar association inquisitions." However, in *Law Students Civil Rights Research Council v. Wadmond* (1971) the Court rejected by another five to four vote a contention that the "character and general fitness" requirement for admission to the New York bar was unconstitutional.

THE NAACP

Aside from the Communist party, the only organization whose associated rights have been seriously litigated before the Supreme Court is the NAACP. After the *Brown* decision in 1954, the activities of the NAACP in seeking to promote school desegregation aroused great hostility in most of the Southern states. Its members were subjected to economic coercion and often to physical violence. There were also many efforts through legislation and court action to hamper or terminate the work of the organization.

Alabama, like other states, has a statute requiring out-of-state corporations to register and meet certain requirements before doing business in the state. The NAACP, organized under the laws of New York, had a regional office in Alabama, but did not comply with the statute, from which it considered itself exempt. After 1954 the organization was particularly active in the state seeking enforcement of the Supreme Court's ruling against racial segregation in the public schools. In retaliation Alabama officials brought court action in 1956 to enjoin the association from conducting business in the state, in the course of which the organization was ordered to produce its records, including names and addresses of all members in Alabama. The association filed the qualifying forms required by statute and produced all records requested except the membership lists, the

---

[17] The Court reached the same result in *In re Anastaplo* (1961). For an account of the *Anastaplo* case by the protagonist, see George Anastaplo, *The Constitutionalist: Notes on the First Amendment* (Dallas, Tex.: Southern Methodist University Press, 1971), Appendix F.

disclosure of which it contended the state could not constitutionally compel. For this failure the organization was held in contempt and fined $100,000.

The Supreme Court ruled in *NAACP v. Alabama* (1958) that compelled disclosure of the membership lists would abridge the rights of members to engage in lawful association in support of their common beliefs. For the association was able to make

> . . . an uncontroverted showing that on past occasions revelation of the identity of its rank-and-file members has exposed these members to economic reprisal, loss of employment, threat of physical coercion, and other manifestations of public hostility. . . . Under these circumstances, we think it apparent that compelled disclosure of . . . membership is likely to affect adversely the ability of petitioner and its members to pursue their collective effort to foster beliefs which they admittedly have the right to advocate, in that it may induce members to withdraw from the Association and dissuade others from joining it because of fear of exposure of their beliefs shown through their associations and of the consequences of this exposure.

The Court had to deal with an embarrassing precedent, *Bryant v. Zimmerman* (1928), which had upheld, as applied to the Ku Klux Klan, a New York law requiring disclosure of membership lists. But the 1928 ruling had stressed the nature of Klan activities, involving unlawful intimidation and violence, which the Court contrasted with the lawful nature of NAACP activities.[18]

The NAACP has concentrated much of its effort on court suits to compel desegregation, and here also it has been subjected to pressure. A Virginia law, typical of those in many other states, forbids the stirring up of litigation or the improper solicitation of legal business. This legislation was aimed at "ambulance chasing" and other unethical legal practices, but because the NAACP admittedly seeks out test cases on which it can go to court, it was accused of violating the statute in Virginia.

In *NAACP v. Button* (1963) the Supreme Court upheld the association's litigation procedures, and in the decision recognized litigation as "a form of political expression." The Court said that, "in the context of NAACP objectives, litigation is not a technique of resolving private differences; it is a means of achieving the lawful objectives of equality of treatment by all government, federal, state, and local, for the members of the Negro community in this country." Indeed, "for such a group, association for litigation may be the most effective form of political association."[19]

---

[18] For subsequent developments in this case, see *NAACP v. Alabama* (1964).

[19] In *Brotherhood of Railroad Trainmen v. Virginia ex rel. Virginia State Bar* (1964) and *United Mine Workers v. Illinois State Bar Assn.* (1967) the Court followed the *Button* case in upholding forms of group legal service to organization members.

7
Religious Freedom and Establishment

Freedom to worship God according to the dictates of individual conscience was one of the dominant motives in the founding of the American Colonies, and it might have been expected that provisions guaranteeing that right would have an important place in the Constitution. In fact, the Founders left the original Constititution almost devoid of language on the relationships of government and religion, thus conforming with their general practice in the civil liberties field. The sole exception was the provision of Article VI that "no religious test shall ever be required as a qualification to any office or public trust under the United States." Even this language was protested by Roger Sherman of Connecticut, who thought prohibition of religious tests for office was unnecessary, "the prevailing liberality being a sufficient security against such tests."

Actually, the "prevailing liberality" had not kept religious tests from being rather common in the Colonies and states. The early constitutions of several states disfranchised or excluded from office Catholics, Jews, and nonbelievers. In Massachusetts and Maryland, the office of governor was closed to all except Christians. In four more states, the governor had to be a Protestant. New York and Virginia were exceptional in taking no account of religious opinion for officeholding.

The adoption of the First Amendment repaired the omissions of the original Constitution on religious freedom by the addition of the following language: "Congress shall make no law respecting an establishment of religion, or prohibiting the free exercise thereof." The states were thus specifically excluded from the ambit of the First Amendment, though many states had similar provisions in their own constitutions. In 1940, however, the Supreme Court held that the free exercise clause in the First Amendment had been made applicable to the states by the Fourteenth Amendment's guarantee of "liberty." This step was a logical sequence to the Court's ruling in the 1925 *Gitlow* decision applying the free speech and press provisions of the First Amendment to the states. Clearly, freedom to propagate religious convictions is hardly distinguishable from free speech generally, and the Supreme Court so held in *Cantwell v. Connecticut*.[1]

It was not until 1947, in *Everson v. Board of Education of Ewing Township*, that the Supreme Court had occasion to deal with the state-religion relationships in an establishment context. But when it did so, it assumed without discussion that the establishment provision of the First Amendment was just as binding on the states as the freedom of religion language.

Judicial interpretation of the free exercise and establishment principles has been affected by the differences in their developmental history. The principle of religious freedom or toleration was the older and the more firmly grounded in 1791. The tragic results of religious persecution and discrimination, of punishment for matters of conscience and belief, had long been demonstrated in England and on the continent by the time of the founding of the American nation, and the theoretical and practical case for toleration was well developed in English writing.

The establishment provision, on the other hand, was in flat contradiction to the English practice then current, and some variety of establishment was found in several of the American states at the time the Constitution was adopted. Thus the principle of separation of church and state was an American invention whose application remained to be worked out in practice.[2]

FREE EXERCISE OF RELIGION

The two religion clauses are actually so interrelated that it is difficult to discuss them separately. Free exercise demands that the state avoid

---

[1] Six years earlier, in *Hamilton v. Board of Regents* (1934), Justice Cardozo had anticipated this ruling by writing in a concurring opinion: "I assume for present purposes that the religious liberty protected by the First Amendment against invasion by the nation is protected by the Fourteenth Amendment against invasion by the states."

[2] See generally Richard E. Morgan, *The Supreme Court and Religion* (New York: Free Press, 1972; David Fellman, *Religion in American Public Law* (Boston: Boston University Press, 1965); Philip B. Kurland, *Religion and the Law* (Chicago: Aldine, 1962); Leo Pfeffer, *God, Caesar and the Constitution: The Court as Referee of Church-State Confrontation* (Boston: Beacon Press, 1975).

coercion with respect to religious beliefs and activities, and there is little overt or intentional state discrimination of this kind at the present time. But many government programs with purely secular purposes, such as compulsory education or public assistance, have coercive features that some religions or religiously motivated individuals may find objectionable. Yet if the state makes exceptions to take account of religious objections, it may then be viewed as giving positive assistance to religion in violation of the establishment clause. The problem is that too much coercion may deny free exercise, while exemption from coercion in response to religious objections may be favoritism amounting to establishment.

Free Exercise and Freedom of Expression

Free exercise of religion is closely related to freedom of expression generally, and it is natural that principles from the broader field can be used, sometimes without further refinement, to dispose of free exercise issues. In fact, one of the most important actions ever taken by the Supreme Court to guarantee free exercise of religion did not even rely on First Amendment principles. This was the case of *Pierce v. Society of Sisters* (1925), in which a Catholic religious order sued to test the constitutionality of an Oregon law requiring all children to attend only public schools for the first eight grades. In upholding the constitutional right of children to attend nonpublic schools where religious education could be provided, the Court struck down the law simply as an interference with the "business and property" of private and parochial schools.

It is possible for other constitutional provisions to be invoked to protect free exercise. For example, in *Niemotko v. Maryland* (1951), some Jehovah's Witnesses were arrested for making proselyting speeches in a public park without having secured a permit to do so. The Court held that permission had been denied because the city officials disliked the Witnesses and their views, and consequently the convictions violated the equal protection clause. Again, *Lovell v. Griffin* (1938) protected the right of Jehovah's Witnesses to sell the sect's literature from door to door without a permit, on free press grounds. *Saia v. New York* (1948) upheld the right of a Jehovah's Witnesses preacher to use a sound truck in a public park for his sermons, on free speech reasoning.

Another important principle that carries over from the speech field is the ban on prior restraint. In *Cantwell v. Connecticut* (1940) the Court held that a state statute requiring approval of a county official for any person to solicit from house to house for religious or philanthropic causes amounted to "a censorship of religion." *Murdock v. Pennsylvania* (1943) ruled that municipal license fees on transient merchants or book agents could not be applied to Jehovah's Witnesses who went from door-to-door offering religious tracts for sale. A New York ordinance requiring a police permit for public worship meetings on city streets was invalidated in *Kunz v. New York* (1951).

In *Larson v. Valente* (1982) a Minnesota law was held violative of both prior restraint and equal protection. The law, which imposed registration and reporting requirements on religions securing more than half of their contributions from nonmembers, was held by the Court to give preference to "mainstream religions."

By reliance on general free expression principles to handle religious freedom claims, the Court has to that extent avoided the necessity of developing any special doctrinal content or tests for enforcement of the free exercise clause. It has assumed that the right to distribute religious pamphlets is no different from the right to distribute pamphlets dealing with other kinds of ideas. It has assumed that religious meetings in public parks deserve the same claim to protection as political rallies.

There are some obvious reasons for equating political and religious freedoms. If religious freedom is not the same as political freedom, then it must enjoy either less or more protection. The first alternative would result in discrimination against religious groups, which is not compatible with the free exercise clause. The second would amount to preference for religious freedom over general speech and press claims, and would raise possible establishment problems. This is the dilemma the Court must face when and if it undertakes to discuss religious freedom as a value separate from the general context of other civil liberties.[3]

The Secular Regulation Rule

The most general principle that has been developed to achieve neutrality of the state with respect to religion is the secular regulation rule. This rule holds that there is no constitutional right to an exemption, on free exercise of religion grounds, from the compulsion of general regulations dealing with nonreligious matters.

The secular regulation rule is based on the distinction between belief and action. Religious beliefs admittedly must have absolute protection, but actions, even though purporting to be taken for religious reasons or as part of religious observances, must conform with the regulations established by the community to protect public order, health, welfare, and morals. This interpretation of the free exercise clause can be traced back to Jefferson who, in a letter to the Danbury Baptists, praised the religion clauses of the First Amendment as permitting "the legislative powers of the government [to] reach actions only, and not opinions . . ."

---

[3] See Donald A. Giannella, "Religious Liberty, Nonestablishment, and Doctrinal Development: Part 1. The Religious Liberty Guarantee," 80 HARVARD LAW REVIEW 1381 (1967).

He saw no interference with natural rights, because the individual "has no natural right in opposition to his social duties."[4]

Jefferson was too optimistic. Experience has shown only too clearly that religious beliefs often require, or are used to justify, unorthodox, bizarre, or even dangerous kinds of practices ranging all the way from polygamy to use of drugs and snake handling. De Tocqueville referred to the large number of "strange sects" in the United States, and observed that "religious insanity is very common."[5]

A regulation that is alleged to impinge on religious belief can be challenged under the secular regulation rule on two grounds: (1) that the regulation is not reasonably related to a valid secular purpose and (2) that there is a religious discrimination on the face of the statute or regulation.

The secular regulation rule was first developed and applied in dealing with the Mormon practice of polygamy. A congressional statute had made polygamy illegal in the territories of the United States, and in *Reynolds v. United States* (1878) the Court upheld the constitutionality of the statute against the Mormon contention that polygamy was required by their religion and that consequently punishing polygamy would deny them the free exercise of their religion. The Court thought the situation was exactly the reverse. Since a law against polygamy in the territories was clearly within the constitutional powers of Congress as a general secular regulation, the Mormons were actually asking for favored treatment from the law—namely, exemption from a statute that would be enforced on all others whose religious principles did not include polygamy.

Compulsory vaccination for smallpox was resisted, sometimes on religious grounds, but in *Jacobson v. Massachusetts* (1905) the Court upheld the legislation as a secular regulation reasonably in accord "with the common belief and . . . maintained by high medical authority."

The resistance of Jehovah's Witnesses to the compulsory flag salute in the public schools presented the Supreme Court with a particularly perplexing secular regulation issue. The Witnesses instruct their children that saluting the flag constitutes worship of a "graven image," and is contrary to Bible teaching. The conflict in conscience thus set up in schools requiring the salute was brought to the Supreme Court in *Minersville School District v. Gobitis* (1940), where the Court decided, with only Justice Stone dissenting, that the compulsory flag salute did not infringe the constitutional rights of the protesting children.

Justice Frankfurter argued that this was "legislation of general scope

---

[4] Quoted in *Reynolds v. United States* (1878).

[5] Alexis de Tocqueville, *Democracy in America* (New York: Knopf, 1948), II: 134, note 19. In *Pack v. Tennessee ex rel. Swann* (1976) snake handling and the drinking of poison in a religious ritual were enjoined as a public nuisance.

not directed against doctrinal loyalties of particular sects." The free exercise clause did not, he said, relieve the individual from obedience to a general law not aimed at the promotion or restriction of religious beliefs. The mere possession of religious convictions that contradict the relevant concerns of a political society does not relieve the citizen from the discharge of political responsibilities. The only question was whether a school board was justified in thinking that requiring the flag salute would help to further legitimate educational ends, and Frankfurter did not see how the Supreme Court could deny that the school board might legitimately hold such a view.

Justice Frankfurter's position was thus that the state had a constitutional right to compel all school children to salute the flag. There was no discrimination against those who had religious scruples against this ceremony. In fact, as in the *Reynolds* case, if their religious scruples were regarded as exempting them from the exercise, they would be receiving preference because of their religion over all other students who had no such scruples.

The *Gobitis* decision unleashed a wave of persecution against the Witnesses, and the ruling was rather generally condemned in the press.[6] Justice Stone, the sole dissenter, accepted religious objections as a valid ground for refusing to salute the flag. He thought that, while voluntary expressions of loyalty might promote national unity, compulsory exercises by children in violation of their own and their parents' religious convictions were not so important a method of promoting national unity as to override the constitutional guarantee of free exercise.

Three years later, the second flag salute case, *West Virginia State Board of Education v. Barnette* (1943), accomplished the important result of reversing the *Gobitis* holding while at the same time avoiding Stone's solution of religious preference. Justice Jackson for the new majority stated the issue as whether any child, regardless of religious belief, could be compelled to engage in a compulsory flag-salute exercise. He answered: "We think the action of the local authorities in compelling the flag salute and pledge transcends constitutional limitations on their power and invades the sphere of the intellect and spirit which it is the purpose of the First Amendment . . . to reserve from all official control." Since the state could not compel *any* student to engage in the flag salute, there was no need to develop a justification for giving preferential treatment to particular religious groups.[7]

[6] David R. Manwaring, *Render unto Caesar: The Flag-Salute Controversy* (Chicago: University of Chicago Press, 1962).

[7] *Wooley v. Maynard* (1977) relied heavily on *Barnette*. A New Hampshire law that required autos to bear license plates carrying the state motto, "Live Free or Die," was challenged by a Jehovah's Witnesses couple who found the motto contrary to their religious and political beliefs and covered it up. The Court agreed that the state could not force individuals to profess an ideological view they find unacceptable.

Prince v. Massachusetts (1944) involved a state law forbidding boys under twelve and girls under eighteen from selling newspapers on the street. A nine-year-old girl, accompanied by her aunt, who was a Jehovah's Witness, sold literature of the Witnesses on downtown street-corners at night. The Court, by a vote of five to four, upheld the statute as reasonable and nondiscriminatory. Propagandizing activities on the public streets were thought likely to result in the same kinds of problems "whether in religious, political or other matters," and Massachusetts was justified in concluding that an absolute prohibition of involvement of children was necessary to accomplish the state's purpose.

Justice Murphy, one of the dissenters, did not doubt the right of the state to have general child welfare regulations, but he insisted that when they infringed on a religious exercise, then there had to be a grave, immediate, and substantial danger as justification. He could see no such dangers in this situation. He thought that the evils a legislature might normally envisage with children on the streets would not be present when there was a religious motivation involved.

Religious fund raisers, particularly those of certain sects, have created considerable annoyance by persistent solicitation in crowded areas such as airports, and many cities have adopted regulations to limit their activities. In *Heffron v. International Society for Krishna Consciousness* (1981) all organizations on the Minnesota state fair grounds were allowed to solicit funds only at their booths. The Court upheld this ban on peripatetic solicitation as a legitimate crowd control measure, saying that religious organizations do not "enjoy rights to communicate, distribute, and solicit on the fairgrounds superior to those of other organizations."

The right of states to require licensing of private schools, state certification of teachers, and curriculum controls has been challenged by the increasing number of conservative Christian day schools, which allege that such state laws are a violation of religious freedom and the federal civil rights act. Initially, these schools lost most of their constitutional challenges. For example, in Nebraska a sheriff under court order padlocked during weekdays a church building in which an unaccredited school was being conducted; the church's appeal was dismissed by the Court in *Faith Baptist Church v. Douglas* (1981). But the controversy over this issue is a continuing one.

Alternatives to the Neutrality Principle

While the secular regulation rule is appealing in its simplicity and apparent evenhandedness, in application it may prove senselessly harsh, failing to take into account the impact of regulations on the religious life of individuals or groups or the relative importance of the public purpose served by the regulation. A significant recognition of the undesirability of such rigidity occurred in 1961, when the secular regulation rule was applied to uphold Sunday closing laws, but with a qualification that was to result in a substantial modification in the Court's subsequent attitude on free exercise problems. Two of the *Sunday Closing Cases—Gallagher v. Crown Kosher Super Market* and *Braunfeld v. Brown*—involved challenges to Sunday closing laws in two states by Orthodox Jewish merchants who contended that, since their religion required that they close their shops on Saturday, a Sunday closing law limited them to a five-day work week and was a restraint of the free exercise of their religion.

Two justices agreed with this position. Justice Stewart thought that the state could not constitutionally compel "an Orthodox Jew to choose between his religious faith and his economic survival." Justice Douglas felt that when a state uses its coercive powers "to compel minorities to observe a second Sabbath, not their own," the state was aiding and preferring one religion over another, contrary to the Constitution.

The Court majority, however, speaking through Chief Justice Warren, upheld the Sunday closing laws as secular regulations. While they had admittedly been religious in their origin, the Court regarded them now as purely an effective device for providing a uniform day of rest. Moreover, the laws were secular regulations that did not make any religious activity unlawful, merely more expensive.

However, Warren's opinion made an important addition to the secular regulation rule. This is the key sentence: "If the State regulates conduct by enacting a general law within its power, the purpose and effect of which is to advance the State's secular goals, the statute is valid despite its indirect burden on religious observances *unless the State may accomplish its purpose by means which do not impose such a burden.*" (Italics added.) This is substantially a new test for secular regulations, which now will be upheld against claims of interference with free exercise only if there appear to be no practicable alternative means whereby the legislative purpose can be accomplished. Applying the test in *Braunfeld*, the Chief Justice evaluated the availability of alternative means for achieving the secular goal of a common day of rest, and found none that seemed practicable.

The potentialties for this new test became apparent when in *Sherbert v. Verner* (1963) its effect was to invalidate a state law. A Seventh Day Adventist textile worker was discharged for refusal to work on Saturday, and no other work was available in the area for one who would not work on Saturday. She filed a claim for unemployment compensation, which was denied on the ground that her refusal to accept suitable work meant that she was not "available for work" as required by statute.

Justice Brennan for the Court ruled that this denial of benefits was a burden on the free exercise of the woman's religion. Admittedly the law had a valid secular purpose. But the pressure on her to violate her Sabbath was as much an infringement on the free exercise of her religion as a fine imposed for Saturday worship. Sunday observers are protected from having to make such a choice. The opinion does not rely on this claim of discrimination, however. It rests rather on the ground that there is an available alternative here which will preserve the free exercise of religion—namely, to grant exemption from the statute for refusal to work for religious reasons. This requirement that a state must grant preference to religious reasons for refusing to work over nonreligious reasons disturbed Justices Harlan and White, dissenting, who would have applied the traditional secular regulation rule.[8]

The Civil Rights Act of 1964 added statutory support to the free exercise clause by forbidding employers to discriminate against an employee or prospective employee on the basis of religion. Administrative regulations issued under the act require that employers make "reasonable accommodations" to the religious needs of their employees, short of "undue hardship." In *Trans World Airlines, Inc. v. Hardison* (1977) the Court agreed that the airline was not required to force employees with more seniority to accommodate an employee who refused to work on Saturday. But in *Thomas v. Review Board* (1981) denial of unemployment benefits to a member of Jehovah's Witnesses, who because of his religious beliefs quit his job with a machine company when he was transferred to the production of turrets for tanks, was held to burden his free exercise.

In addition to the "less drastic means" test, the secular regulation rule may be ameliorated by judicial balancing of interests. *Wisconsin v. Yoder* (1972) presented a classic confrontation between state compulsory education laws and the adamant insistence of the Old Order Amish that their children cease public school attendance after the eighth grade. Further education, they contended, was unnecessary for the simple agricultural life led by the sect and would, in fact, expose the children to secular influences imperiling their religious values. Experience in several states demonstrated that the Amish would not yield on their principles, no matter how much coercion was applied.

The Court concluded, almost unanimously (Douglas was in partial dissent), that enforcement of the law would deny free exercise of the Amish religion and that there was no state interest of sufficient magnitude to override their claims for protection. The Amish beliefs were not matters of personal preference but "of deep religious conviction, shared by an organized group, and intimately related to daily living," pervading and determining "virtually their entire way of life." Secondary schooling, by exposing Amish children to "worldy influences" contrary to their beliefs, would substantially

---

[8] The *Sherbert* holding was subsequently applied in state courts to overturn the conviction of Navajo members of the Native American Church for using peyote in their religious ceremonies (*People v. Woody* [1964]), to free a woman from a contempt sentence for refusal on religious grounds to serve on a jury (*In re Jenison* [1963]), and to hold that children could not be compelled to stand while the national anthem was played in school (*Sheldon v. Fannin* [1963]).

interfere with their religious development and their "integration into the way of life of the Amish faith community at the crucial adolescent state of development."

In *McDaniel v. Paty* (1978) a Tennessee constitutional provision barred ministers of the Gospel from membership in the state legislature or state constitutional conventions. The state supreme court defended the exclusion as a secular regulation aimed at avoiding divisive channeling of political activity along religious lines (and John Locke could be quoted to support this view). But Madison had protested "punishing a religious profession with the privation of a civil right," and the Supreme Court agreed.

An earlier instance of judicial recognition of religious claims occurred in *Murdock v. Pennsylvania* (1943), where the Court held that Jehovah's Witnesses' practice of their religion by offering their literature for sale from door to door did not subject them to municipal license taxes. "The hand distribution of religious tracts is an age-old form of missionary evangelism," said Justice Douglas, and "selling" the literature to defray expenses did not make it a commercial operation.[9]

Congress as well as the Court has authorized religiously motivated exceptions to secular regulations, most notably in connection with conscientious objection to military service.[10] Every American conscription law has granted exemption from military service to conscientious objectors who met the statutory definition. The Draft Act of 1917 gave exemption to objectors affiliated with a "well-recognized religious sect or organization . . . whose existing creed or principles [forbid] its members to participate in war in any form." This limitation of exemption to members of particular sects seems clearly invalid as a discrimination against other religions, but in fact the secretary of war ruled that "personal scruples against war" would be considered as constituting conscientious objection.[11]

In adopting the 1940 Selective Training and Service Act, Congress made it unnecessary to belong to a pacifist religious sect if the claimant's own opposition to war was based on "religious training and belief." This phrase was defined in the 1948 act as follows: ". . . an individual's belief in a relation to a Supreme Being involving duties superior to those arising from any human relation, but [not including] essentially political, sociological, or philosophical views or a merely personal moral code."

The Supreme Court construed this language in *United States v. Seeger*

---

[9] *Murdock* reversed the Court's holding in *Jones v. Opelika* (1942), decided only a year earlier.

[10] Decisions denying naturalization to alien conscientious objectors unwilling to swear that they would defend the United States by force of arms—*United States v. Schwimmer* (1929), *United States v. Macintosh* (1931), *United States v. Bland* (1931)—were reversed in *Girouard v. United States* (1946).

[11] The general constitutionality of the draft act was upheld in *Arver v. United States (Selective Draft Law Cases)* (1918).

(1965). The case involved three young men, none of whom was a member of an orthodox religious group or willing to declare a belief in a Supreme Being. However, none was "an avowedly irreligious person or . . . an atheist." All were found by the Court to have a sincere and meaningful belief that occupied a place in their lives "parallel to that filled by the orthodox belief in God." The Court interpreted the statutory phrase "Supreme Being" as meaning not the orthodox God but a "broader concept of a power or being, or a faith, 'to which all else is subordinate or upon which all else is ultimately dependent.'" The language denying the rights of conscientious objection based upon a "merely personal moral code" meant "a moral code which is not only personal but which is the sole basis for the registrant's belief and is in no way related to a Supreme Being."

Following *Seeger,* Congress amended the statute to delete the reference to a "Supreme Being" but continued to provide that "religious training and belief" did not include "essentially political, sociological or philosophical views, or merely personal moral code." In *Welsh v. United States* (1970) the registrant was explicit in denying that his views were religiously based. But Justice Black for the Court read Welsh's statement of beliefs against the taking of life as being held "with the strength of more traditional religious convictions" and interpreted the statute as exempting "from military service all those whose consciences, spurred by deeply held moral, ethical, or religious beliefs, would give them no rest or peace if they allowed themselves to become a part of an instrument of war."

Although Harlan concurred in the result, he believed that Black had "performed a lobotomy" on the act by reading out of it the theistic religious requirement that Congress had clearly intended as a condition for exemption. However, such a theistic basis of classification seemed to Harlan contrary to the establishment clause, and so, rather confusingly, he concurred in Black's test, "not as a matter of statutory construction, but as a touchstone for salvaging a congressional policy of long standing that would otherwise have to be nullified." White, Burger, and Stewart dissented.[12]

Although the Court finessed the religious preference dilemma in *Welsh,* other cases in which exemption from secular rules was granted to religious devotees came perilously close to unconstitutional favoritism to religion. As Justice Frankfurter protested in the second flag salute case: "The validity of secular laws cannot be measured by their conformity to religious doctrines. It is only in a theocratic state that ecclesiastical doctrines measure legal right or wrong."

---

[12] "The Legal Relationship of Conscience to Religion: Refusals to Bear Arms," 38 UNIVERSITY OF CHICAGO LAW REVIEW 583 (1971).

State Definition of Religion

Recognition of the right of religious claimants to override secular regulations inescapably involves determining what religion is. To carry out a policy of preference for religious freedom, the Supreme Court must either define religion itself, or allow groups and individuals to make their own definitions of religion.[13]

The Court's initial tendency was to undertake its own definition of religion, as was demonstrated in the Mormon cases. In *Davis v. Beason* (1890) the territory of Idaho had made it a prerequisite to exercise of the franchise that the voter take an oath he was not a member of any organization that advised or practiced the "crime of bigamy or polygamy." Davis, a Mormon, was denied the right to vote. Since he was not himself a polygamist, he had lost the franchise because of his belief in polygamy as expressed in his church membership. To uphold the statute the Court had to deny that polygamy could be a religious belief, and to do this it sought to develop an objective test or definition of religion: "The term 'religion' has reference to one's views of his relations to his Creator, and to the obligations they impose of reverence for his being and character, and of obedience to his will." Religious liberty permits each individual "to entertain such notions respecting his relations to his Maker and the duties they impose as may be approved by his judgment and conscience, and to exhibit his sentiments in such form of worship as he may think proper, not injurious to the equal rights of others."

On the basis of this definition, the Court somehow concluded that polygamy could not be "a tenet of religion." Rather it was, by "the general consent of the Christian world in modern times," a crime, and "crime is not the less odious because sanctioned by what any particular sect may designate as religion." Similarly, in *Church of Jesus Christ of Latter-day Saints v. United States* (1890) the Court found that the Mormon Church could not be considered a religious corporation, because one of its principal tenets, polygamy, was merely supposed or imagined to be religious. As a parallel, the Court pointed to the Thugs of India, who "imagined that their belief in the right of assassination was a religious belief; but their thinking so did not make it so."

In its later rulings, however, the Court has tended to allow groups and individuals to define religion for themselves, and to recognize opinion and action religiously motivated in good faith as constitutionally protected, even though this means accepting views that seem, as Justice Douglas said in *United States v. Ballard* (1944), "incredible, if not pre-

---

[13] See "Toward a Constitutional Definition of Religion," 91 HARVARD LAW REVIEW 1056 (1978). Theism appears to be no longer a necessary element in religion. In *Torcaso v. Watkins* (1961) a Maryland requirement of a "declaration of belief in the existence of God" as a qualification for public office was held unconstitutional.

posterous, to most people." In *Murdock v. Pennsylvania,* as we have seen, the Court allowed Jehovah's Witnesses to decide for themselves that selling their literature from door to door was part of their religion. In *Fowler v. Rhode Island* (1953), the Court said: "It is no business of courts to say that what is a religious practice or activity for one group is not religion under the protection of the First Amendment."

Black Muslim prison inmates were initially denied the right to practice their religion in prison. The reasons given by prison administrators were that the sect was not a religion but rather a political and racist movement and that their preachings of hatred for white people would be dangerous in prison. But in *Cooper v. Pate* (1963), the Supreme Court reversed the refusal of a lower court to hear the complaint of a Black Muslim that he was denied access to religious publications and certain other privileges because of his religious beliefs. Subsequent decisions have established that Muslims must be allowed to have the Koran, to be visited by Islamic ministers, and to hold religious services. Similar rights for Buddhists were recognized in *Cruz v. Beto* (1972). American Indian prisoners belonging to the Native American Church have won the right to wear their hair longer than prison rules normally allow and to build "sweat lodges" for religious rites.[14]

The Supreme Court has yet to confront the major free exercise issue presented by religious "cults" whose beliefs and practices seem in important respects antisocial and dangerous. It did deal with a cult issue in *United States v. Ballard,* holding that a cult leader could be prosecuted for mail fraud, provided the jury was not allowed to pass on the truth of the religious claims he made but only his good faith in professing to believe them. Current concerns were dramatized by the horrifying mass suicides at Jonestown, Guyana, in 1978; and charges against cults include brainwashing,[15] harassment of ex-members, extortion from relatives of members, amassing stores of weapons, infiltrating government agencies and stealing documents, denial of medical help, assault, and murder.

Denial of Religious Claims

In spite of the new permissiveness, the Supreme Court does, of course, reserve the right to disallow claims for religious status. In *Gillette v. United States* (1971), the Court declined to stretch the statutory exemption for conscientious objectors to cover draftees who did not object to all

---

[14] In 1974 the U. S. Army recognized the right of members of the Sikh religion to wear turbans and have long hair and beards, but in 1982 the Army withdrew its dress code exemption for religious groups (*New York Times,* December 7, 1982).

[15] See Robert N. Shapiro, "'Mind Control,' or Intensity of Faith: The Constitutional Protection of Religious Beliefs," 13 HARVARD CIVIL RIGHTS-CIVIL LIBERTIES LAW REVIEW 751 (1978). In 1983 a young California woman was awarded $32.5 million from the Hare Krishnas for brainwashing and imprisonment.

wars but only to particular wars (specifically, the war in Vietnam). While the moral case against participation in "unjust wars" has an ancient and honorable lineage in religious thought,[16] the Court could not reconcile it with the express statutory command that exemption be based only on opposition "to participation in war in any form."

Similarly, *Johnson v. Robison* (1974) rejected the claim that statutory denial of veterans' educational benefits to conscientious objectors who had performed alternate civilian service violated religious freedom and equal protection. The American Friends Service Committee and two of its employees failed in their effort to secure refund, as a method of bearing witness to their religious opposition to participation in war in any form, of that part of their taxes used for military purposes.[17]

The refusal of Jehovah's Witnesses to permit blood transfusions because of the Biblical injunction against "eating blood" has created tragic dilemmas. There have been many cases where, because the patient or family members refused consent, hospital authorities or doctors have sought court orders authorizing transfusions. If a child is involved (even an unborn child[18]), the courts have invariably ordered the tranfusion. With adults, the problem is more difficult, but again most courts have acted on the theory that there is no constitutional right to die and that attempted suicide is a crime. If there are minor children who might become charges of the state in case of the death of a parent, that is a further consideration.

The Supreme Court has regularly denied certiorari in cases raising this issue.[19] Only one state supreme court appears to have held that the state should not intervene. *In re Brooks' Estate* (1965) was an Illinois case where an adult woman without minor children was dying and the hospital obtained a court order appointing a conservator who approved the transfusion, but she died in spite of it. The state supreme court, hearing the case after her death, ordered the appointment expunged on the ground that her refusal had created no clear and present danger and that the order had interfered with her basic constitutional rights.

The opposing view, taken by most courts, is exemplified by the New Jersey supreme court in *John F. Kennedy Memorial Hospital v. Heston* (1971), involving a twenty-two-year-old unmarried woman. The court upheld the court-ordered transfusion, suggesting that the hospital might have been guilty of malpractice had it failed to use established medical procedures and that it was reasonable to resolve the issue by permitting

---

[16] See John A. Rohr, *Prophets without Honor: Public Policy and the Selective Conscientious Objector* (Nashville, Tenn.: Abingdon, 1971).

[17] *United States v. American Friends Service Committee* (1974).

[18] *Raleigh Fitkin–Paul Morgan Memorial Hospital v. Anderson* (1964).

[19] For example, *State v. Perricone* (1962), *George v. United States* (1966).

the hospital and staff "to pursue their functions according to their professional standards."[20]

An emerging issue of the deepest moral and religious significance is whether persons who have suffered irreversible brain damage should be kept alive by massive artificial means. In 1975 a suit filed in the New Jersey courts by the parents of Karen Ann Quinlan, asking that she be permitted to "die with dignity," stimulated national consideration of the right to die. On the one hand, it is argued that a failure to use all available means to preserve life amounts to murder and opens the door to "mercy killings." On the other hand, there is the alarming prospect of hospitals and nursing homes filling up with machine-sustained organisms devoid of all human qualities whose "life" is maintained by a huge commitment of societal resources.

The Liberty of Churches

While courts will become involved in the internal affairs of churches only with the greatest reluctance, there are disputes, particularly those involving property rights, which they cannot avoid. State courts have accepted suits brought by individuals for reinstatement of membership, suits filed for reinstatement of a pastor or to prevent a discharged pastor from conducting services, cases involving the right of a church to buy and sell property,[21] and cases concerning burial rights. In suits between competing factions of a local congregation, the general rule is that the will of the majority prevails, and courts will limit their inquiry to determining which is the majority. But where hierarchical or centrally organized churches are involved, the courts will follow the decision of the proper institutional authority.[22]

ESTABLISHMENT OF RELIGION

There have been two general views as to the intention of the establishment clause. One position holds that it was meant to outlaw only the

[20] See also *Application of President and Directors of Georgetown College* (1964); John J. Paris, "Compulsory Medical Treatment and Religious Freedom," 10 UNIVERSITY OF SAN FRANCISCO LAW REVIEW 1 (1975).

[21] In *United Methodist Church v. Barr* (1979) the Supreme Court let stand California court rulings allowing the church to be sued for alleged fraud in connection with the bankruptcy of a church-related retirement home chain.

[22] *Watson v. Jones* (1872), *Kedroff v. St. Nicholas Cathedral of Russian Orthodox Church* (1952), *Kreshik v. St. Nicholas Cathedral* (1960), *Serbian Eastern Orthodox Diocese v. Milivojevich* (1976). See Paul G. Kauper and Stephen C. Ellis, "Religious Corporations and the Law," 71 MICHIGAN LAW REVIEW 1499 (1973). In 1982 the New Hampshire Supreme Court held that four Roman Catholic nuns had the right to sue their bishop for a public hearing on the church's decision to dismiss them as parochial school teachers (*New York Times*, December 25, 1982).

kind of establishment that existed in Europe in 1791—namely, an official, publicly supported church. This view contends that the evil in establishment is the preferential treatment of one religion over others. It argues that the establishment clause does not forbid state contacts with religion or state support of religious activities so long as all religions are treated equally and no discrimination is involved.

The other view contends that establishment refers to any government support of or connection with religion. This position holds that the no-establishment principle requires the complete separation of church and state, and forbids any public financial support to religious institutions, even if made available on a nonpreferential basis. The Supreme Court has consistently espoused this second position, and the supporting arguments for this interpretation can be summarized briefly.

First there is the evidence supplied by the framing of the First Amendment. Congress considered and rejected language that would clearly have adopted the first position stated above. In the Senate three motions, all aimed directly and narrowly against laws preferring one "sect" or "denomination" over others, were defeated. However, the Senate then adopted another comparatively narrow ban: "Congress shall make no law establishing articles of faith or a mode of worship." The House, which had previously adopted broad prohibitory language against laws "establishing religion," rejected the Senate's version. A conference committee of the two houses, including James Madison as chairman of the House conferees, abandoned the Senate proposal and drafted the present language, which forbids "an establishment of religion" rather than merely an established church.

Second, the phrase "establishment of religion" must be given the meaning that it had in the United States in 1791, rather than its European connotation. In America there was no establishment of a single church, as in England. Four states had never adopted any establishment practices. Three had abolished their establishments during the Revolution. The remaining six states—Massachusetts, New Hampshire, Connecticut, Maryland, South Carolina, and Georgia—changed to comprehensive or "multiple" establishments. That is, aid was provided to all churches in each state on a nonpreferential basis, except that the establishment was limited to churches of the Protestant religion in three states and to those of the Christian religion in the other three states. Since there were almost no Catholics in the first group of states, and very few Jews in any state, this meant that the multiple establishment practices included every religious group with enough members to form a church. This nonpreferential assistance to organized churches constituted "establishment of religion" in 1971, and the amendment forbade Congress to adopt this practice.

Third, Jefferson and Madison were the dominant figures in developing the constitutional policy on establishment, and they both espoused strict separation of church and state. A bill providing for tax support of religion had been presented to the Virginia Legislature in 1784. Those who professed no religion were permitted by the bill to direct that their tax be used for general educational purposes. Madison attacked this bill in his famous "Memorial and Remonstrance against Religious Assessments," which was so persuasive that the bill was not even presented in the 1785 session. Instead, Jefferson's Act for Establishing Religious Freedom was passed by the Virginia legislature.

During their terms as President, moreover, both Jefferson and Madison took very strict positions on establishment. Both believed that presidential proclamations of Thanksgiving Day were contrary to the Constitution. They also regarded as unconstitutional tax exemption for churches, payment from government funds to chaplains in Congress and the armed services, and nonpreferential land grants for the support of churches. It is significant that a 1796 treaty with Tripoli, a Moslem country, negotiated under President Washington and ratified by the Senate, stated that there was no ground for religious differences between the two nations because "the government of the United States of America is not, in any sense, founded on the Christian religion."

Current understanding sees the no-establishment principle as based upon two interrelated values.[23] One is religious voluntarism, a recognition that the growth and advancement of a religious sect must come from the voluntary support of its members. The second is political noninvolvement, the best interests both of the state and the church demanding that the political process be substantially insulated from religious pressures and interfaith dissension. The mixture of religion with politics is an explosive one, an historic evil that the establishment clause recognized and sought to defuse.[24] On the other hand, religion is a vital force in society, and its manifestations cannot be hermetically sealed off from secular life. Consequently, even though the goal of political noninvolvement in religion is generally accepted, there has been a wide variety of views and practices in applying the principle.

Benevolent Neutrality

The Supreme Court's first full discussion of the establishment problem[25] came in the case of *Everson v. Board of Education of Ewing Town-*

[23] Donald A. Gianella, "Religious Liberty, Nonestablishment, and Doctrinal Development: Part II, The Nonestablishment Principle," 81 HARVARD LAW REVIEW 513 (1968).

[24] Mark DeWolfe Howe, *The Garden and the Wilderness: Religion and Government in American Constitutional History* (Chicago: University of Chicago Press, 1965).

[25] The issue was ignored in a 1930 case, *Cochran v. Louisiana State Board of Education,* where it might have been exploited. The state of Louisiana under a free textbook program was supplying books to students in parochial as well as public schools. The constitutional objection raised was that this involved a taking of property for private use contrary to the due process clause. The Court ruled, however, that the appropriation of tax funds was for a public purpose, and thus upheld the program.

ship (1947), where the five-judge majority embraced what may be called the "benevolent neutrality" theory. A New Jersey statute authorized local boards of education to make rules and contracts for transportation of children to and from schools, whether public or private. Under this statute the Ewing township board arranged to reimburse parents of public and Catholic school pupils for money expended by them for transportation of their children on the regular public transportation system.

A taxpayer brought suit challenging on constitutional grounds the right of the board to reimburse parents of parochial school students, but lost in the Supreme Court by a five to four vote. Justice Black's opinion for the majority (including Douglas, Murphy, Vinson, and Reed) dealt principally with the objection that the statute amounted to an establishment of religion. To assist in applying the establishment clause to the New Jersey bus problem, Black reviewed European and American colonial history of government-supported churches, concluding that the First Amendment means at least this much:

> Neither a state nor the Federal Government can set up a church. Neither can pass laws which aid one religion, aid all religions, or prefer one religion over another. Neither can force nor influence a person to go to or to remain away from church against his will or force him to profess a belief or disbelief in any religion. No person can be punished for entertaining or professing religious beliefs or disbeliefs, for church attendance or nonattendance. No tax in any amount, large or small, can be levied to support any religious activities or institutions, whatever they may be called, or whatever form they may adopt to teach or practice religion.

On the basis of these principles Black acknowledged that the New Jersey statute approached the "verge" of constitutional power. Indeed, looking at the establishment of religion clause as forbidding the contribution of "tax-raised funds to the support of an institution which teaches the tenets and faith of any church"—and Black admitted this is what the provision means—it would be hard to support the statute. But he escaped from the necessity of reaching this conclusion by moving over to the free exercise of religion clause, which he interpreted as commanding New Jersey not to "hamper its citizens in the free exercise of their own religion." The state must not exclude any individuals, "because of their faith, or lack of it, from receiving the benefits of public welfare legislation."

Fearful that this argument might prove too much, Black hurried on to say that of course a state could limit its provision of transportation assistance to public school children only. But in fact, he added, the states have generally not taken this line. They already furnish many services to church schools with general approval, such as fire and police protection, sidewalks, and public highways. The First Amendment "requires the state to be a neutral in its relations with groups of religious believers and non-believers; it does not require the state to be their adversary. State power is no more to be used so as to handicap religions than it is to favor them." His argument closed with the contention that this New Jersey action did not constitute "the slightest breach" in the wall between church and state, which "must be kept high and impregnable."

The principle of the *Everson* case, then, is that it does not violate the establishment clause to permit religious institutions to share in social gains from government programs that are religiously neutral. The benefits here went to the children and their parents, not to the religious schools. It was a similar "child benefit" theory that the Court embraced in *Board of Education v. Allen* (1968) to uphold a New York statute requiring school districts to purchase and "loan" textbooks to pupils in parochial and private as well as in public schools. Justice White saw this as simply making "available to all children the benefits of a general program to lend school books free of charge."

Justice Black disagreed that the *Everson* principle covered *Allen*. Schoolbooks were different from bus fares. Though required to be secular, the books selected would "inevitably tend to propagate the religious views of the favored sect." He was also alarmed at the incursion into politics of the "powerful sectarian religious propagandists who have succeeded in securing passage of the present law to help religious schools carry on their sectarian religious purposes." However, the Court reiterated its approval of textbook-loan programs in *Meek v. Pittenger* (1975).[26]

The pupil benefit theory was the justification for the provisions in the "GI Bill" passed by Congress in 1944, under which returning veterans could attend denominational schools to which federal payments were made directly. Similarly, all children who attend tax-emem_pt schools were made eligible for the benefits of the National School Lunch Act. Under various federal statutes, such as the National Defense Education Act, Congress has provided for loans or grants to colleges and universities for buildings or educational programs. Religious institutions of higher learning have generally been eligible for such aid, with the limitation that no funds can go for buildings used for religious instruction or for chapels or for schools of divinity or theology.

Prior to 1965, no substantial federal financial aid in the elementary and secondary education field had ever been provided. The principal reason why all the proposals for federal aid to education failed of enactment in Congress was Catholic refusal to support legislation that did not include aid for religious schools. President Johnson successfully bypassed

---

[26] "Sectarian Books, the Supreme Court, and the Establishment Clause," 79 YALE LAW JOURNAL 111 (1969); Paul A. Freund, "Public Aid to Parochial Schools," 82 HARVARD LAW REVIEW 1680 (1969).

this barrier and secured passage of the Elementary and Secondary Education Act of 1965 by proposing a variation of the pupil benefit theory under which funds would go primarily to schools serving children from low-income families. The act as passed made grants available under various programs for improving the education of students in both religious and public schools.

The High Wall–No Aid Theory

The strict, as opposed to the benevolent, view on church-state separation draws its symbolic support from Jefferson's warning that a "high wall" must be maintained between the government and religion. It was this wall that Black insisted he was preserving "high and impregnable" in *Everson*, but the four dissenters there felt that Black's rhetoric was inconsistent with his conclusion. It reminded Jackson of Byron's Julia, who, while "whispering 'I will ne'er consent,'—consented." Rutledge's masterly dissent in *Everson* invoked what he held to be the true teaching of Jefferson and Madison, whose writings were analyzed at length. As a practical matter Rutledge contended that no line could be drawn between payment of bus fare and payment for larger, but no more necessary, items in religious education.

One year later, in *McCollum v. Board of Education* (1948), all the justices except Reed agreed that the high wall had been breached. The public schools of Champaign, Illinois, had a "released-time" program of religious education under which public school children, on consent of their parents, attended classes of Protestant, Catholic, or Jewish religious instruction during school hours and in the school building. The religious teachers were not paid by the schools, but were under the supervision of the school superintendents, and attendance was compulsory for participants in the program.

Justice Black, speaking for six justices, held that under this plan tax-supported school buildings were being used in disseminating religious doctrines, and the state's public school machinery was being employed to provide pupils for religious classes—a clear violation of the *Everson* principle. Justice Jackson, concurring, agreed that the Champaign religious classes went beyond permissible limits, but he was worried over the prospect of the Supreme Court's becoming a "super board of education for every school district in the nation." Without a clearer statement of legal principles to provide guidance to both educators and judges than Black's opinion provided, he feared that the wall of separation between church and state was likely to become "as winding as the famous serpentine wall designed by Mr. Jefferson for the University he founded."

The *McCollum* decision created a furore in church circles, for similar released-time programs were widely in effect throughout the country. It was against this background that the Court was offered a second opportunity to consider the issue, in ruling on the New York program of released-time religious education in *Zorach v. Clauson* (1952). The New York plan called for religious instruction outside the schools, thus differing sufficiently from the Champaign arrangement to win the approval of six justices, including three who had voted against the Champaign plan (Douglas, Vinson, and Burton) and two who had not been on the Court at the time of the earlier decision (Clark and Minton).[27]

Under the New York City program, students were released from classes during the school day, on written request of their parents, in order to attend religious exercises or classes in religious centers off the school grounds. Those not released stayed in the school classrooms. The churches made weekly reports to the schools of children who had not reported for religious instruction. Because the program involved "neither religious instruction in public school classrooms nor the expenditure of public funds," Douglas ruled for the majority that the *McCollum* case was not controlling. The situation was merely that of schools closing their doors or suspending their operations "as to those who want to repair to their religious sanctuary for worship or instruction. . . . The public schools do no more than accommodate their schedules to a program of outside religious instruction." But this latter statement cannot possibly be squared with the facts, as the dissenters (Black, Jackson, and Frankfurter) promptly pointed out. The schools do not close their doors or suspend their operations. Students who do not participate in the religious program are compelled to attend other school activities. Thus the state in the New York program was clearly making "religious sects beneficiaries of its power to compel children to attend secular schools." As Jackson put it, the school "serves as a temporary jail for a pupil who will not go to Church."[28]

Two outstanding "high wall" decisions are *Engel v. Vitale* (1962) and *School District of Abington Township v. Schempp* (1963). The first arose out of the action of the New York State Board of Regents, which has general supervisory authority over the state public schools, in composing a twenty-two-word prayer so bland that it was thought to be nonsectarian and recommending its daily recital in the public schools as part of a general program of moral and spiritual training. By a vote of six to one (Stewart), the Supreme Court held that a prayer "composed by

---

[27] See "The 'Released Time' Cases Revisited: A Study of Group Decisionmaking by the Supreme Court," 83 YALE LAW JOURNAL 1202 (1974).

[28] See Frank J. Sorauf, "*Zorach v. Clauson:* The Impact of a Supreme Court Decision," 53 AMERICAN POLITICAL SCIENCE REVIEW 777 (1959); "The Released Time Case," in C. Herman Pritchett and Alan F. Westin, eds., *The Third Branch of Government* (New York: Harcourt Brace Jovanovich, 1963), pp. 118–148. In *Smith v. Smith* (1976) the Court refused to reconsider the *Zorach* decision.

governmental officials as a part of a governmental program to further religious beliefs" was clearly an establishment of religion.[29]

At issue in the *Schempp* case were the practices in two Pennsylvania and Maryland schools of beginning the day with reading of the Bible or recitation of the Lord's Prayer. The Court held these likewise to be unquestionably religious exercises and so, again with only Stewart dissenting, unconstitutional.

Justice Black's opinion in *Engel* relied largely on the unhappy history of evils resulting from establishment, in both England and the American Colonies. He did not invoke the free exercise clause for two reasons. First, the prayer was considered "denominationally neutral" or nonsectarian. Second, participation in the prayer on the part of pupils was voluntary, which might be regarded as taking care of those who objected to the prayer. Justice Black apparently thought that under these conditions it would be difficult to demonstrate an interference with any pupil's free exercise of religion, although he admitted that "indirect coercive pressure upon religious minorities" could exist under the plan.

The reaction to the *Engel* decision, particularly since it came only three months after the controversial ruling in *Baker v. Carr*, was explosive in the extreme. Only a minority of those expressing their opinions—and this minority notably included President Kennedy—appeared to have made an effort to understand the Court's position. For most, their conclusion was simply that the Supreme Court was against prayer. The Court was variously charged with "tampering with America's soul," with having stated its "disbelief in God Almighty." A representative in Congress from Alabama cried out: "They put the Negroes in the schools and now they've driven God out." Constitutional amendments were immediately introduced in Congress to authorize prayers in the public schools.

Time was to show that sober second thought would yield more understanding of and support for the Court's position than the initial reactions indicated. The Court itself, unmoved by the outcry against *Engel*, in the next term reiterated its position in the *Schempp* case. From the Court's previous decisions Clark drew this rule: "To withstand the strictures of the Establishment Clause there must be a secular legislative purpose and a primary effect that neither advances nor inhibits religion." The constitutional command is for a "wholesome" neutrality. Such neutrality would not prevent study of the Bible or of religion in public schools "when presented objectively as part of a secular program of education." Nor did "the concept of neutrality, which does not permit a State to require a religious exercise even with the consent of the majority of those affected, collide with the majority's right to free exercise of

[29] See Louis H. Pollak, "Public Prayers in Public Schools," 77 HARVARD LAW REVIEW 62 (1963).

religion." The free exercise clause prohibits the use of state action to deny the rights of free exercise to anyone, but "it never meant that a majority could use the machinery of the State to practice its beliefs."

The *Schempp* decision also spelled out why the Court was invoking the establishment rather than the free exercise clause. As Justice Clark said, "It is necessary in a free exercise case for one to show the coercive effect of the enactment as it operates against him in the practice of his religion," whereas no coercion need be shown to support an establishment violation. Consequently, it is much easier to satisfy the "standing" requirement in an establishment suit than in a free exercise case. In fact, the issue of standing, which in *Doremus v. Board of Education* (1952) the Court used to avoid deciding a Bible-reading case, was practically ignored by the Court in the *Engel* and *Schempp* cases.

In spite of continuing opposition to the prayer rulings, the Supreme Court maintained its position. In *Treen v. Karen B.* (1982) the Court affirmed a lower court ruling that state laws providing for voluntary prayer sessions in public schools are unconstitutional. *Lubbock Independent School District v. Lubbock Civil Liberties Union* (1983) declined to review a lower court ban on voluntary religious activities before or after school hours, in spite of a motion and amicus brief by 24 U.S. senators urging the Court to grant review.[30]

Evidence indicates that the prayer rulings have been ignored or evaded in many school districts,[31] and continuous efforts have been made to secure a constitutional amendment to permit voluntary prayers in the public schools, the most recent having been promoted by President Reagan.[32]

Compulsory chapel at the nation's military academies, an obvious challenge to the high wall, was declared unconstitutional by the Court of Appeals for the District of Columbia in 1972, and the Supreme Court refused certiorari in *Laird v. Anderson* (1972). However, the Court has

[30] But universities are different. *Widmar v. Vincent* (1981) ruled that public universities that let secular organizations meet in their buildings must also make facilities available to campus religious groups.

[31] See Kenneth M. Dolbeare and Phillip E. Hammond, *The School Prayer Decisions: From Court Policy to Local Practice* (Chicago: University of Chicago Press, 1971); W. K. Muir, Jr., *Prayer in the Public Schools: Law and Attitude Change* (Chicago: University of Chicago Press, 1967). By 1983 at least eighteen state legislatures had required a daily minute of silence in the schools as a way of circumventing the Supreme Court rulings. A 1982 Alabama statute required classroom prayers, and an Alabama federal judge upheld the law, asserting that the states have a legal right to establish a religion. Justice Powell stayed this ruling pending appeal; *Jaffree v. Board of School Commissioners* (1983).

[32] The logic of the prayer decisions was followed in *Stone v. Graham* (1980), which ruled, five to four, that a Kentucky law requiring public schools to post copies of the Ten Commandments (privately financed) in their classrooms was unconstitutional. *Bradshaw v. Hall* (1981) declared that North Carolina's practice of printing a "Motorist's Prayer" on the official highway maps was an unconstitutional establishment of religion.

made clear that it has no intention of opposing all manifestations of religion in public life, such as chaplains in Congress and in the armed forces, Thanksgiving Day proclamations, or "In God We Trust" on coins.[33]

In *Larkin v. Grendel's Den* (1982) Chief Justice Burger gave full support to the high wall as "a useful figurative illustration to emphasize the concept of separateness." Here the Court declared unconstitutional as a breach in the high wall a Massachusetts statute empowering churches to veto issuance of liquor licenses for premises within 500 feet of the church.

Strict Neutrality

A different formula for achieving the strict separation sought by the high wall theory was proposed by Philip B. Kurland in an influential 1961 law review article,[34] a position subsequently adopted by Justice Harlan as a rule for decision. Kurland proposed that "the freedom and separation clauses should be read as a single precept that government cannot utilize religion as a standard for action or inaction because these clauses prohibit classification in terms of religion either to confer a benefit or to impose a burden." In other words, neutrality would be achieved by never mentioning religion in a statute or taking it into account in an administrative decision.

Harlan employed this approach in his *Allen* concurrence, asserting that the New York textbook law did not "employ religion as its standard for action or inaction." He justified tax exemption for churches in *Walz v. Tax Commission* (1970) by the same neutrality rationale. The Court, he warned, must be alert to spot "religious gerrymanders, that is, legislation singling out religious institutions for favored treatment." But in *Walz* the exemption included educational and charitable institutions as well as religious, and so he concluded that "the radius of legislation encircles a class so broad that . . . religious institutions could be thought to fall within the natural perimeter."

The decision in *Epperson v. Arkansas* (1968) also employed strict neutrality reasoning. In that case a state statute forbidding the teaching of evolution in public schools and publicly supported colleges and univer-

---

[33] See Justice Brennan's opinion in the *Schempp* case; *Aronow v. United States* (1970); *O'Hair v. Cooke* (1981). In *Florey v. Sioux Falls* (1980), the Court refused to hear a challenge to the observance of Christmas and other religious holidays in the public schools. But in *Marsh v. Chambers* (1983) the Court held, six to three, that the Nebraska legislature could pay a chaplain to open each day's session with a prayer.

[34] "Of Church and State and the Supreme Court," 29 UNIVERSITY OF CHICAGO LAW REVIEW 1 (1961). The Kurland approach is supported in Paul J. Weber and Dennis A. Gilbert, *Private Churches and Public Money* (Westport, Conn.: Greenwood Press, 1981).

sities was held to violate the rule that government "must be neutral in matters of religious theory, doctrine, and practice." The Court said, "the overriding fact is that Arkansas' law selects from the body of knowledge a particular segment which it proscribes for the sole reason that it is deemed to conflict with . . . a particular interpretation of the Book of Genesis by a particular religious group."[35]

It should be understood that the Kurland-Harlan position, while attractive in its simplicity, would prevent any accommodation of religious claims such as the Court approved in releasing the Amish from school attendance laws and would render invalid the exemption granted by Congress in 1965 to the Amish—who believe that any form of insurance shows a lack of faith in God—from the social security system.[36]

Secular Tests

More appealing to most members of the Court than the strict neutrality test has been some formula for distinguishing secular from religious purposes. Justice Clark was the first to propose a simple test for this purpose in his *Schempp* opinion: "To withstand the strictures of the Establishment Clause there must be a secular legislative purpose and a primary effect that neither advances nor inhibits religion." Also in *Schempp*, Brennan tried his hand at a somewhat more complex set of standards; what the establishment clause forbids, he said, are "those involvements of religious with secular institutions which (*a*) serve the essentially religious activities of religious institutions; (*b*) employ the organs of government for essentially religious purposes; or (*c*) use essentially religious means to serve governmental ends, where secular means would suffice." Obviously Bible reading and school prayers were condemned by either the Clark or Brennan formulas.

Brennan repeated his three-part rule in the *Walz* case, where he discovered two basic secular justifications for granting real property tax exemptions to religious organizations. First, along with other private, nonprofit organizations, they "contribute to the well-being of the community in a variety of nonreligious ways, and thereby bear burdens that would otherwise have to be met by general taxation, or be left undone, to the detriment of the community." Second, religious organizations "uniquely contribute to the pluralism of American society by their religious activities."

[35] In 1982 a federal judge, after a highly publicized trial, held unconstitutional an Arkansas law that required "evolution-science" and "creation-science" to be presented equally in public schools whenever "origins" were discussed (*McLean v. Arkansas Board of Education* [1982]).

[36] But members of the Old Order Amish who, as individuals are exempted from Social Security tax by federal statute, as operators of businesses must pay Social Security and unemployment taxes required of all employers, despite their belief that paying taxes is a sin (*United States v. Lee* [1982]).

Free Exercise Accommodation

Still another rationale stresses the obligation to avoid governmental action that would interfere with the free exercise of religion. *Sherbert v. Verner* held that an infringement of free exercise rights can only be justified by a "compelling state interest"—moreover, a compelling state interest that cannot be satisfactorily achieved by some less drastic means that will avoid the free exercise burden. This would not amount to "establishing" a religion by giving it a preferential position; rather, it would simply recognize "the governmental obligation of neutrality in the face of religious differences." Similarly, in *Wisconsin v. Yoder,* the Court found that, "however strong the State's interest in universal compulsory education, it is by no means absolute" and in this situation not of "sufficient magnitude to override the interest claiming protection under the Free Exercise Clause."

Establishment on the Burger Court

The initial contribution of the Burger Court was an additional test for the constitutionality of state involvement in religion—namely, "excessive entanglement," announced by the Chief Justice in *Walz v. Tax Commission* (1970). In this case the time-honored practice of tax exemption for church property was held to involve no such entanglement.

The Court's major church-state problems in the 1970s, however, did not involve tax exemption but rather grew out of widespread and continuing state efforts to provide financial aid for religious schools or tuition payments for parents of their students. *Lemon v. Kurtzman* (1971) involved a Rhode Island program of salary supplements paid to teachers of secular subjects in nonpublic schools and a Pennsylvania program of reimbursement to nonpublic schools for teachers' salaries, textbooks, and instructional materials used in the teaching of specific subjects. The programs were invalidated because entanglement would result from the "comprehensive, discriminating, and continuing state surveillance" that would inevitably be required to enforce the secular purpose limitations, as well as from the "divisive political potential" of these programs. "The potential for political divisiveness related to religious belief and practice is aggravated in these two statutory programs by the need for continuing annual appropriations and the likelihood of larger and larger demands as costs and populations grow." Only White dissented.

On the same day that *Lemon* was decided, however, the federal program of construction grants for colleges and universities, which included church-related institutions, passed the entanglement test in *Tilton v. Richardson* (1971). Naturally no grants were available for buildings used for worship or sectarian instruction, but it was contended that in a church-related college sectarian influences would permeate the entire institution. Burger's opinion rejected this view. There was a substantial difference in this regard between institutions of higher education and parochial elementary and secondary schools. Religious indoctrination is not a substantial purpose of the church-related colleges, and in any event "college students are less impressionable and less susceptible to religious indoctrination." Also, many church-related institutions have a "high degree of academic freedom." Douglas, Black, and Marshall, dissenting, were not convinced. Government surveillance would have to continue, Douglas asserted, as long as the buildings lasted.[37]

These issues returned to the Court in 1973 and were decided in almost identical fashion. *Committee for Public Education and Religious Liberty v. Nyquist* involved three financial aid plans for New York nonpublic schools—money grants for maintenance and repair of buildings, tuition reimbursement for parents of pupils in nonpublic schools, and tax relief to parents failing to qualify for tuition reimbursement. Powell, commenting on "the ingenious plans for channeling state aid to sectarian schools that periodically reach this Court," held that the New York aid plans so clearly had the "impermissible effect of advancing religion, it is not necessary to consider whether such aid would yield an entanglement with religion."

Sloan v. Lemon (1973) brought up to the Court a Pennsylvania parent reimbursement plan to replace the teacher salary plan invalidated by *Lemon v. Kurtzman.* As in *Nyquist,* the program was declared unconstitutional as advancing religion. The third case, *Levitt v. Committee for Public Education and Religious Liberty* (1973), struck down a New York program to reimburse nonpublic schools for costs incurred in connection with examinations and maintenance of student records. Burger held that such services, "some secular and some potentially religious," were constitutionally different from bus rides or state-loaned textbooks. But there was a fourth case—*Hunt v. McNair* (1973), involving a college building construction program in South Carolina—which included church-related institutions; it was approved on the precedent of *Tilton v. Richardson.*

Pennsylvania, undaunted, came back to the Court with still another program in *Meek v. Pittenger* (1975). This time the state proposed to finance for nonpublic schools auxiliary services such as counseling, testing, speech and hearing therapy, and "other secular, neutral, nonideological services," to lend instructional materials and equipment, and to lend textbooks acceptable for use in public schools. The Supreme Court upheld the textbook loan but declared the other parts of the program unconstitutional. Stewart took the occasion to provide still another "con-

---

[37] On the *Tilton* precedent, *Roemer v. Board of Public Works of Maryland* (1976) upheld (five to four) a program of annual grants to colleges in the state, including four church-related colleges.

venient, accurate distillation" of the Court's rules on establishment, which came down to three tests: the statute must have a secular legislative purpose, it must have a primary effect that neither advances nor inhibits religion, and the statute and its administration must avoid excessive government entanglement with religion.

At this point the Court was divided into three equal groups: "accommodationists" (White, Burger, and Rehnquist) seeking a relaxed interpretation of the First Amendment that would yield maximum acceptance for religious practices and claims; "separationists" (Brennan, Marshall, and Stevens) favoring something close to a high wall between church and state; and "moderates" (Blackmun, Powell, and Stewart) taking a middle position. Not surprisingly, this division produced some confusing results. *Wolman v. Walter* (1977) dealt with an Ohio statute providing public funds for students of nonpublic schools. The Court upheld provisions for lending secular texts and supplying standardized tests (six to three), providing speech, hearing, and psychological services (eight to one), and guidance and remedial services (seven to two). But the Court declared unconstitutional provisions in the same statute providing public money for purchase of instructional materials and equipment for students (six to three) and transportation for field trips (five to four).[38]

Tax Exemption for Churches

The long-established principle of tax exemption for church property was ratified by *Walz v. Tax Commission* (1970), as already noted. Brennan stressed that the exemption was not favoritism to churches; the government routinely grants tax exemption to all manner of voluntary associations that are supposed by legislators to serve beneficent purposes. To require disclosure of property and payment of taxes would result in entanglement of church and state, thought Burger. The exemption, said Harlan, neither encouraged nor discouraged participation in religious life, though he warned that some sorts of exemptions might involve government so deeply with religious institutions as to contravene the establishment clause. Only Douglas insisted that tax exemption was the equivalent of state subsidy to religion.[39]

Property tax exemption becomes more complicated when church properties are used for income-producing purposes; but the issue, while much litigated, has not reached the Supreme Court. Of more concern is

---

[38] The trend seemed to favor the accommodationists' position, however. In *Committee for Public Education v. Regan* (1980) they picked up the votes of Stewart and Powell, and upheld (five to four) a New York law reimbursing nonpublic schools for performing testing and reporting services mandated by state law.

[39] Schools that are church-related, but not an integral part of a church, are subject to unemployment tax (*St. Martin Lutheran Church v. South Dakota* [1981]).

widespread property and income tax evasion by "ministers" with mail order degrees of doctor of divinity who set themselves up as churches and preach "sermons" to a few friends on Sunday in their garages. In the town of Hardenburgh, New York, 200 of the 236 residents became "ministers" and claimed property tax exemption on their homes. A state law ending this fraud was upheld by state courts.[40]

Tax exemption for racially discriminatory private schools has been understood to be barred by the Constitution, judicial rulings, and Title VI of the 1964 Civil Rights Act, as well as by regulations of the Internal Revenue Service. But in 1982 President Reagan announced that the regulations had "no basis in law" and instructed the Department of Justice to withdraw from the Supreme Court two cases in which the government had challenged tax exemption for such schools. His proposal to grant the exemptions aroused such a storm that he asked Congress to clarify the situation by passing a law that would specifically deny tax exemption to schools that discriminate; in the meantime the exemptions would be granted. But a month later a federal court barred such exemptions, and the administration then restored the two cases to the Supreme Court docket.[41] The Court appointed a special counsel to argue the position the government had abandoned.[41]

The eight to one decision in *Bob Jones University* upheld denial of tax exemption in the strongest possible terms. The statute authorized tax exemption for "charitable" institutions. A charitable institution, wrote Burger, "must serve a public purpose and not be contrary to established public policy." For a quarter of a century it has been "a firm national policy to prohibit racial segregation." Educational institutions which, for whatever reason, practice racial discrimination should not "be encouraged by having all taxpayers share in their support by way of special tax status." As for the contention that the racial policy of these institutions was based on religious beliefs, Burger said that religious liberty may be limited "by showing that it is essential to accomplish an overriding governmental interest."

In 1982 President Reagan proposed legislation giving tuition tax credits of $500 per child to families with incomes up to $75,000 for children attending private elementary and secondary schools. The constitutionality of the plan was challenged. The Supreme Court had held a New York law providing tuition reimbursement to parents unconstitutional in *Committee for Public Education v. Nyquist* (1973).[42]

---

[40] *Hardenburgh v. New York* (1981); the Supreme Court denied review. In 1982 the New York Court of Appeals ruled that the Unification Church of Rev. Sun Myung Moon was indeed a church and eligible for tax-exempt status. Since 1977 it had been denied tax exemption on the ground that its activities were chiefly economic and political (*New York Times*, May 7, 1982).

[41] *Bob Jones University v. United States, Goldsboro Christian School v. United States.*

[42] But see "Government Neutrality and Separation of Church and State: Tuition Tax Credits," 92 HARVARD LAW REVIEW 696 (1979).

The issue was raised again in *Mueller v. Allen* (1983). A Minnesota law permitted parents of elementary and secondary school children to deduct up to $700 in school expenses for each child from their income for state tax purposes. Public school parents could deduct certain expenses such as the cost of driver education classes or rental of musical instruments, but the principal beneficiaries were parents of children attending private or parochial schools that charge tuition. The Supreme Court, by a five to four vote, upheld the law, denying that tax credits improperly advanced the religious aims of sectarian schools.

Issues of church-state relations, always of high volatility, have been exacerbated by recent controversies over school prayer, abortion, cult activities, tuition tax credits, education vouchers, and the like. Increasingly these issues have been carried to the courts. Two researchers found that in the decade from 1946 to 1956 there were only 66 reported state and federal court cases in which a free exercise claim was made, while the decade from 1970 to 1980 produced 384 such cases.[43] Though there are many reasons for this increase, especially the growth in marginal religions, easier access to the courts, as provided by *Flast v. Cohen*, has played a part. *Valley Forge Christian College v. Americans United* (1982) may somewhat reduce the flood of cases. The opinion not only ruled that a citizen group had no standing to challenge a government donation of surplus property to a church-run college. The Court went on to warn federal judges not to pass on alleged errors or violations of the Constitution unless a specific, immediate controversy was at stake.

---

[43] Frank Way and Barbara J. Burt, "The Free Exercise Clause and Marginal Religious Groups" (mimeo.). A valuable study of all the important court decisions on church-state issues from 1951 to 1971, including consideration of the community contexts in which the cases developed and the strategies and goals of the persons or groups bringing the suits, is Frank J. Sorauf, *The Wall of Separation: The Constitutional Politics of Church and State* (Princeton: N.J.: Princeton University Press, 1976).

8

Procedural Due Process

The concept of due process, introduced into the Constitution in the Fifth Amendment as a limitation on Congress and repeated in the Fourteenth Amendment as a limitation on the states, is perhaps the most expansive and adaptable of the Constitution's many broad phrases. As Justice Frankfurter has eloquently said:

> "Due process," unlike some legal rules, is not a technical conception with a fixed content unrelated to time, place and circumstances. Expressing as it does in its ultimate analysis respect enforced by law for that feeling of just treatment which has been evolved through centuries of Anglo-American constitutional history and civilization, "due process" cannot be imprisoned within the treacherous limits of any formula. Representing a profound attitude of fairness between man and man, and more particularly between the individual and government, "due process" is compounded of history, reason, the past course of decisions, and stout confidence in the strength of the democratic faith which we profess. Due process is not a mechanical instrument. It is not a yardstick. It is a process.[1]

The due process concept does not depend for its constitutional foundation solely on the two clauses of the Fifth and Fourteenth Amendments. All of the amendments from the Fourth through the Eighth embody important due process rights, mostly concerned with protection against abuses in criminal prosecutions. The existence in the Constitution

[1] *Joint Anti-Facist Refugee Committee v. McGrath* (1951).

of both general and specific due process provisions has presented the Supreme Court with some interesting and difficult issues of interpretation. In this chapter we will be concerned, first, with the Court's enunciation of the procedural rights of persons in their adverse relationships to the state under the general due process clauses and, second, with the Court's initial efforts to reconcile the general with the more specific procedural protections in the Fourth through Eighth Amendments.

DUE PROCESS AND LEGISLATION

The due process clause of the Fifth Amendment, as pointed out in Chapter 1, is generally traced to the Magna Carta of 1215, in one chapter of which the king promised: "No freeman shall be arrested, or imprisoned, or disseized, or outlawed, or exiled, or in any way molested; nor will we proceed against him, unless by the lawful judgment of his peers or by the law of the land." In England it was thus the king who was limited by due process. By constrast, anything Parliament enacted was "the law of the land" and not subject to judicial check. But in one of its first opinions interpreting the due process clause, *Murray's Lessee v. Hoboken Land & Improvement Co.* (1865), the Supreme Court held that in America due process was a limitation on the legislature as well as on the executive and the judiciary.

The problem in the *Murray* case was whether legislation providing for distress warrant levies on the property of federal tax collectors found to be indebted to the United States amounted to constitutional procedure. The Court said:

> That the warrant now in question is legal process, is not denied. It was issued in conformity with an act of Congress. But is it "due process of law"? The Constitution contains no description of those processes which it was intended to allow or forbid. It does not even declare what principles are to be applied to ascertain whether it be due process. It is manifest that it was not left to the legislative power to enact any process which might be devised. The article is a restraint on the legislative as well as on the executive and judicial powers of the government, and cannot be construed as to leave Congress free to make any process "due process of law" by its mere will.

A second contribution of the *Murray* decision, written by Justice Curtis, was its effort to ascertain and state the principles upon which the Court would rely in deciding whether a particular process was "due" process. Curtis thought there were two tests that should be used. First, "we must examine the constitution itself, to see whether this process be in conflict with any of its provisions." He did not say where he would look in the Constitution, but obviously he must have been thinking of the specific "process" guarantees found primarily in the Bill of Rights. If this search turned up a conflict, then of course the process was not "due process," and that would be the end of it.

In the *Murray* situation, however, no such conflict was found, and so Curtis went on to announce a second test: "those settled usages and modes of proceeding existing in the common and statute law of England, before the emigration of our ancestors, and which are shown not to have been unsuited to their civil and political condition by having been acted on by them after the settlement of this country." This was a test based on English and early American practice. A process otherwise unforbidden by the Constitution might still turn out to be contrary to Anglo-Saxon traditions, and if so it would not be due process of law. For the purposes of the *Murray* case Curtis conducted a search which showed that a summary method for the recovery of debts due to government had been provided for "by the common and statute law of England prior to the emigration of our ancestors, and by the laws of many of the States at the time of the adoption of this amendment," and consequently the statute "cannot be denied to be due process of law."

By the *Murray* decision, then, Congress was brought under the purview of the due process clause, and a standard for determining whether legislative action constituted due process was stated. The adoption of the Fourteenth Amendment meant that state legislatures were placed in a similar position. Thus the Supreme Court became responsible for testing the procedures stipulated by both federal and state statutes, so far as they affected life, liberty, or property, on due process grounds.

DUE PROCESS IN JUDICIAL AND ADMINISTRATIVE PROCEEDINGS

Due process in judicial proceedings, the Supreme Court said in *Pennoyer v. Neff* (1877), required principally that litigants have the benefit of a full and fair trial in the courts and that their rights be measured not by laws made to affect them individually but by general provisions applicable to all those in like condition. Judicial procedures might vary according to circumstances, but they would be *due* procedures if they followed the established forms of law or if, adapting old forms to new problems, they preserved the principles of liberty and justice.

Jurisdiction

Of the basic components in judicial due process, perhaps the most fundamental is jurisdiction. Jurisdiction has been defined as the power to create legal interests. The jurisdiction of the federal courts is conferred on them and defined by acts of Congress. Without jurisdiction, they cannot act. As the Supreme Court said in *Ex parte McCardle* (1869):

> Jurisdiction is power to declare the law, and when it ceases to exist, the only function remaining to the court is that of announcing the fact and dismissing the case.

The jurisdiction of state courts, however it may be defined by their constitutions and legislature, is necessarily limited by their geography. Legal interests cannot be created if they cannot be enforced. The state must have actual physical power over persons or things if its courts are to render effective decrees concerning them. A state has jurisdiction over a person (such proceedings are called *in personam* actions) if he or she is physically present within the state, or is domiciled in the state but is temporarily absent, or has consented to the exercise of jurisdiction.

Corporations, being fictitious persons, can manifest their presence in states outside their state of origin only by activities carried on in their behalf. In general, such activities must be "continuous and systematic" in order to meet the "presence" test.[2] However, in some situations occasional acts of a corporate agent may be deemed sufficient to render the corporation liable to suit.[3]

Jurisdiction over things, usually exerted by actions *in rem,* may be exercised over property within the state, even though the owner is not within the state and control over the person is never obtained. Thus a state can permit attachment of property within its borders owned by a nonresident, for the purpose of satisfying a debt owed by the nonresident to a citizen of the state, or in settlement of a claim for damages by the citizen against the nonresident.

---

[2] See *International Shoe Co. v. Washington* (1945). *World-Wide Volkswagen Corp. v. Woodson* (1980) held that where corporate defendants carried on no activity whatever in Oklahoma and availed themselves of no privileges or benefits of Oklahoma law, the mere fortuitous circumstance that a single automobile sold in New York to New York residents happened to suffer an accident while passing through Oklahoma did not constitute "minimum contact" with Oklahoma sufficient to permit Oklahoma courts to exercise jurisdiction in a products liability suit. See also *Rush v. Savchuk* (1980).

[3] See *Travelers Health Assn. v. Virginia* (1950). In the case of *New York Times Co. v. Sullivan* (1964), the Alabama courts asserted jurisdiction over a libel suit against the newspaper because 394 copies containing the alleged libel out of an edition of 650,000 had been circulated in Alabama, 35 of them in Montgomery County where the suit arose. The *New York Times* contended that this was an inadequate basis for jurisdiction, but entered a general appearance in the action; the Supreme Court ruled that under Alabama law this amounted to waiving the jurisdictional objection.

Notice and Hearing

Jurisdiction, though potentially possessed, may not be exercised in a judicial proceeding until it has been perfected by appropriate notice that acquaints all parties of the institution of proceedings calculated to affect their rights. It is contrary to due process for a person to be deprived of property rights by a decree in a proceeding in which he or she does not appear, or is not served with process or effectively made a party to the case. The standard method of giving notice is by personal service—i.e., summons delivered to the defendant personally. However, various forms of substituted service, as by mail or newspaper publication, may meet the legal requirements. In general, due process requires the best notice that is possible under the circumstances.[4]

Due process requires that a party to judicial proceedings be afforded an opportunity to be heard at some stage before final judgment is entered. This includes the right to present such arguments, testimony, or evidence as may be pertinent to the case before a fair and impartial tribunal.

Illustrative of the notice and hearing requirement are two Supreme Court decisions involving actions for garnishment (seizures of wages for debt) and replevin (recovery of property, typically by creditors to repossess tangible goods purchased under installment sales contracts). Statutes authorizing such actions have historically provided for summary procedures. In *Sniadach v. Family Finance Corp.* (1969) service on the garnishee had the effect of freezing the wage-earner's salary prior to opportunity to be heard or to tender a defense. *Fuentes v. Shevin* (1972) involved a replevin statute authorizing a seizure of property on the ex parte application to a court clerk and the filing of a security bond by the person claiming the right to possession of the property. In both instances the Court held that the absence of notice and hearing prior to seizure violated due process.[5]

Administrative agencies and officers often have considerable authority to take action affecting the rights of property and of person. Where they are given such powers, the obligations of due process also become

---

[4]See *Mullane v. Central Hanover Bank & Trust Co.* (1950), *Walker v. Hutchinson* (1956), *Armstrong v. Manzo* (1965). In *Greene v. Lindsay* (1982) the Court held that where tenants were to be ousted from a public housing project, notice by posting on the apartment door was not adequate, since children might tear down the notice. In the absence of personal service, notice by mail was required. Justice O'Connor, dissenting, said there was no evidence in the record "regarding the speed and reliability of the mails."

[5]While *Fuentes* was apparently undermined by *Mitchell v. W. T. Grant Co.* (1974), it was reconfirmed in *North Georgia Finishing, Inc. v. Di-Chem, Inc.* (1975). The *Sniadach* case was relied on in *Stanley v. Illinois* (1972), where an unwed father's children, on the mother's death, were declared state wards and placed in guardianship. The Supreme Court held that the father was entitled to a hearing on his fitness as a parent before his children were taken away from him. See also *Mennonite Board v. Adams* (1983).

applicable to them. This means that the requirements of jurisdiction, notice, hearing, and general fairness of procedure must be observed in administrative actions, though administrative procedures typically do not afford all the protections that would apply in a court proceeding. In the Administrative Procedure Act of 1946, Congress undertook to codify and standardize the procedural protections to be observed in federal actions affecting persons and property.[6]

Some significant Supreme Court decisions have brought new types of administrative decisions within the ambit of due process. *Goldberg v. Kelly* (1970) held that before welfare payments could be discontinued, there had to be an evidentiary hearing at which the recipient could appear personally to present evidence. *Goss v. Lopez* (1975) invalidated the suspension of students from the public school system without a hearing. *Perry v. Sinderman* (1972) ruled that a teacher who was fired after ten years in a state college system in violation of what he contended was a de facto tenure system was entitled to a hearing where he could be informed of the grounds for his nonretention and challenge their sufficiency.[7]

THE INCORPORATION CONTROVERSY

The general due process requirements of jurisdiction, notice, and fair hearing apply to civil proceedings in all American courts, both federal and state. For criminal proceedings, however, the situation is more complicated. Federal courts must observe all the process provisions of the Fourth through Eighth Amendments. State courts, however, have only the general due process language of the Fourteenth Amendment as their guide. This difference in the constitutional situation of the two sets of courts has generated one of the most celebrated controversies in American constitutional law.

The Supreme Court's initial position was that in criminal proceedings state courts were obliged to observe only the general concept of due process and its historical requirements. Due process did not require

---

[6] See Kenneth C. Davis, *Administrative Law and Government* (St. Paul, Minn.: West Publishing Company, 1975).

[7] But *Mathews v. Eldridge* (1976) held that the Social Security Administration was not required to hold a full hearing before cutting off disability insurance benefits. *Smith v. Organization of Foster Families* (1977) held that hearings were not required before removal of children from foster homes. In *Blum v. Yaretsky* (1982) the action of nursing homes in discharging or transferring Medicaid patients without notice or hearing was upheld on the ground that no "state action" was involved. A hearing is not required before inflicting corporal punishment by school authorities *(Ingraham v. Wright* [1977]). *Dixon v. Love* (1977) upheld an Illinois system under which a driver's license is automatically revoked without a hearing if the license had been suspended three times within a ten-year period.

the states to adopt specific measures of procedure or doctrines of law. Its effect was negative—to keep state courts within broad bounds—rather than positively to enforce certain mandatory procedures. The Court summed up this position in *Snyder v. Massachusetts* (1934) when it said that a state was "free to regulate the procedure of its courts in accordance with its own conception of policy and fairness unless in so doing it offends some principle of justice so rooted in the traditions and conscience of our people as to be ranked as fundamental."

The Court did not encounter this problem immediately on adoption of the Fourteenth Amendment, for at first litigation centered on the privileges and immunities clause, which was thought to be more promising in its protective potentialities than the due process clause. But in the *Slaughterhouse Cases* (1873) the Court confined the privileges and immunities clause to the narrow protection of those rights peculiar to national citizenship, making it inapplicable to property rights and trials in the state courts.

Attention then turned to the due process clause of the Fourteenth Amendment, which got its first significant examination in *Hurtado v. California* (1884). Instead of being indicted by a grand jury, Hurtado had been brought to trial for murder on information after examination and commitment by a magistrate, as permitted by the California constitution. Thus the question before the Supreme Court was whether such departure from grand jury indictment violated due process of law.

On the basis of Justice Curtis's first test in the *Murray* case, due process had clearly been violated, for the Fifth Amendment makes indictment by grand jury mandatory for all capital or otherwise infamous crimes. However, Justice Matthews made the *Murray* rule seem to approve the *Hurtado* result. The "real syllabus" of the Curtis holding, Matthews said, is "that a process of law, which is not otherwise forbidden, must be taken to be due process of law, if it can show the sanction of settled usage both in England and in this country; but it by no means follows that nothing else can be due process of law." Then, having recognized Curtis's first test by the clause, "which is not otherwise forbidden," he proceeded to ignore it and to work from the last thought in the sentence, which is substantially Curtis's second test—the test of historical practice.

Matthews was able to show that grand jury indictment was not even known at the time of Magna Carta, or for centuries thereafter. In fact, some of the early practices had been so barbarous that he suggested "it is better not to go too far back into antiquity for the best securities for our 'ancient liberties.'" In any case, it would not be wise for the states to be bound to any fixed set of procedures in criminal cases.

It is more consonant to the true philosophy of our historical legal institutions to say that the spirit of personal liberty and individual right, which they embodied, was preserved and developed by a progressive growth and wise adaptation to new circumstances and situations of the forms and processes found fit to give, from time to time, new expression and greater effect to modern ideas of self-government.

For those who might find this liberal philosophy unconvincing, Matthews had a more pedantic argument. Since the Fifth Amendment contains both the guarantee of due process and of indictment by grand jury, and since it must be assumed that no part of the Constitution is superfluous, it follows that due process as used in the Fifth Amendment does not include indictment by grand jury. When the same phrase is repeated in the Fourteenth Amendment, it must be given the same meaning. Thus Matthews emerged with the remarkable conclusion, directly opposed to that of Curtis, that the due process clauses in both the Fifth and Fourteenth Amendments must be interpreted to *exclude* any rights specified elsewhere in the Constitution.

Justice Harlan was the only dissenter in the *Hurtado* case; he was an incorporationist. To him the Fourteenth Amendment evinced "a purpose to impose upon the States the same restrictions, in respect of proceedings involving life, liberty and property, which had been imposed upon the general government." Again, in *Maxwell v. Dow* (1900), he dissented in the most extensive examination the Fourteenth Amendment had received up to that time. He was thoroughly aroused by the fact that the development of substantive due process had made it possible for the Court to protect property rights against state legislative action, while procedural rights in state courts remained unprotected, and he commented bitterly:

> If then the "due process of law" required by the Fourteenth Amendment does not allow a State to take private property without just compensation, but does allow the life or liberty of the citizen to be taken in a mode that is repugnant to the settled usages and the modes of proceeding authorized at the time the Constitution was adopted and which was expressly forbidden in the National Bill of Rights, it would seem that the protection of private property is of more consequence than the protection of the life and liberty of the citizen.

This entire argument was resumed in *Twining v. New Jersey* (1908). The state practice under fire in *Twining* was self-incrimination; the jury, under state law, had been instructed that they might draw an unfavorable inference from the defendant's failure to testify in denial of evidence offered against him. Justice Moody for the Court upheld the law, but recognizing the weakness of the *Hurtado* decision, announced that the Court preferred to rest its decision "on broader grounds" than were there stated. The important thing was whether exemption from self-incrimination was "a fundamental principle of liberty and justice which inheres in the very idea of free government and is the inalienable right of a citizen of such a government."

How can judges proceed to answer such a question? One way, Moody asserted, was "to inquire how the right was rated during the time when the meaning of due process was in a formative state and before it was incorporated in American constitutional law." He found that it was omitted from the great declarations of English liberty, and that in fact English courts and Parliaments dealt with the exemption "as they would have dealt with any other rule of evidence." Moreover, only four of the thirteen original states insisted that this rule should be included in the Constitution, and two of these states did not have it in their own constitutions at the time. Thus the historical evidence demonstrated that "the privilege was not conceived to be inherent in due process law, but on the other hand a right separate, independent, and outside of due process." Moody went on to note that the exemption was unknown outside the common-law countries, and was not observed "among our own people in the search for truth outside the administration of the law." So, "salutary as the principle may seen to the great majority, it cannot be ranked with the right to hearing before comdemnation, the immunity from arbitrary power not acting by general laws, and the inviolability of private property."

After the *Twining* decision the incorporation controversy was relatively quiescent at the Supreme Court level for three decades. Then in 1937 *Palko v. Connecticut* offered an opportunity for reexamining the issue. In the interim the incorporation theory had achieved a very great success in another area. As already noted, *Gitlow v. New York* (1925) had admitted that the "liberty" protected by the Fourteenth Amendment against deprivation without due process included the freedoms of speech and press guaranteed by the First Amendment. If the First Amendment was incorporated into the Fourteenth, why were not the other guarantees in the Bill of Rights similarly situated?

It fell to Justice Cardozo to answer this question in the *Palko* case. The defendant had been convicted of second-degree murder and given a life sentence, but the state appealed the conviction, as was authorized by state law; and the state supreme court, finding there had been error in the trial to the prejudice of the state, ordered a new trial. The second time the defendant was convicted of murder in the first degree and sentenced to death. The question was whether the effect of the second trial was to place the defendant twice in jeopardy for the same offense.

Cardozo began by once more flatly rejecting the incorporation thesis. To the extent that some of the first eight amendments had been made effective against the states, that was not because they were incorporated into the Fourteenth Amendment when it was adopted, but because they had been found by the Supreme Court "to be implicit in the concept of ordered liberty." Cardozo admitted that when one looked at the line drawn by the Court between rights that meet this test and those that do not, it might seem "wavering and broken." But "reflection and analysis" would disclose a "rationalizing principle."

> The right to trial by jury and the immunity from prosecution except as the result of an indictment may have value and importance. Even so, they are not of the very essence of a scheme of ordered liberty. To abolish them is not to violate a "principle of justice so rooted in the traditions and conscience of our people as to be ranked as fundamental." . . . Few would be so narrow or provincial as to maintain that a fair and enlightened system of justice would be impossible without them. What is true of jury trials and indictments is true also . . . of the immunity from compulsory self-incrimination. . . . This too might be lost, and justice still be done.

On the other hand, freedom of thought and speech, as guaranteed by the First Amendment, is on "a different plane of social and moral values. . . . Of that freedom one may say that it is the matrix, the indispensable condition, of nearly every other form of freedom." So these freedoms have been "absorbed" into the Fourteenth Amendment, for "neither liberty nor justice would exist if they were sacrificed."

With this groundwork, it remained only for Cardozo to conclude that double jeopardy of the type presented in this case was not a value on the high plane represented by the First Amendment. All the state was asking was that the case against the defendant go on "until there shall be a trial free from the corrosion of substantial legal error." If there had been an error adverse to the accused, admittedly he could get another trial. To give the state a reciprocal privilege was "no seismic innovation. The edifice of justice stands, its symmetry, to many, greater than before."

Justice Black was in his first term on the Court when the *Palko* decision was made, and he did not dissent, though Butler did. This is interesting, for ten years later Black, in *Adamson v. California* (1947), led an assault on this entire line of cases that lacked only one vote of achieving success. The issue was again self-incrimination, this time as presented by a state statute permitting the failure of a defendant to explain or to deny evidence against him to be commented on by the court and by counsel and to be considered by the judge and the jury. For the defendant with a previous criminal record, the problem posed by this rule is that if he chooses to go on the witness stand to explain or deny evidence, he is then subject to cross-examination that can bring out his prior convictions. If he fails to take the stand, the assumption is that he cannot refute the evidence or has something to hide.

By a five to four vote, the Court held this statutory provision not contrary to due process. Justice Reed for the majority stood by the *Palko* rejection of the incorporation argument. The only question was whether a state statute permitting comment on the refusal of a defendant to take the stand met the Supreme Court's notions as to allowable procedure. Reed made practically no effort to answer by reference to standards outside the value systems of the individual justices, such as historical practice. Instead, he said very frankly, "We see no reason why comment should not be made upon his silence. . . . When evidence is before a jury that threatens conviction, it does not seem unfair to require him to choose between leaving the adverse evidence unexplained and subjecting himself to impeachment through disclosure of former crimes."

Black's dissent, which spoke for Douglas, Murphy, and Rutledge as well, was a powerful defense of the incorporation theory. In a lengthy appendix to his opinion, he marshaled the historical data favorable to the incorporation view; such as the speeches of Bingham and Howard already referred to, and concluded: "My study of the historical events that culminated in the Fourteenth Amendment . . . persuades me that one of the chief objects that the provisions of the Amendment's first section, separately, and as a whole, were intended to accomplish was to make the Bill of Rights applicable to the states." The Court, he went on, had repeatedly declined to appraise this historical evidence. Instead, it had reiterated a "natural law" formula under which it had substituted "its own concepts of decency and fundamental justice for the language of the Bill of Rights. . . . I would follow what I believe was the original purpose of the Fourteenth Amendment—to extend to all the people of the nation the complete protection of the Bill of Rights."

Justice Frankfurter, concurring in the Court's majority opinion, devoted himself to answering Black and to ridiculing the "notion that the Fourteenth Amendment was a covert way of imposing upon the States all the rules which it seemed important to Eighteenth Century statesmen to write into the Federal Amendments." Actually, substantial victory for the incorporation position was only a decade away. The story of those developments, however, must await the more detailed examination of due process requirements for criminal prosecutions, which is the subject of the following chapter.[8]

[8] For an excellent treatment of the entire incorporation development, see Richard C. Cortner, *The Supreme Court and the Second Bill of Rights: The Fourteenth Amendment and the Nationalization of Civil Liberties* (Madison: University of Wisconsin Press, 1981).

9
Criminal Prosecutions

One of the Supreme Court's most important functions is to maintain constitutional standards for the criminal prosecutions conducted in both federal and state courts. The significance that the Constitution attaches to such protection is indicated by the fact that five of the ten amendments comprising the Bill of Rights are largely devoted to specifying the standards and procedures to be observed in criminal prosecutions. These amendments contain not only the broad guarantee of due process of law, but numerous specific procedural protections such as indictment by grand jury and speedy and public trial, as well as safeguards against self-incrimination, unreasonable searches and seizures, double jeopardy, and cruel and unusual punishments. In addition to enforcing these constitutional provisions, the Supreme Court has the general responsibility over administration of justice in the federal courts that comes from its position at the apex of the judicial hierarchy. This supervisory authority, the Court has said, "implies the duty of establishing and maintaining civilized standards of procedure and evidence." [1]

CRIMES AGAINST THE UNITED STATES

There are four principal references to federal crimes in the Constitution: "counterfeiting the securities and current coin of the United States,"

---

[1] *McNabb v. United States* (1943). In *Yates v. United States* (1958) the Court made a highly unusual use of its supervisory power by itself reducing a sentence for contempt of court after the district judge who imposed the original sentence had failed to respond to the Supreme Court's "gentle intimations" that the sentence should be reduced.

"piracies and felonies committed on the high seas," and "offences against the law of nations," all found in Article I, section 8; and "treason against the United States," which is defined in Article III, section 3. Obviously these four crimes do not account for the content of the United States Criminal Code, and there is no federal common law of crimes.[2] All the other multitudinous crimes on the federal statute books have been defined and made punishable by congressional exercise of implied power. Any law that Congress has the power to adopt, it also has the power to enforce by making violation a crime. Thus the power "to establish post offices and post roads" clearly implies the power to punish theft from the mails. Of the crimes that achieve the distinction of constitutional mention, only one, treason, has a history and a constitutional significance justifying consideration here.

The constitutional provision on treason is short. "Treason against the United States shall consist only in levying war against them, or in adhering to their enemies, giving them aid and comfort. No person shall be convicted of treason unless on the testimony of two witnesses to the same overt act, or on confession in open court." The intent of the framers in these words is well known: they were seeking to make convictions for treason very difficult to obtain. The members of the Convention "almost to a man had themselves been guilty of treason under any interpretation of British law."[3] They had been "taught by experience and by history to fear abuse of the treason charge almost as much as they feared treason itself." They believed that a government had to deserve the loyalty of its citizens, and that opposition to the abuses of a tyrannical government was justified and should not be punished as treason.

Consequently the Convention wrote into the Constitution every limitation on treason convictions "that the practice of governments had evolved or that politico-legal philosophy to that time had advanced." The result of this restrictive approach has been to render treason litigation comparatively unimportant in American constitutional development. The Supreme Court never had occasion to review a treason conviction until the case of *Cramer v. United States* in 1945. In the brief for that case, all previous proceedings in which construction of the treason clause had been involved were collected, and they totaled nineteen. As Justice Jackson said in his *Cramer* decision: "We have managed to do without treason prosecutions to a degree that probably would be impossible except while a people was singularly confident of external security and internal stability."

The treason provision has, however, been invoked often enough to demonstrate its problems of interpretation. The Aaron Burr conspiracy led to two treason rulings by Chief Justice Marshall. In *Ex parte Bollman* (1807)

---

[2] *United States v. Hudson and Goodwin* (1812).

[3] This quotation and those immediately following are from *Cramer v. United States* (1945).

he warned that "the crime of treason should not be extended by construction to doubtful cases." He confined the meaning of levying war to the actual waging of war or the actual assembling of men for that purpose. In presiding over the trial of Burr,[4] Marshall ruled that Burr, not having been present at the actual assemblage of men, could be convicted of procuring or levying of war only upon the testimony of two witnesses to his having procured the assemblage. The result was practically to limit convictions for "levying war" to actual participants in armed hostilities.

In more recent times treason charges have usually been based not on the "levying war" clause, but on the offense of "adhering" to the nation's enemies, "giving them aid and comfort." In *Cramer v. United States* (1945) the Supreme Court divided five to four in applying this constitutional provision. Cramer had befriended two of the German saboteurs who were landed in the United States by submarine in 1942 for the purpose of sabotaging the American war effort. He met and lunched with them in public places, and took a large sum of money from one for safekeeping. The only overt acts established by two witnesses were the public meetings. The Court majority concluded that Cramer's eating and drinking in a public place "was no part of the saboteurs' mission and did not advance it."

Two years later the Supreme Court for the first time in its history sustained a treason conviction. *Haupt v. United States* (1947) grew out of the same incident of the German saboteurs, the defendant being the father of one of them. When the son turned up in Chicago on his mission, the father took him into his house, accompanied him when he sought employment in a plant manufacturing bomb sights, and purchased an automobile for him. This time the Court held the constitutional standard of treason had been met. The "harboring and sheltering" that Haupt had provided his son, an overt act established by two witnesses, was of direct value to his traitorous enterprise, in a way that Cramer's public meetings with the saboteurs had not been.

Since 1947 only one additional treason case has reached the Supreme Court, *Kawakita v. United States* (1952), and it added little to the law. Following the Korean War the Defense Department referred over two hundred cases of possible treason arising out of that conflict to the Department of Justice, but actual prosecutions were few. They seem likely to continue to be few.

In fact, to a considerable degree prosecutions under various antisubversive and espionage laws, which do not present such difficult problems of proof, have substituted for treason prosecutions. In the famous case of the Rosenbergs, who were executed in 1952 after conviction under the Espionage Act for giving aid to a country, not an enemy, the offense was held to be

---

[4] *United States v. Burr* (1807).

distinct from treason, so that neither the two-witness rule nor the overt act requirement was applicable.[5]

CRIMINAL PROCEDURE IN THE ORIGINAL CONSTITUTION

For the most part the original Constitution did not concern itself with spelling out the procedural protections in federal prosecutions, but there were four exceptions. One is the prohibition on suspension of the writ of habeas corpus.[6] A second, the jury trial provisions of Article III, was quickly superseded by the Sixth Amendment. Only the prohibitions on bills of attainder and ex post facto laws need be examined here.

Bills of Attainder

Both Congress and the states were forbidden by Article I, sections 9 and 10, to pass any "bill of attainder." These provisions were adopted to outlaw the practice of legislative punishment common in England, where individuals could be condemned to death by special act of Parliament called a bill of attainder. Legislative acts inflicting lesser punishments were designated "bills of pains and penalties." As interpreted by the Supreme Court, the bill of attainder provisions forbid all legislative acts, "no matter what their form, that apply either to named individuals or to easily ascertainable members of a group in such a way as to inflict punishment on them without a judicial trial."[7]

The bill of attainder provisions were first applied after the Civil War. A congressional act requiring attorneys practicing in the federal courts to take an oath that they had never given aid to persons engaged in hostility to the United States was held unconstitutional in *Ex parte Garland* (1867). In *Cummings v. Missouri* (1867) a state constitutional provision seeking to exclude persons who had aided the Confederacy from following certain professions—a minister was involved in this case—was invalidated on similar grounds.

No other legislation was held to constitute a bill of attainder until 1946, when in *United States v. Lovett* the Court voided an act of Congress that had prohibited the payment of compensation to three named govern-

---

[5] *United States v. Rosenberg* (1952). On the general subject, see James Willard Hurst, "Treason in the United States," 58 HARVARD LAW REVIEW 226, 395, 806 (1944–1945), and *The Law of Treason in the United States: Collected Essays* (Westport, Conn.: Greenwood Press, 1971).

[6] See discussion in C. Herman Pritchett, *Constitutional Law in the Federal System* (Englewood Cliffs, N.J.: Prentice-Hall, 1983), Chapter 17.

[7] *United States v. Lovett* (1946). See John Hart Ely *"United States v. Lovett: Litigating the Separation of Powers,"* 10 HARVARD CIVIL RIGHTS–CIVIL LIBERTIES LAW REVIEW 1 (1975).

ment employees who had been charged with subversive activities by the House Un-American Activities Committee. In *Communist Party v. SACB* (1961) Justice Black, dissenting, contended that the Internal Security Act of 1950 was a "classical bill of attainder" because it constituted a legislative finding of guilt against members of the Communist party. The majority said in rebuttal: "The Act is not a bill of attainder. It attaches not to specified organizations but to described activities in which an organization may or may not engage."

However, Black's view became that of the Court majority in *United States v. Brown* (1965) where, as already reported, a 1959 statute making it a crime for a member of the Communist party to serve as an officer or employee of a labor union was held unconstitutional. It would be legitimate, said Chief Justice Warren, for Congress to adopt a generally applicable rule decreeing that any person who commits certain acts or possesses certain characteristics should not hold union office, leaving to courts and juries the task of deciding what persons fell in those categories. But this act designated the persons who possessed the feared characteristics—members of the Communist party—and this made the act a bill of attainder.[8]

Ex Post Facto Laws

The passage of ex post facto laws is also forbidden to both Congress and the states. An ex post facto law is "a law made after the doing of the thing to which it relates, and retroacting upon it." The reason for inserting such sweeping prohibitions in the Constitution was apparently to be found in the freedom with which state legislatures in that era had passed paper money or legal tender laws setting aside existing contracts, so that what had been lent in gold and silver could be repaid in paper. However, in *Calder v. Bull* (1798) the Supreme Court construed the ex post facto clauses as covering only penal and criminal laws.

Every law that makes criminal an act done before the passage of such law that was innocent when done, or that aggravates a crime or makes it greater than when it was committed, or that changes the punishment and inflicts a greater penalty than the law annexed to the crime when committed, or that alters the rules of evidence, permitting less or different evidence to convict a person of an offense committed prior to its passage, or that operates in any way to the disadvantage of one accused of a crime committed prior to the enactment of the law is an ex post facto law. The clause is directed against legislative action only. It does not reach erroneous or inconsistent decisions of the courts.

A law cannot be held to be ex post facto unless it imposes punishment

---

[8] In *Nixon v. Administrator of General Services* (1977) the Court held that the congressional statute providing for government control of Nixon's papers was not a bill of attainder.

in the legal sense for past acts. A deportation law authorizing the secretary of labor to expel aliens for criminal acts committed before its passage was held not ex post facto, since deportation is not classified as punishment, but as a discretionary exercise of sovereign power.[9] Similarly, a statute terminating payment of Social Security benefits to an alien following deportation for Communist affiliation was declared not ex post facto on the ground that it was not a penalty.[10]

The right to practice a business or profession may be denied to one who was convicted of an offense before the statute was enacted, if the offense can reasonably be regarded as a continuing disqualification. Thus *DeVeau v. Braisted* (1960) upheld a statute excluding convicted felons from offices in New York waterfront unions, unless pardoned or holding a parole board's good conduct certificate. But the Civil War test oaths invalidated as bills of attainder in *Garland* and *Cummings* were also held to be ex post facto, on the assumption that they bore no reasonable relation to fitness to perform professional duties.[11]

UNREASONABLE SEARCHES AND SEIZURES

The Fourth Amendment is the most specific recognition of the right of privacy in the Constitution. It reflects the strong resentment felt by the American colonists against the "general warrants" or "writs of assistance" that the British had employed to search private homes and other premises in enforcement of their tax laws and commercial regulations. Such searches were not permitted at common law. To be sure, English law did recognize broad powers of arrest; even private citizens could make arrests, and all felony arrests could be made without warrant. In fact, arrest warrants were accepted only reluctantly and primarily for the purpose of protecting those making arrests from tort liability. But the common law, with its strong bias toward property rights, did not grant any right to search the premises of suspected offenders on the grounds of "reasonable suspicion." English insistence that a man's home is his castle has been forever memorialized in William Pitt's speech on the Excise Bill:

> The poorest man may in his cottage bid defiance to all the force of the Crown. It may be frail; its roof may shake; the wind may blow through it; the storms may enter, the rain may enter,—but the King of England cannot enter; all his forces dare not cross the threshold of the ruined tenement.

[9] *Mahler v. Eby* (1924).

[10] *Flemming v. Nestor* (1960).

[11] Florida violated the ban on ex post facto laws when it changed the rules for computing prisoner's time off for good behavior, and then applied the new rules to the disadvantage of prisoners whose crime was committed before the law was changed (*Weaver v. Graham* [1981]).

The provisions in the Bill of Rights, as we know, apply only to the federal government unless they are extended to the states by the Fourteenth Amendment. Chapter 8 traced the developments in the early period of the "incorporation" controversy, as the Court rejected various efforts to make the criminal prosecution provisions of the Bill of Rights applicable to the states. The Supreme Court had no occasion to consider the relationship of the Fourth Amendment to the states until 1949, when it decided *Wolf v. Colorado.* Then the justices readily agreed, in an opinion by Justice Frankfurter, that freedom from unreasonable search and seizure was an essential element in the concept of "ordered liberty."

> The security of one's privacy against arbitrary intrusion by the police—which is at the core of the Fourth Amendment—is basic to a free society. . . . The knock at the door, whether by day or by night, as a prelude to a search, without authority of law but solely on the authority of the police, did not need the commentary of recent history to be condemned as inconsistent with the conception of human rights enshrined in the history and the basic constitutional documents of English-speaking peoples.

Another preliminary comment should be made concerning the coverage of the Amendment. It applies in arrests and searches of individuals' persons, their living quarters, offices, or the hotel rooms they are occupying, and even their automobiles. The basic elements bringing search and seizure protection into effect have historically been two: there must be a physical invasion of or trespass on a constitutionally protected area, and there must be a seizure of a physical object. But, as we shall see, there have now been substantial modifications in both these standards.[12]

Arrests and Probable Cause

Because of the close connection between searches and arrests, a few words are in order concerning the power to arrest. The Fourth Amendment recognizes warrants of arrest, which can be issued only on "probable cause." However, the amendment does not mean that warrants are required for an arrest. That would be completely impractical, because it would preclude officers from making arrests for offenses committed in their presence or where immediate action was necessary to apprehend a law violator. In *United States v. Watson* (1976) the Court even upheld a warrantless arrest in

---

[12] A critical analysis of the Supreme Court's Fourth Amendment decisions from 1969 to 1973 is found in Leonard W. Levy, *Against the Law: The Nixon Court and Criminal Justice* (New York: Harper & Row, Pub., 1974), Chapter 2. See, more generally, Jacob W. Landynski, *Search and Seizure and the Supreme Court* (Baltimore: Johns Hopkins Press, 1966).

a public place on probable cause, although the officer had had time to secure a warrant and no exigency justified his failure to do so. As we shall see, a search would not have been valid under these conditions.

Probable cause for arrest exists where facts and circumstances within the officer's knowledge or of which he has "reasonably trustworthy information [are] sufficient in themselves to warrant a man of reasonable caution in the belief that an offense has been or is being committed."[13] In *Terry v. Ohio* (1968), the Court said that it had consistently refused to sanction arrests "based on nothing more substantial than inarticulate hunches." In *Papachristou v. City of Jacksonville* (1972), Douglas wrote, "Arresting a person on suspicion, like arresting a person for investigation, is foreign to our system." But in *Draper v. United States* (1959), an arrest by federal narcotics agents was ruled valid where the agents had only a tip that a man arriving on a certain train, dressed in a certain way, walking fast, and carrying a tan bag would be transporting narcotics.[14]

An arrest occurs not only when the traditional forms are followed but, according to *Terry*, "whenever a police officer accosts an individual and restrains his freedom to walk away." Similarly, in *Henry v. United States* (1959), the Court held that an arrest had occurred when two FBI agents stopped a suspect's car, though the formal arrest did not take place until two hours later, after the suspect had been taken to their office and cartons he had been transporting had been found to contain stolen radios.

The Search Warrant

As the test of reasonableness in a search, the Fourth Amendment relies primarily upon the requirement of a search warrant, issued "upon probable cause, supported by oath or affirmation, and particularly describing the place to be searched, and the persons or things to be seized." Warrants are issued by judicial officers, who are brought into the procedure to exert a neutral or at least modifying influence upon the police. As Justice Murphy said, "In their understandable zeal to ferret out crime and in the excitement of the capture of a suspected person, officers are less likely [than judges] to

---

[13] *Brinegar v. United States* (1949). A Florida procedure whereby a person arrested without a warrant and charged by information may be jailed without an opportunity for probable cause determination. It is unconstitutional (*Gerstein v. Pugh* [1975]).

[14] *Hampton v. United States* (1976) held it was not entrapment when federal agents supplied suspected drug dealers with heroin and set them up for arrest, because they were "predisposed" to commit crime. In *Michigan v. Summers* (1981) the Court ruled that police officers with a valid search warrant for a home may detain residents for possible later arrest in case the officers find illegal substances in the home. Stewart, dissenting, said that "the requirement of probable cause for arrest has been turned upside down."

possess the detachment and neutrality with which the constitutional rights of the suspect must be viewed."[15]

A judicial officer has probable cause for issuance of a warrant if presented with an affidavit setting forth apparent facts that would lead a reasonably discreet and prudent person to believe that the offense charged had been committed.[16] According to *Jones v. United States* (1960) and *Aguilar v. Texas* (1964), an affidavit resting on hearsay—that is, one which relies on the observations of an informer rather than an officer—meets the probable cause test if the informer has previously given correct information and if there is corroboration from other sources, or if the magistrate is informed of some of the underlying circumstances on which the informant's conclusions were based and from which the officer determined that the information was reliable.

In *Spinelli v. United States* (1969), the Warren Court held that an anonymous tip was not acceptable as probable cause even though it had been corroborated by a detailed FBI affidavit. But the Burger Court, by a five to four decision in *United States v. Harris* (1971), undermined *Spinelli* by eliminating the requirement that the police must demonstrate the credibility of an anonymous informer, and it authorized the magistrate to rely on an officer's assertion about a suspect's reputation. *Illinois v. Gates* (1983) overruled both *Aguilar* and *Spinelli*, holding constitutional a search warrant based in part on an anonymous tip about drug dealers.[17]

---

[15] *Trupiano v. United States* (1948). See also *Johnson v. United States* (1948). In *Coolidge v. New Hampshire* (1971), a warrant for search of an automobile in a murder case was issued by the chief law-enforcement officer of the state—the attorney general—who acted in his capacity as a justice of the peace at the same time that he personally directed police investigation of the murder; later he was chief prosecutor at the trial. The Court held he was not a "neutral and detached magistrate." *Shadwick v. Tampa* (1972) held that municipal court clerks are "neutral and detached magistrates" for Fourth Amendment purposes. It violated the Fourth Amendment when a Georgia justice of the peace was paid five dollars each time he signed a search warrant for a policeman but nothing if he refused (*Connally v. Georgia* [1977]). *Franks v. Delaware* (1978) held that a defendant has a right to challenge evidence on the ground that prosecutors obtained a search warrant by making false statements to the issuing judge. An "open-ended" search warrant allowing police to seize anything they pleased in an alleged pornographic shop was ruled unconstitutional (*Lo-Ji Sales v. New York* [1979]).

[16] There was probable cause for issuance of a search warrant when officers had seen large amounts of sugar and five-gallon cans being taken into a house and had smelled fermenting mash when walking past the house. (*United States v. Ventresca*[1965]). Generally, the fact that evidence is available to officers which would justify issuance of a search warrant does not relieve them of the necessity to secure such a warrant. In *Jones v. United States* (1958), the Court held that protracted observation by federal agents of mash flowing from a house did not justify search and seizure of contraband distilling equipment without a warrant. Similarly, in *Johnson v. United States* (1948), the odor of burning opium coming from a hotel room was held insufficient to justify entry without a warrant.

[17] Arson investigators must obtain search warrants before they enter a building except during and immediately after a fire (*Michigan v. Tayler* [1978]). Likewise warrants must be obtained by inspectors for the Occupational Safety and Health Administration before making spot searches of employers' premises (*Marshall v. Barlow's* [1978]).

Whatever the Supreme Court's standards may be, it is unfortunately true that many magistrates issue search warrants either automatically or after only the most perfunctory inquiry.

Search without a Warrant

Most constitutional issues as to search and seizure arise, however, not out of failure to observe the requirements in securing warrants but out of failure to secure any search warrants at all. Such failure does not necessarily void a search or seizure. It depends upon the circumstances.

Search without a warrant may be made in connection with a valid arrest. An officer making an arrest with a warrant of arrest, or on the basis of trustworthy information, or for a crime committed in the officer's presence, may search the person of the suspect for weapons and seize any evidence of crime in plain sight within the immediate area of the arrest.

The "plain sight" and the "immediate area" rules have been the subject of intense controversy. In *Harris v. United States* (1947), the Court by a five to four vote upheld a search of a four-room apartment with only an arrest warrant. But the following year, in *Trupiano v. United States*, the Court, again divided five to four, invalidated a seizure without a warrant of a still on a New Jersey farm where the illegal equipment was in plain sight, the reason being that the agents had had plenty of time to secure a warrant and seemed to have willfully disregarded the warrant requirement.

Then in *United States v. Rabinowitz* (1950), the Court swung back toward the *Harris* position. A stamp dealer had been arrested on a warrant in his one-room office for selling stamps fraudulently overprinted to give them a higher value for philatelists. A search was then made of the office for additional fraudulent stamps, over five hundred of which were found. Although the officers had thought to bring experts along to identify the stamps, they had not thought to secure a search warrant. The Court, by a five to three vote, held that the search was nevertheless reasonable, since the office was open to the public, small, and under the immediate control of the occupant. *Trupiano* was overruled, to the extent that it required "a search warrant solely upon the basis of the practicability of procuring it rather than upon the reasonableness of the search after a lawful arrest."

But both *Harris* and *Rabinowitz* were overruled by *Chimel v. California* (1969). Here the officers, with an arrest warrant but no search warrant, had nevertheless searched an entire three-bedroom house. The Court returned to a more literal interpretation of the rule that on an arrest warrant the officers can conduct only "a search of the person arrested and the area within his reach."[18]

---

[18] In *Coolidge v. New Hampshire* (1971) an arrest inside a house was held not to justify a search of the arrestee's automobile outside on the driveway (which was not in fact searched until two days later, after it had been seized and taken to the police station). *Vale v. Louisiana*

The Burger Court took a surprisingly strong position against warrantless searches in connection with arrests. In *Payton v. New York* (1980), a state statute authorized police to enter private residences without a warrant and with force if necessary to make a routine felony arrest. The Court held, six to three, that the sanctity of the home was too substantial to invade without a warrant even under statutory authority and where probable cause was present.[19] Following *Payton, Steagald v. United States* (1981) ruled that even with a valid arrest warrant the police also need a search warrant to enter the home of someone other than the person they want to arrest.

However, in *Washington v. Chrisman* (1982) police entry and arrest without a warrant was upheld because of the peculiar circumstances. An officer, having detained a student on a college campus for possible liquor law violation, accompanied him to his dormitory so the student could secure proof of age. Once in the room, the officer saw plain-sight evidence of drug possession by the other occupant of the room, which the Court held justified his arrest.

A search can be made without a warrant with the consent of the occupant of the quarters searched, who is thereby considered to have waived his or her Fourth Amendment rights. In *United States v. Matlock* (1974), an arrest was made in the front yard of a home. The officers were then admitted to the house by a woman living there and with her consent searched the bedroom that she told them was occupied jointly by the arrestee and herself. The Supreme Court held that this was adequate consent for the search.

A suspect who is asked to consent to a search need not be told that there is a right to refuse; so the Court ruled in *Schneckloth v. Bustamonte* (1973) and *United States v. Watson* (1976). Justice Brennan, dissenting in *Schneckloth*, wrote, "It wholly escapes me how our citizens can meaningfully be said to have waived something as precious as a constitutional guarantee without ever being aware of its existence."

Conviction for murder by strangulation in *Cupp v. Murphy* (1973) rested on scrapings from under the suspect's fingernails taken in spite of his protests when he went voluntarily to the police station for questioning. The

---

(1970) ruled that arrest of a man outside his house did not justify search of the home. But *United States v. Santana* (1976) held that a suspect sighted in a doorway in public view could be pursued into the house without a warrant. A warrantless four-day search of a defendant's apartment following his arrest after the shooting of a police officer in the apartment could not be justified on the basis of any "murder scene exception" (*Mincey v. Arizona* [1978]).

[19] *United States v. Johnson* (1982) applied *Payton* retroactively to all Fourth Amendment convictions that were not final at the time *Payton* was handed down. But the Fourth Amendment does not prevent federal agents from breaking and entering to install bugging equipment authorized by a judge under the Crime Control Act (*Dalia v. United States* [1979]). Police do not need a warrant before installing a "pen register" that records the numbers dialed on a telephone (*Smith v. Maryland* [1979]). Neither do they need a search warrant to track a moving object by monitoring the signal from an implanted radio transmitter (*United States v. Knotts* [1983]).

Court held there was probable cause for this search, though the police had neither an arrest nor search warrant.

The Fourth Amendment can be violated by guileful as well as forcible or stealthy intrusions into a constitutionally protected area. In *Gouled v. United States* (1921) a business acquaintance, acting under orders of federal officers, obtained entry into Gouled's office by falsely purporting only to pay a social visit. In Gouled's absence, the intruder ransacked the office and seized certain private papers of an incriminating nature. The Court held this an unconstitutional search and seizure.[20]

This precedent did not help James Hoffa, who was convicted in 1964 of jury tampering on the basis of evidence provided by one of his associates, Partin, who had been a frequent visitor to Hoffa's hotel room but who was secretly an informer for the government. Hoffa contended that Partin's role vitiated the consent Hoffa had given for Partin's repeated entries into the suite, and that by listening to Hoffa's statements Partin had conducted an illegal search for verbal evidence. The Supreme Court, however, in *Hoffa v. United States* (1966), held that the security of his hotel room on which Hoffa was entitled to rely had not been breached. Partin was present by invitation, and Hoffa's revelations were voluntary.

Stop and Frisk

The common police practice of stopping and frisking suspicious persons without a warrant or probable cause was upheld in *Terry v. Ohio* (1968), though within certain limits. Many considerations may arouse an officer's suspicion but fall short of establishing probable cause for an arrest. In *Terry*, a veteran police officer patrolling in downtown Cleveland noted two men who were intently and repeatedly looking into a particular store window. Convinced that they were "casing" the store for a robbery and might be armed, he stopped them, grabbed one man, patted the outside of his clothing, and felt a gun in the overcoat pocket. Chief Justice Warren approved such a search by an officer provided it was limited to "outer clothing . . . in an attempt to discover weapons which might be used to assault him."[21] But in *Sibron v. New York* (1968), decided the same day, the Court refused to approve a stop and frisk where the officer had no reason to believe the drug suspect he stopped was armed or dangerous. The officer had thrust his hand into the suspect's pocket searching for drugs, which he

[20] The Court also ruled in *Gouled* that, even in a lawful search, the police could seize only illegal articles, such as narcotics, weapons, or fruits of a crime, and not "mere evidence" of crime such as articles of clothing. In 1967 the Court overruled the "mere evidence" rule in *Warden v. Hayden*, holding that the principal object of the Fourth Amendment is the protection of privacy rather than the protection of property.

[21] In a companion case, *Peters v. New York* (1968), the Court upheld a stop and frisk where an officer had found burglar's tools when he frisked for a weapon after grabbing a furtive suspect who tried to flee from him.

found. But, noted Warren, "the police officer is not entitled to seize and search every person whom he sees on the street."[22]

A Burger Court ruling, *Adams v. Williams* (1972), approved a stop and frisk even though it was not based on the officer's personal observation. An informant had advised the officer that a man sitting in a nearby car was carrying narcotics and had a gun at his waist. The officer went to the vehicle and, when the occupant rolled down the window rather than complying with the officer's request to open the door, reached in and seized a loaded gun from the occupant's waistband. Douglas, Brennan, and Marshall dissented.

Entry

Even though armed with a warrant, officers have generally been required to announce and identify themselves before demanding entry into a house.[23] However, they can enter in "hot pursuit" of a suspect and search the house for the felon, the felon's weapons, and the fruits of the crime.[24]

In *Wong Sun v. United States* (1963) an agent, on the basis of information too vague to sustain a request for an arrest warrant, sought entry to a Chinese laundry at 6:00 A.M. by pretending he had some laundry there; after being refused admission he identified himself, broke open the door, and seized the fleeing suspect. The Court by a five to four vote held this to be an unlawful entry and an unauthorized arrest.

By contrast, in *Ker v. California* (1963), officers without warrants but with probable cause to suspect narcotics violations entered an apartment quietly and without announcement, using a passkey supplied by the building manager, because they feared the narcotics would be destroyed if they knocked and demanded entry. By another five to four vote, and apparently because these were state rather than federal officers, this justification for a no-knock intrusion was accepted.

In a "law and order" mood, Congress in 1970 included no-knock provisions in the District of Columbia Court Reform Act and also in the Drug Abuse Prevention and Control Act. After several horrifying incidents in which agents broke into the wrong houses and terrorized occupants, Congress repealed the provision in the drug abuse act.

---

[22]*Brown v. Texas* (1979) held that where an officer stopped a pedestrian and required him to identify himself when there was no reasonable ground for suspecting criminal conduct, this was a "seizure" of the person in violation of the Fourth Amendment.

Kolender v. Lawson (1983) negated a California vagrancy law that allowed police to arrest anyone who "refused to identify himself and to account for his presence" when requested to do so by a peace officer, where public safety reasonably demanded such identification. Lawson, a black man of "unconventional appearance" who liked to walk, was repeatedly detained or arrested in white neighborhoods when he refused to identify himself.

[23]*Miller v. United States* (1958).

[24]*Warden v. Hayden* (1967), *United States v. Santana* (1976).

Entry by Other than Police Officers

Search warrants must be secured by city officials seeking to inspect private premises for possible violations of fire, health, and building regulations, but the warrants do not need to meet the same "probable cause" tests required in a criminal investigation. The Court so held in two 1967 cases, *Camara v. Municipal Court,* where a city public health inspector without a warrant had been refused entrance to an apartment, and *See v. Seattle,* involving an effort to inspect a commercial warehouse under the fire code. In these opinions, decided by a vote of six to three, the Court overruled the earlier five to four holding in *Frank v. Maryland* (1959).[25]

In a controversial opinion, *Wyman v. James* (1971), the Court held by a vote of six to three that mandatory caseworker visits into homes receiving welfare assistance are rehabilitative, not investigative, searches in the traditional criminal law sense, and so the Fourth Amendment does not apply. The visits were made during regular daytime working hours, and forcible entry and snooping were prohibited by law. Justice Marshall, dissenting, said: "A paternalistic notion that a complaining citizen's rights can be violated so long as the State is somehow helping him is alien to our Nation's philosophy."

Automobile Arrests and Searches

The interests of an automobile driver who is stopped and whose car is subjected to a search are three: mobility, which is restrained; control over personal property, which is invaded; and expectations of privacy for the contents of the car, which are breached.[26] Consequently, the Fourth Amendment does apply to automobiles, as the Supreme Court recognized in the leading case of *Carroll v. United States* (1925). However, because the mobility of autos would normally make it impossible to secure search warrants, the Court in *Carroll* upheld stopping and searching without a warrant where there is probable cause to believe that the car will yield contraband or evidence useful for prosecution of crime. In *Carroll* the search was for liquor in enforcement of the national prohibition laws.[27]

The search preceded the arrest in *Carroll.* When occupants of a car are placed under arrest before a search is made, the case for a warrantless search is weaker, for the car no longer has free mobility. Thus in *Preston v. United*

---

[25] *Air Pollution Variance Board v. Western Alfalfa Corp.* (1974) ruled that a government inspector did not need a search warrant to go onto the outdoor property of a manufacturing plant to observe smoke plumes emitted from chimneys.

[26] See "Warrantless Searches and Seizures of Automobiles," 87 HARVARD LAW REVIEW 835 (1974).

[27] See also *Brinegar v. United States* (1949).

States (1964), after arresting a man in his car for vagrancy, the police took custody of the car because they did not want to leave it on the street. The Court held that this gave them no right to search the car.[28] However, *Chambers v. Maroney* (1970) validated an automobile search after the driver's arrest, while the car was in police custody. Justice White claiming that "the mobility of the car . . . still obtained in the station house."

In *Cooper v. California* (1967), the car of a man arrested on narcotics charges was held as evidence pending forfeiture proceedings as required by statute. After holding the car for one week, during which time a warrant could have been obtained, the police searched the car without a warrant. The Supreme Court by a five to four vote ruled that police may search a car, with or without probable cause, if they have a continuing right to possess it.

After an accident, an off-duty Chicago policeman was arrested in Wisconsin for drunken driving, and his car was towed to a private garage. Assuming that as a policeman he was required to carry a gun, officers searched the car for it and instead found evidence of a murder. The Court in *Cady v. Dombrowski* (1973) upheld the search, since its purpose had been benign and not aimed at discovering criminal evidence. A warrantless examination of the exterior of an auto and a taking of exterior paint samples while the car was in a public parking lot was upheld in *Cardwell v. Lewis* (1974). No expectation of privacy was thereby violated.

Delaware v. Prouse (1979) ruled that the police cannot stop an auto for the purpose of checking the driver's license of the operator or the registration of the car when there is neither probable cause to believe nor reasonable suspicion that the car is violating motor vehicle laws or any of its occupants is subject to detention for law violation.[29] But *Pennsylvania v. Mimms* (1977) held that police can compel a driver to get out of the car when stopped for a minor traffic violation; and two 1973 decisions, *United States v. Robinson* and *Gustafson v. Florida,* had opened up alarming possibilities for searching the persons of automobile drivers arrested for minor traffic offenses. A police officer in the District of Columbia made a full custody arrest of an auto driver whom he knew to be driving without a license. The officer frisked the arrestee and pulled from one pocket a cigarette pack, which he opened and found to contain heroin. The *Robinson* decision held this to be a lawful search incident to a lawful arrest. In *Gustafson,* a driver arrested for not having his driver's license in his possession was subjected to a full search, which yielded marijuana. The doctrine of these cases, according to Justice Powell, is that "an individual lawfully subjected to a

---

[28] See also *Whiteley v. Warden* (1971). But *South Dakota v. Opperman* (1976) approved a warrantless search of a glove compartment in a car impounded for parking violations.

[29] *Rakas v. Illinois* (1978) held that passengers cannot challenge police search of a car in which they are riding.

custodial arrest retains no significant Fourth Amendment interest in the privacy of his person."[30]

The constitutional status of articles in automobiles subjected to search has caused the Court great confusion. In 1977 *United States v. Chadwick* held that a footlocker was protected by an expectation of privacy requiring a warrant for its seizure, but an automobile search was only incidentally involved. Much more on point was *Arkansas v. Sanders* (1979), where the Court ruled that, absent any exigent circumstances, the police must first obtain a warrant before opening a suitcase taken from an auto properly stopped and searched for contraband. Justice Powell declared that the *Carroll* "automobile exception" should not be extended to a warrantless search of personal luggage merely because it was located in an auto lawfully stopped by police. "Luggage . . . is inevitably associated with the expectation of privacy."

But the Court's consensus began to erode in *Robbins v. California* (1981). Justice Stewart extended the *Chadwick-Sanders* holdings on luggage to cover any "closed, opaque container" (in this case containing marijuana), which may not be opened without a warrant even if found during a lawful search of an automobile. But two justices concurred only in the result and three dissented. Then on the same day Stewart, for another plurality of four, and with three dissents, held in *New York v. Belton* (1981) that when a policeman had made a lawful custodial arrest he could, as an incident of that arrest, search the passenger compartment of the vehicle and any "containers" therein, whether open or closed. In this case the "container" was the pockets of the defendant's jacket, which when unzipped revealed cocaine.

Stewart's retirement upset the Court's delicate balance, and in *United States v. Ross* (1982) Stevens massed a six-judge majority in support of a new rule intended to end the confusion about types of containers and authority to search. The *Ross* rule states that police officers

> who have legitimately stopped an automobile and who have probable cause to believe that contraband is concealed somewhere within it—may conduct a probing search of compartments and containers within the vehicle whose contents are not in plain view.

Since under the *Carroll* exception no warrant is required, the police "may conduct a search of the vehicle that is as thorough as a magistrate could authorize in a warrant." But, Stevens added, "the probable cause determina-

---

[30] For analyses of the *Robinson* case, see Wayne R. La Faye, "Case-by-Case Adjudication' versus 'Standardized Procedures: The Robinson Dilemma," and James B. White, "The Fourth Amendment as a Way of Talking about People: A Study of Robinson and Matlock," in Philip B. Kurland, ed., *The Supreme Court Review, 1974* (Chicago: University of Chicago Press, 1974), pp. 127-232.

tion must be based on objective facts that could justify the issuance of a warrant by a magistrate and not merely on the subjective good faith of the police officers." The opinion shifted analysis from "the nature of the container" to "the object of the search," and *Robbins* was overruled, along with the portion of *Sanders* on which *Robbins* relied. Marshall, speaking also for Brennan and White, excoriated the ruling:

> The majority today not only repeals all realistic limits on warrantless automobile searches, it repeals the Fourth Amendment warrant requirement itself. By equating a police officer's estimation of probable cause with a magistrate's, the Court utterly disregards the value of a neutral and detached magistrate.

Border and Airline Passenger Searches

Border searches have never been considered subject to the Fourth Amendment. Since 1789, customs officials have been authorized to search, without warrant or demonstration of probable cause, anyone entering the United States. In *Boyd v. United States* (1886), the Court reasoned that since the statute was passed by the same Congress that proposed the Bill of Rights, border searches were never intended to come within the scope of the Fourth Amendment.

The U.S. Border Patrol, finding it impossible to control illegal Mexican immigration by border searches, has regularly conducted roving patrols and maintained fixed inspection checkpoints miles inside California and other border states. *Almeida-Sanchez v. United States* (1973) held, five to four, that the Fourth Amendment prohibits the search of vehicles by roving patrols, without a warrant or probable cause. *United States v. Brignoni-Ponce* (1975) extended this ruling to forbid roving patrols to stop autos for questioning of occupants unless there was reasonable suspicion that they were aliens. *United States v. Ortiz* (1975) applied the same rule to stopping and questioning at fixed checkpoints. Closed by *Ortiz*, the checkpoints were reopened when the Court reversed *Ortiz* in *United States v. Martinez-Fuerte* and *Sifuentes v. United States* (1976), which upheld the stopping of autos at fixed checkpoints for brief questioning of occupants regarding citizenship, without warrants or reason to suspect the occupants of a particular car. It was also constitutional for officers to refer some motorists stopped to a secondary inspection area for further questioning, "even if it be assumed that such referrals are made largely on the basis of apparent Mexican ancestry."[31]

The requirement that airline passengers submit to a search of their baggage and their persons is an obvious challenge to the rule of probable

---

[31] *United States v. Cortez* (1981) held that the training and experience of border patrol officers justified them in stopping a suspicious vehicle and questioning its occupants.

cause. It can be argued that prevention of high-jacking is a compelling interest of such magnitude as to justify the searches, and acquiscence in the searches is practically universal. The Court avoided a ruling on the constitutionality of airport searches in *United States v. Mendenhall* (1980), where federal narcotics agents had stopped a young woman disembarking from a plane who fit a "drug courier profile." They asked her to accompany them to their office, where she submitted to search with no obvious protest. The Court ruled, five to four, that her action had been voluntary and that she had not been "seized" within the meaning of the Fourth Amendment.[32] [But *Florida v. Royer* (1983) rejected an arrest based on the profile.

Supporting the war on drugs, the Court in *United States v. Villamonte-Marquez* (1983) approved the random stopping and boarding of boats on any waters connecting to the open seas. Rehnquist reasoned that because boats were more difficult to apprehend than autos, persons on board were entitled to less constitutional protection than auto passengers.

The Exclusionary Rule

The principal sanction against unconstitutional search and seizure is the "exclusionary rule," which forbids evidence secured in violation of the Fourth Amendment from being used against the defendant in court. The rule has been the subject of intense controversy. There is disagreement as to its justification and its purpose. One theory is that it is intended to act as a deterrent to police misconduct. A second argument is that it preserves the integrity of the courts, for accepting unconstitutionally secured evidence would make them partners in the illegality. Still a third position is that the rule gives effect to a personal constitutional right which the government cannot infringe, and that the rule needs no other justification.[33]

There has been much respectable criticism of the rule. The English do not accept it. The outstanding American authority on evidence, John Wigmore, argues against it. Justice Cardozo thought it unacceptable that "the criminal should go free because the constable has blundered."

The exclusionary rule was first stated by the Supreme Court in a federal case, *Weeks v. United States* (1914). The impression has prevailed that the Court promulgated it there only as a rule of evidence in federal courts, not as a requirement derived from the Fourth Amendment. But in fact Justice Day's opinion for a unanimous Court said explicitly that the

[32] See "The Constitutionality of Airport Searches," 72 MICHIGAN LAW REVIEW 128 (1973); "Reformulating Seizures in Airport Drug Stops and the Fourth Amendment," 69 CALIFORNIA LAW REVIEW 1486 (1981). Canine search for drugs was upheld in *United States v. Place* (1983).

[33] For an eloquent defense of this third position, see Thomas S. Schrock and Robert C. Welsh, "Up from Calandra: The Exclusionary Rule as a Constitutional Requirement," 59 MINNESOTA LAW REVIEW 251 (1974). See also Anthony Amsterdam, "Perspectives on the Fourth Amendment," 58 MINNESOTA LAW REVIEW 349 (1974); John Kaplan, "The Limits of the Exclusionary Rule," 26 STANFORD LAW REVIEW 1027 (1974).

refusal to repress illegally seized evidence was "a denial of the constitutional rights of the accused."

Originally this exclusionary rule applied only if federal agents were the guilty parties in procuring the evidence. If the evidence was illegally secured by state police or stolen by private parties and then turned over to federal officers on a "silver platter," it could be employed in a federal trial. But in *Elkins v. United States* (1960) the Supreme Court by a vote of five to four abandoned the "silver platter" doctrine.

The Supreme Court did not consider whether the exclusionary rule applied in state courts until *Wolf v. Colorado* (1949). As already noted, the Fourth Amendment was there held binding on the states, but six members of the Court voted not to embody the exclusionary rule in the Fourteenth Amendment. Justice Frankfurter, after a survey of practice on this point, concluded that "most of the English-speaking world does not regard as vital . . . the exclusion of evidence thus [illegally] obtained." Accordingly the Court "must hesitate to treat this remedy as an essential ingredient of the right." The sanctions suggested by Frankfurter, if evidence secured by illegal invasion of privacy was nonetheless used in court, were "the remedies of private action and such protection as the internal discipline of the police, under the eyes of an alert public opinion, may afford."

A strong dissent came from Justices Murphy, Rutledge, and Douglas. Justice Holmes had once said that without the exclusion of evidence as a sanction, the Fourth Amendment "might as well be stricken from the Constitution." Now the Court was reversing that view with a "bland citation of 'other remedies.'" Murphy proceeded to demonstrate that these other remedies were either unavailable or unrealistic, and he summed up: "The conclusion is inescapable that but one remedy exists to deter violations of the search and seizure clause. That is the rule which excludes illegally obtained evidence."[34]

The Court's subsequent dilemmas in applying the *Wolf* rule may be illustrated by three decisions. The first, *Rochin v. California* (1952), was a prosecution for illegal possession of narcotics. Having information that Rochin was selling dope, three deputy sheriffs entered his house and forced open his bedroom door. Rochin was sitting on the bed partly dressed, and his common-law wife was in bed. There were two capsules on the nightstand, which Rochin seized and put in his mouth. The deputies jumped on him and tried to extricate the capsules. This failing, they handcuffed him and took him to a hospital, where at the direction of the officers a doctor pumped his stomach and produced the capsules, which contained morphine. The capsules were the chief evidence on which he was convicted.

Justice Frankfurter for a unanimous Court invalidated the conviction.

---

[34] *Haring v. Prosise* (1983) held that a person who pleaded guilty to a crime retained the right to sue police for an unconstitutional search of his home.

The *Wolf* rule would have admitted evidence secured illegally, but the conduct here went beyond any acceptable bounds.

> It is conduct that shocks the conscience. Illegally breaking into the privacy of the petitioner, the struggle to open his mouth and remove what was there, the forcible extraction of his stomach's contents—this course of proceeding by agents of government to obtain evidence is bound to offend even hardened sensibilities. They are methods too close to the rack and the screw to permit of constitutional differentiation.

Next came *Irvine v. California* (1954), where official conduct was also shocking, but not too shocking to permit application of the *Wolf* rule. The police suspected Irvine of illegal bookmaking. In his absence from home, they had a locksmith go there and make a door key. Two days later they entered the house with his key and installed a concealed microphone, boring a hole in the roof through which wires were strung to a neighboring garage, where officers were posted with listening devices. Subsequently they twice reentered the house to move the microphone into better positions. At the trial, the officers were allowed to testify to conversations heard by this method.

The Court majority, Justice Jackson writing the opinion, said that this was "trespass, and probably a burglary," but according to *Wolf* there was no basis for denying the state's right to get a conviction by use of such methods. "We adhere to *Wolf* as stating the law of search-and-seizure cases."

Four justices thought the *Irvine* procedure was unconstitutional regardless of the *Wolf* rule, and Frankfurter, author of *Wolf*, was included in the four. he contended that the *Wolf* ruling did not affect the decision on exclusion of the evidence in this case, because here there was "additional aggravating conduct which the Court finds repulsive," as there had also been in the *Rochin* case. There had been no direct physical violence in *Irvine*, as there had been in *Rochin*, but there had been "a more powerful and offensive control over the Irvines' life," a control which enabled police to hear every word said in a private home for an entire month.

The third case was *Breithaupt v. Abram* (1957). A truck driven by Breithaupt in New Mexico collided with another car and three persons were killed. An almost empty whiskey bottle was found in the truck. Breithaupt, seriously injured, was taken to a hospital unconscious. When liquor was detected on his breath, the police directed a doctor to secure a sample of his blood by use of a hypodermic needle. Testimony regarding the blood test was admitted in evidence at the trial, and an expert gave his opinion that the amount of alcohol found in the blood was sufficient to induce intoxication.

By a six to three vote the Court distinguished these circumstances from those in the *Rochin* case and upheld the conviction. Justice Clark pointed out that blood tests are "routine"; they do not shock the conscience or offend the sense of justice; there is nothing brutal or offensive about them. Intoxication is one of the reasons for the "increasing slaughter on our highways," and the interests of society in reducing these hazards outweigh "so slight an intrusion" on the person.

The Court's effort to distinguish the *Rochin* case was unconvincing, as the three dissenters (Warren, Black, and Douglas) pointed out. In each case the operation was performed by a doctor in a hospital. In each case body fluids were extracted. Both operations are common, "scientific," and cause no lasting ill effects. In both cases evidence that had been obtained from a man on an involuntary basis was used to convict him.

The *Wolf* rule on evidence had apparently emerged unscathed from this series of encounters, but actually its days were numbered. In *Mapp v. Ohio* (1961), the Court by a five to three vote overruled *Wolf*. Cleveland police officers, suspecting that a law violator was hiding in a certain house, broke in the door, manhandled a woman resident, searched the entire premises, and discovered some obscene materials in a trunk. The woman was convicted of possession of these materials. The state court, pointing out that the objects had not been taken from the defendant's person by brutal or offensive physical force (as in *Rochin*), permitted their use in evidence on the basis of *Wolf*. But the Supreme Court disposed of *Wolf*, Justice Clark saying:

> The ignoble shortcut to conviction left open to the State [by *Wolf*] tends to destroy the entire system of constitutional restraints on which the liberties of the people rest. Having once recognized that the right to privacy embodied in the Fourth Amendment is enforceable against the States, and that the right to be secure against rude invasions of privacy by state officers is, therefore, constitutional in origin, we can no longer permit that right to remain an empty promise.

When a new constitutional standard is laid down by the Court, it is generally given retroactive effect. But in *Linkletter v. Walker* (1965) the Court ruled that the *Mapp* doctrine would not be applied to invalidate state criminal convictions that had become final before the decision was rendered. The existence of the *Wolf* rule prior to *Mapp* had had consequences that could not be ignored. "The past cannot always be erased by a new judicial declaration."[35]

The exclusionary rule has continued to be controversial. The general public undoubtedly sees it as one of the "technicalities" of the law that

---

[35] See discussions of the retroactivity issue by G. Gregory Fahlund, "Retroactivity and the Warren Court," 35 JOURNAL OF POLITICS 570 (1973); Ralph A. Rossum, "New Rights and Old Wrongs: The Supreme Court and the Problem of Retroactivity," 23 EMORY LAW JOURNAL 381 (1974); and Paul J. Mishkin, "The High Court, the Great Writ, and the Due Process of Time and Law," 79 HARVARD LAW REVIEW 56 (1965).

handcuffs police and lets criminals go free. But scholars and judges also join in the criticism. In a major article, Dallin H. Oaks concluded that the rule did not deter police misconduct and that it had the negative effects of fostering false testimony by law-enforcement officers, seriously delaying and overloading criminal proceedings and diverting attention from the search for truth on the guilt or innocence of the defendant. But in spite of these weaknesses and disadvantages, Oaks would not abolish the rule "until there is something to take its place. . . . It would be intolerable if the guarantee against unreasonable search and seizure could be violated without practical consequence."[36]

Oaks would replace the exclusionary rule "by an effective tort remedy against the offending officer or his employer. . . . A tort remedy could break free of the narrow compass of the exclusionary rule, and provide a viable remedy with direct deterrent effect upon the police whether the injury party was prosecuted or not." In *Bivens v. Six Unknown Named Agents* (1971), Chief Justice Burger took the same position. Opposing the exclusionary rule, he likewise agreed that it could not be abandoned "until some meaningful alternative can be developed." He recommended that "Congress should develop an administrative or quasijudicial remedy against the government itself to afford compensation and restitution for persons whose Fourth Amendment rights have been violated."

There are two problems with these recommendations. The first is the practical one of drafting and funding a feasible plan of tort remedies, which would present great difficulties. The second is the moral problem of permitting individuals to be convicted of crime by the use of evidence secured in violation of their constitutional rights.

In the meantime, even though no discernible progress was being made toward providing a suitable tort remedy, the Burger Court began to dismantle the exclusionary rule piecemeal. In *United States v. Calandra* (1974), the Court held that the rule did not apply to grand juries and that witnesses could not refuse to answer questions merely because they were prompted by illegally obtained evidence. Justice Brennan, dissenting, had the "uneasy feeling that today's decision may signal that a majority of my colleagues have positioned themselves to . . . abandon altogether the exclusionary rule," and he repeated this concern in *United States v. Peltier* (1975). However, the rule survived a severe test in *Stone v. Powell* (1976), in spite of Justice Powell's expressed doubt that it had much deterrent effect on police, and Burger's severe attack on "this draconian, discredited device."

The exclusionary rule had another narrow escape in *Taylor v. Alabama* (1982), where in a five to four vote Justice O'Connor joined the opposition. The majority, applying the precedents of *Brown v. Illinois*

[36] "Studying the Exclusionary Rule in Search and Seizure," 37 UNIVERSITY OF CHICAGO LAW REVIEW 665 (1970).

(1975) and *Dunaway v. New York* (1979), found a causal connection between an illegal arrest and the subsequent confession which required its exclusion.

The exclusionary rule won another reprieve in *Illinois v. Gates* (1983), where a narcotics arrest warrant had been based in part on an anonymous tip. The Court had called for an unusual second hearing in the case for argument as to whether the rule should be modified to permit the use of evidence secured by police in "good faith" but illegal searches. Later, with "apologies to all," the Court announced the case was not suitable for a holding on the exclusionary rule.

Wiretapping and Electronic Surveillance

When the Supreme Court first confronted the wiretapping problem in *Olmstead v. United States* (1928), it concluded that the Fourth Amendment was not applicable because there had been no trespass on a constitutionally protected area and no physical object had been seized. Federal prohibition agents had secured evidence against a gang of rumrunners by tapping their telephones and recording the conversations, and convictions were secured on the basis of this evidence. The Court majority determined that there had been no actual search and seizure in this case. The agents had never entered the quarters of the suspects, but had done the tapping in the basements of apartment buildings. "The evidence was secured by the use of the sense of hearing and that only."

Justice Holmes, dissenting, noted that wiretapping was a crime in the state of Washington, where these acts occurred, and said that the United States should have no part in such a "dirty business." Justice Brandeis, also dissenting, felt that the conception of a "search" should not be confined to actual physical entry.

> The progress of science in furnishing the Government with means of espionage is not likely to stop with wire-tapping. Ways may some day be developed by which the Government, without removing papers from secret drawers, can reproduce them in court. . . . Advances in the psychic and related sciences may bring means of exploring unexpressed beliefs, thoughts and emotions. . . . Can it be that the Constitution affords no protection against such invasions of individual security?

The Court did, however, point out in *Olmstead* that Congress had power to adopt "controlling legislation" in this field, and in the 1934 Communications Act Congress followed this suggestion by providing that "no person not being authorized by the sender shall intercept any communication and divulge or publish the . . . contents . . . of such intercepted communication to any person." Subsequently the Court in *Nardone v. United States* (1937) held that this law rendered inadmissible in federal trials evidence as to an interstate communication secured by wiretapping. Later the Court extended this interpretation to apply also to intrastate communications and to indirect or derivative use of evidence secured in this fashion.[37]

It might have been expected that the Roosevelt Court, which was so largely guided by the views of Holmes and Brandeis, would have taken the first opportunity to adopt their dissenting position in *Olmstead*. But when the occasion presented itself in *Goldman v. United States* (1942), only Frankfurter, Stone, and Murphy were prepared to do so. Douglas confessed ten years later, in *On Lee v. United States*, that his failure to join them had been an error. Black supported *Olmstead* because of his literalist interpretation of the Fourth Amendment as applying only to tangible objects.

In the *Goldman* case the Court for the first time encountered the practice of electronic eavesdropping or "bugging." No use is made of telephone lines; instead, bugs are planted in locations permitting conversations to be overheard at a distance. In *Goldman* government agents had used a detectaphone sensitive enough to pick up conversations in an adjoining office, the words being heard through the wall with no physical intrusion into the adjacent office. Since *Olmstead* had ruled that words are not protected against seizure, and since there had been no search involving physical trespass, the Court majority held that the Fourth Amendment had not been violated.[38]

The Communications Act did not stop wiretapping. In fact, the Department of Justice, relying on an interpretation of the act by Attorney General Jackson, contended it was not a criminal violation to intercept conversations by wiretapping so long as the results were not used in court. Consequently federal agencies carried on wiretapping on a large scale, though supposedly only with the express consent of the attorney general and principally in cases of national security or where life was in danger.

Continuous efforts were made in Congress to pass legislation authorizing wiretapping, but they all failed. A number of states, however, passed laws permitting wiretapping if authorized in advance by a judge, judicial consent serving as the functional equivalent of a search warrant. But the Supreme Court in *Berger v. New York* (1967) declared a law of this type unconstitutional by a vote of five to four. The wiretapping, each instance of which could continue for two months, was condemned as the equivalent of

---

[37] *Weiss v. United States* (1939) and *Nardone v. United States* (1939). See also *Rathbun v. United States* (1957), *Benanti v. United States* (1957).

[38] If trespass does occur during a bugging operation, then of course it becomes an unconstitutional search and seizure under the *Olmstead-Goldman* doctrine. In *Silverman v. United States* (1961), police officers in the District of Columbia had occupied a vacant house and driven a "spike mike" through the party wall of an adjoining row house. The spike made contact with the heating duct of the house, and all conversations in the house were audible to the officers next door. The Supreme Court held that the projection of the spike into the adjoining house, "by even a fraction of an inch," amounted to an unauthorized physical penetration of a constitutionally protected area.

a series of intrusions persuant to a single showing of probable cause, and with no notice to those overheard. The broad sweep of the Court's language left it uncertain whether any practical wiretap law could be adopted.

The Court quickly reconsidered, however. *Katz v. United States* (1967) outlined a procedure by which wiretapping could be constitutionally employed—namely, prior judicial authorization justified by investigation and a showing of probable cause and for a strictly limited law-enforcement purpose.[39] Equally important, *Katz* finally overruled *Olmstead* and *Goldman*, and abandoned the conception that the Fourth Amendment forbids only physical invasions and physical seizures. What the Fourth Amendment actually protects, said Justice Stewart, is "people, not places. What a person knowingly exposes to the public, even in his own home or office, is not a subject of Fourth Amendment protection. But what he seeks to preserve as private, even in an area accessible to the public, may be constitutionally protected."

In *Katz*, government agents had eavesdropped on a gambler by bugging a public telephone booth that he habitually used to place bets. But the fact that he was in a glass-enclosed booth where he could be readily seen was irrelevant. He was constitutionally entitled to make a private telephone call that would not be broadcast to government agents by a bug on top of the phone booth. The fact that there was no physical penetration of the agents into the phone booth was also irrelevant. The Court, Stewart said, has departed from the "narrow view" of the *Olmstead* case that property interests or technical notions of trespass control the right of the government to search and seize. "The Government's activities in electronically listening to and recording the petitioner's words violated the privacy upon which he justifiably relied while using the telephone booth and thus constituted a 'search and seizure' within the meaning of the Fourth Amendment."

With the support of the *Katz* decision, Congress in the Crime Control Act of 1968 provided for a system of judicially approved wiretapping for certain classes of crime on the request of the attorney general. The provisions were carefully drawn to meet the requirements of *Berger* and *Katz;* applications for consent to wiretap or bug had to be detailed and particularized, and conditions for use of the order were carefully circumscribed.[40] Applications had to be signed by the attorney general or an

---

[39] The Court referred for support to its favorable decision in *Osborn v. United States* (1966), where on the basis of a sworn statement that one of James Hoffa's attorneys had endeavored to bribe a prospective juror, the two federal judges in the district where the trial was being conducted had authorized the use of a tape recorder for the specific and limited purpose of ascertaining the truth of the allegation.

[40] In *United States v. Kahn* (1974) a court-approved wiretap on the phone of a man suspected of gambling yielded information about his wife, who had not been named in the application or suspected of complicity. The Court held that information concerning her was nonetheless validly obtained. For other problems arising in connection with authorized wiretaps, see *United States v. New York Telephone Co.* (1977), *Scott v. United States* (1978), and *United States v. Donovan* (1977).

assistant attorney general specially designated by him for this purpose. However, Attorney General John Mitchell permitted his executive assistant to sign applications, a procedure the Supreme Court held illegal in *United States v. Giordano* (1974), thereby nullifying the prosecution of over six hundred defendants.

Attorney General Mitchell contended that the requirements of the 1968 act did not apply to wiretapping in "national security" investigations, citing a provision in the statute that nothing contained therein should "be deemed to limit the constitutional power of the President" to protect the United States. However, in *United States v. United States District Court* (1972) the Supreme Court unanimously held that this language was not a grant of power, and that so far as domestic security measures were concerned, the prior judicial warrant procedures had to be followed. As already noted, in 1978 Congress created the Foreign Intelligence Surveillance Court to review government requests for electronic surveillance of suspected spies, terrorists, and, in exceptional cases, American citizens with information deemed essential to national security.

Unauthorized national security wiretaps were placed on seventeen newspersons and former government officials by the Nixon administration for twenty-one months between 1969 and 1971. The District of Columbia Court of Appeals ruled that the wiretaps violated both the Fourth Amendment and Title III of the 1968 Crime Control Act, a decision affirmed by the Supreme Court on an equally divided vote (Rehnquist not participating.)[41]

Third-Party Bugging

In *On Lee v. United States* (1952) the Court held admissible statements made by the accused to a supposed friend on his own premises which, through a transmitter concealed on the person of the "friend," were broadcast to a federal agent outside. The Court majority regarded this as simply "eavesdropping on a conversation, with the connivance of one of the parties"; but Justice Frankfurter thought that, like *Olmstead*, it was "dirty business." However, the *On Lee* ruling, to which four justices dissented, was reaffirmed in *Lopez v. United States* (1963). Here a federal agent investigating possible evasion of excise taxes by a restaurant owner was offered a bribe to call off the investigation. The agent returned with a pocket wire recorder on his person and secured a recording that was used at the trial. The Court majority denied this was eavesdropping. The agent was lawfully on the premises, and the recording was simply corroborating evidence of what he had heard with his own ears.

After the new notions of privacy enunciated in *Berger* and *Katz*, it seemed reasonable to conclude that *On Lee* and *Lopez* could not survive.

[41] *Kissinger v. Halperin* (1981).

But in *United States v. White* (1971), the Court accomplished the feat of reconciling *On Lee* with *Katz*, over the protests of Douglas, Harlan, Brennan, and Marshall. Again, a government informant had carried a transmitter on his person that broadcast incriminating statements of the suspect to concealed agents. The Court majority approved this method of supplying "relevant and probative evidence which is also accurate and reliable," but Harlan condemned third-party bugging as violating the general principle that "official investigatory action that impinges on privacy must typically, in order to be constitutionally permissible, be subjected to the warrant requirement."

Private Papers and Records

In *Boyd v. United States* (1886), a proceeding for nonpayment of customs duties, a court order required the production of invoices covering the goods. The Supreme Court declared the statute authorizing this order unconstitutional on the ground that "any forcible and compulsory extortion of a man's . . . private papers . . . to convict him of crime" was a violation of both the Fourth and Fifth Amendments. But under *Andresen v. Maryland* (1976) the Fifth Amendment no longer protects private papers. Moreover, when personal papers are out of the possession of their owner and in the hands of another person who is ordered to surrender them by subpoena, there is no Fourth Amendment protection.

Provisions of the Bank Secrecy Act requiring banks to keep records and make reports on transactions of their clients were held in *California Bankers Assn. v. Shultz* (1974) not to violate the Fourth Amendment, for the government could get access to these records only "by existing legal process." But this turned out to be quite easy. *United States v. Miller* (1976) upheld the government's right to demand from the banks microfilmed copies of checks and deposit slips, for a customer has "no legitimate expectation of privacy when he does business with a bank."[42]

SELF-INCRIMINATION

The Fifth Amendment provides that no one "shall be compelled in any criminal case to be a witness against himself."[43] There has been much diversity of opinion concerning the privilege against self-incrimination. On the one hand, it has been regarded as "one of the great landmarks in man's struggle to make himself civilized."[44] Justice Field said: "The essential and

[42] See the analysis by David M. O'Brien, *Privacy, Law, and Public Policy* (New York: Praeger, 1979), Chapter 2.

[43] See generally Leonard W. Levy, *Origins of the Fifth Amendment* (New York: Oxford University Press, 1968).

[44] Erwin N. Griswold, *The Fifth Amendment Today* (Cambridge, Mass.: Harvard University Press, 1955), p. 7.

inherent cruelty of compelling a man to expose his own guilt is obvious to every one."[45] On the other hand, the privilege was subjected to a classic attack by Jeremy Bentham, and Charles Evans Hughes recommended serious consideration of its abolition.

The first, and most obvious, effect of the Fifth Amendment is that the defendant in a criminal trial cannot be required to take the witness stand. It is improper for the opposing counsel or the judge to call attention to failure of a defendant to take the stand; and *Carter v. Kentucky* (1981) held that whenever a defendant requests it, the judge must instruct the jury that defendant's failure to testify cannot be viewed as evidence of guilt. A defendant who chooses to take the stand risks having damaging evidence brought out on cross-examination.[46]

Before a grand jury, congressional committee, or administrative tribunal, the situation is different. Because there has been no indictment for crime, a person from whom evidence is sought cannot refuse to be a witness; but once on the stand a witness can decline to answer particular questions on the ground of self-incrimination.[47] It is normally very difficult to challenge witnesses who refuse to testify on Fifth Amendment grounds without forcing them to reveal the conduct which the Constitution entitles them to conceal. It is agreed that a witness may refuse to give not only answers that constitute admission of guilt but also those that merely furnish evidence of guilt or supply leads to obtaining such evidence. However, a witness may not refuse to talk when the danger of incrimination is "of an imaginary and unsubstantial character, having reference to some extraordinary and barely possible contingency, so improbable that no reasonable man would suffer it to influence his conduct."[48]

The Fifth Amendment does not justify refusal to testify about matters that would merely impair reputation or tend to disgrace.[49] The Court has held that a witness or defendant who has voluntarily answered some questions may not refuse to answer related questions on the ground of self-incrimination.[50]

An individual who has acquired income in an illegal manner cannot refuse on self-incrimination grounds to make out an income tax return, but

[45] *Brown v. Walker* (1896).

[46] In *Jenkins v. Anderson* (1980) a defendant had taken the stand and testified that he killed in self-defense. To impeach his credibility, the prosecution asked why, if that was true, he had not gone to the police to report the circumstances. The Court held that by taking the stand the defendant had waived any Fifth Amendment objection to use of his prior silence for purposes of impeachment.

[47] Mark Berger, *Taking the Fifth, the Supreme Court, and the Privilege against Self-Incrimination* (Lexington, Mass.: Lexington Books, 1980).

[48] Quoted in *Emspak v. United States* (1955) from an 1861 decision by the Court of Queen's Bench, *The Queen v. Boyes*, 1 B. & S. 311.

[49] *Hale v. Henkel* (1906).

[50] *Rogers v. United States* (1951), *Brown v. United States* (1958).

can refuse to answer incriminating questions concerning it.[51] Even though criminal conduct would be disclosed by the answers, a person may not refuse to testify if the conduct is no longer punishable because the statute of limitations has run or because immunity from prosecution has been granted by statute.

Grant of Immunity

Compatibly with the Fifth Amendment, there is a method of compelling witnesses to testify against themselves. Under appropriate statutory authority, the state can grant immunity from prosecution to persons for any incriminating evidence they may give under compulsion. Immunity is granted by court order on application of prosecuting officials, and if witnesses refuse to testify after being granted immunity, they can be jailed for contempt.[52] Immunity is typically sought for minor criminal suspects whose evidence will help to convict major malefactors.

The first federal immunity statute was upheld by a five to four vote of the Supreme Court in *Brown v. Walker* (1896). The majority admitted that, interpreted literally, the self-incrimination clause authorizes a witness "to refuse to disclose any fact which might tend to incriminate, disgrace or expose him to unfavorable comments," and as so interpreted would render the immunity act unconstitutional. But the Fifth Amendment could also be read as having for its object only "to secure the witness against a criminal prosecution, which might be aided directly or indirectly by his disclosure." The Court regarded this second interpretation as yielding a better balance between private right and public welfare. "If [a witness] secure legal immunity from prosecution, the possible impairment of his good name is a penalty which it is reasonable he should be compelled to pay for the common good."

The frequent blockage of government inquiries into subversion by claims of the privilege against self-incrimination led the Eisenhower administration to propose, and Congress to adopt, the Immunity Act of 1954, under which witnesses can be compelled to testify before courts, grand juries, or congressional committees in national security cases by granting them immunity from prosecution for any criminal activities they may confess. The act was upheld in *Ullmann v. United States* (1956) on the authority of *Brown v. Walker*. Justice Douglas, dissenting with Black, thought that *Brown v. Walker* should be overruled. Under its doctrine, the constitutionally guaranteed privilege of silence was being traded away "for a partial, undefined, vague immunity." The 1954 statute protected individuals from criminal punishment but exposed them to the punishment of

---

[51] *United States v. Sullivan* (1927).
[52] See *United States v. Wilson* (1975).

infamy and disgrace. "My view is that the Framers put it beyond the power of Congress to *compel* anyone to confess his crimes. The evil to be guarded against was partly self-accusation under legal compulsion. But that was only part of the evil. The conscience and dignity of man were also involved."

Until 1970 all immunity statutes granted "transactional immunity"— that is, they entirely barred subsequent prosecution for any "transaction, matter or thing" to which the witness testified. However, the Organized Crime Control Act of 1970 provided for a more limited form of immunity, called "use" or "testimonial" immunity, which only bars use of the witnesses' testimony (or any information derived directly or indirectly from such testimony) in any criminal case. If evidence of crime can be secured independently from the compelled testimony, the witness is not protected from prosecution.

Such partial, as compared with complete, immunity was held not to violate the Fifth Amendment in *Kastigar v. United States* (1972). The Court thought that the witness given use immunity was sufficiently protected because in any subsequent prosecution the state would have to assume "the affirmative duty to prove that the evidence it proposes to use is derived from a legitimate source wholly independent of the compelled testimony." But, as Levy says, these admissions, though technically not incriminating, "are an open invitation for the state to conduct its own investigation against him, secure in the knowledge that he is implicated, if not guilty, by his own admission."[53] Justice Douglas, dissenting in *Kastigar,* said: "Government acts in an ignoble way when it stoops to the end which we authorize today."[54]

Self-Incrimination in State Courts

We have already seen that the Fifth Amendment was long regarded as inapplicable to state prosecutions. Two major decisions, *Twining v. New Jersey* (1908) and *Adamson v. California* (1947), upheld state statutes permitting the drawing of unfavorable inferences from the defendant's failure to take the witness stand. To similar effect was *Feldman v. United States* (1944), where by a four to three vote the Court held that the Fifth Amendment did not protect a person in refusing to give testimony in a hearing before a state body that might lead to a federal prosecution.

Cohen v. Hurley (1961) by a five to four margin held that New York could disbar an attorney who invoked the privilege and refused to testify before a judicially established committee of inquiry looking into "ambu-

---

[53] Leonard W. Levy, op. cit., p. 184, and Chapter 3 generally.

[54] *New Jersey v. Portash* (1979) held that a defendant's testimony before a grand jury under a grant of immunity could not be used to impeach him during his subsequent criminal trial.

lance chasing." The majority held that the attorney's disbarment was based not on the exercise of the self-incrimination privilege but on his refusal to discharge obligations which as a lawyer he owed the court.

But only two months after *Cohen,* the *Mapp* decision began a constitutional revolution that eventually dethroned the "ordered liberty" test and absorbed the major protections of the Bill of Rights into the Fourteenth Amendment. In due course *Malloy v. Hogan* (1964), by another five or four vote, overruled the long-established doctrine of *Twining* and *Adamson.* Justice Brennan for the majority wrote: "The Twining view of the privilege has been eroded. . . . It would be incongruous to have different standards determine the validity of a claim of privilege . . . depending on whether the claim was asserted in a state or federal court."

Justice Harlan, one of the dissenters, agreed that principles of justice inherent in due process should forbid a state to imprison a person solely because he refused to give evidence that might incriminate him. But he objected to the majority's "wholesale incorporation" of federal requirements into the Fourteenth Amendment, for this would make applicable to the states the entire body of federal law that had grown up in this field, in inevitable "disregard of all relevant differences which may exist between state and federal criminal law and its enforcement."

On the same day that *Malloy* was decided, the Court overruled *Feldman* and held in *Murphy v. Waterfront Commission of New York Harbor* (1964) that evidence which a person was compelled to give before a state tribunal under guarantee of immunity from state prosecution could not be used against him in a federal prosecution. The basis for the *Feldman* decision, questionable enough when it was handed down in 1944, had been completely undercut by the *Elkins* ruling that evidence illegally seized by state officials could not be used in federal courts.

One week after *Malloy* and *Murphy,* the Warren Court handed down its famous decision in *Escobedo v. Illinois* (1964). While *Escobedo* and its even more famous twin, *Miranda v. Arizona* (1966), have a bearing on self-incrimination, they are more appropriately discussed in connection with the right to counsel. The *Malloy-Murphy* holdings were given effect in a number of later Warren Court cases. Self-incrimination was one of the protections extended to juvenile court proceedings in *In re Gault* (1967). *Spevack v. Klein* (1967) overruled *Cohen v. Hurley,* holding that lawyers were as much entitled to protection against self-incrimination as other persons, and should not have to suffer "the dishonor of disbarment and the deprivation of a livelihood as a price for asserting it."[55]

[55] In *Garrity v. New Jersey* (1967), a companion case to *Spevack v. Klein,* the Court ruled that where police officers were given the choice of incriminating themselves or forfeiting their jobs and pension rights, and they chose to make confessions, the confessions were not voluntary and could not be used in subsequent criminal prosecutions in state courts. *Lefkowitz v. Cunningham* (1977) held unconstitutional a New York statute under which an attorney who refused to waive immunity when subpoenaed to appear before a special grand jury was divested of his state political party offices.

A line of cases going back to Justice Holmes holds that compelled identification of suspects through physical characteristics is not self-incrimination. In *Holt v. United States* (1910) he wrote that the Fifth Amendment prohibited "the use of physical or moral compulsion to extort communication . . . not an exclusion of [the] body as evidence when it would be material." *Schmerber v. California* (1966) upheld compulsory blood tests for drunken drivers involved in accidents, and *South Dakota v. Neville* (1983) ruled that a state can use a driver's refusal to take a blood alcohol test in a prosecution for drunk driving. *United States v. Wade* (1967) approved requiring a suspect in a lineup to speak before witnesses to a bank robbery the words used by the robber. In *Gilbert v. California* (1967) another suspected bank robber had to submit a handwriting sample for comparison with a note given to a bank teller during a robbery. *United States v. Dionisio* (1973) ruled that the Fifth Amendment did not protect a person from a court order to make a voice recording to be played before a federal grand jury seeking to identify a criminal by the sound of a voice on a legally intercepted phone conversation. The rationale in all these cases was that the Fifth Amendment by its reference to "witness" was intending to cover only "testimonial" evidence—that is, communication of information based on one's own knowledge.

California v. Byers (1971) upheld a hit-and-run law requiring a motorist involved in an accident to stop at the scene and give name and address. And *United States v. Washington* (1977) ruled that it was not self-incrimination when the government used, in a trial, evidence before a grand jury given by a witness who was suspected of wrongdoing but had not been warned in advance that he was a potential defendant in danger of indictment. But *Estelle v. Smith* (1981) held that the defendant in a capital case should have been warned before consenting to a psychiatric examination that the results might be used against him in fixing his sentence.

Private Papers and Records

Boyd v. United States (1886) held that "the seizure of a man's private books and papers to be used against him is [not] substantially different from compelling him to be a witness against himself."[56] But subsequent decisions have undermined *Boyd* and made it clear that only personal compulsion of the accused is forbidden.[57] The Fifth Amendment does not prevent the government from violating an accused's claims of privacy for books or papers in the possession of another person. Thus *Couch v. United States*

---

[56] With respect to the production of records, *Boyd* held that the Fourth and Fifth Amendments "run almost into each other."

[57] *Hale v. Henkel* (1906), *Johnson v. United States* (1913), *Perlman v. United States* (1918).

(1973) held that a taxpayer who regularly turned her business and tax records over to an independent accountant had divested herself of the records to such a degree that she could not resist a government subpoena to the accountant for production of the records in a tax investigation. Similarly, *Fisher v. United States* (1976) upheld a subpoena requiring an attorney to surrender records prepared by the taxpayer's accountant. The Fifth Amendment, said White, "protects a person only against being incriminated by his own compelled testimonial communications." *Andresen v. Maryland* ruled that there is no self-incrimination if a person's handwritten notes and business records are secured by a search warrant rather than by subpoena.

Hale v. Henkel (1906) held that a corporation cannot resist a subpoena on Fifth Amendment grounds, though it may do so on the basis of the Fourth Amendment. Nor can a custodian of corporate or labor union books withhold them on the ground of possible personal incrimination by their production.[58]

COERCED CONFESSIONS

The Fifth Amendment forbids the use in federal courts of confessions secured under conditions of physical or mental coercion, for in such cases defendants would obviously have been under compulsion to testify against themselves.[59] In recent years additional limitations have been placed by the Supreme Court upon the use of confessions in federal prosecutions.

Federal statutes require suspects on apprehension to be taken before the nearest judicial officer "without unnecessary delay" for hearing, commitment, or release on bail. When suspects are taken before a committing magistrate, the law officers must show probable cause for the arrests, and the suspects must be informed of their right to remain silent and to have counsel. The motive of the police in delaying this process is usually to attempt to secure a confession before suspects learn of their rights.[60]

In *McNabb v. United States* (1943) two men suspected of shooting a revenue officer were taken into custody by federal officials and questioned over a period of two days, without the presence of friends or counsel, until a confession was secured. The Supreme Court voided the conviction, not on the ground that the confession was coerced, but because of violation of the "without unnecessary delay" provision.

---

[58] *Wilson v. United States* (1911), *United States v. White* (1944). Similarly, public documents must be produced by the official in possession though they tend to incriminate (*Shapiro v. United States* [1948]).

[59] *Bram v. United States* (1897).

[60] Since the *Escobedo* and *Miranda* decisions, of course, suspects must be informed of these rights as soon as they are arrested or subjected to interrogation.

There was considerable criticism of the *McNabb* rule as placing a substantial impediment in the path of law enforcement, but the Court reaffirmed it in *Mallory v. United States* (1957). This decision, which voided a death sentence for rape in the District of Columbia, set off a concerted effort in Congress to revise the *McNabb* rule by new legislation providing that a confession or other evidence otherwise admissible should not be excluded solely because of delay in the arraignment. These initial efforts failed, but in 1967 Congress passed an act revising the *McNabb-Mallory* rule by permitting police in the District of Columbia to detain suspects for up to three hours of interrogation before having them arraigned.

Coerced Confessions in State Courts

Confessions extorted by force and violence are contrary to the most elemental notions of due process and any convictions based on them are void. The Supreme Court was first confronted with such a situation in *Brown v. Mississippi* (1936). The facts of brutality and torture by state officers were uncontroverted, and no evidence other than the coerced confessions of murder was presented at the trial. The state's defense was the *Twining* argument that immunity from self-incrimination was not an essential element in due process of law. Chief Justice Hughes replied for a unanimous Court that *Twining* simply gave a state some freedom to experiment with the procedures of criminal prosecution. But that freedom is "the freedom of constitutional government and is limited by the requirement of due process of law. Because a State may dispense with a jury trial, it does not follow that it may substitute trial by ordeal. The rack and torture chamber may not be substituted for the witness stand."

More difficult questions arise where confessions are secured by coercion that is mental rather than physical. At first the Court was reluctant to move against psychological coercion.[61] But in *Ashcraft v. Tennessee* (1944) a Court majority adopted the rule of "inherent coerciveness." Ashcraft had been convicted of murder on a confession elicited by thirty-six hours of continuous questioning under electric lights by relays of officers, investigators, and lawyers. Such a situation was held to be "so inherently coercive that its very existence is irreconcilable with the possession of mental freedom by a lone suspect against whom the full coercive force is brought to bear."

This stand against psychological coercion was generally maintained in subsequent decisions, though usually by a divided Court.[62] To give only one example, *Fikes v. Alabama* (1957) involved a black of low mentality who

---

[61] *Lisenba v. California* (1941).

[62] *Malinski v. New York* (1945), *Haley v. Ohio* (1948), *Watts v. Indiana* (1949), *Turner v. Pennsylvania* (1949), *Harris v. South Carolina* (1949), and *Leyra v. Denno* (1953) were all decided by five to four votes.

had been kept incommunicado for a week, had not been arraigned, and had been questioned intermittently. Justice Frankfurter's conclusion for the Court was that none of these circumstances standing alone would justify a reversal, but that "in combination they bring the result below the Plimsoll line of 'due process.'"

Whether a confession was voluntary or coerced must be decided without reference to its probable truth. The Court briefly departed from this rule in *Stein v. New York* (1953), which assumed that involuntary confessions are excluded solely because they are untrustworthy and that if there is independent evidence of the reliability of a confession it need not be rejected because it was involuntary. However, the Court rejected this view in *Rogers v. Richmond* (1961), and overruled *Stein* in *Jackson v. Denno* (1964). The latter decision held that the voluntariness of a decision must be determined prior to its admission into evidence before the jury.[63]

As the *Fikes* case indicated, the Court at that time, contrary to the *McNabb-Mallory* rule in the federal courts, did not regard confessions secured while a suspect was illegally detained by the police as unconstitutional for that reason alone. A divided Court upheld confessions secured between arrest and arraignment in *Gallegos v. Nebraska* (1951), *Stroble v. California* (1952), and *Brown v. Allen* (1953). In the latter case a preliminary hearing was not given until eighteen days after the arrest.

In 1958 the question was first raised as to whether a confession would be regarded as coerced that was secured after a suspect had been denied the opportunity to consult a lawyer during his questioning by the police. In *Crooker v. California* (1958) and *Cicenia v. La Gay* (1958), the Court treated this as a denial of counsel rather than as a coercion issue, and by votes of five to four and five to three in the two cases held that denial of access to counsel did not automatically invalidate the confessions. These decisions were reversed in *Escobedo v. Illinois* (1964), which along with the related case of *Miranda v. Arizona* (1966) will be discussed in the following section.

THE RIGHT TO COUNSEL

In establishing an accused person's right to have "the assistance of counsel for his defense," the Sixth Amendment represented an important advance over common-law practices. The actual wording of the amendment implies that the assistance of counsel is a privilege of which the accused has a right to avail himself, but not a mandatory feature of all criminal trials. In the Federal Crimes Act of 1790, Congress imposed a statutory duty on the courts

---

[63] See also *Sims v. Georgia* (1967). In *Lego v. Twomey* (1972), the Court held that the voluntariness of a confession may be determined by the preponderance of evidence; it need not be established by the stricter standard of proof beyond a reasonable doubt.

to assign counsel to represent the defendant in capital cases, from which it could be logically implied that there was no such obligation in other types of cases. Up until 1938 it was the general understanding that where persons desired counsel, but for lack of funds or any other reason were not able to obtain counsel, the court was under no obligation in a noncapital case to secure counsel for them.

The Supreme Court abruptly and decisively changed this rule in *Johnson v. Zerbst* (1938), a counterfeiting prosecution in which it held that "the Sixth Amendment withholds from federal courts, in all criminal proceedings, the power and authority to deprive an accused of his life or liberty unless he has or waives the assistance of counsel." The Court justified this new interpretation of the amendment by adding that the "right to be heard would be, in many cases, of little avail if it did not comprehend the right to be heard by counsel." The right to counsel can be waived, but the waiver must be intelligent and understanding, and judicial determination on this point depends "upon the particular facts and circumstances . . . including the background, experience, and conduct of the accused."[64]

Right to Counsel in State Trials

The Supreme Court first considered the issue of right to counsel in state court trials in the famous First Scottsboro case, *Powell v. Alabama* (1932).[65] The case involved seven black youths, ignorant and illiterate, who were charged with the rape of two white girls in an open gondola car of a freight train passing through Alabama. They were taken from the train near Scottsboro and jailed there. Public excitement was high, and they were guarded by state militia at all stages of the proceedings. At the arraignment they pleaded not guilty. They were not asked whether they had, or were able to employ, counsel, or wished to have counsel appointed. The presiding judge did appoint "all the members of the bar" as counsel for the purpose of arraigning the defendants, but this "expansive gesture" produced no results.

The first case came to trial with no counsel for the defense. As the trial began an out-of-state lawyer said some people had asked him to come down, and that he would be willing to appear along with local counsel that the court might appoint. A member of the local bar then agreed that he would help the out-of-state lawyer. As the Supreme Court subsequently noted:

> With this dubious understanding, the trials immediately proceeded. The defendants, young, ignorant, illiterate, surrounded by hostile sentiment, haled

---

[64] See *Von Moltke v. Gillies* (1948). In *Faretta v. California* (1975), the Court held that a competent person accused of crime has a constitutional right to reject free, court-appointed legal assistance and conduct his or her own defense. *Middendorf v. Henry* (1976) held that persons in the armed services have no right to counsel at a summary court-martial.

[65] See Dan T. Carter, *Scottsboro: A Tragedy of the American South* (Baton Rouge: Louisiana State University Press, 1969).

back and forth under guard of soldiers, charged with an atrocious crime regarded with especial horror in the community where they were to be tried, were thus put in peril of their lives within a few moments after counsel for the first time charged with any degree of responsibility began to represent them.

The state supreme court ruled that this arrangement met the requirements of the state constitution. The Supreme Court, however, said that did not decide the matter under the Fourteenth Amendment. "The right to the aid of counsel," wrote Justice Sutherland, is of a "fundamental character." In this country, "historically and in practice," a hearing has always included "the right to the aid of counsel when desired and provided by the party asserting the right." The Court went on to indicate why this should be so:

> The right to be heard would be, in many cases, of little avail if it did not comprehend the right to be heard by counsel. Even the intelligent and educated layman has small and sometimes no skill in the science of law. If charged with crime, he is incapable, generally, of determining for himself whether the indictment is good or bad. He is unfamiliar with the rules of evidence. Left without the aid of counsel he may be put on trial without a proper charge, and convicted upon incompetent evidence, or evidence irrelevant to the issue or otherwise inadmissible. He lacks both the skill and knowledge adequately to prepare his defense, even though he have a perfect one. He requires the guiding hand of counsel at every step in the proceedings against him. Without it, though he be not guilty, he faces the danger of conviction because he does not know how to establish his innocence.

All these factors would operate even with literate and informed defendants. Considering all the additional prejudicial circumstances in this case, the Court was clear that "the failure of the trial court to give . . . reasonable time and opportunity to secure counsel was a clear denial of due process."

But the Court did not stop there. If these defendants were unable to get counsel, even though opportunity were offered, then the due process clause required the trial court "to make an effective appointment of counsel." This was new law, and so it was natural that the Court should state careful limits for the new principle:

> Whether this would be so in other criminal prosecutions, or under other circumstances, we need not determine. All that it is necessary now to decide, as we do decide, is that in a capital case, where the defendant is unable to employ counsel, and is incapable adequately of making his own defense because of ignorance, feeble-mindedness, illiteracy, or the like, it is the duty of the court, whether requested or not, to assign counsel for him as a necessary requisite of due process of law; and that duty is not discharged by an assignment at such a time or under such circumstances as to preclude the giving of effective aid in the preparation and trial of the case.

To an unusual degree the principle of the *Powell* case was tied to the individual circumstances of that case. In *Betts v. Brady* (1942) the circumstances were different and the Court's holding was different. Betts, under indictment for robbery in Maryland, requested the court to appoint counsel for him, since he was financially unable to secure legal aid. The judge refused, on the ground that it was not the practice in that county to appoint counsel for indigent defendants except in murder and rape prosecutions. The trial proceeded before the judge, acting without a jury.

Bett's contention was that the *Powell* case required appointment of counsel in all state criminal cases. Justice Roberts, who spoke for the Supreme Court, admitted there was some ground for such a conclusion in the *Powell* opinion, but pointed out that the actual holding in the case had been limited to its specific facts. The question whether the *Powell* rule applied to all criminal cases was therefore a new one. "Is the furnishing of counsel in all cases whatever dictated by natural, inherent, and fundamental principles of fairness?"

The Court then proceeded to make the same kind of examination of the constitutions and statutes of the original states which, as applied in *Powell*, had resulted in the conclusion that aid of counsel "when desired and provided by the party asserting the right" was a fundamental requirement of a fair hearing. However, the Court's conclusion as to the mandatory *furnishing* of counsel was that "in the great majority of the States, it has been the considered judgment of the people, their representatives and their courts that appointment of counsel is not a fundamental right, essential to a fair trial. On the contrary, the matter has generally been deemed one of legislative policy." Whereas in *Powell* the Court had pointed out the great disadvantages any layman would encounter without legal guidance in a court of law, here Roberts said the defendant was "of ordinary intelligence and ability to take care of his own interests on the trial of [a] narrow issue." Therefore no constitutional error had been made.

Justice Black was joined by Douglas and Murphy in a vigorous dissent against this holding. Black of course believed that the Sixth Amendment was incorporated in the Fourteenth, but he was willing to argue the matter on the ground of fundamental fairness chosen by the majority, saying: "A practice cannot be reconciled with 'common and fundamental ideas of fairness and right,' which subjects innocent men to increased dangers of conviction merely because of their poverty." The majority opinion had admitted that in eighteen states the statutes required the courts to appoint in all cases where defendants were unable to procure counsel, and "any other practice seems to me to defeat the promise of our democratic society to provide equal justice under the law."

State counsel cases continued to come to the Court in unusual numbers, well over twenty in the decade following *Betts v. Brady*. The Court under the *Betts* rule had to consider the "special circumstances" in each case to determine whether the denial of counsel had amounted to a constitutional defect in the trial.[66] In several instances absence of counsel was held unobjectionable even though the possibility of serious unfairness seemed to exist.[67] But in most cases the Court did find that the circumstances required the furnishing of counsel. This was generally true, for example, where the offense was a capital one;[68] where the conduct of the trial judge appeared to be questionable;[69] where the defendant was young or ignorant or otherwise handicapped;[70] or where the points of law involved were too technical for a layman to grasp.[71] In fact, after 1950 the Supreme Court never affirmed a state criminal conviction where denial of counsel was claimed.

Clearly the Court was moving toward a firmer position on the necessity for counsel in state trials. Finally, in the celebrated case of *Gideon v. Wainwright* (1963) the Court overruled *Betts v. Brady* and held that representation by counsel is a constitutional necessity in all state criminal trials.[72] Justice Black wrote the opinion in *Gideon,* and thus had the opportunity to turn his *Betts* dissent into the law of the Constitution. Gideon was an uneducated ne'er-do-well who, convicted of a minor crime in Florida without the assistance of counsel, stubbornly and unaided from his prison cell drafted a petition printed painfully with pencil on lined paper to the Supreme Court. The Court agreed to hear his claim and appointed a member of a leading Washington law firm, Abe Fortas, who in 1965 was himself to be appointed to the Court, to represent Gideon.

The Court was unanimous in concluding that the right to counsel was fundamental and essential to a fair trial. In fact, twenty-two states had filed briefs as friends of the Court arguing for this position, while only two states had come forward to support Florida's position. Even Justice Harlan agreed that the "special circumstances" rule had been "substantially and steadily eroded" and that *Betts* should be overruled; he only objected that it was entitled to "a more respectful burial" than Justice Black had given it.[73] The

---

[66] For an interesting analysis of the factors considered by the Court in making these decisions, see Fred Kort, "Predicting Supreme Court Decisions Mathematically: A Quantitative Analysis of the Right to Counsel Cases," 51 AMERICAN POLITICAL SCIENCE REVIEW 1 (1957).

[67] See *Canizio v. New York* (1946), *Bute v. Illinois* (1948).

[68] See *Tomkins v. Missouri* (1945).

[69] See *Townsend v. Burke* (1948) and *White v. Ragen* (1945).

[70] See *De Meerleer v. Michigan* (1947), *Marino v. Ragen* (1947), *Moore v. Michigan* (1957).

[71] See *Rice v. Olson* (1945).

[72] This decision is the subject of a fascinating book by Anthony Lewis, *Gideon's Trumpet* (New York: Random House, 1964).

[73] See Jerold H. Israel, "Gideon v. Wainwright: The 'Art' of Overruling," in Philip B. Kurland, ed., *The Supreme Court Review: 1963* (Chicago: University of Chicago Press, 1963), pp. 211–72. The decision was given retroactive effect because, as later explained in *Linkletter v. Walker* (1965), the principle applied in *Gideon* "went to the fairness of the trial—the very integrity of the fact-finding process," and there could be no assurance that a defendant convicted without the aid of counsel had received a fair trial.

decision was generally well received in the legal profession, and programs for supplying counsel to indigent defendants were promptly inaugurated or existing programs improved throughout most of the states.

Escobedo and Miranda

The issue in the famous case of *Escobedo v. Illinois* (1964) had to do with the right to counsel in the pretrial period, but the concerns expressed by the Court in *Escobedo* about abuses of police investigatory methods led to a full-fledged examination of that problem in *Miranda v. Arizona* (1966). These two decisions have had a major impact on subsequent thinking about criminal procedure.

As already noted, the Court denied in two 1958 cases, *Crooker v. California* and *Cicenia v. La Gay,* the right of suspects to consult counsel during police interrogation "irrespective" of the particular circumstances involved. An "inflexible rule" of this sort, the Court said in *Cicenia,* would be inconsistent with the latitude the states needed in administering their systems of criminal justice.

The "special circumstances" rule, however, was to suffer the same fate here as in *Gideon.* The process began in *Spano v. New York* (1959), where the Court ruled that counsel could not be denied a defendant after indictment.[74] But the major decision came five years later. Escobedo, under suspicion of murder, was questioned intensively by police officers who repeatedly denied his request to see his attorney and likewise rebuffed the persistent attempts of the attorney to see his client. Escobedo was not informed of his right to refuse to answer police questions, and eventually he made a confession.

The Supreme Court, having already agreed in *Spano* that counsel could not be denied after indictment, now concluded by a vote of five to four that no "meaningful distinction" could be drawn between interrogation before and after formal indictment. Justice Goldberg spoke for the Court majority:

> We hold, therefore, that where, as here, the investigation is no longer a general inquiry into an unsolved crime but has begun to focus on a particular suspect, the suspect has been taken into police custody, the police carry out a process of interrogations that lends itself to eliciting incriminating statements, the suspect has requested and been denied an opportunity to consult with his lawyer, and the police have not effectively warned him of his absolute constitutional right to remain silent, the accused has been denied "the assistance of counsel" in violation of the Sixth Amendment to the Constitution

---

[74]*Massiah v. United States* (1964), a federal narcotics case, followed *Spano* in holding that the securing of incriminating statements from a defendant under indictment, by a ruse of government agents that involved electronic eavesdropping, was a denial of the right to counsel under the Sixth Amendment.

as "made obligatory upon the States by the Fourteenth Amendment," *Gideon v. Wainwright . . .* and that no statement elicited by the police during the interrogation may be used against him at a criminal trial.

Justice Goldberg took account of objections that this rule would greatly reduce the number of confessions secured because, as Justice Jackson had once said, "any lawyer worth his salt will tell the suspect in no uncertain terms to make no statement to police under any circumstances." Goldberg replied that "no system worth preserving" should have to fear that an accused would be made aware of his constitutional rights. Moreover, officers could still gather evidence from witnesses and undertake other "proper investigative efforts." The Court's holding was only that "when the process shifts from investigatory to accusatory—when its focus is on the accused and its purpose is to elicit a confession—our adversary system begins to operate, and, under the circumstances here, the accused must be permitted to consult with his lawyer."

The *Escobedo* ruling was clear evidence of the Supreme Court's great concern about police abuses in interrogating suspects and its belief in the virtues of the adversary process, the protections of which it was extending from the trial to the pretrial period. *Escobedo* also represented an effort to substitute an objective test for the constitutionality of interrogation in place of the subjective, balancing, case-by-case examination of circumstances that the Court had been forced into in its previous decisions.

But *Escobedo* left may questions unanswered. When did warning of their rights have to be given to suspects? Did *Escobedo* preclude any questioning at all in the absence of counsel? Must counsel be supplied for indigents or others unable to secure counsel? And did *Escobedo* operate retroactively to invalidate every prior prosecution where conviction had been secured in violation of its standards? *Escobedo* quickly became the focus of a nationwide debate on law enforcement and the whipping boy of all who blamed the increase in crime on the "coddling of criminals" by such Court decisions.

The Supreme Court took an important step toward clarifying its standards and stepping up its war on police abuses in *Miranda v. Arizona* (1966) and three companion cases, all involving the use of confessions obtained by police interrogation without informing the suspects of their right to remain silent and to see counsel. The Court reversed the convictions in all these cases by a vote of five to four, on the ground that incommunicado police detention is inherently coercive. In the process it laid down a stiff code of conduct for police interrogation, including the following requirements:

1. Persons held in custody for interrogation must first be informed in clear and unequivocal terms that they have the right to remain silent.
2. They must be warned that anything they say can and will be used against them in court.

3. They must be given the right to consult with counsel prior to questioning and to have counsel present during questioning if they desire.
4. Failure to request counsel does not constitute a waiver of the right to have counsel.
5. If the accused is unable to secure a lawyer, one must be appointed.

The *Miranda* decision added new fuel to the flames started by *Escobedo*. Many law-enforcement officers contended that the new rules would make it impossible any longer to solve crimes by securing confessions. On the other hand, it was argued that police have concentrated on confessions because that is easier than going out to look for evidence, and that *Miranda* would force them to do a more creative job. Also, several studies purported to show that confessions are not presently involved in the great majority of convictions.

Some commentators who shared the Court's goals were nonetheless critical of the *Miranda* decision, on the ground that the Court had undertaken the essentially legislative task of adopting a complete code of law-enforcement procedures, a responsibility which belongs to legislatures, and on which substantial progress was being made in some areas. But the Supreme Court obviously felt that police malpractices were so widespread that the normal procedure of criticizing past abuses in individual cases was inadequate to correct them, and that consequently it must spell out in detail a code of constitutional conduct for the police. Chief Justice Warren gave assurance that the decision was not intended to hamper the traditional function of police officers in investigating crime; persons not under restraint could be questioned; any statements freely and voluntarily given would be admissible in evidence. He also suggested that the role of confessions in securing convictions had been overplayed; in all four of these cases there was very good evidence against the suspects besides the confessions. Finally, he encouraged "Congress and the States to continue their laudable search for increasingly effective ways of protecting the rights of the individual while promoting efficient enforcement of our criminal laws."

One week after *Miranda*, the Court held in *Johnson v. New Jersey* (1966) that neither the *Escobedo* nor the *Miranda* decision was to be applied retroactively. Law-enforcement agencies had fairly relied on prior cases in obtaining incriminating statements during the years preceding these two cases, and retroactivity in their application would serious disrupt administration of the criminal laws, the Court held; but they would apply to prosecutions begun after the cases were announced. For persons whose trials were already completed, the case law on coerced confessions would still be available as a basis for appeals.[75]

---

[75] See comments on the decision by Yale Kamisar, ["A Dissent from the *Miranda* Dissents," 65 MICHIGAN LAW REVIEW 59 (1966); Neil T. Romans,] "The Role of State Supreme Courts in Judicial Policy Making: *Escobedo, Miranda* and the Use of Judicial Impact Analysis," 27 WESTERN POLITICAL QUARTERLY 38 (1974).

In subsequent cases the Warren Court, in spite of violent criticism from many quarters, stood by the position taken in *Escobedo* and *Miranda* and even extended it. *United States v. Wade* (1967) and *Gilbert v. California* (1967) held that a defendant must have counsel present if required to take part in a police lineup for identification before trial. *Mempa v. Rhay* (1967) ruled that a probationer was entitled to be represented by appointed counsel at a combined probation revocation and sentencing hearing. *Mathis v. United States* (1968) held that a defendant who was questioned by an internal revenue agent while imprisoned in a state jail was entitled to *Miranda*-type warnings and to presence of counsel. *Coleman v. Alabama* (1970) ruled that a preliminary court hearing to determine whether there was sufficient evidence to warrant presenting the case to the grand jury was a critical stage of the criminal process, where those accused were entitled to counsel.[76]

Attacks on *Miranda* peaked during the 1968 "law and order" political campaign. Congress in the 1968 Crime Control Act undertook to restore to judges the right to decide on the admissibility of confessions on the basis of the "totality of circumstances" rather than on adherence to the *Miranda* rules. Specifically, the statute provided that confessions were admissible in federal courts if the trial judge found them "voluntary" (limiting *Miranda*) and despite delay in arraignment (repealing *Mallory*); it made eyewitness testimony admissible even if the defendant did not have counsel during a police lineup (reversing *Wade*).

The Burger Court was by no means hostile to the right to counsel.[77] In fact, in *Argersinger v. Hamlin* (1972), the Court unanimously extended *Escobedo* to require counsel in misdemeanors and petty offenses if imprisonment for any length of time was possible. But the Burger Court did deny a right to counsel claim in several instances. Thus, in *Kirby v. Illinois* (1972), counsel was held not to be required in an identification lineup conducted before indictment; *Wade* was distinguished because there the lineup was after indictment. *United States v. Ash* (1973) more directly attacked *Wade* by ruling that counsel was not required when the prosecution, after indictment, conducted a photographic display containing the defendant's picture to determine whether witnesses to the crime could identify him.

As for *Miranda*, the Crime Control Act covered only federal courts and the District of Columbia, leaving it fully applicable to the states. But in *Harris v. New York* (1971), the Court by a five to four vote made a substantial inroad on *Miranda* by holding that a statement inadmissible in the prosecution's case, because no *Miranda* warning had been given, was

---

[76] But a magistrate's determination of probable cause to charge a person arrested without a warrant is not a critical stage requiring appointed counsel (*Gerstein v. Pugh* [1975]).

[77] See Levy, op cit., Chapter 4.

nonetheless usable for impeachment of the defendant's testimony should the defendant take the witness stand.[78]

The counsel issue continues to be very controversial and the decisions go both ways, depending largely on the fact situations. In *Brewer v. Williams* (1977) the Court held five to four that a man convicted of a brutal child murder must be retried because police had induced him in the absence of counsel to lead them to the victim's body. Burger attacked the decision as "intolerable" and "weird." *Estelle v. Smith* (1981) unanimously voided a death sentence; the Court held that the defendant should have been warned in advance of his consent to a psychiatric examination, held to determine whether he was competent to stand trial, that the results might be used against him in determining his sentence and that he had a right to consult an attorney before agreeing to such an interview. *Edwards v. Arizona* (1981) ruled that police may not continue to interrogate a suspect who has asked for an attorney.

On the other hand, *Oregon v. Mathiason* (1977) held that a suspect who went to the police station voluntarily and was not under arrest could be questioned without being given the *Miranda* warning. In *California v. Prysock* (1981) the Court said that police officers need not read the precise words of the *Miranda* warning before questioning a suspect, so long as they make it clear the suspect has a right to a lawyer. *Fare v. Michael C.* (1979) upheld police who continued to interrogate a juvenile suspect in their custody after he asked to speak to his probation officer. *United States v. Mandujano* (1976) held that the *Miranda* rules do not extend to witnesses before grand juries, even though they are criminal suspects.

Plea Bargaining and Effective Representation by Counsel

Plea bargaining is the practice under which, by agreement between prosecutor and defendant's counsel, the defendant enters a plea of guilty to a lesser charge than the one originally made. The state's interest is in avoiding a long and expensive trial. If all criminal charges had to proceed to trial, the court system would be hopelessly overloaded. The defendant's interest in a reduced sentence may seem obvious, but the price is great. It involves forfeiting the Fifth Amendment right against self-incrimination; the Sixth Amendment rights to public trial, confrontation, and presentation of witnesses; and possibly the Fourth Amendment right to have unlawfully seized evidence excluded. Pressures brought on the defendant by threat of a

---

[78] In *Oregon v. Hass* (1975) the Court permitted the use for impeachment purposes of statements made to police by a suspect in custody, after he had asked for a lawyer but before the lawyer was present.

heavier sentence, and often by the defendant's counsel, raise questions about the voluntary character of the confession.[79]

Nevertheless, the Supreme Court has ruled that plea bargaining is constitutional. In *Brady v. United States* (1970), Justice White spoke of the "mutuality of advantage" in the system. For the state, there is "the more promptly imposed punishment" and the conservation of "scarce judicial and prosecutional resources." For the defendant, "his exposure is reduced, the correctional processes can begin immediately, and the practical burdens of a trial are eliminated." So it was not unconstitutional "for the State to extend a benefit to a defendant who in turn extends a substantial benefit to the State."[80]

In agreeing to a plea bargain, defendants of course have the advice of counsel, but this is not necessarily to their benefit. In the first place, counsel in many such instances are court-appointed or overworked public defenders who find a guilty plea the most expeditious solution. Second, the fact that the guilty plea is made on advice of counsel makes it very difficult to challenge in a later proceeding. In *McMann v. Richardson* (1970), three defendants alleged that their confessions were secured by coercion and that their court-appointed counsel had incompetently represented them. But the Supreme Court ruled that a plea of guilty made by defendants who were represented by "reasonably competent" counsel could not be subsequently attacked. Defendants must accept the risk of "ordinary error" by their attorneys in their assessment of the law and facts. Only "serious derelictions" by counsel would vitiate a plea of guilty as not "a knowing and intelligent act."[81]

The reluctance of the Court to accept charges of incompetence of counsel is demonstrated in another plea-bargaining case, *Tollett v. Henderson* (1973). Here the defendant had not been informed of the constitutional rights with respect to the composition of the grand jury or the possibility of challenging the indictment. But the Court rejected the contention that counsel was incompetent, saying that a counseled plea of guilty could not be vacated "because the defendant was not advised of every conceivable constitutional plea in abatement he might have to the charge."[82]

---

[79] *Bordenkircher v. Hayes* (1978) enhanced the plea-bargaining power of prosecutors by ruling that they may threaten a defendant with a second more serious indictment if the defendant refuses to plead guilty on an initial charge and demands to be tried.

[80] *Santobello v. New York* (1971) held that where the state, due to a change in prosecutors, had broken its bargain with a defendant, the principle of due process had been violated and the bargain must be honored or the guilty plea allowed to be withdrawn.

[81] See also *Brady v. United States* (1970) and *Parker v. North Carolina* (1970). *Morris v. Slappy* (1982) held that a rape defendant's rights were not violated when the public defender assigned a new lawyer to the case only a few days before trial.

[82] Contrary to *Powell v. Alabama* (1932) and *Hawk v. Olson* (1945), *Chambers v. Maroney* (1970) rejected a claim of ineffective representation by counsel who had had no adequate opportunity to confer with defendant prior to trial. But *Henderson v. Morgan* (1976) set aside a conviction of a defendant who had pleaded guilty to second-degree murder without being fully informed on the consequences of the plea. See also *Jones v. Barnes* (1983).

INDICTMENT BY GRAND JURY

English practices with respect to indictment by grand jury and trial by jury, which were still in process of transition in the period of colonization, were not transferred bodily to the New World. There was initially a period of pronounced hostility toward the legal profession and its methods, and the law was applied in a rude and nontechnical fashion. There thus arose "the great difference between the limits of the jury trial in different States" that Alexander Hamilton commented on in *The Federalist*, No. 83, with the result that "no general rule could have been fixed upon by the Convention which would have corresponded with the circumstances of all the States." Consequently in its provisions for federal criminal prosecutions the Constitution made no mention of the grand jury whatever. The Fifth Amendment filled in this gap by the provision that "no person shall be held to answer for a capital or otherwise infamous crime, unless on a presentment or indictment of a grand jury."

The purpose of the grand jury provision is to require prosecuting officers to prove to a body of laymen that there is a prima facie case of criminal violation so that citizens will not be subjected to the expense and indignity of a criminal trial without reasonable cause. If the grand jury finds the evidence sufficiently strong, it votes an indictment or a "true bill."

This is one area where the states are not required to follow federal standards. In some twenty-eight states the grand jury had been abolished, and a prosecuting officer may bring a person to trial by filing an "information" against him. The Supreme Court upheld this practice in *Hurtado v. California* (1884), and has never reversed this decision.

A grand jury generally consists of from twelve to twenty-three members; the jurors are selected by lot from the voting rolls or are chosen by judges or other local officials. The district attorney meets with the grand jury, whose sessions are secret. It has the power to inquire into any alleged offense called to its attention by the judge's charge to the jury, but the usual practice is for the group to confine its attention to issues presented by the district attorney, and that official is often accused of dominating the grand jury.[83]

TRIAL BY JURY

Jury trial came to American with the English colonists. Though now used in perhaps only 1 percent of English criminal prosecutions, it remains a

---

[83] See Roger T. Brice, "Grand Jury Proceedings: The Prosecutor, the Trial Judge, and Undue Influence," 39 UNIVERSITY OF CHICAGO LAW REVIEW 761 (1972); David J. Fine, "Federal Grand Jury Investigation of Political Dissidents," 7 HARVARD CIVIL RIGHTS–CIVIL LIBERTIES LAW REVIEW 432 (1972); Charles E. Goodell, "Where Did the Grand Jury Go?" 246 HARPERS 14 (May 1973).

vital instrument of American justice in both civil and criminal cases. The justification is not primarily that untrained lay jurors are reliable fact finders, although the principal empirical study of the jury system concluded that judges agreed with jury findings in over three-fourths of the jury trial cases studied.[84] Rather, the case for the jury, as eloquently stated by Justice White in *Duncan v. Louisiana* (1968), is that "jury trial is granted to criminal defendants in order to prevent oppression by the Government. [It is] an inestimable safeguard against the corrupt or overzealous prosecutor and against the compliant, biased, or eccentric judge." Another important consideration is that juries temper the application or enforcement of unpopular, outdated, or overstrict laws.

Jury Trial in Federal Courts

The Constitution provides for jury trials in criminal cases by the Sixth Amendment (and also by Article III, section 2, of the original Constitution), and in civil cases "where the value in controversy shall exceed twenty dollars" by the Seventh Amendment.[85] Since the Sixth Amendment merely says that the accused "shall enjoy the right" to a trial by jury, jury trial in federal courts is not an institutional requirement, but only a "valuable privilege" that a person accused of crime may forego at his election. However, "before any waiver can become effective, the consent of government counsel and the sanction of the court must be had, in addition to the express and intelligent consent of the defendant."[86]

The right to trial by jury in federal criminal cases has been held to be limited to those who, under the Fifth Amendment, are subject to indictment or presentment by grand jury. This means that there is a class of petty crimes for which jury trial cannot be claimed. *Cheff v. Schnackenberg* (1966) was somewhat tentative in drawing the line between serious and petty crimes, saying: "The prevailing opinion today suggests that a jury is required where the sentence imposed exceeds six months but not when it is less than that period." Other situations in which jury trial may not be claimed include charges of criminal contempt of court[87] and petititons for the writ of habeas corpus; deportation proceedings for aliens and disbarment proceedings for

---

[84] Harry Kalven, Jr. and Hans Zeisel, *The American Jury* (Boston: Little, Brown, 1966).

[85] *Lehman v. Nakshian* (1981) made clear that the Seventh Amendment right to jury trial does not apply in actions against the federal government.

[86] *Patton v. United States* (1930). See also *Singer v. United States* (1965). The death penalty provision of the Federal Kidnapping Act, which stated that a defendant shall be punished by death if the kidnapped person has not been liberated unharmed and if the verdict of the jury shall so recommend, was held unconstitutional in *United States v. Jackson* (1968) as tending to deter exercise of the right to demand a jury trial as well as to discourage assertion of the Fifth Amendment right not to plead guilty.

[87] But see the conditions under which jury trials may be required in criminal contempt cases, in *United States v. Barnett* (1964) and *Cheff v. Schnackenberg* (1966).

attorneys, which are civil, not criminal; and extradition proceedings, which are administrative, not judicial. Moreover, trials by courts-martial are not affected by the Sixth Amendment, the provision of the Fifth Amendment waiving the grand jury requirement "in the land or naval forces" having been also read into the Sixth.[88]

Jury Trial in State Courts

The laws of every state require a right to jury trial in serious criminal cases, but the Supreme Court until 1968 had declined to hold that jury trial in state courts was a federal constitutional right. In fact, in *Maxwell v. Dow* (1900), the Court said by way of dictum: "Trial by jury has never been affirmed to be a necessary requisite of due process of law." This position was reiterated in *Palko v. Connecticut* (1937). However, in *Duncan v. Louisiana* (1968), after so many other provisions of the Bill of Rights had been absorbed into the Fourteenth Amendment, the Court concluded that the right to jury trial in criminal cases was also "fundamental to the American scheme of justice." Consequently, *Duncan* ruled that "the Fourteenth Amendment guarantees a right of jury trial in all criminal cases which— were they to be tried in a federal court—would come within the Sixth Amendment's guarantee."[89] Only Harlan and Stewart dissented.[90]

Adoption of the federal court rule meant that petty crimes would be exempt from the state jury trial requirement. In *Baldwin v. New York* (1970), the Court confirmed that petty crimes were those punishable by no more than six months in prison.

Jury Selection

The jury, according to the Sixth Amendment, must be "impartial." This raises the whole question of jury composition and method of selection. Bias, although difficult to guard against, may be thought of (1) as being simply a matter of opinion, or (2) as growing out of or being associated with social or economic status of jurors. Bias in the first sense is protected against by the right to challenge prospective jurors for cause. At the Aaron Burr trial for treason, his attorney argued that a juror to be selected must have a mind "perfectly indifferent and free from prejudice," but Chief Justice Marshall said this was too stringent a standard. A closed mind would be objectionable, but casual opinions on the subject should not disqualify a venireman. Obviously the challenged bias must have some direct relation to the issues of the case. In capital cases, the general practice was to exclude

---

[88] *Ex parte Milligan* (1866).

[89] But *Ludwig v. Massachusetts* (1976) held that a defendant may be denied a jury in his or her initial trial provided the state allows through appeal a second trial in which there is a jury.

[90] *De Stefano v. Woods* (1968) held that *Duncan* did not apply retroactively.

persons with constitutional scruples against the death penalty from the jury. But *Witherspoon v. Illinois* (1968) declared this practice unconstitutional. A jury drawn only from that minority that has no doubts about imposing capital punishment would not be impartial, the Court thought. Indeed, it would be a "hanging jury," said Justice Stewart.

In Chapter 4 we discussed the situation where an entire community is so inflamed by publicity about a crime that securing an impartial jury seems impossible. A change of venue is required in those circumstances. *Groppi v. Wisconsin* (1971) held that a statute prohibiting change of venue for a criminal jury trial in any misdemeanor case, regardless of the extent of local prejudice against the defendant, violated the right to trial by an impartial jury.

The main protection against bias resulting from a juror's race or employment or class status is the "cross-section" principle that forbids any systematic exclusion of identifiable segments of the community from jury panels or from the juries ultimately drawn from these panels.[91] In *Smith v. Texas* (1940) the Court said: "it is part of the established tradition in the use of juries as instruments of public justice that the jury be a body truly representative of the community"; and in *Taylor v. Louisiana* (1975) the Court reaffirmed "the fair cross-section requirement as fundamental to the jury trial guaranteed by the Sixth Amendment." This principle was incorporated in the Federal Jury Selection and Service Act of 1968, which requires random selection from "a fair cross-section of the community," and bars discrimination on account of race, color, religion, sex, national origin, or economic status.[92]

Prior to 1968, each federal district court followed its own methods in jury selection; these were not always in accord with the cross-section principle. One was the "key man" system, under which outstanding citizens recommended the veniremen. Or the venire might be drawn from lists of telephone subscribers, property owners, even church members—not sources that would provide a representative cross-section. The 1949 Smith Act prosecution of Communists in New York was bogged down for seven weeks by unsuccessful defense efforts to establish that poor people were deliberately excluded from federal jury panels in New York.

Both the due process clause and the equal protection clause of the Fourteenth Amendment require the Supreme Court to review state jury

[91] The Supreme Court struck down some restrictive jury practices even when their purpose was benign. In *Thiel v. Southern Pacific Co.* (1946) the practice invalidated was that of automatically excusing from jury service all persons working for a daily wage, since the fee for jurors was inadequate to compensate them for loss of wages. In *Glasser v. United States* (1942) the Court indicated that intentional selection of jurors from among women who had taken League of Women Voters "jury classes" would not be approved.

[92] *Test v. United States* (1975) held that under this act the defendant has a right to inspect jury lists to determine whether a disproportionate number of people with Spanish surnames, students, and blacks have been systematically excluded.

selection practices where charges of discrimination are made. The chief problems, both in the selection of grand and trial juries, have resulted from discrimination against blacks. As early as 1880, a Virginia judge charged with excluding blacks from jury lists because of their race and color was found guilty of denying equal protection.[93] In the same year, a West Virginia statute requiring juries to be composed exclusively of white male citizens was likewise held unconstitutional.[94] However, where a state statute made no discrimination against blacks, the fact that no blacks had sat on the grand and trial juries in a murder case was not a constitutional objection to conviction. Petitioners had no right to have blacks on the jury, the Court said.[95] Thus, so long as open discrimination against blacks was avoided, it was possible for the Southern states to follow a successful exclusion policy based on practice and custom.

This system operated undisturbed by the Supreme Court until 1935, when it was challenged in *Norris v. Alabama,* known as the Second Scottsboro case. Following the Supreme Court's reversal in the first case on grounds of denial of counsel, a second trial had been held in another county and the defendants again convicted. This second conviction was attacked on the ground that blacks were systematically excluded from the grand jury in the county where the indictment was found, and from the trial jury in the county where the trial was held. The Supreme Court unanimously sustained this contention, finding that in each of the two counties no blacks had ever been called for jury service within the memory of the oldest inhabitants or any officer of the courts. This was in spite of the fact that there were black citizens in each county well able to render jury service, and that black citizens had been called on to serve on federal juries in that district. "For this long-continued, unvarying, and wholesome exclusion of Negroes from jury service," Chief Justice Hughes concluded, "we find no justification consistent with the constitutional mandate." The great advance of the *Norris* decision was that it permitted discriminatory practices to be inferred from the facts showing the actuality of unequal treatment.

The *Norris* rule was a fairly clear one, and for a time it took care of the situation.[96] Soon, however, things got more complicated as techniques were developed for evading the spirit of the Court's rulings. In the case of *Akins v. Texas* (1945) the jury commissioners had carefully placed one black on the grand jury. The commissioners freely admitted that the limitation of black representation to one juror was intentional, but the Supreme Court was unable to find any loophole in this technical compliance with constitutional requirements. Mathematical exactitude or proportional representation of

[93] *Ex parte Virginia* (1880).
[94] *Strauder v. West Virginia* (1880).
[95] *Virginia v. Rives* (1880).
[96] See *Smith v. Texas* (1940), *Hill v. Texas* (1942), *Eubanks v. Louisiana* (1958).

races or groups, the Court said, was not required to meet the equal protection guarantee. But *Cassell v. Texas* (1950) held a grand jury panel illegal because in twenty-one consecutive grand jury panels there had never been more than one black.

The Court found discrimination to exist in *Avery v. Georgia* (1952), where the names of prospective black jurors were placed in the jury box on yellow tickets, and in *Whitus v. Georgia* (1967), where the names of prospective jurors were selected from the books of the county tax receiver, which were maintained on a racially segregated basis. But in *Brown v. Allen* (1953), the Court approved selection of jurors from taxpayers' lists. Blacks amounted to 33 percent of the county population but only 16 percent of the taxpayers. The Court majority thought this was a "good faith effort to secure competent juries."

In *Swain v. Alabama* (1965), an average of six or seven blacks was placed on trial jury venires, but no black had actually served since 1950, every one apparently having been eliminated by the prosecutor on peremptory challenges. The Court held that this record did not make out a prima facie case of invidious discrimination; there had not been "total exclusion" of a racial group.

Carter v. Jury Commission of Greene County (1970) was the first case to reach the Supreme Court in which an attack on alleged racial discrimination in choosing juries was made by plaintiffs seeking affirmative relief rather than by defendants challenging judgments of criminal conviction. The district court, finding invalid racial discrimination, had enjoined the jury commissioners from systematically excluding blacks from the jury rolls; it ordered prompt action to compile lawful jury lists. The district judge, however, had declined to enjoin the enforcement of Alabama jury selection laws or to order the governor to appoint blacks to the jury commission. The Supreme Court affirmed on all points.

In *Hernandez v. Texas* (1954), the Court found that persons of Mexican descent had been systematically excluded from jury service; this was the first time the rule against racial discrimination had been extended to a group other than blacks.

The issue of racial bias was considered in *Ham v. South Carolina* (1973), where the Court ruled that the trial judge had erred in refusing to examine jurors as to possible prejudice arising from the fact that the defendant was black. But in *Ristaino v. Ross* (1976), the Court retreated from *Ham*, holding that questions about potential racial bias were constitutionally required only if there were "a significant likelihood" that racial prejudice might infect the trial.[97]

___

[97] In agreement, *Rosales-Lopez v. United States* (1981) held that a defendant has an automatic right to demand questioning of jurors about racial prejudice only where the defendant is accused of a violent crime or the defendant and the victim are members of different racial groups. In *Rosales-Lopez* the charge was alien smuggling.

Fay v. New York (1947) upheld the constitutionality of New York's "blue ribbon" juries, which were allegedly chosen from "the upper economic and social stratum" to the exclusion of manual workers. Noting that proportional representation was not required on juries, even for racial groups, the Court said: "how much more imprudent would it be to require proportional representation of economic classes."[98]

Following the common-law practice, women were originally ineligible for jury service in all states. *Strauder v. West Virginia* (1880) explicitly held that a state could constitutionally confine jury service to males. Utah was the first state to break the barrier in 1898, and eventually all other states followed. However, access of women to the jury box was often qualified. They could claim automatic exemption in many states. Florida law provided that women were not to be included on jury lists unless they registered their desire to serve with the court clerk. In *Hoyt v. Florida* (1961) the Court upheld this law as based on a reasonable classification. Since "woman is still regarded as the center of home and family life," she should have the right to determine whether jury service was compatible with her "special responsibilities." But only fourteen years later, in *Taylor v. Louisiana* (1975), the Court recognized "the current judgment of the country" and declared unconstitutional a comparable Louisiana statute, saying: "the exclusion of women from jury venires deprives a criminal defendant of his Sixth Amendment right to trial by an impartial jury drawn from a fair cross-section of the community."[99]

Jury Size

The common-law jury was composed of twelve persons; and in *Thompson v. Utah* (1898) the Supreme Court held that the Sixth Amendment jury was a jury "constituted, as it was at common law, of twelve persons, neither more nor less."[100] After *Duncan* was decided in 1968, holding that jury trial in state courts was a fundamental constitutional right, it seemed logical to assume that state juries would have to conform to the rules for federal juries. In fact, the Court did take this position in *Williams v. Florida* (1970), but not in the way anticipated.

Florida had adopted a statute in 1967 providing that "six men" should constitute the jury to try all criminal cases except for capital crimes, for

[98] The contention that government employees should be excluded from jury service in the District of Columbia because they would be biased in favor of the government was rejected in *Dennis v. United States* (1950).

[99] However, automatic exemption of women from service on their request was still the law in two states, resulting in Missouri in jury venires averaging less than 15 percent female. In *Duren v. Missouri* (1979) this result was held to violate the fair cross-section requirement.

[100] This ruling was reaffirmed in *Maxwell v. Dow* (1900), *Rasmussen v. United States* (1905), and *Patton v. United States* (1930).

which the twelve-member jury was retained. By a vote of six to two, the Court came to the surprising conclusion that the Sixth Amendment did *not* require twelve-member federal criminal juries, and so obviously the states were under no obligation to continue using them. Justice White thought there was no firm evidence that the framers intended "to equate the constitutional and common law characteristics of the jury." Perhaps "the usual expectation was that the jury would consist of 12," but that number was an "historical accident." The important thing was to preserve the essential function that the framers expected the jury to perform, and that

> obviously lies in the interposition between the accused and his accuser of the common-sense judgment of a group of laymen, and in the community participation and shared responsibility which results from that group's determination of guilt or innocence. The performance of this role is not a function of the particular number of the body which makes up the jury. To be sure, the number should probably be large enough to promote group deliberation, free from outside attempts at intimidation, and to provide a fair possibility for obtaining a representative cross-section of the community. But we find little reason to think that these goals are in any meaningful sense less likely to be achieved when the jury numbers six, than when it numbers twelve. . . .[101]

White dealt to his satisfaction with arguments that fewer jurors would be more likely to convict and reduce the number of viewpoints represented in a randomly selected jury. But his basic position was that jury size was "incidental to the real purpose of the [Sixth] Amendment."

Black and Douglas concurred in this result, but Harlan was appalled at such cavalier overruling of precedents and dismissal of the common-law tradition in favor of a "functional" analysis. "History," he said, "continues to be a wellspring of constitutional interpretation." Once the umbilical cord is cut, what controls? "For if 12 jurors are not essential, why are six?" Why not three? Marshall agreed with Harlan, and Blackmun did not participate.

Harlan got his answer in *Ballew v. Georgia* (1978), where state law allowed five-member juries in criminal cases. Readily admitting the Court's inability "to discern a clear line between six members and five," Justice Blackmun concluded that the purpose and functioning of a jury in a criminal trial would be "seriously impaired, and to a constitutional degree, by a reduction in size below six members." Surprisingly, Blackmun relied heavily on over a score of research studies which purported to establish that proportionately smaller juries result in less effective group deliberation, affect the accuracy of results achieved, and imbalance verdicts to the

---

[101] See the demonstration to the contrary by Hans Zeisel, ". . . And Then There Were None: The Diminution of the Federal Jury," 38 UNIVERSITY OF CHICAGO LAW REVIEW 710 (1971); Peter W. Sperlich, "And Then There Were Six: The Decline of the American Jury," 63 JUDICATURE 262 (1980).

detriment of the defense. The Court was unanimous, though Powell questioned Blackmun's "heavy reliance on numerology derived from statistical studies."[102]

Federal Jury Size

While White's stripping of the twelve-member requirement from the Sixth Amendment was an essential step in upholding the six-member Florida jury, it was dictum in that no federal jury issue was before the Court. Moreover, no subsequent move has been made toward reducing the size of federal criminal juries. But well before the *Williams* decision, six-member *civil* juries had been authorized in a number of federal district courts.

The Supreme Court gave its approval in *Colgrove v. Battin* (1973). It might seem that *Williams* had settled this issue, but in fact the Court had recognized in the *Williams* opinion that the federal civil jury problem might be complicated by the specific recognition in the Seventh Amendment of the right to jury trial in suits at "common law" where the value in controversy exceeds twenty dollars. But in a five to four decision, Justice Brennan proved no less adept than White in extricating the Court from history and its precedents. He held that the Seventh Amendment had not meant to freeze the common-law jury into the Constitution. It only meant to protect the principle of civil juries.

The rather odd assortment of Douglas, Marshall, Stewart, and Powell dissented. Marshall picked up the torch of the fallen Harlan and in a powerful opinion protested this "wholesale abolition" of the civil jury and its replacement by a "six-man mutation . . . a different institution which functions differently, produces different results, and was wholly unknown to the Framers of the Seventh Amendment."

The Unanimity Rule

Since at least 1367, the unanimous jury verdict has been considered an established and integral part of common-law criminal procedure. It was recognized as an indispensable feature of federal jury trials in an unbroken line of cases, virtually without dissent, the latest being *Patton v. United States* (1930). So far as state courts were concerned, there were dicta in two earlier cases, *Maxwell v. Dow* (1900) and *Jordan v. Massachusetts* (1912), holding that the unanimity requirement was not obligatory; but of course these decisions came long before the Court held in *Duncan* that jury trial in state courts was a fundamental constitutional right.

We have just seen what a surprising impact the implementation of

---

[102] See Peter W. Sperlich, "Trial by Jury: It May Have a Future," in Philip B. Kurland and Gerhard Casper, eds., *The Supreme Court Review: 1978* (Chicago: University of Chicago Press, 1979), pp. 191–224.

Duncan had on jury size in *Williams v. Florida.* Two years later, in *Johnson v. Louisiana* (1972) and *Apodaco v. Oregon* (1972), Justice White sought to complete the dismantling of the Sixth Amendment that he had begun in *Williams.* The legislatures of both Louisiana and Oregon had authorized dispensing with the unanimity requirement in criminal cases. In the Louisiana case the jury vote on conviction for armed robbery was nine to three. In the Oregon case the two defendants were found guilty by votes of eleven to one and ten to two. The Court upheld these verdicts as against charges of denial of due process and equal protection.

Justice White repeated the antihistorical and jury-functional arguments he had originated in *Williams.* In that opinion he had foreseen that his case against the twelve-member jury could just as readily apply to the unanimity rule, but in a *Williams* footnote he had expressly reserved that question:

> We intimate no view whether or not the requirement of unanimity is an indispensable element of the Sixth Amendment. While much of the above historical discussion applies as well to the unanimity as to the 12-man requirement, the former, unlike the latter, may well serve an important role in the jury function, for example, as a device for insuring that the Government bear the heavier burden of proof.

But two years later, in *Johnson* and *Apodaco,* this virtue of unanimity was no longer compelling for White. Unanimity might not be a historical accident, like size, but it was to be judged on its contemporary function, not its history. Was unanimity necessary to give effect to the "reasonable doubt" standard that criminal convictions must satisfy? No. If nine jurors found guilt beyond a reasonable doubt, it was the three dissenting jurors who should consider whether their doubts were reasonable. Would not majority jurors, once they had achieved their nine or ten votes, refuse to listen to counterarguments and simply terminate the deliberations? No. "Appellant offers no evidence that majority jurors simply ignore the reasonable doubts of their colleagues or otherwise act irresponsibly in casting their votes in favor of conviction." Is not unanimity a necessary precondition for effective application of the cross-section principle, making it impossible for convictions to occur without the acquiescence of minority elements in the community? No. Every distinct voice in the community does not have "a right to be represented on every jury and a right to prevent conviction of a defendant in any case."[103]

Justice Stewart, one of the four dissenters, rejected these assurances as

---

[103] Although White spoke for the five-judge majority in eliminating the unanimity requirement for state criminal juries, he failed to convince one of the five, Justice Powell, that the Sixth Amendment did not require unanimity on federal juries. Unanimity in the federal courts, Powell contended, was "mandated by history." Consequently the principle of unanimity on federal criminal juries was narrowly preserved.

completely "impervious to reality." He thought it more likely that "under today's judgment, nine jurors can simply ignore the view of their fellow panel members of a different race or class." Unanimity "provides the simple and effective method endorsed by centuries of experience and history to combat the injuries to the fair administration of justice that can be inflicted by community passion and prejudice."[104]

The Court's retreat from unanimity came to a halt in *Burch v. Louisiana* (1979), where state law permitted conviction by five out of six jurors. The state claimed the system saved time and money, but Rehnquist held that nonunanimous verdicts by six-person juries "threaten the constitutional principles that led to the establishment of the size threshold."[105]

OTHER SIXTH AMENDMENT PROTECTIONS

The Sixth Amendment spells out certain other protections of trial procedure. An accused is entitled to a "speedy and public trial." Of necessity speed is a relative concept, subordinate to the broader protections of the amendment. The federal Speedy Trial Act of 1974, adopted over opposition of the Department of Justice, requires that a person arrested be charged within thirty days of the arrest and arraigned within ten days of being charged and that trial begin within sixty days of the arraignment. The act provides for some circumstances under which elapsed time would not be counted toward the 100-day period. Charges would be dismissed against any defendant who moved for dismissal after the speedy trial period had elapsed and trial had not begun.[106] *Klopfer v. North Carolina* (1967) held that the speedy trial provision is also applicable to the states.

[104] In 1973 unanimity in criminal cases was still required in the courts of most states. In addition to Louisiana and Oregon, four other states permitted less than unanimous decisions, but in all four such verdicts could be rendered only in trials for offenses less than a felony. One of these states, Montana, permitted conviction by vote of two-thirds of the jurors. Justice Blackmun, concurring in *Johnson* and its acceptance of a nine to three vote, said he would find it difficult to approve a seven to five conviction, though it is difficult to see what the distinguishing principle is between the two majorities.

A 1967 English statute authorized ten to two verdicts in criminal cases but required the jury to deliberate for at least two hours, or longer if required by the court. Scotland allows convictions by a bare majority (eight to seven), but rules of evidence there are much stricter than in the United States, making the burden of proof about twice as great.

[105] Two useful jury studies are Rita James Simon, *The Jury: Its Role in American Society* (Lexington, Mass.: Lexington Books, 1980); Jon Van Dyke, *Jury Selection Procedures* (Cambridge, Mass.: Ballinger, 1977).

[106] The Speedy Trial Act was in part a response to the Supreme Court's decision in *Barker v. Wingo* (1972). In defining the right to a speedy trial, the time period to be considered is the period between trial and either arrest or indictment, whichever comes first (*Dillingham v. United States* [1975]). In the notorious "Green Beret murder case," *United States v. MacDonald* (1982), the Court held that the time between dismissal of military charges in 1970 and a subsequent indictment on civilian criminal charges in 1975 was not to be considered in determining whether the delay in bringing respondent to trial violated his right to a speedy trial.

The requirement of the Sixth Amendment that "the accused shall enjoy the right . . . to be informed of the nature and cause of the accusation" is intended to make it possible for the defendant to prepare his defense adequately. Failure to meet this standard may be the result of either the statute defining the crime or the indictment charging it. However, vagueness in the statute is more properly attacked on the basis of the due process clause of the Fifth Amendment, thus limiting the purview of the Sixth Amendment to the indictment process.

The right to be informed of the nature and cause of the accusation also has some relevance to the Supreme Court's insistence that criminal statutes must be sufficiently specific in their terms to define and give adequate notice of the kind of conduct which they forbid. This is the familiar rule that criminal statutes may be held "void for vagueness." The applicable principle has been stated by the Supreme Court:

> That the terms of a penal statute creating a new offense must be sufficiently explicit to inform those who are subject to it what conduct on their part will render them liable to its penalties, is a well-recognized requirement, consonant alike with ordinary notions of fair play and the settled rules of law. And a statute which either forbids or requires the doing of an act in terms so vague that men of common intelligence must necessarily guess at its meaning and differ as to its application, violates the first essential of due process of law.[107]

The Sixth Amendment right of a defendant "to be confronted with the witnesses against him" was held in *Pointer v. Texas* (1965) to be a "fundamental right" obligatory on the states. Here the transcript of testimony given by a witness at the preliminary hearing was introduced at the trial because the witness had left the state and was unavailable to testify. The Supreme Court ruled that this denied the defendant's right to confront the witness and cross-examine him by counsel.[108]

In *Turner v. Louisiana* (1965) the jury during a three-day period of sequestration in a murder trial was in the charge of two deputy sheriffs who were also witnesses for the state. The Court held that this close association undermined the basic guarantees of trial by jury, including confrontation and cross-examination.

The Immigration and Nationality Act of 1952 automatically, without prior judicial or administrative proceedings, imposed the penalty of forfeiture of citizenship on persons who, in time of war or emergency, leave or

---

[107] *Connally v. General Construction Co.* (1926). For illustrative decisions, see *Lanzetta v. New Jersey* (1939) and *Winters v. New York* (1948). In *Rose v. Locke* (1975) the Court reversed a lower court ruling that Tennessee's "crimes against nature" statute did not give adequate notice that it applied to the act of cunnilingus.

[108] See also *Douglas v. Alabama* (1965), *Brookhart v. Janis* (1966), *Smith v. Illinois* (1968), and *Chambers v. Mississippi* (1973).

remain outside the United States to evade military service. In *Kennedy v. Mendoza-Martinez* (1963) the Court held this provision void as withholding a cluster of rights guaranteed by the Fifth and Sixth Amendments—namely, notice, confrontation, trial by jury, compulsory process for obtaining witnesses, and aid of counsel.

The unique "one-man grand jury" system of Michigan was held by the Court in *In re Oliver* (1948) to deny several Sixth Amendment trial rights. The case arose when a Michigan judge, sitting as a grand jury, concluded that a witness testifying before him in a secret session was not telling the truth. He thereupon assumed his role as judge, and with no break in the proceedings, charged the witness with contempt, immediately convicted him, and sentenced him to sixty days in jail. The only other persons present during this weird procedure were two other judges who sat as advisers, plus the court staff. The trial had, of course, proceeded without counsel, but there had also been a failure to give the accused anything definite as to the nature and cause of the accusation against him—the charge was that his story did not "jell." Moreover, although this charge was based in part on testimony of another witness before the judge-grand jury the same day, the accused was denied any opportunity to be confronted with the witnesses against him. On all these points the Supreme Court held the proceeding unconstitutional.[109]

Finally, the Sixth Amendment right of a defendant to have compulsory process for obtaining witnesses in his favor was held in *Washington v. Texas* (1967) to be incorporated into the due process clause and made binding on the states. *Webb v. Texas* (1972) ruled that a judge who badgered the defendant's principal witness and effectively drove him off the witness stand had denied the defendant his Sixth Amendment right to offer witnesses.

DUE PROCESS, FAIR TRIAL, AND EQUAL PROTECTION

Both federal and state trials are subject to requirements of fairness that may be grounded in general conceptions of due process or equal protection rather than in the more specific procedural language of the Bill of Rights. It is a denial of due process if a prosecutor knowingly offers false evidence or suppresses evidence favorable to a defendant.[110] In *Miller v. Pate* (1967) a

---

[109] See Robert G. Scigliano, *The Michigan One-Man Grand Jury* (East Lansing: Governmental Research Bureau, Michigan State University, 1957).

[110] *Mooney v. Holohan* (1935). But *Imbler v. Pachtman* (1976) threw out a damage suit against a public prosecutor for allegedly using perjured testimony in a murder trial, on the ground that prosecutors must have absolute immunity from suit if they are to carry out their duties vigorously and courageously.

sex-murder conviction was reversed because the prosecutor had deliberately misrepresented paint on a pair of men's shorts as blood. But *Smith v. Phillips* (1982) held there was no violation of due process when a juror in a murder case was at the same time applying for a job in the prosecutor's office.

Although it had long been understood that the common-law standard of proof of a criminal charge "beyond a reasonable doubt" was a constitutional due process requirement, the Court did not specifically so hold until *In re Winship* (1970). In *Sandstrom v. Montana* (1979) a homicide conviction was reversed because the judge's instructions did not require that the prosecution prove every element of the crime beyond a reasonable doubt.[111]

"Presumption of innocence" is equally basic. In *Estelle v. Williams* (1976) the Court said that the "presumption of innocence, although not articulated in the Constitution, is a basic component of a fair trial under our system of criminal justice." *Taylor v. Kentucky* (1978) appeared to hold that a trial judge must charge the jury that a defendant is presumed to be innocent, not merely that the prosecution must prove guilt beyond a reasonable doubt. But *Kentucky v. Whorton* (1979) ruled that failure to charge the jury did not in and of itself violate the Constitution; such failure must be evaluated in the light of all the circumstances, such as jury instructions and weight of evidence.

A conviction based on insufficient evidence, or totally devoid of evidentiary support, is a denial of due process. In *Thompson v. Louisville* (1960) a conviction for loitering and disorderly conduct, in *Garner v. Louisiana* (1961) a conviction for disturbing the peace by a civil rights sit-in, and in *Gregory v. Chicago* (1969) a conviction for disorderly conduct in a march around Mayor Daley's home, all were held completely devoid of support in the evidence. Moreover, due process limits the power of Congress or state legislatures to make the proof of one fact or group of facts evidence of the ultimate fact on which guilt is predicated.[112]

Tumey v. Ohio (1927) held invalid an arrangement under which city mayors tried bootlegging cases and received compensation for their "costs" only when defendants were convicted. The Supreme Court thought this gave the mayor-judge "a direct, personal, substantial, pecuniary interest" in convictions. The *Tumey* principle was applied in *Ward v. Village of Monroeville, Ohio* (1972), where the revenue produced by fines in the mayor's court provided a substantial part of the municipality's revenues.

North v. Russell (1976) held that it does not deny due process for criminal cases to be tried by judges without legal training, provided the

---

[111] See also *Jackson v. Virginia* (1979).

[112] *Tot v. United States* (1943). *United States v. Romano* (1965) held unconstitutional a federal statute providing that the mere presence of a person at an illegal still should be deemed sufficient evidence to authorize conviction for possession and custody of the still, unless the defendant explained such presence to the satisfaction of the jury.

defendant through appeal can get a second trial before a judge who is a lawyer.

A more complex problem of Supreme Court supervision over state criminal justice arises when the charge of unfairness in the trial is based on allegations that the verdict was affected by outside pressures not apparent on the record. There was a slogan on the frontier. "Give him a fair trial and then hang him." Is a lynching transformed into a fair trial when the requisite forms of legal action are gone through? In *Frank v. Mangum* (1915), the Court, over the protest of Holmes and Hughes, refused to review a conviction in a case of anti-Semitism from Georgia. But in *Moore v. Dempsey* (1923), growing out of race riots and a mob-dominated trial of blacks in Arkansas, Holmes had a chance to assert for the Court its responsibility for guaranteeing a fair trial:

> . . . if the case is that the whole proceeding is a mask—that counsel, jury and judge were swept to the fatal end by an irresistible wave of public passion, and that the State Courts failed to correct the wrong, neither perfection in the machinery for correction nor the possibility that the trial court and counsel saw no other way of avoiding an immediate outbreak of the mob can prevent this Court from securing to the petitioners their constitutional rights.

As we know, defendants can invoke the Fifth Amendment and decline to take the witness stand in a criminal trial. But in *Lakeside v. Oregon* (1978), when the trial judge cautioned the jury not to draw adverse inferences from the defendant's failure to testify in his own behalf, counsel for the defense objected, fearing that this warning would actually encourage the jury to draw such inferences. In *United States v. Grayson* (1978) the defendant did take the stand, and the trial judge imposed a more severe sentence on the ground that his testimony was a fabrication. The Court held that the sentence did not violate due process by punishing the defendant for the crime of perjury, for which he had not been indicted or tried, but the dissenters charged that such sentencing practices would inhibit defendants from testifying in their own behalf. *Henry v. Colorado* (1978) affirmed that asking a defendant on the witness stand about previous felony convictions does not violate due process.

Constitutional Rights of Indigents

A fairly recent concern of the Supreme Court has been to assure that indigents will not be denied due process and equal protection because of their inability to pay for justice. The leading case is *Griffin v. Illinois* (1956), which held it unconstitutional discrimination for a state to furnish free stenographic transcripts of trials only for review of constitutional questions and to indigent defendants under death sentence. This restriction prevented other defendants, unable to purchase a transcript, from exercising their right to appellate review.[113]

In *Douglas v. California* (1963) the Court for similar reasons struck down a state criminal procedure under which appellate courts could deny an indigent's request for appointment of counsel if they believed the appointment would be valueless.[114] *Swenson v. Bosler* (1967) held that poor defendants must be provided with lawyers when they appeal to higher state courts, even if they do not specifically request such aid. But *Ross v. Moffitt* (1974) ruled that, after the first appeal as of right, counsel did not have to be supplied for further discretionary state appeals or for application for review in the Supreme Court. And *Fuller v. Oregon* (1974) upheld a state recoupment statute requiring indigent criminal defendants who had been provided counsel to reimburse the state for the cost of counsel if they subsequently acquired the means to do so.

Williams v. Illinois (1970) ruled that indigents cannot be held in jail because of their inability to pay their fines beyond the maximum period of confinement fixed by statute. *Tate v. Short* (1971) held that fines for traffic offenses that an indigent was unable to pay could not be converted into a jail sentence.

In *Boddie v. Connecticut* (1971), the Court held that indigents could not be denied access to the divorce courts because of inability to pay the various fees involved. Justice Harlan concluded that "given the basic position of the marriage relationship in this society's hierarchy of values and the concomitant monopolization of the means for legally dissolving this relationship, due process does prohibit the State from denying, solely because of inability to pay, access to its courts to individuals who seek judicial dissolution of their marriages." But *United States v. Kras* (1973) held that the payment of filing fees for access to federal bankruptcy court had a rational basis and did not deny indigents equal protection of the laws. Justice Stewart, dissenting, said, "The Court today holds that Congress may say that some of the poor are too poor even to go bankrupt." *Ortwein v. Schwab* (1973) followed *Kras* in upholding Oregon's $25 appellate court filing fee.

Due Process in Juvenile Courts

The general conception of juvenile courts has been that the state is acting through them as *parens patriae* and not as adversary, and that the proceedings against juveniles are civil and not criminal. Consequently it

---

[113] See also *Burns v. Ohio* (1959), *Douglas v. Green* (1960), and *Rinaldi v. Yeager* (1966). But *United States v. MacCollom* (1976) denied free trial transcripts in a habeas corpus proceeding.

[114] See also *Draper v. Washington* (1963), *Lane v. Brown* (1963), *Anders v. California* (1967), *Entsminger v. Iowa* (1967).

has been the usual practice that the child is not entitled to the constitutional rights of adult offenders, such as bail, indictment, public or jury trial, immunity against self-incrimination, or counsel, but can claim only the fundamental due process right to fair treatment.

In the case of *In re Gault* (1967), a fifteen-year-old boy who had made a lewd telephone call was committed to the state industrial school as a delinquent, with the possibility of remaining there until the age of twenty-one. For an adult, the maximum punishment for such an offense would have been a fine of fifty dollars or imprisonment for not more than two months. The boy's parents brought a habeas corpus action, alleging that they had been given inadequate notice of the charges, that the complainant had not testified, that they had not been offered the assistance of counsel, that the boy had not been warned his testimony could be used against him, that no transcript had been made of the trial, and that Arizona law did not permit appeal of a juvenile court decision.

Justice Fortas, though recognizing the benign purposes which the informal procedures of juvenile courts had been intended to achieve, felt that the intelligent enforcement of due process standards would not compel the states to displace the substantive benefits of the juvenile process and would correct such grievous disregard of procedural protections as was demonstrated by this case. "Under our Constitution," said Fortas, "the condition of being a boy does not justify a kangaroo court." Specifically, he held that in a juvenile proceeding there must be notice of charges; notice of right to be represented by counsel and appointment of counsel if the parents are unable to afford counsel; the right to confront and cross-examine complainants and other witnesses; and adequate warning of the privilege against self-incrimination and the right to remain silent.[115]

Subsequently the Court ruled in *In re Winship* (1970) that juvenile courts must apply the same standard of proof for guilt as that governing criminal proceedings—namely, the rule of guilt "beyond a reasonable doubt." *Breed v. Jones* (1975) applied the prohibition against double jeopardy to juvenile courts. However, *McKeiver v. Pennsylvania* (1971) decided that the right to trial by jury is not constitutionally required in juvenile courts.[116]

Two controversial 1979 decisions upheld state laws permitting voluntary admission of minor children to mental hospitals by parents or guardians without a hearing, but the Court did impose a requirement for a "neutral fact-finder" to determine whether statutory requirements for admission were satisfied.[117]

---

[115] See also *Kent v. United States* (1966).

[116] For critical analyses of juvenile court practices, see Peter S. Prescott, *The Child Savers: Juvenile Justice Observed* (New York: Knopf, 1981); and Ellen Ryerson, *The Best-Laid Plans: American's Juvenile Court Experiment* (New York: Hill and Wang, 1978).

[117] *Secretary v. Institutionalized Juveniles* (1979), *Parham v. J.R.* (1979).

Legal Incompetence

The conviction of an accused person who is legally incompetent violates due process, and state procedures must be adequate to protect this right.[118] The first formulation of an insanity test for judging criminal responsibility was the "right-wrong" criterion promulgated in *M'Naghten's Case* (1843)—namely, that "at the time of the committing of the act, the party accused was labouring under such a defect of reason, from disease of the mind, as not to know the nature and quality of the act he was doing; or, if he did know it, that he did not know he was doing what was wrong." The federal courts adopted the *M'Naghten* rule, and then supplemented it with the "irresistible impulse" test after this modification had been approved by the Supreme Court in *Davis v. United States* (1895).

This remained the basis for judging criminal responsibility in all the federal courts until 1954, when the District of Columbia Court of Appeals adopted a new test for insanity in *Durham v. United States.* This rule was "simply that an accused is not criminally responsible if the unlawful act was the product of mental disease or mental defect." The *Durham* rule set off a vigorous debate, but was not adopted by other courts and was expressly repudiated by three federal circuits. *Durham* was criticized because of the inherent vagueness in its terms, its overemphasis on the causal relationship between "disease" and "product," and its lack of utility for juries, which must make a social judgment, not a medical analysis.

In 1962 the American Law Institute proposed another test that strikes a balance between the more restrictive *M'Naghten* and irresistible impulse rules and the *Durham* test. It provides:

> A person is not responsible for criminal conduct if at the time of such conduct as a result of mental disease or defect he lacks substantial capacity either to appreciate the criminality [wrongfulness] of his conduct or to conform his conduct to the requirements of law.[119]

Apart from its approval in the 1895 *Davis* case of jury instructions embodying the irresistible impulse test, the Supreme Court had not found any of these four standards to be constitutionally required or preferred over the others.[120] However, the 1982 verdict of "innocent by reason of insanity" against John W. Hinckley, Jr., who attempted to assassinate President Reagan, stirred up a national frenzy of opposition to the insanity defense.

---

[118] *Bishop v. United States* (1956), *Pate v. Robinson* (1966).

[119] This standard was adopted by the Ninth Circuit Court of Appeals in *Wade v. United States* (1970).

[120] For a general discussion, see Abraham S. Goldstein, *The Insanity Defense* (New Haven, Conn.: Yale University Press, 1967); Herbert Fingarette, *The Meaning of Criminal Insanity* (Berkeley: University of California Press, 1972); Norval Morris, *Madness and the Criminal Law* (Chicago: University of Chicago Press, 1982).

Two states, Idaho and Montana, abolished it. Other states authorized verdicts of "guilty but mentally ill," which would permit imprisonment after release from a mental institution. The American Bar Association recommended that the burden of proving insanity by a preponderance of the evidence be shifted from the state to the defendant. The American Psychiatric Association proposed that psychiatrists should not be asked to make conclusive judgments on the sanity or insanity of a defendant. In 1983 President Reagan submitted to Congress a crime control bill that would restrict the insanity defense only to persons unable to distinguish between right and wrong.

A heightened national concern over commitment practices[121] and scandalous treatment of the inmates of state mental hospitals led to a unanimous Supreme Court decision in *O'Connor v. Donaldson* (1975) that mental patients who were not dangerous to others could not be confined in institutions against their will if they did not receive therapy and if they could survive in the outside world with the aid of relatives or friends. But a Bill of Rights Act for the developmentally disabled, adopted by Congress in 1975, was held in *Pennhurst State School and Hospital v. Halderman* (1981) not to create in favor of the mentally retarded any substantive right to "appropriate treatment" in the "least restrictive" environment, which Blackmun characterized as creating "the odd and perhaps dangerous precedent of ascribing no meaning to a congressional enactment."

Constitutional Rights of Prisoners

The treatment of prison inmates was historically regarded as strictly a matter for correctional administrators, and courts followed a "hands-off" policy. In 1871 a Virginia judge said in *Ruffin v. Commonwealth* that a convict is "for the time being the slave of the state." As late as 1954 the Court of Appeals for the Tenth Circuit held that "courts are without power to supervise prison administration or to interfere with the ordinary prison rules or regulations."[122]

But the situation began to change in the 1960s, first in the lower courts without notable leadership from the Supreme Court. In 1965 an Arkansas district judge held that persons convicted of crime were covered by the due process and equal protection clauses,[123] and in 1966 the Court of Appeals for

---

[121] See the comprehensive analysis, "Civil Commitment on the Mentally Ill," 87 HARVARD LAW REVIEW 1190–1406 (1974); *Specht v. Patterson* (1967). *Addington v. Texas* (1979) held that for an involuntary civil commitment to a mental hospital, due process requires "clear and convincing" standard of proof, greater than the "preponderance of evidence" standard in other categories of civil cases, but not as strict as the "reasonable-doubt" standard.

[122] *Banning v. Looney* (1954).

[123] *Talley v. Stephens* (1965).

the Fourth Circuit guaranteed inmates access to courts[124] and to medical care.[125] In *Holt v. Sarver* (1970), an Arkansas district judge held that barbaric conditions in the state's prisons violated the ban on cruel and unusual punishment and ordered prison authorities to submit a plan for bringing the system within constitutional standards.[126] In 1976 Judge Frank Johnson held that Alabama's prisons were "unfit for human habitation" and threatened to close them unless a long list of minimum constitutional standards was met. By 1982 federal courts had found prison conditions to be unconstitutional in three dozen states.

The Supreme Court appeared less sensitive to these conditions than the lower courts. In *Bell v. Wolfish* (1979) the Court upheld jailer's broad discretion to limit the privacy of persons held in jail awaiting trial, usually because they cannot afford bail, their presumption of innocence giving them no constitutional right to protection against "double-bunking" or checking of their bodily cavities for drugs or weapons after receiving visitors. Likewise, *Rhodes v. Chapman* (1981) rejected complaints of "double-celling" for long-term convicts who were told that "the Constitution does not mandate comfortable prisons."

The Supreme Court did, of course, have an established interest in protecting the right of convicted prisoners to pursue postconviction remedies by way of habeas corpus. In *Smith v. Bennett* (1961), the Court held that states could not refuse the writ to prisoners unable to pay the filing fee, and *Johnson v. Avery* (1969) struck down a prison regulation barring inmates from assisting other prisoners in preparation of petitions for postconviction relief.

As already noted, the Supreme Court has guaranteed minority religious faiths access to reading material and ministers. *Procunier v. Martinez* (1974) held that censorship of prisoners' mail must be no greater than required to protect security interests.[127] But while granting that prisoners retained those First Amendment rights not inconsistent with legitimate penological objectives, *Pell v. Procunier* (1974) denied that these included the right to demand face-to-face interviews with news media representatives.

Wolff v. McDonnell (1974) held that prison misconduct proceedings, which could cause the loss of "good-time" credits, must observe minimal

---

[124] *Coleman v. Peyton* (1966). In *Bounds v. Smith* (1977) the Supreme Court held that prison officials are obligated to assist prisoners in preparing legal claims, either by providing adequate law libraries or outside legal assistance.

[125] *Edwards v. Duncan* (1966). *Estelle v. Gamble* (1976) ruled that deliberate indifference to serious medical needs of an inmate would be cruel and unusual punishment.

[126] See Case Note, 84 HARVARD LAW REVIEW 456 (1970).

[127] Prison officials may not be sued for damages for negligently failing to mail a prisoner's letters seeking legal assistance, so long as they had not acted maliciously (*Procunier v. Navarette* [1978]).

due process requirements.[128] But *Jones v. Prisoners' Labor Union* (1977) ruled that organizations of prison inmates need not be allowed to conduct meetings and solicit members inside prison. *Greenholtz v. Inmates* (1979) assured states that they are free to administer their parole systems in any way they wish.

DOUBLE JEOPARDY

The Fifth Amendment in archaic language forbids the government to put any person twice "in jeopardy of life or limb" for the same offense. The underlying idea, as Justice Black has said, "is that the State with all its resources and power should not be allowed to make repeated attempts to convict an individual for an alleged offense, thereby subjecting him to embarrassment, expense and ordeal and compelling him to live in a continuing state of anxiety and insecurity, as well as enhancing the possibility that even though innocent he may be found guilty." [129]

Palko v. Connecticut held in 1937 that the states were not bound by the double jeopardy rule, on the ground that it was not essential to a scheme of "ordered liberty." But, like most of the other "ordered liberty" decisions, *Palko* was overruled during the "incorporationist" tide of the 1960s. In *Benton v. Maryland* (1969), the Warren Court asserted that the ban on double jeopardy "represents a fundamental ideal in our consitutional heritage" and was consequently binding on the states through the Fourteenth Amendment.[130]

Enforcement of the double jeopardy provision depends upon the views taken as to what constitutes "jeopardy" in a legal proceeding and what constitutes "sameness" in an offense. On the first question, an accused person has of course been placed in jeopardy when tried by a court of competent jurisdiction and either acquitted or convicted.[131] *Crist v. Bretz* (1978) held that states must follow the federal rule that jeopardy attaches in a jury trial at the moment the jury is empaneled and sworn, invalidating a Montana statute under which jeopardy did not attach until the first witness was sworn.

---

[128] But *Montayne v. Haymes* (1976) and *Meachum v. Fano* (1976) held that prison inmates do not have a constitutional right to a hearing before transfer to a maximum security penitentiary, whether or not the transfer was punitive. And *Hewitt v. Helms* (1983) ruled that an informal, nonevidentiary review was sufficient for deciding to confine an inmate to administrative segregation as a security threat.

[129] *Green v. United States* (1957). Courts-martial are governed by the double jeopardy provision; see *Wade v. Hunter* (1949).

[130] The *Benton* decision was given retroactive effect in *North Carolina v. Pearce* (1969).

[131] Trial by a court that is subsequently found to lack jurisdiction cannot place a defendant in jeopardy, no matter how far the proceedings are carried.

The government may not appeal a verdict of acquittal and institute a second prosecution for the same offense, no matter how erroneous the legal ruling that led to acquittal.[132] But when a jury fails to agree on a verdict and is discharged by the judge, a second trial is permissible, the theory being that it is merely a continuation of the first.[133]

Where a defendant successfully seeks to avoid trial prior to its conclusion by a motion for mistrial, this is a deliberate election by the defendant not to have guilt or innocence determined by the first trier of fact, and the government may appeal.[134] A defendant who secures a mistrial on ground of misbehavior by the prosecutor may be tried again on the same charge unless it is proved that the prosecutor intentionally aborted the trial.[135] The same thing is true where the defendant's motion for mistrial is necessitated by error of the trial judge.[136] But a trial judge who on his own motion declared a mistrial to enable the government's witnesses to consult with their own attorneys abused his discretion in discharging the jury and reprosecution was a violation of double jeopardy.[137]

The accused may waive constitutional immunity against double jeopardy by requesting a new trial or appealing from a verdict of guilty. If a conviction is set aside on appeal, the defendant may be tried a second time for the same offense,[138] but not if the reversal was based on insufficient evidence.[139] Nor can a more serious charge be brought than in the first trial.[140] However, the second trial can proceed on a different theory; in *Forman v. United States* (1960) a defendant was convicted of a subsidiary conspiracy after the statute of limitations had run on the main conspiracy involved in the first trial.

The "same offense" provision means the identical offense as defined by the same governmental jurisdiction. The test of identity of offenses is whether the same evidence is required to prove them. If not, the fact that two charges grow out of one transaction does not make a single offense where two or more are defined by the statutes.[141] Thus Congress may provide for

---

[132] *Sanabria v. United States* (1978). See also *Fong Foo v. United States* (1962) and *Breed v. Jones* (1975).

[133] *United States v. Perez* (1824).

[134] *United States v. Scott* (1978). This decision overruled *United States v. Jenkins* (1975).

[135] *Oregon v. Kennedy* (1982).

[136] *United States v. Dinitz* (1971).

[137] *United States v. Jorn* (1971). But when a judge declared a mistrial because of a defective indictment, before any evidence was presented, a subsequent trial did not constitute double jeopardy (*Illinois v. Somerville* [1973]).

[138] *United States v. Ball* (1896).

[139] *Burks v. United States* (1978), *Hudson v. Louisiana* (1981). Retrial is permissible if reversal of the conviction on appeal was based on the weight of the evidence (*Tibbs v. Florida* [1982]).

[140] *Green v. United States* (1957), *Price v. Georgia* (1970).

[141] *Morgan v. Devine* (1915), *United States v. Ewell* (1966).

both civil and criminal prosecution for the same act or failure to act, or it may separate a conspiracy to commit a substantive offense from the actual commission of the offense, and attach a different penalty to each. A person who refused to testify before a Senate committee was not subjected to double jeopardy by being punished for contempt of the Senate and also indicted for a misdemeanor for such refusal.[142]

The "same evidence" rule makes it possible to file multiple charges arising out of a single transaction (or, in Chief Justice Burger's phrase in *Ashe v. Swenson,* "one frolic"). In *Hoag v. New Jersey* (1958) a man who was alleged to have robbed five tavern patrons was tried for the robbery of three of them and was acquitted because of the unexpected failure of four of the state's witnesses to identify the defendant. The state then tried Hoag for robbery of a fourth patron, who was the only witness at the first trial to identify the defendant, and this time the jury convicted. By a five to three vote the Supreme Court upheld the state's action on the ground that, while a single trial would have been "preferable practice," the Fourteenth Amendment did not lay down an inflexible rule making multiple trials unconstitutional, and the circumstances of this case did not result in "fundamental unfairness." Chief Justice Warren, dissenting, thought that the state had relitigated "the same issue on the same evidence before two different juries."

Ciucci v. Illinois involved a man accused of killing his wife and three children. The initial prosecution for one of the murders brought conviction and a twenty-year sentence. Dissatisfied with this outcome, the prosecutor instituted a second trial for another of the murders, which yielded a forty-five-year sentence. The state then made a third effort, and was finally rewarded by a death sentence. The Court upheld these tactics by a five to four vote in 1958.

Comparable prosecution methods were finally declared unconstitutional by the Court in *Ashe v. Swenson* (1970) by reading the technical doctrine of "collateral estoppel" into the double jeopardy provision.[143] But three justices, speaking through Brennan, directly attacked the "same evidence" rule. They favored the "same transaction" rule, requiring the prosecution "to join at one trial all the charges against a defendant which grow out of a single criminal act, occurrence, episode, or transaction." Potential prosecutorial abuses in bringing multiple trials under the same evidence rule were "simply intolerable."

The double jeopardy rule does not apply to sentencing decisions after retrial with the same force that it does to redeterminations of guilt or

---

[142] *In re Chapman* (1897). See also *Gore v. United States* (1958), *Brown v. Ohio* (1977).

[143] Collateral estoppel "means simply that when an issue of ultimate fact has once been determined by a valid and final judgment, that issue cannot again be litigated between the same parties in any future lawsuit," said Justice Stewart in *Ashe v. Swenson.*

innocence. A defendant whose conviction is reversed may receive a more severe sentence upon retrial than at the first trial. But in *North Carolina v. Pearce* (1969) a threefold increase in punishment on retrial was held by the Court to be punishment of the defendant for getting his original conviction set aside and so violative of due process.

United States v. DiFrancesco (1980) by a five to four vote upheld a provision of the Organized Crime Control Act granting the government the right to appeal sentences imposed on "dangerous special offenders." The dissenters contended that "a punishment enhanced by an appellate court is an unconstitutional multiple punishment." But by another five to four vote in the same term, *Bullington v. Missouri* (1981) held that a defendant sentenced to life imprisonment who was granted a new trial could not be sentenced to death on the second conviction.

Where both federal and state governments make the same act an offense, the Supreme Court has held that it is not double jeopardy for each government to prosecute and punish. This rule provoked considerable dissatisfaction during the era of national prohibition, but the Court justified dual prosecution in *United States v. Lanza* (1922) as resulting from our system of "two sovereignties, deriving power from different sources, capable of dealing with the same subject-matter within the same territory . . . It follows that an act denounced as a crime by both national and state sovereignties is an offense against the peace and dignity of both."[144]

A bizarre form of double jeopardy problem came to the Court's attention in *Louisiana ex rel. Francis v. Resweber* (1947). Francis had been duly convicted of murder and sentenced to death. He was placed in the electric chair, but because of some mechanical difficulty, it did not operate, and the prisoner was returned to his cell. Redress was then sought in the courts on the ground that a second trip to the electric chair would constitute double jeopardy contrary to the Fifth Amendment and cruel and unusual punishment in violation of the Eighth Amendment. The Court rejected both claims by a vote of five to four.[145]

---

[144] See *Abbate v. United States* (1959) and *Bartkus v. Illinois* (1959) for interesting instances of federal and state prosecutions for the same offenses. The attorney general announced, as reported in *Petite v. United States* (1960), that it would not be the general policy of the government to make several offenses arising from a single transaction the basis of multiple prosecutions. *Waller v. Florida* (1970) held that a defendant who had been convicted in municipal court for violation of city ordinances could not be tried by the state on a charge of grand larceny based on the same acts. See also *Missouri v. Hunter* (1983).

[145] The importance of the double jeopardy rule is indicated by the fact, as pointed out by Justice Blackmun in *United States v. DiFrancesco* (1980), that the Supreme Court had handed down twenty-one decisions on double jeopardy between 1971 and 1980. See Peter Westen and Richard Drubel, "Toward a General Theory of Double Jeopardy," in Philip B. Kurland and Gerhard Casper, eds., *The Supreme Court Review: 1978* (Chicago: University of Chicago Press, 1979), pp. 81–169.

EXCESSIVE BAIL

"Excessive bail shall not be required," the Eighth Amendment says, copying a similar provision in the English Bill of Rights of 1689. Bail is the pledge of money or property by an accused person or his sureties in order to guarantee appearance for trial. Admission to bail provides a means whereby an individual may obtain freedom while awaiting trial. Apart from humanitarian considerations and the presumption that a person is innocent until proved guilty, it provides the accused with a better opportunity to prepare a defense. The constitutional provision has been construed as a limitation both on Congress, in adopting statutes governing admission to bail, and on federal courts, in fixing bail in individual cases.

Bail is excessive, the Supreme Court has said, when it is set "at a figure higher than an amount reasonably calculated" to fulfill the purpose of assuring the presence of the accused at the trial. The Federal Rules of Criminal Procedure itemize the factors to be considered by the court in fixing bail as follows: "The nature and circumstances of the offense charged, the weight of the evidence against him, the financial ability of the defendant to give bail and the character of the defendant." In *Stack v. Boyle* (1951) the Court held that bail of $50,000 for each of twelve Communist party members was excessive, but since that time bail in much higher amounts has become common.

There are two conflicting tendencies in current attitudes toward bail. One stresses the fact that almost half the national jail population consists of defendants awaiting trial, many eligible for release but lacking the money to post bond. Concern about abuses in the bail system led Congress to pass the Bail Reform Act of 1966, which requires the release on personal recognizance or on unsecured bond of persons charged with noncapital federal offenses unless a judicial officer finds that release would "not reasonably assure" appearance as required. Release on "own recognizance" is also widely practiced in the states.

But much of the current national concern about crime has focused on alleged abuses of the bail system. Statistics are presented on the number of crimes committed by repeat offenders out on bail. One legislative reaction has been to define certain crimes for which bail can be denied. A Nebraska law making violent sex crimes nonbailable came up to the Supreme Court in *Murphy v. Hunt* (1982), but after hearing argument the Court dismissed the case as moot because the prisoner had already been convicted and so was no longer eligible for pretrial bail.

The Court likewise avoided passing on a District of Columbia pretrial detention law that allowed judges to order defendants held for up to sixty days without bail on a finding that release would be a danger to the community. In *Edwards v. United States* (1980) the Court allowed the lower court opinion upholding the statute to stand without review.

CRUEL AND UNUSUAL PUNISHMENT

The Eighth Amendment's ban on "cruel and unusual punishment" has raised some very difficult moral issues. Prior to the landmark capital punishment decision, *Furman v. Georgia*, in 1972, the Supreme Court had applied various standards in interpreting the provision. First, punishment considered grossly disproportionate to the offense was considered cruel and unusual in several cases. In *Weems v. United States* (1910), a Philippine law providing for a punishment of twelve years in chains at hard labor was held greatly excessive for the crime of falsifying an official document. In *Trop v. Dulles* (1958), the Court ruled that imposing loss of citizenship on a member of the armed forces convicted by court-martial of wartime desertion was cruel and unusual. Chief Justice Warren said this was "a form of punishment more primitive that torture," for it involved "the total destruction of the individual's status in organized society."

Again, a California law making it a crime to be a drug addict was held in *Robinson v. California* (1962) to be cruel and unusual punishment. The statute did not require any proof that the defendant bought or used drugs or had any in his possession. The mere status of being an addict, which could be established by needle marks in the arm, was sufficient. The Court regarded addiction as an illness rather than a crime and thought that ninety days in jail for being ill was cruel and unusual punishment.[146] However, in *Powell v. Texas* (1968) the Court by a vote of five to four declined to rule that criminal conviction of chronic alcoholism was cruel and unusual. The majority thought that knowledge about alcoholism and the record in this case were inadequate for a "wide-ranging new constitutional principle."

Two Burger Court decisions allowed grossly disproportionate sentences. *Hutto v. Davis* (1982) upheld forty years for possession and distribution of nine ounces of marijuana. *Rummel v. Estelle* (1980) approved a life sentence for three thefts totalling $289. While these cases seemed to make length of sentence purely a legislative prerogative, the Court reconsidered and by a five to four vote in *Solem v. Helm* (1983) held that a life sentence without possibility of parole was cruel and unusual and significantly disproportionate for a $100 bad check charge plus six previous nonviolent offenses.

Second, the Court has considered whether punishment is cruel and unusual because barbaric in some absolute sense.[147] Clearly death by torture

---

[146] See Herbert Fingarette, "Addiction and Criminal Responsibility," 84 YALE LAW JOURNAL 413 (1975), and "The Perils of Powell: In Search of a Factual Foundation for the 'Disease Concept of Alcoholism,'" 83 HARVARD LAW REVIEW 793 (1970).

[147] See Hugo Adam Bedau, ed., *The Death Penalty in America* (New York: Doubleday, 1967); Michael Meltsner, *Cruel and Unusual: The Supreme Court and Capital Punishment* (New York: Random House, 1973); Arthur J. Goldberg and Alan M. Dershowitz, "Declaring the Death Penalty Unconstitutional," 83 HARVARD LAW REVIEW 1773 (1970). In 1982 Texas carried out an execution by lethal injection, and a Massachusetts law gives condemned prisoners the choice of death in the electric chair or by lethal injection.

or various forms of lingering death are forbidden. But the Court has accepted more "humane" forms of capital punishment. In *Wilkerson v. Utah* (1878), public execution by musketry was upheld. *In re Kemmler* (1890) approved the new method of electrocution as apparently instantaneous and painless. The second trip to the electric chair in the *Francis* case was regarded as acceptable by the Court majority in part because it was the result of an "unforseeable accident" and not any intentional cruelty.

Concerted legal attacks on the constitutionality of capital punishment began in the 1960s, stimulated in part by the fact that those receiving death sentences were disproportionately blacks. One result was the *Witherspoon* decision already noted. But other challenges to court procedures in capital cases were less successful. In *McGautha v. California* (1971) and *Crampton v. Ohio* (1971), the practice under which state statutes left the death verdict to the absolute discretion of the jury, with no standards of any sort to guide them, was held not to violate due process. Justice Harlan thought it would be impossible to draft statutory standards for this purpose:

> To identify before the fact those characteristics of criminal homicides and their perpetrators which call for the death penalty, and to express these characteristics in language which can be fairly understood and applied by the sentencing authority, appear to be tasks which are beyond present human ability.

California law called for a two-stage trial, one to determine guilt and the second to hear evidence and argument on the issue of punishment. In Ohio guilt and punishment were determined at a single trial. The bifurcated procedure might well be preferable, the Court said in *Crampton*, but it was not constitutionally required.

These decisions gave little warning of the ruling that was to come a year later in *Furman v. Georgia* (1972), where by a vote of five to four the Court held that the imposition of the death penalty in three cases, one for murder and two for rape, constituted cruel and unusual punishment in violation of the Eighth and Fourteenth Amendments.[148] The Court issued a brief per curiam opinion, which was followed by substantial statements by every member of the Court.

The five justices who made up the majority were divided into two groups. Douglas, Stewart, and White took an analytic and empirical approach, appraising the practice under the Eighth Amendment in the light of due process and equal protection. Their concern was whether the death

---

[148] See Daniel D. Polsby, "The Death of Capital Punishment? Furman v. Georgia," in Philip B. Kurland, ed., *The Supreme Court Review, 1972* (Chicago: University of Chicago Press, 1972), pp. 1-40. The California supreme court had declared capital punishment unconstitutional under that state's constitution four months earlier (*People v. Anderson* [1972]).

penalty was evenly applied, and of course they found that it was not. Stewart's comment is quotable:

> These death sentences are cruel and unusual in the same way that being struck by lightning is cruel and unusual. For, of all the people convicted of rapes and murders in 1967 and 1968, many just as reprehensible as these, the petitioners are among a capriciously selected random handful upon whom the sentence of death has in fact been imposed.

Douglas contended that the death penalty was cruel and unusual because applied irregularly and "selectively to minorities whose members are few, who are outcasts of society, and who are unpopular, but whom society is willing to see suffer though it would not countenance general application of the same penalty across the boards."

White conceded that the death penalty, while cruel in "the dictionary sense," would nevertheless be justified if it served "social ends." But he did not believe "that society's need for specific deterrence justifies death for so few when for so many in like circumstances life imprisonment or shorter prison terms are judged sufficient, or that community values are measurably reenforced by authorizing a penalty so rarely invoked."

The other two majority justices, Brennan and Marshall, took a normative approach. For them, the Eighth Amendment posed a core question of values; they were concerned less with fairness and equality and more with mercy and charity. For them, capital punishment, no matter how often or how infrequently applied, was uncivilized, excessive, unacceptable. For Brennan, "the primary principle. . . . is that a punishment must not by its severity be degrading to human dignity." Marshall, in by far the longest opinion of the day, not only made what he called "a long and tedious journey" through history and the precedents but also reviewed a great number of studies and reports bearing upon the "six purposes conceivably served by capital punishment: retribution, deterrence, prevention of repetitive criminal acts, encouragement of guilty pleas and confessions, eugenics, and economy." His impassioned conclusion was that ending the death sentence would recognize "the humanity of our fellow beings" and achieve "a major milestone in the long road up from barbarism."

Powell wrote the major opinion in dissent, and it was basically a plea for judicial restraint in this enormously difficult area. Stressing the "enormity of the step taken by the Court today," he said: "Not only does it invalidate hundreds of state and federal laws, it deprives those jurisdictions of the power to legislate with respect to capital punishment in the future, except in a manner consistent with the cloudily outlined views of those Justices who do not purport to undertake total abolition." This was "a classic case for the exercise of our oft-announced allegiance to judicial restraint."

After *Furman* it was widely assumed that the Court had not declared capital punishment unconstitutional per se, but only its unpredictable and fortuitous use. Consequently the legislatures of thirty-five states acted to tighten the laws under which the death penalty was to be inflicted. They took two different approaches. Some states, including Georgia, Florida, and Texas, established new procedures for capital cases, requiring sentencing judges and juries to consider certain specified aggravating or mitigating circumstances of the crime and the offender. Courts of appeal were given broader authority to decide whether the death penalty was fair in the light of the sentences for similar offenses. These laws were intended to reduce the arbitrariness and possible racial prejudice denounced in *Furman*.

But ten other states, including North Carolina, Louisiana, and Oklahoma, sought to meet the *Furman* objections by removing all flexibility from the sentencing process, though limiting the offenses for which the death sentence could be imposed. Anyone found guilty of the specified offenses was to be sentenced to death automatically. There would be no more unpredictable lightning bolts.

On July 2, 1976, by which time there were some 600 persons on death rows under the new laws, the Supreme Court made the judgment it had postponed a year earlier. By a vote of seven to two in *Gregg v. Georgia* it ruled that the death penalty was not inherently cruel and unusual. Justice Stewart's opinion relied heavily on "society's endorsement of the death penalty for murder" as evidenced by action of the thirty-five state legislatures; "a heavy burden rests on those who would attack the judgment of the representatives of the people." The Georgia law, moreover, had met and remedied the *Furman* objections. "No longer can a jury wantonly and freakishly impose the death sentence; it is always circumscribed by the legislative guidelines." The Texas and Florida statutes were upheld by the same reasoning.[149]

However, the "automatic" statutes of North Carolina, Louisiana, and Oklahoma were held unconstitutional by votes of five to four.[150] Brennan and Marshall, who had dissented in the Georgia, Texas, and Florida decisions, now joined Stewart, Powell, and Stevens in striking down mandatory death sentences for specified crimes as "unduly harsh and unworkably rigid," incompatible with "contemporary values." These statutes simply "papered over the problem of unguided and unchecked jury discretion," and provided no way for appellate courts to check arbitrary and capricious exercise of discretion.[151] They treated "all persons convicted of a

---

[149] *Jurek v. Texas, Proffitt v. Florida.*

[150] *Woodson v. North Carolina, Roberts v. Louisiana, Green v. Oklahoma.*

[151] On the impossibility of eliminating prosecutory or jury discretion by automatic death sentences, see Charles L. Black, Jr., *Capital Punishment: The Inevitability of Caprice and Mistake* (New York: W. W. Norton & Co., Inc., 1974).

designated offense not as uniquely individual human beings, but as members of a faceless, undifferentiated mass to be subjected to the blind infliction of the penalty of death." Consequently death sentences from these three states were vacated.

White, Burger, Blackmun, and Rehnquist were the dissenters in the mandatory sentence cases; and while voting to make up the majority in *Gregg*, they were sharply critical of Stewart's "muddled reasoning" in all the cases. White contended that legislatures should have the right to decide whether mandatory death sentences deter crime and whether "the commission of certain crimes conclusively establishes that the criminal's character is such that he deserves death." By refusing to honor these legislative judgments, White thought the Court had "again surrendered to the temptation to make policy for and to attempt to govern the country through a misuse of [its] powers."

Application and interpretation of the 1976 rulings brought a stream of state death sentences to the Court for review, which must be summarized briefly. *Davis v. Georgia* (1976) and *Adams v. Texas* (1980) reversed convictions because of failure to apply the *Witherspoon* rule on jury selection properly. *Beck v. Alabama* (1980) reversed because the jury was not permitted to consider a verdict of guilt on a lesser included noncapital offense. *Coker v. Georgia* (1977) held that a death sentence for the rape of an adult woman was grossly disproportionate and excessive punishment.

Lockett v. Ohio (1978) and *Bell v. Ohio* (1978) ruled that Ohio law did not permit the type of individualized consideration of mitigating circumstances required by *Gregg*, and Louisiana law encountered the same objection in *Roberts v. Louisiana* (1977). *Green v. Georgia* (1979) ruled that exclusion of testimony during the punishment phase denied a fair trial, and *Gardner v. Florida* (1977) held that a judge may not impose the death penalty on the basis of a secret presentence report that the defendant had no chance to refute. In *Presnell v. Georgia* (1978) there was inadequate jury finding of forcible rape.

As noted earlier, *Estelle v. Smith* (1981) held that the defendant should have had the advice of counsel before consenting to a psychiatric examination; this ruling voided at least twenty Texas death sentences. *Godfrey v. Georgia* (1980) overturned a death sentence because the murder was not sufficiently horrible and inhumane to meet statutory requirements. *Enmund v. Florida* (1982) ruled that a person may not be sentenced to death for participation in a crime resulting in death caused by someone else—a so-called "felony murder." *Eddings v. Oklahoma* (1982) reversed the death sentence of a defendant who was sixteen at the time of the crime because of failure to consider mitigating circumstances, but without deciding whether the Constitution bars execution of all juveniles.

Dobbert v. Florida (1977), upholding a conviction under Florida law, was one of the few death sentence cases to escape reversal on review. Justice

Rehnquist, a strong supporter of capital punishment, took the occasion of *Coleman v. Balkcom* (1981) to castigate the repeated opportunities for appeals in capital punishment cases that have created a "stalemate" in which people are sentenced to die but are not executed. In fact, by 1983, at a time when there were about one thousand prisoners on death rows throughout the country, only six persons had been executed, and four of those had not challenged the imposition of the penalty. However, the appeals process, which averages about eight years, was running out for these death row inmates in 1983; and the country faced the grim prospect of scores of executions in the 1980s.

The prospect was increased by the Court's six to three decision in *Barefoot v. Estelle* (1983) that federal judges may use special, speeded-up procedures to handle appeals by death row inmates; it also warned that stays of execution would not always be granted to hear these appeals. At the same time a five to four ruling in *California v. Ramos* upheld a state law requiring that juries considering life sentence versus death penalty must be told by the judge that the governor could commute a life sentence, opening the way to parole.

CONCLUSION

The Warren Court was responsible for a dramatic rethinking and strengthening of the constitutional rights of defendants in federal criminal trials. As for state courts, an inexorable process, whether called "incorporation" or "absorption," made binding most of the provisions of the Fourth through the Eighth Amendments. The new, stricter federal standards were thus given nationwide application; through such decisions as *Escobedo* and *Miranda,* they reached down into every police station in the nation. The line of decisions from *Mapp* to *Furman* ranks as one of the major assertions of judicial power in the Court's long history.

This experience also vividly demonstrates the political limits on the Court's authority. While Congress sometimes shared the Court's concern for improving the standards of criminal justice, as in adoption of the Bail Reform Act of 1966, the Jury Selection and Service Act of 1968, and the Speedy Trial Act of 1974, more often it was joining with much of the public in attacking the Court and the entire judicial system for "coddling criminals."

Inevitably, the Burger Court subjected Warren Court criminal justice decisions to reconsideration. While the spirit of the new Court majority was considerably more skeptical concerning constitutional claims, there was no wholesale overruling of precedents. In fact, right to counsel was extended in *Argersinger.* The *Miranda* rules were preserved, though limited in application. The *Mapp* exclusionary rule likewise survived, though not intact. While accepting the constitutionality of capital punishment, the Court preserved a basis for judicial control of its imposition.

One area where there was substantial erosion of Warren Court standards was in federal habeas corpus review of state criminal convictions. *Stone v. Powell* (1976) and subsequent rulings[152] substantially closed the federal courts to claims of Fourth Amendment violations in state convictions, the Burger Court preferring to leave enforcement of those constitutional rights to state courts. As a result, in some states defendants and judges have found it preferable to rely on state constitutional provisions rather than on the Bill of Rights as interpreted by the Burger Court.[153]

It is well to remember, as Justice Frankfurter said in *Stein v. New York* (1953), that constitutional guarantees for criminal defendants are provided "not out of tenderness for the accused but because we have reached a certain stage of civilization"—a civilization, Douglas added, which "by respecting the dignity even of the least worthy citizen, raises the stature of all of us."

---

[152] *Francis v. Henderson* (1976), *Estelle v. Williams* (1976), *Rose v. Lundy* (1982), *Engle v. Isaac* (1982), *United States v. Frady* (1982).

[153] See William J. Brennan, Jr., "State Constitutions and the Protection of Individual Rights," 90 HARVARD LAW REVIEW 489 (1977).

10

Equal Protection: Racial

"Equal protection of the laws" is a phrase born with the Fourteenth Amendment, the first specific recognition of the doctrine of equality in the Constitution. The dictum of the Declaration of Independence that "all men are created equal," which was effectively used in the antislavery campaign, had a somewhat different import. Charles Sumner came closer to the equal protection notion with his phrase "equality before the law," which he developed in 1849 in contending before the Massachusetts supreme court that separate public schools for black children would be unconstitutional. Later he sought to get the principle of equal rights into the Constitution by way of the Thirteenth Amendment, his suggestion being: "All persons are equal before the law, so that no person can hold another as a slave."

But it was Representative Bingham who gave final form to the idea. In December 1865, he proposed a constitutional amendment authorizing Congress "to secure to all persons in every State of the Union equal protection in their rights, life, liberty, and property." Within the same month Senators Wilson and Trumbull introduced the bill that became the Civil Rights Act of 1866, in which all inhabitants were guaranteed "full and equal benefit of all laws and proceedings for the security of person and estate." When Bingham came to prepare his draft of the Fourteenth Amendment, "equal protection in their rights" and "equal benefit of all laws" were merged to produce "equal protection of the laws."

THE ORIGINAL UNDERSTANDING

Obviously Congress was thinking primarily of the newly freed blacks when it drafted the Fourteenth Amendment. Their problems were of two sorts. The first was political. How could they be guaranteed the right to vote and to full political participation in the Southern states? Congress sought to include some formula for this purpose in the Fourteenth Amendment, but ultimately all it was able to produce was the provision in section 2 of the amendment reducing representation in the House for any state that denied the vote to qualified citizens.

The second problem was guaranteeing the civil, as distinct from the political, rights of the freedmen. This was the area that equal protection was meant to cover—but what fields, and how fully? There can be no doubt that the equal protection clause was meant to end discrimination enforced upon blacks by the "Black Codes" of certain states which limited their right to hold property, specified criminal offenses for blacks only, and hampered their access to the courts in a variety of ways. In 1862 Congress had repealed the Black Codes in the District of Columbia and prohibited exclusion of witnesses on account of color in court cases there. The Civil Rights Act of 1866, passed just prior to congressional adoption of the Fourteenth Amendment, spelled out clearly the purpose to guarantee blacks equality in courts and commerce, by giving

> . . . citizens, of every race and color . . . the same right, in every State and Territory . . . to make and enforce contracts, to sue, be parties, and give evidence, to inherit, purchase, lease, sell, hold, and convey real and personal property, and to full and equal benefit of all laws and proceedings for the security of person and property, as is enjoyed by white citizens, and shall be subject to like punishment, pains, and penalties, and to none other.

Congressional intent in other areas of discrimination is less clear. The impact that equal protection was intended to have on segregation is certainly open to doubt. The problem of segregation was never squarely faced during the incubation period of the amendment. There was a widespread assumption of a dichotomy between "civil" equality and "social" equality. The former was a matter that the law must control, but the latter was a matter of taste, with which the law had nothing to do. Just where the dividing line was between the two areas was not too clear, however.

Geographical segregation—that is, governmental restriction of blacks to certain sections of a city or their exclusion from areas by limiting their right to buy or live on particular pieces of property—was clearly forbidden under congressional interpretations of that period. Segregation in transportation, it would seem, was almost equally condemned by congressional attitudes of the time, which held that transportation companies had a common-law duty to take all comers, and that making any distinctions in the operation of this duty because of color denied an equal right to contract for transportation.

Concerning hotels and theaters, there was substantially more disagreement. Hotels were generally thought, like railroads, to have a common-law obligation to serve all comers, but there were problems of location as to rooms and at dining tables where preferences in tastes could legitimately be indulged. Theaters were scarcely in the same public utility category as railroads and hotels, but they were nevertheless subject to extensive regulation of various sorts.

On segregation in education, the situation was the most confused of all. At the close of the Civil War, blacks were generally excluded from education altogether in both North and South. The primary problem was to get any kind of education at all for blacks, not whether the schools were to be separate or mixed. In the District of Columbia, separate schools for blacks were established as they were freed during the war, so that a pattern of segregation was established before Congress could take a position on the subject. Several abortive efforts were made subsequently to legislate against school segregation, but the main battle was in connection with the Civil Rights Act of 1875. On May 22, 1874, an amendment permitting separate but equal schools was defeated in the Senate, twenty-six to twenty-one, and the next day the Senate passed the bill forbidding school segregation by a vote of twenty-nine to sixteen. However, when the House considered the measure a year later, it deleted the school clause, and it remained out of the final statute.[1]

The Civil Rights Act of 1875, then, forbade racial separation or discrimination in public conveyances, hotels, and theaters, and also required equality in jury service. The constitutional basis for the statute cited in the congressional debates was primarily the equal protection clause, with privileges and immunities as a subordinate support. There were two matters of major significance to note about this act. The first is that, apart from the jury provisions, it was directed at discriminatory actions not primarily of public officials, but of private individuals operating services traditionally subject to public regulation.

Second, the Civil Rights Act was based on an unquestioned assumption that Congress had plenary legislative power to enforce the protections of the Fourteenth Amendment, that its authority was as broad as was necessary to correct abuses that might be found, and that it could be invoked to punish acts of omission or failure to enforce the law, as well as affirmative discriminatory acts. There was this significant difference

---

[1] See John P. Frank and Robert F. Munro, "The Original Understanding of 'Equal Protection of the Laws,'" 50 COLUMBIA LAW REVIEW 131 (1950); Alexander M. Bickel, "The Original Understanding and the Segregation Decision," 69 HARVARD LAW REVIEW 1 (1955).

in the two situations. When a state discriminated by affirmative state action, redress simply required the negating of that action. But where the discrimination arose out of actions by private individuals that the state failed to prevent or punish, then redress necessarily required the assertion of power to coerce state officials into a positive program of law enforcement. Thus the latter situation involved substantially greater congressional control over state and local government than the former.

Nevertheless, both in the act of 1875 and in the earlier Ku Klux (Second Enforcement) Act of 1871, Congress asserted its power to legislate affirmatively in behalf of a racial group that states might neglect to protect from the actions of private persons. There can be no doubt that a large majority in Congress at this time shared the view that Congress could enforce the Fourteenth Amendment on the states by affirmative legislation, and that a state denied equal protection when it tolerated widespread abuses against a class of citizens because of their color without seriously attempting to protect them by enforcing the law.

Within a decade the Supreme Court decided that Congress had been completely wrong on both these points. There is scarcely a more striking instance in American constitutional history of outright judicial disregard of congressional intent. In the *Civil Rights Cases* of 1883, the Supreme Court concluded that the Congress which had drafted the Fourteenth Amendment and which had provided for its enforcement by major enactments in 1871 and 1875 had not understood the amendment or congressional powers under it. By means of what Justice Harlan in his dissenting opinion called "a subtle and ingenious verbal criticism," the Court proceeded to sacrifice "the substance and spirit" of the amendment.

Justice Bradley's opinion is indeed a masterpiece of ingenuity. He started by giving literal effect to the language that "no state" shall deny equal protection, saying: "It is State action of a particular character that is prohibited. Individual invasion of individual rights is not the subject-matter of the amendment." The congressmen who had drafted and interpreted this language apparently had no such understanding of its meaning, but only one Supreme Court justice, Harlan, agreed with them. Railroads, he said, might be owned by private companies, but they were "none the less public highways," and the state may regulate their entire management. With railroads, and also with inns, "no matter who is the agent, or what is the agency, the function performed is *that of the State*." As to places of public amusement, "the authority to establish and maintain them comes from the public," and "a license from the public . . . imports, in law, equality of right, at such places, among all the members of that public."

The defeat of the Harlan position meant that Congress was stripped of any power to correct or to punish individual discriminatory action. Only *state* action was subject to the amendment. Bradley then undertook a second exercise in strict construction, this time operating on section 5 of the amendment. What did that section give Congress power to do? Why, "to enforce the prohibition" on state legislation or "State action of every kind" denying equal protection of the laws; further,

> . . . to adopt appropriate legislation for correcting the effects of such prohibited State laws and State acts and thus to render them effectually null, void, and innocuous. This is the legislative power conferred upon Congress, and this is the whole of it. It does not invest Congress with power to legislate upon subjects which are within the domain of State legislation; but to provide modes of relief against State legislation, or State action, of the kind referred to. It does not authorize Congress to create a code of municipal law for the regulation of private rights; but to provide modes of redress against the operation of State laws, and the action of State officers . . . when these are subversive of the fundamental rights specified in the amendment.

In other words, Congress was limited to the *correcting* of *affirmative* state action. "Until some State law has been passed, or some State action through its officers or agents has been taken, adverse to the rights of citizens sought to be protected by the Fourteenth Amendment, no legislation of the United States under said amendment, nor any proceeding under such legislation, can be called into activity." The Civil Rights Act was not corrective legislation. It was "primary and direct." It was a code of conduct which ignored state legislation, and assumed "that the matter is one that belongs to the domain of national regulation." Since the law was thus based on a misconstruction of the Fourteenth Amendment, and since it was not regarded by the Court as having any demonstrable relationship with the Thirteenth Amendment, it was unconstitutional.

DE JURE VERSUS DE FACTO DISCRIMINATION

The decision in the *Civil Rights Cases* has never been specifically overruled, and the "state action" theory it adopted remains a factor in equal protection interpretation, though, as we will see, often broadly interpreted. But the spirit of the 1883 ruling was challenged within three years by the decision in *Yick Wo v. Hopkins* (1886). A San Francisco ordinance made it unlawful to operate a laundry, except in a brick or stone building, without securing the consent of the board of supervisors. Masquerading as a safety measure, the ordinance in actual use discriminated against Chinese laundry operators. The fact of discrimination was demonstrated to the satisfaction of the Supreme Court, which determined that there had been a "practical denial" of equal protection.

> Though the law itself be fair on its face and impartial in appearance, yet, if it is applied and administered by public authority with an evil eye and an

unjust hand, so as practically to make unjust and illegal discrimination between persons in similar circumstances, material to their rights, the denial of equal justice is . . . within the prohibition of the Constitution.

In other words, this was discrimination de facto, though not de jure. The law was "fair on its face." But the Court looked behind or beyond the words of the law to its motive and its administration, and found a discriminatory purpose and effect. It is well to be aware of this duality before proceeding further with an account of racial discrimination litigation.

De Jure Discrimination

Under the de jure test, a statute provides equal protection if on its face it assures equality of treatment. The amendment is not violated unless a motive or intent to discriminate on a racial basis is apparent to courts in the words of the statute. The classic illustration is the famous case of *Plessy v. Ferguson* (1896). Here a Louisiana statute requiring segregation of the two races on public carriers was upheld by the Supreme Court. Said Justice Brown:

The object of the amendment was undoubtedly to enforce the absolute equality of the two races before the law, but in the nature of things it could not have been intended to abolish distinctions based upon color, or to enforce social, as distinguished from political equality, or a commingling of the two races upon terms unsatisfactory to either.

The Court denied that the enforced separation of the races stamped the colored race with a "badge of inferiority." "If this be so, it is not by reason of anything found in the act, but solely because the colored race chooses to put that construction upon it."

Plessy is ancient history, but the de jure test for equal treatment remains a viable rationale for judicial decisions, as more recent examples illustrate. In *Palmer v. Thompson* (1971) the city of Jackson, Mississippi, ordered the closing of all municipal swimming pools after a court order to desegregate them had been issued. Justice Black found no unequal treatment: "the city has closed the public pools to black and white alike." As for the contention that the action was motivated by a desire to avoid integration of the races, he said that a law must be judged by its "facial content," not on allegations about the motivation of its sponsors.

Washington v. Davis (1976) concerned the constitutionality of an examination for police officers in the District of Columbia, which blacks failed at a rate four times that of whites. Justice White wrote that for a law or other official act to deny equal protection it must reflect a "racially discriminatory purpose." It cannot be held "unconstitutional *solely* because it has a racially disproportionate impact." In *Village of Arlington Heights v. Metropolitan Housing Development Corp.* (1977) a developer desiring to build racially integrated low- and moderate-income housing in a suburban community was denied a zoning permit. The Court held that the developer had failed to carry the burden of proving that racially discriminatory intent or purpose was a motivating factor in the zoning decision.

On the other hand, the Court can of course find evidence of de jure discrimination; *Brown v. Board of Education* (1954), soon to be considered, is a monumental example. In the early case of *Strauder v. West Virginia* (1880) the Court was confronted by a statute limiting jurors to "white males." A more recent case of de jure discrimination is *Hunter v. Erickson* (1969), where the city charter provided that no fair housing law enacted by the city council could become law until approved by a popular referendum.

De Facto Discrimination

The de facto test for discrimination looks beyond statutory language to its effect, and judges whether any race-dependent consequences were intentional. As we have just seen, this is what the *Yick Wo* Court did. And this is what the Court did in the Second Scottsboro case, *Norris v. Alabama* (1935), finding that in the Alabama counties involved no blacks had even been called for jury service within the memory of the oldest inhabitants. And unlike the decision in *Washington v. Davis,* the Court in *Griggs v. Duke Power Co.* (1971) found an employment test discriminatory because unrelated to job performance and operating to disqualify blacks at a significantly higher rate than white applicants.[2]

Race as a Suspect Classification

While "equal protection of the laws" gives courts a sweeping mandate, race enjoys a special protection against discrimination by reason of its explicit mention in the Fifteenth Amendment and its implicit role in the Thirteenth and Fourteenth. Consequently it is not surprising that race has generally occupied the top position in the Court's hierarchy of equal protection concerns.

De jure racial classifications are automatically suspect. When racial quotas are utilized in affirmative action programs, as we shall soon see, they create serious problems of rationalization. Another exception to the

[2] See Barry A. Miller, "Proof of Racially Discriminatory Purpose under the Equal Protection Clause," 12 HARVARD CIVIL RIGHTS–CIVIL LIBERTIES LAW REVIEW 725 (1977); John Hart Ely, "Legislative and Administrative Motivation in Constitutional Law," 79 YALE LAW JOURNAL 1205 (1970).

rule against racial classifications is *United Jewish Organizations v. Carey* (1977), which upheld the use of racial quotas in reapportioning New York legislative districts where the purpose was to increase the voting strength of nonwhites as required by the Voting Rights Act. The reapportionment had divided a community of Hasidic Jews between two districts to assure blacks and Puerto Ricans a 65 percent majority.

In *Korematsu v. United States* (1944) Justice Black wrote that "all legal restrictions which curtail the civil rights of a single racial group are immediately suspect." Nevertheless, in that case the Court found no ground for challenging executive action in expelling persons of Japanese ancestry, many of them American citizens, from the West Coast after Pearl Harbor.[3]

RACIAL SEGREGATION IN HOUSING

The equal protection clause, we have seen, was clearly intended to protect equal rights in buying or disposing of property. After the *Civil Rights Cases* (1883), this protection would still be effective against state action that violated equal rights in property ownership, and the Supreme Court so held when cases came up for review. Baltimore, in 1910, was apparently the first city to adopt a municipal segregation ordinance. Shortly afterward, the same procedure was followed by other Southern cities. The Louisville ordinance came before the Supreme Court in *Buchanan v. Warley* (1917) and was invalidated on the ground that it was an unconstitutional interference with the right of a property owner to dispose of his real estate. Attempts to circumvent the *Buchanan* decision were defeated in both state and federal courts, and by 1930 the unconstitutionality of municipal segregation ordinances was firmly established.[4]

The field was thus left to a second protective device—restrictive covenants entered into by property owners binding themselves not to sell or lease their property to blacks or certain other social, national, or religious groups. Because this type of agreement results from action by private persons, not by the state, it was at first generally successful in meeting constitutional tests.

The first restrictive covenant case to reach the Supreme Court, *Corrigan v. Buckley* (1926), was dismissed on grounds of lack of jurisdiction, but Justice Sanford for the Court did hold that such private covenants were not contrary to the Constitution or to public policy. Not until 1948

[3] Note that *United States v. Martinez-Fuerte* (1976) permitted the Border Patrol to stop autos at fixed checkpoints within California and question occupants, even though those questioned were selected "on the basis of apparent Mexican ancestry."

[4] See *Harmon v. Tyler* (1927), *City of Richmond v. Deans* (1930), *City of Birmingham v. Monk* (1951).

did the Supreme Court reconsider this position. Then it handed down two unanimous decisions upholding the validity of restrictive covenants but denying them judicial enforcement. The first decision, *Shelley v. Kraemer,* concerned actions brought to enforce restrictive covenants in the states of Missouri and Michigan. Chief Justice Vinson found it relatively easy to reconcile the Court's new view with its previous decisions. *Corrigan v. Buckley,* he pointed out, had concerned only the right of private individuals to enter into such covenants, and he here reiterated the conclusion of the *Corrigan* case that "restrictive agreements standing alone cannot be regarded as violative of any rights guaranteed . . . by the Fourteenth Amendment."

But in *Shelley v. Kraemer* the Court was willing to push beyond this point and to consider the status of action by state courts to enforce these covenants. "It cannot be doubted," said the Chief Justice, "that among the civil rights intended to be protected from discriminatory state action by the Fourteenth Amendment are the rights to acquire, enjoy, own and dispose of property." The question, then, was whether judicial enforcement of restrictive convenants amounted to "state action." The Court answered:

> We have no doubt that there has been state action in these cases in the full and complete sense of the phrase. The undisputed facts disclose that petitioners were willing purchasers of properties upon which they desired to establish homes. The owners of the properties were willing sellers; and contracts of sale were accordingly consummated. It is clear that but for the active intervention of the state courts, supported by the full panoply of state power, petitioners would have been free to occupy the properties in question without restraint.

The fact that "the particular pattern of discrimination, which the State has enforced, was defined initially by the terms of a private agreement" made no difference. "State action, as that phrase is understood for the purposes of the Fourteenth Amendment, refers to exertions of state power in all forms."

The second decision, *Hurd v. Hodge* (1948), involved two cases arising in the District of Columbia, where the equal protection clause could not be invoked. Consequently, it was contended that judicial enforcement was forbidden by the due process clause of the Fifth Amendment. The Court, speaking again through the Chief Justice, found it unnecessary to base its decision upon constitutional grounds at all. Primary reliance was placed upon section 1 of the Civil Rights Act of 1866, which guarantees to "all citizens" the same rights as white citizens "to inherit, purchase, lease, sell, hold, and convey real and personal property." The Court held that judicial enforcement of restrictive covenants would be a violation of this section. Even in the absence of the statute, however, the Court indicated that judicial enforcement would be contrary to the public policy of the United States, which the Supreme Court would have power to enforce in the exercise of its supervisory powers over the courts of the District of Columbia.

Since these two decisions left restrictive convenants legal, even though unenforceable, the question soon arose as to whether a signer of a convenant who breached its provisions could be sued for damages by other participants in the covenant. In *Barrows v. Jackson* (1953) a California property owner who had failed to live up to the conditions of a covenant was sued by three neighbors on the ground that the value of their property had dropped sharply since blacks moved in. But six justices thought that the Supreme Court should not permit or require California to coerce a property owner to pay damages for failure to observe a covenant that California had no right to incorporate in a statute or enforce in equity and which federal courts could not enforce because contrary to public policy.

SEGREGATION IN EDUCATION

The fraudulent character of the protection afforded by the "separate but equal" rule was perhaps most obvious in the field of education. By any test that might be applied, black schools in states where segregation was the rule were markedly inferior to white schools. For many years, however, the Supreme Court persistently avoided getting itself into situations where it would have to recognize this fact.

The story starts in 1899, with *Cumming v. Richmond County Board of Education.* This case arose out of the decision of a Georgia school board to discontinue the existing black high school in order to use the building and facilities for black elementary education. No new high school for blacks was established, though the existing white high schools were continued. Black taxpayers sought to restrain the school board from using money to support white high schools until equal facilities for black students were provided. The unanimous Supreme Court decision avoided discussion of the segregation issue. It denied that discontinuance of the black high school was a violation of equal protection of the laws, but laid more stress on the conclusion that an injunction which would close the white high schools was not the proper legal remedy and would not help the black children. Justice Harlan concluded with a reminder that the management of schools was a state matter in which the federal government could intervene only in the case of a "clear and unmistakable disregard" of constitutional rights.

A Kentucky law requiring segregation of white and black students in all educational institutions, private and public, was upheld as applied to a private institution in *Berea College v. Kentucky* (1908). Again the Court found a way to avoid passing on the segregation issue. It argued that this was merely a matter between Kentucky and a corporation which it had created, and that the state could withhold privileges from one of its corporations which it could not constitutionally withhold from an individual.

Having successfully avoided the issue twice, the Court then felt able to act as though established practice had foreclosed discussion of the question. *Gong Lum v. Rice* (1927) concerned a child of Chinese descent who was required to attend a black school in Mississippi under the state constitutional obligation that separate schools be maintained for children of "the white and colored races." As to the equal protection problem posed by this arrangement, Chief Justice Taft said for the Court: "Were this a new question, it would call for very full argument and consideration, but we think it is the same question which has been many times decided to be within the constitutional power of the state legislature to settle without intervention of the federal courts under the Federal Constitution." The fifteen state and lower federal court decisions cited by the Chief Justice to support this conclusion, however, could not hide the fact that there had been no Supreme Court ruling directly on the issue of segregation in educational institutions and that there had never been "full argument and consideration" by that body.

The pattern of segregation in education thus achieved a solid constitutional foundation. The more liberally oriented Court of the later 1930s was able, however, to effect a substantial change of direction within the confines of the doctrine by stressing the need for *equality* in segregation. Missouri refused to admit blacks to its state law school, providing instead that the state would pay tuition fees for any of its black citizens who could obtain admission to law schools in neighboring states where segregation was not enforced. In *Missouri ex rel. Gaines v. Canada* (1938) the Court ruled that Missouri could not shift its responsibility for providing equal education to another state.

Missouri met this ruling by setting up a separate, and inferior, law school for blacks, and other Southern states adopted the same device. How far was the Supreme Court prepared to go in insisting upon equality of facilities? The test came in 1950. *McLaurin v. Oklahoma State Regents* involved a black who sought admission to the state university as a Ph.D. candidate in education. The Legislature, under pressure of the *Gaines* ruling, had amended the state law to permit the admission of blacks to institutions of higher learning in cases where such institutions offered courses not available in the black schools. However, the program of instruction for such black students was to be given "upon a segregated basis." Accordingly, McLaurin was admitted to the University of Oklahoma graduate school but was subjected to certain segregation practices in classrooms, library, and cafeteria. These separations, which the state defended as "merely nominal," were declared unconstitutional by a unanimous Court. Such restrictions on McLaurin, Chief Justice Vinson wrote. "impair and inhibit his ability to study, to engage in discussions and exchange views with other students, and, in general, to learn his profession."

Sweatt v. Painter (1950) involved the petition of a black who had refused to attend the separate law school for blacks that Texas had set up for admission to the University of Texas Law School. The Texas courts, denying his petition, had claimed that the "privileges, advantages, and opportunities for the study of law" at the black law school were "substantially equivalent" to those available at the university law school.

The Supreme Court disagreed. Chief Justice Vinson's opinion contrasted the faculty, the student body, the library, the alumni, and the other facilities of the two institutions. In comparison with the University of Texas Law School, judged by the Court to be "one of the nation's ranking law schools," was the black law school with five full-time professors, a student body of twenty-three, a library of 16,500 volumes, and one alumnus who had become a member of the Texas bar. "It is difficult to believe that one who had a free choice between these law schools would consider the question close." Above all, the Court considered that a law school limited to blacks, a minority of the Texas population, could not be an effective "proving ground for legal learning and practice."

By this time the pressure against segregation was shifting from university and graduate professional education, where the breaking-down of segregation barriers presented a lesser problem because of the comparatively few black students involved, to public education at the primary and secondary levels. In December 1952, the Court held hearings on five appeals in such cases, in all of which the lower courts had upheld segregation laws but demanded that educational facilities be made equal. On June 8, 1953, the Court announced the cases would be reargued on October 12 and set out a series of five questions to which counsel were requested to address themselves. Two of the five questions related to the intent of the Congress and the state legislatures which drafted and ratified the Fourteenth Amendment and whether they understood that it would abolish segregation in public schools.

Brown v. Board of Education of Topeka and the other school segregation cases[5] were finally decided on May 17, 1954. The vote was unanimous, an unexpected development that was immediately hailed as a

---

[5] *Briggs v. Elliott, Davis v. County School Board of Prince Edward County, Gebhart v. Belton, Bolling v. Sharpe.* For a detailed account of the development of the Court's ruling, see Richard Kluger, *Simple Justice* (New York: Knopf, 1975).

diplomatic triumph for Chief Justice Warren, who wrote the opinion. It was a surprisingly brief statement of thirteen paragraphs. First, Warren noted that the historical background and the circumstances surrounding the adoption of the Fourteenth Amendment were at best "inconclusive" as to the intention of the drafters. But in any case the Court could not "turn the clock back to 1868 when the Amendment was adopted, or even to 1896 when *Plessy v. Ferguson* was written." The decision had to consider public education "in the light of its full development and its present place in American life throughout the Nation." Warren continued:

> Today, education is perhaps the most important function of state and local governments. Compulsory school attendance laws and the great expenditures for education both demonstrate our recognition of the importance of education to our democratic society. It is required in the performance of our most basic responsibilities, even service in the armed forces. It is the very foundation of good citizenship. Today it is a principal instrument in awakening the child to cultural values, in preparing him for later professional training, and in helping him to adjust normally to his environment. In these days, it is doubtful that any child may reasonably be expected to succeed in life if he is denied the opportunity of an education. Such an opportunity, where the state has undertaken to provide it, is a right which must be made available to all on equal terms.

Thus the Court finally came to grips with the constitutionality of the "separate but equal" doctrine, which it had avoided in six preceding public education cases. "Does segregation of children in public schools solely on the basis of race, even though the physical facilities and other 'tangible' factors may be equal, deprive the children of the minority group of equal educational opportunities? We believe that it does." For this precedent-shattering conclusion, the Court's justification was surprisingly brief and simple. "To separate children in grade and high schools from others of similar age and qualifications solely because of their race generates a feeling of inferiority as to their status in the community that may affect their hearts and minds in a way unlikely ever to be undone." Consequently, "separate educational facilities are inherently unequal."[6]

Bolling v. Sharpe was handled in a separate decision from the other four cases, since is arose in the District of Columbia where the equal protection clause was not applicable. In a brief opinion, Warren held that the due process clause of the Fifth Amendment required the same result.

---

[6] As evidence that this conclusion was "amply supported by modern authority," Warren cited in the famous footnote 11 Gunnar Myrdal's *An American Dilemma* and six psychological and sociological studies, which led to charges that the opinion was based on sociology rather than law. See Herbert Garfinkel, "Social Science Evidence and the School Segregation Cases," 21 JOURNAL OF POLITICS 37 (1959).

It would be "unthinkable" that the Constitution imposed a lesser duty on the federal government than on the states. Equal protection is a more specific safeguard than due process, to be sure, and the concepts are not "interchangeable." But the liberty protected by the due process clause includes "the full range of conduct which the individual is free to pursue, and it cannot be restricted except for a proper governmental objective. Segregation in public education is not reasonably related to any proper governmental objective, and thus it imposes on Negro children of the District of Columbia a burden that constitutes an arbitrary deprivation of their liberty in violation of the Due Process Clause."

These holdings still left the problem of putting this potentially explosive doctrine into effect. Further hearings were held in April 1955, and on May 31 the Supreme Court announced its plan of action. The cases would be remanded to the courts where they had originated, which would fashion decrees of enforcement on equitable principles and with regard for "varied local school problems." The local courts would consider whether the actions or proposals of the various school authorities constituted "good faith implementation of the governing constitutional principles." They would require "a prompt and reasonable start toward full compliance" with the 1954 ruling, but once such a start had been made, the courts might find that additional time was necessary to carry out the ruling in an effective manner. Such delays, however, would have to be proved "necessary in the public interest and . . . consistent with good faith compliance at the earliest practicable date." During this period of transition to full compliance, the courts where the cases originated would retain jurisdiction of them under obligation to take such proceedings "as are necessary and proper to admit to public schools on a racially nondiscriminatory basis with all deliberate speed the parties to these cases." Thus the Supreme Court committed its prestige to an experiment in judicially enforced revision of human behavior patterns without precedent in American experience.

ENFORCEMENT OF THE *BROWN* DECISION

At first it seemed that the prestige of the Court might substantially temper the expected resistance to the *Brown* decree. The Court may have expected that it would receive some support from Congress and the President in winning acceptance for the ruling, but no such aid was forthcoming. On the contrary, ninety-six Southern congressmen signed a manifesto in 1956 challenging the legality of the Court's decision; and President Eisenhower, while declaring that he would enforce the law, persistently declined to attempt any organization of support for the ruling.

After the 1955 mandate, the Court endeavored to give the lower courts the maximum opportunity and the maximum responsibility for pressing toward the constitutional goal of integration, not only for the schools but for other public facilities. The desegregation requirement was extended to bus transportation, public parks and golf courses, swimming pools, public auditoriums, courtroom seating, and airport restaurants by Supreme Court rulings which merely reversed or affirmed lower court decisions by per curiam opinions or without any opinion.[7] Since the *Brown* opinion had been limited to demonstrating why segregation in education was unconstitutional, there were some who felt that the Court was neglecting its responsibility to spell out constitutional principles by failing to provide a reasoned argument against segregation in other areas of public activity.[8]

In the states of the "Old South" the legislatures, led by Virginia, promptly adopted complete batteries of new laws aimed to frustrate efforts to achieve integration. In many instances these laws were recognized even by their sponsors to be unconstitutional, but they were gestures of defiance and testing them in court would take time.

In addition to legal barriers to desegregation, delay was occasioned by threatened or actual violence. Major incidents occurred at Clinton, Tennessee, in 1956; at Little Rock, Arkansas, in 1957; at New Orleans in 1960; and at the University of Mississippi in 1962. In *Cooper v. Aaron* (1958) the Supreme Court held that the violent resistance to the Little Rock school board's desegregation plan was "directly traceable" to the Governor and state Legislature and warned that the constitutional rights of children not to be discriminated against in school admission because of race "can neither be nullified openly and directly by state legislators or state executive or judicial officers, nor nullified indirectly by them through evasive schemes for segregation."

Achieving desegregation of the public schools by lawsuits was inevitably a slow and difficult process. In the first place, the issue of segregation had to be raised in each individual school district by persons or groups who would take the responsibility, run the risks, and incur the costs of filing a suit. Usually this task had to be assumed by organized black groups, typically the NAACP. In some sections of the South reprisals against those active in the NAACP were so severe and effective that no one would initiate action against school segregation.

[7] *Mayor of Baltimore v. Dawson* (1955), public recreation; *Holmes v. City of Atlanta* (1955), municipal golf courses; *Gayle v. Browder* (1956), buses; *New Orleans City Park Improvement Assn. v. Detiege* (1958), public parks; *State Athletic Cmsn. v. Dorsey* (1959), athletic contests; *Turner v. Memphis* (1962), airport restaurants; *Johnson v. Virginia* (1963), courtroom seating; *Schiro v. Bynum* (1964), auditoriums; *Lee v. Washington* (1968), jails.

[8] See Herbert Wechsler, "Toward Neutral Principles of Constitutional Law," 73 HAR-VARD LAW REVIEW 1, 22 (1959).

Second, the local school boards, acting either on their own initiative or under the compulsion of a federal district court order, had to prepare a desegregation plan. School boards, even when they were willing to act, usually preferred to wait for a court mandate in order to justify themselves to the segregationists in the community.

Third, the federal district judges had to order the desegregation plans into effect. At the time enforcement of the *Brown* decision got under way there were forty-eight federal district judges in the eleven Southern states. They were nearly all native Southerners, sharing the views of the white Southern establishment, subject to the social pressures of their communities, personally unsympathetic to the *Brown* ruling. It is not surprising that they tended to move very slowly, and in some cases not at all, in implementing school desegregation plans.

Fourth, the Federal Courts of Appeals for the Fourth and Fifth Circuits, located in Richmond and New Orleans, composed of ten judges, had the responsibility of reviewing the decisions of the district judges. Generally the appellate court judges, somewhat further removed from the pressures of local situations than the district judges, took a conscientious view of their obligations to enforce the Supreme Court's ruling, and they overturned many of the district court decisions.[9]

The Positive Duty to Desegregate

The *Brown* mandate could be interpreted to mean only that school districts must stop using discriminatory practices, not that they had a positive duty to undertake desegregation plans. This interpretation found support in *Shuttlesworth v. Birmingham Board of Education* (1958), which upheld a pupil placement plan that purported to assign students to schools on various bases, with race carefully excluded. In fact, transfers out of black schools were administratively impossible, but the Supreme Court upheld a lower court's "presumption" that the law was not being used to discriminate against black pupils.

Prince Edward County, Virginia, one of the parties covered by the *Brown* decision, undertook to meet its obligation not to discriminate by simply closing all public schools in the county and providing tuition grants for pupils attending private schools. The county maintained it had no constitutional obligation to operate a public school system, but in *Griffin v. County School Board of Prince Edward County* (1964), the Court ruled that the decision not to operate a public school system had a clearly unconstitutional object.

Another "nondiscriminatory" technique was freedom of choice,

[9] See the excellent study by J. W. Peltason, *Fifty-eight Lonely Men* (New York: Harcourt Brace Jovanovich, 1961).

under which each pupil was supposed to be free to choose the school to be attended. *Green v. County School Board of New Kent County* (1968) found that under this plan very little transfer out of a black school had occurred; but, more important, the Court took the occasion to announce that school boards had a positive duty to formulate plans promising prompt conversion to a desegregated system. The goal was complete integration, achievement of a "unitary, nonracial system of public education."

In a Mississippi case the following year, *Alexander v. Holmes County Board of Education* (1969), the Court was even more brusque, warning that the standard of "all deliberate speed" was "no longer constitutionally permissible" and demanding that every district "terminate dual school systems at once and . . . operate now and hereafter only unitary schools."

These decisions left no escape from the obligation to adopt positive desegregation plans. In Montgomery, Alabama, Judge Frank M. Johnson had been supervising the progress of desegregation since 1964. In 1968 he added to his earlier orders the desegregation of school faculties by imposing racial quotas, requiring, for example, that in schools with twelve or more teachers, the race of at least one of every six faculty and staff members must be different from the race of the majority at the school. In *United States v. Montgomery County Board of Education* (1969), this provision was upheld as a reasonable step toward desegregation.

Swann v. Charlotte-Mecklenburg Board of Education (1971), in an opinion by Chief Justice Burger, went much further in providing guidelines for the lower courts. First, the Supreme Court held that where one-race schools existed in a system with a history of segregation, there was a presumption that this was the result of present or past discriminatory action. Second, the Court made clear that the "neighborhood school" might have to be partially sacrificed to achieve desegregation.

> All things being equal, with no history of discrimination it might well be desirable to assign pupils to schools nearest their homes. But all things are not equal in a system that has been deliberately constructed and maintained to enforce racial segregation.

Third, the Court recognized the need for massive busing to achieve integration. "Desegregation plans cannot be limited to the walk-in school." Fourth, the Court reiterated its acceptance of teacher assignment by race to achieve faculty desegregation. Finally, to avoid any misunderstanding, Chief Justice Burger firmly announced that the Court's goal was not racial balance. "The constitutional command does not mean that every school in every community must always reflect the racial composition of the school system as a whole." Mathematical ratios were to be only an instrument in the process of shaping a remedy for segregation. The constitutional goal was to abolish dual school systems, not to achieve racial balance.

Up to this date all the Court's school segregation decisions had been unanimous, even after the first two Nixon appointments. But in 1972 the Nixon justices, by then four, broke away from the majority in *Wright v. Council of City of Emporia* (1972). The city of Emporia, Virginia, had been part of the county school system which operated segregated schools. After the *Green* decision, integration of the county schools was ordered. Emporia, where there were fewer blacks than in the surrounding county, then sought to withdraw from the county system and set up its own separate schools. The Court majority held that such a realignment of school districts in an area with a history of state-enforced segregation would impede the process of dismantling the segregated system and could not be allowed. The four-judge minority contended that Emporia had a lawful right to provide for the education of its own children and charged that the Court was pursuing a "racial balancing" approach.[10]

The reverse situation—city-county consolidation—proved even more controversial. In 1972 Judge Robert R. Merhige ordered the Richmond school system, which was about 70 percent black, merged with those of the two surrounding counties, which were about 90 percent white. The court of appeals rejected this plan, and the Supreme Court, with Justice Powell, a Virginian, not participating, divided four to four, thereby leaving the appellate rejection of the merger in effect.[11]

The same issue returned to the Court the next year, this time from Detroit. In *Milliken v. Bradley* (1974), consolidation was rejected by a vote of five to four, with Stewart joining the four Nixon justices. A federal district judge had found the Detroit board of education guilty of creating and perpetuating school segregation. Concluding that a Detroit-only plan was inadequate to accomplish desegregation, the judge created an area composed of Detroit plus fifty-three suburban school districts, within which a massive busing program would operate. Chief Justice Burger for the majority held that bringing the outlying districts into the plan was unjustified because there had been no showing of significant violations by them and no evidence of any interdistrict violations. Nor was there any claim that the district boundary lines had been established to foster racial segregation. It would, Burger said, violate the deeply

---

[10] In *United States v. Scotland Neck City Board of Education* (1972), decided the same day, and involving the same kind of effort by a city to withdraw from the county system, the Court was unanimous in voiding the plan, which would have left the county schools 89 percent black.

[11] *School Board of Richmond v. State Board of Education* (1973).

rooted tradition of local control of education for school district lines to be casually ignored or treated as mere administrative conveniences.[12]

The Detroit case was one of the Court's first to come from a northern city. While a deliberate policy to segregate had been found to exist there, in most northern cities segregation was principally caused by neighborhood schools within segregated housing patterns. In legal terms, this was de facto rather than de jure—i.e., state-enforced—segregation. The Court had never decided whether de facto segregation was unconstitutional. Initially, after *Brown*, the Court had been dealing with segregation in the South that was clearly state imposed and could be countered simply by ordering an end to the discriminatory laws and practices. If de jure discrimination were the Court's sole concern, than a segregated system for which the state was not directly responsible would be free from judicial redress. But this would have left segregation in the Northern states largely untouched. Moreover, with the *Green* insistence on positive state action against segregation, it should make no difference whether the segregation was de facto or de jure.

This issue was raised but evaded in *Keyes v. School District No. 1, Denver* (1973). Justice Powell, who as a Virginian was particularly sensitive to the anomaly that the nation's most segregated schools were now in the North, argued that the de facto-de jure distinction had "long since . . . outlived its time" and should be replaced by "constitutional principles of national rather than merely regional application." The Court, however, found that there had been "de jure segregation in a meaningful portion of the [Denver] school system," and so there was no need to consider the de facto rule.

Boston schools were a classic case of deliberate, long-standing de jure segregation. In 1974 Judge Arthur Garrity issued detailed findings to that effect, and in 1975 ordered a remedial program that included busing. The Boston reaction was violent, but the Garrity order was upheld by the court of appeals and the Supreme Court denied review.[13] In cases from Columbus and Dayton, Ohio, the Court upheld the authority of federal judges to impose sweeping desegregation plans in any city where children had been attending mostly all-white or all-black schools as a result of school board policies.[14]

---

[12] However, in *Buchanan v. Evans* (1975), the Court affirmed a lower federal court decision that called for the overwhelmingly black school system of Wilmington, Delaware, to integrate with white schools in the surrounding county.

[13] *White v. Morgan, Doherty v. Morgan, Boston Home and School Assn. v. Morgan* (1976). In 1982 Judge Garrity ended his supervision of the Boston schools and turned over compliance with busing orders to the state board of education.

[14] *Columbus Board of Education v. Penick* (1979), *Dayton Board of Education v. Brinkman* (1979).

In 1980 the Court let stand a lower-court decision requiring extensive school busing between the city of Wilmington and eleven county
school districts, which Rehnquist charged was "a countywide remedy
more Draconian than any ever approved by this Court."[15] But it affirmed
lower-court action barring any form of interdistrict desegregation for
Atlanta area schools.[16]

Busing in the Los Angeles school system, ordered initially in 1963,
came to an end in 1982 as the Court upheld a proposition adopted by
popular vote forbidding mandatory pupil transportation to remedy school
segregation resulting from other than intentional governmental acts.[17] At
the same time, however, the Court struck down a Washington State
initiative that denied local school boards the option of busing as a
legislative classification based on racial criteria.[18] And in *Metropolitan
County Board of Education of Nashville v. Kelley* (1983) the Court unanimously rejected a Justice Department request that it reexamine the
landmark 1971 *Swann* decision.

Congressional and Presidential Action

The first substantial congressional support of school integration came
with the adoption of the Civil Rights Act of 1964. Title IV of that act
authorized the attorney general to bring school desegregation suits in the
name of the United States, and Title VI prohibited racial discrimination
in any local or state program receiving federal financial assistance. This
sanction became of particular importance when in the Education Act of
1965 Congress adopted President Johnson's plan for federal financial
assistance to elementary and secondary schools. To become eligible for
these grants, all public schools had to certify that they were integrated or
file acceptable plans for achieving complete integration. The federal
Office of Education promptly issued guidelines for judging progress
toward integration in terms of quotas and percentages, which were upheld by the Supreme Court.[19] However, under the Nixon administration,
pressure for enforcement of the standards was relaxed, and there was an
almost complete failure to use the fund-cutoff sanction.

Most judicially imposed integration plans involved busing, which

---

[15] *Delaware State Board v. Evans* (1980).

[16] *Armour v. Nix* (1980). *Pasadena City Board of Education v. Spangler* (1976) held that,
once the affirmative duty to desegregate has been accomplished, school authorities cannot be
required to readjust attendance zones each year to keep up with population shifts.

[17] *Crawford v. Board of Education* (1982).

[18] *Washington v. Seattle School District* (1982).

[19] *Caddo Parish School Board v. United States* (1967).

had been approved by the Supreme Court in *Swann*. Opposition to busing was very strong and emotionally charged, however, as much so in the North as it had earlier been in the South. President Nixon took a firm antibusing position in 1972. He asked Congress to pass legislation providing for a moratorium of one year on court-ordered busing and imposing a variety of restrictions and prohibitions on future busing. Such legislative interference with constitutional decrees issued to enforce constitutional rights was regarded by many legislators as unconstitutional,[20] and Congress passed a more limited measure simply halting for eighteen months any school desegregation ordered by federal courts until all appeals had been exhausted. Nixon's plan to seek a constitutional amendment forbidding the assignment of any pupil to a school on the basis of race or color was aborted by Watergate.

In 1974 and 1975 Congress adopted some limits on busing, but they did not attempt to control court action if required to enforce constitutional rights. President Ford took a strong antibusing stance. In 1976 he encouraged the Department of Justice to file a friend of the court brief in the Boston case, but Attorney General Edward Levi ultimately decided against it. While opposition to busing continued to grow during the Carter administration, no effective antibusing legislation was adopted by Congress, and the Justice Department continued to seek desegregation by lawsuit.

The Reagan administration, however, opposed busing as counterproductive; and in a case involving East Baton Rouge, Louisiana, the Department of Justice for the first time petitioned a federal court of appeals to reconsider a mandatory busing plan. In the Seattle School District case, where the Carter administration had argued in the lower courts that the state antibusing law was unconstitutional, the Reagan Justice Department urged the Supreme Court to uphold the law, a position the Court rejected by a vote of five to four. The Department did announce plans to file suits against school districts charged with providing inferior education to minority schools. Both the House and Senate in the Ninety-seventh Congress adopted separate antibusing measures which would have prohibited the Justice Department from participating in cases that could lead to busing, and appropriations to finance the desegregation of public schools were sharply reduced in 1982.[21]

[20] See the analysis in "The Nixon Busing Bills," 81 YALE LAW JOURNAL 1542 (1972).

[21] For useful discussions, see J. Harvie Wilkinson III, *From Brown to Bakke: The Supreme Court and School Integration, 1954–1978* (New York: Oxford University Press, 1979); Gary Orfield, *Must We Bus? Segregated Schools and National Policy* (Washington, D.C.: Brookings Institution, 1978); Lino A. Graglia, *Disaster by Decree: The Supreme Court, Race and the Schools* (Ithaca, N.Y.: Cornell University Press, 1976).

AFFIRMATIVE ACTION

The Supreme Court's insistence in the school segregation cases that state neutrality was not enough, and that positive action must be taken to terminate racial segregation, raises the difficult constitutional question as to whether racial classifications can be employed for benign and ameliorative purposes. We have just seen that the Court did approve racial quotas for teaching staffs in the *Montgomery County* case. In American higher education and in professional schools such as law and medicine, the 1960s saw the inauguration of programs for recruiting minority students by special financial aid and preferential admissions policies.

The concern of the federal government to implement the antidiscrimination provisions of Title VI of the Civil Rights Act of 1964 was expressed in President Johnson's 1965 Executive Order No. 11246 and led in 1967 to the Department of Labor's development of preferential hiring requirements on the basis of race and sex in the construction industry and later for the entire business community. Enforcement of the Department of Labor's order in federal dealings with colleges and universities was delegated to the Department of Health, Education, and Welfare. By 1970 HEW began to issue "guidelines" for nondiscriminatory faculty and staff employment, with the threat of withdrawal of federal financial grants if hiring goals were not met.

The practical justification offered for preferential admissions or employment was that the consequences of century-old discrimination could be remedied only by deliberate discrimination in the opposite direction. The constitutional justification offered was generally that racial classifications are prohibited only when they are invidious and used to stigmatize, and that *Brown* did not reject racial classifications per se, only their improper use. The opposing view holds that race can never be used as a basis for classification, even with worthy motives, and that the case for compensatory justice must always be made on the basis of individual circumstances, not on class status.

The constitutionality of affirmative action was squarely presented to the Supreme Court in the case of *DeFunis v. Odegaard* (1974). The law school of the University of Washington had decided that the only way to secure a reasonable representation of minorities in its student body was to modify admission requirements and procedures to give certain advantages to minority applicants. DeFunis, a white, was denied admission in 1971, while less qualified blacks, he contended, were admitted. A state superior court held that DeFunis had been denied equal protection and ordered his admission. Though the state supreme court reversed and upheld the law school procedures, DeFunis was permitted to continue in school pending his appeal to the Supreme Court. By the time the Court dealt with his case in the spring of 1974, DeFunis was in his last semester of law school and assured of graduation. By a five to four vote the Supreme Court took advantage of this situation to declare the case moot.

Four years later the issue returned to the Court in the case of *Regents of the University of California v. Bakke* (1978).[22] The medical school of the University of California at Davis had reserved 16 out of 100 places in its annual entering class for blacks, Mexican-Americans, and two other minority groups. Allan Bakke was twice rejected by Davis, as well as by other medical schools. After his second rejection he brought suit claiming racial discrimination on the ground that minority applicants admitted under the quota were less qualified than he. The California supreme court agreed that the Davis racial quota involved unconstitutional classification and ordered the admission of Bakke.

On appeal to the Supreme Court, the admission of Bakke and invalidation of the quota were upheld. But the Court's ruling was considerably more complicated, and in effect it approved affirmative-action programs that do not employ numerical quotas. Four members of the Court, headed by Justice Brennan, would in fact have upheld the Davis plan as a remedy for "the effects of past societal discrimination." Another four, speaking through Justice Stevens, avoided the constitutional issue and held the Davis plan to be in flat violation of Title VI of the Civil Rights Act.

Justice Powell, the ninth member, was squarely in the middle, agreeing in part with each side. He joined the Stevens bloc in holding that the Davis quota was invalid as an explicit racial classification. But he also held that under the First Amendment colleges and professional schools need to have a diverse student body, and to achieve that goal it would be proper to "take race into account." Race or ethnic background could be deemed a "plus" in a particular applicant's file, provided that it did not insulate the individual from comparison with all other candidates. Powell specifically cited and recommended the admission procedures at Harvard College, which succeeded in securing a substantial minority enrollment without any apparent or announced use of numerical quotas. The general view was that the Court had achieved a satisfactory compromise in *Bakke* and that carefully designed race-conscious programs in

---

[22] In the meantime *Lau v. Nichols* (1974) construed the Civil Rights Act as commanding the San Francisco school system to provide bilingual instruction to some 1,800 non-English-speaking students of Chinese ancestry in the public schools. *Franks v. Bowman Transportation Co.* (1976) ruled that blacks denied jobs because of their race should be granted special seniority rights and move ahead of white workers hired in place of them. But see *McDonald v. Santa Fe Trail Transportation Co.* (1976).

education, employment, and other areas could proceed with assurance of their constitutionality.[23]

Fullilove v. Klutznick (1980) gave the Court a further opportunity to apply its *Bakke* rationale. The Public Works Employment Act of 1977 required that at least 10 percent of federal funds granted for local public works projects must be used by the state or locality to procure services or supplies from minority businesses. The Court upheld the act by vote of six to three. While Burger wrote the Court's opinion, Powell's concurrence provided the most effective argument.

All racial classifications are suspect and subject to strict judicial scrutiny, because race is irrelevant to almost every governmental decision. To distinguish a permissible race-conscious remedy from an impermissible racial preference, wrote Justice Powell, two requirements must be met. First, the governmental body that attempts to impose a race-conscious remedy must have the authority to act in response to identified discrimination. Here Congress had been given "the unique constitutional power" of legislating to enforce the provisions of the Thirteenth, Fourteenth, and Fifteenth Amendments.

Second, the governmental body must make findings that demonstrate the existence of illegal discrimination. In passing this statute Congress had established that purposeful discrimination contributed significantly to the small percentage of federal contracting funds received by minority business enterprises. Congressional choice of a remedy must be upheld if the means selected are equitable and reasonably necessary to the redress of the identified discrimination.[24]

The major test of affirmative action programs in private employment came in *Kaiser Aluminum & Chemical Co. v. Weber* (1979). Weber, a white employee, had attacked the Kaiser plan of reserving for minorities half of all positions in its nationwide training program for skilled craft jobs. Weber, though he had more seniority than several black employees chosen, was not selected. As a private employer Kaiser was not bound by the equal protection clause enforced in the *Bakke* case, but Title VI of the 1964 Civil Rights Act bars racial discrimination in private employment. By a vote of five to two the Supreme Court held that Congress did not intend to interfere with programs giving special preference to minorities, saying: "It would be ironic indeed if a law triggered by a nation's

[23] In a sequel to *Bakke*, the Court in *DeRonde v. Regents of the University of California* (1981) let stand a state court decision upholding the affirmative-action program of the law school at Davis. Developed after the *Bakke* decision, the plan takes account of "ethnic minority status" along with test scores, rigor of undergraduate studies, economic hardship, maturity, personal growth, and recommendations.

[24] In *Bakke*, Powell contended, the Regents had met neither test. "They were entrusted only with educational functions, and they made no findings of past discrimination."

concern over centuries of racial injustice . . . constituted the first legislative prohibition of all voluntary, private, race-conscious efforts to abolish traditional patterns of racial segregation and hierarchy."[25]

In 1981 Boston's fiscal problems caused the city to lay off 400 police and firefighters, and state law required firing in reverse order of seniority. Those affected were predominantly blacks and Latinos hired under court orders in the 1970s to remedy the overwhelming white police and fire departments. A federal judge ruled that percentages of minority members must be maintained, even though this meant that white officers with more seniority had to be laid off. After the case had gone to the Supreme Court, the city fortuitously found the money to cancel the firings, which allowed the Supreme Court to dismiss the case as moot.[26]

RACIAL DISCRIMINATION IN EMPLOYMENT

Title VII of the Civil Rights Act of 1964 makes it unlawful for employers to deprive any individual of employment opportunities "because of such individual's race, color, religion, sex, or national origin." The act excluded from its coverage many employers and imposed strict procedural requirements. Thus a charge of discrimination had to be filed first with a state or local fair employment practices agency, if one existed, for sixty days, and subsequently with the federal Equal Employment Opportunities Commission (EEOC), for another sixty days. The EEOC can take cases that cannot be settled through conciliation to federal district courts for a finding of discrimination. Complainants are also authorized to bring class actions for enforcement of the act.

The leading cases of *Griggs v. Duke Power Co.* (1971) and *Washington v. Davis* (1976) have already been noted. *Franks v. Bowman Transportation Co.* (1976) ruled that blacks denied jobs because of their race should be granted special seniority rights and moved ahead of white workers hired in place of them. Seniority plans have often been alleged to have discriminatory effects, but *American Tobacco Co. v. Patterson* (1982)

---

[25] Among the many sources on affirmative action, see Allan P. Sindler, *Bakke, DeFunis, and Minority Admissions* (New York: Longman, 1978); Ralph A. Rossum, *Reverse Discrimination: The Constitutional Debate* (New York: Marcel Dekker, 1980); John C. Livingston, *Fair Game? Inequality and Affirmative Action* (San Francisco: W. H. Freeman, 1979); John Hart Ely, "The Constitutionality of Reverse Racial Discrimination," 41 UNIVERSITY OF CHICAGO LAW REVIEW 723 (1974); Robert M. O'Neil, "Preferential Admissions," 80 YALE LAW REVIEW 699 (1971).

[26] *Boston Firefighters Union v. Boston Chapter, NAACP* (1983). But the Court agreed to hear a similar case from Memphis *(Firefighters v. Stotts)*. The Reagan administration filed a brief in support of the Boston firefighters and against promotion plans for minorities in the Detroit and New Orleans police departments.

ruled that such plans are constitutional regardless of their impact on women and minorities as long as they are not adopted for a discriminatory purpose. An industry requirement that employees must work for forty-five weeks a year to secure permanent status, a requirement no black employee had ever met, was nevertheless held to be a bona fide seniority rule in *California Brewers v. Bryant* (1980).

STATE MISCEGENATION LAWS

In many states interracial marriage has been a criminal offense. The Supreme Court had never passed on the constitutionality of such laws, although in *Pace v. Alabama* (1882) it upheld an Alabama statute whose penalties for fornication between a white person and a black were more severe than those provided in the general fornication statute.

After the *Brown* decision, an encounter with state miscegenation laws seemed inevitable. In 1955 the Virginia supreme court in *Naim v. Naim* upheld that state's law. Distinguishing the *Brown* ruling, the state court reasoned that intermarriage, unlike education, was not a foundation of good citizenship or a right that must be available to all on equal terms. The Fourteenth Amendment, the court said, did not foreclose the states from preserving the "racial integrity" of their citizens or preventing a "mongrel breed." The Supreme Court twice, in transparently evasive maneuvers, avoided review of this ruling.

Presumably the Supreme Court felt that the *Brown* decision had created enough problems for one decade without adding the issue of mixed marriages. But by 1964 it was ready to move cautiously. In *McLaughlin v. Florida* the Court unanimously declared unconstitutional a statute that made it a crime for a white person and a black, not married to each other, to habitually live in and occupy the same room at night. The state court had upheld the law on authority of the *Pace* decision, but the Supreme Court now ruled that *Pace* had embodied too narrow a view of the equal protection clause. Any classification based solely on race, said Justice White for the Court, must bear a heavy burden of justification. He found no such justification here, but his opinion seemed to assume that a justification might conceivably be possible. Justice Stewart thought this was too cautious; he would not admit that under any circumstances a state law could make "the color of a person's skin the test of whether his conduct is a criminal offense."

Florida also had a law against mixed marriages, but the Court in *McLaughlin* was careful to avoid expressing any opinion on its validity. However, this issue was squarely raised by a 1966 Virginia supreme court decision, and in *Loving v. Virginia* (1967) the Supreme Court unanimously declared the Virginia antimiscegenation law unconstitutional. Holding that marriage is one of the "basic civil rights of man," Chief Justice Warren said: "To deny this fundamental freedom on so unsupportable a basis as . . . racial classifications . . . so directly subversive of the principle of equality at the heart of the Fourteenth Amendment, is surely to deprive all the state's citizens of liberty without due process of law."

STATE ACTION

An important factor in the expanding effectiveness of the equal protection clause against racial discrimination has been the Supreme Court's recent interpretation of the "state action" requirement of the Fourteenth Amendment. The Court's initial statement on state action in the *Civil Rights Cases* (1883) was that the Fourteenth Amendment forbade only those denials of due process or equal protection "sanctioned in some way by the state" or "done under state authority." But whether an act falls within these categories is not always easy to determine.

Actions of State Officials

Normally there is no doubt that actions by state or local officials in their official capacity constitute state action. This is obvious when they act under authorization of a specific state law, but it is also generally true when they take discriminatory action without authorization of law or even contrary to law. An early holding of the Supreme Court was in *Ex parte Virginia* (1880), where a county judge had been indicted for excluding blacks from jury service. The Court said: "Whoever . . . acts in the name and for the State, and is clothed with the State's power, his act is that of the State."

The Civil Rights Act of 1866, passed before adoption of the Fourteenth Amendment, made punishable racial discrimination by persons acting "under color of any law." This phrase has since been rather generally employed in civil rights statutes, and it has come to be accepted as one of the tests of state action. The Supreme Court in *United States v. Classic* (1941) applied the statute to officials guilty of election fraud, saying: "Misuse of power, possessed by virtue of state law and made possible only because the wrongdoer is clothed with the authority of state law, is action taken 'under color of' state law."

In the gruesome case of *Screws v. United States* (1945), where a sheriff had beaten a black prisoner to death in his jail, the defense against a federal civil rights prosecution was that the sheriff, having acted in abuse of his official capacity, could not be regarded as having acted under color of law. The Court majority rejected this view, Justice Rutledge contending that the sheriff had acted with the "power of official place," but Justice Roberts, dissenting, could not see how conduct "in flagrant defiance of State law, may be attributed to the State."

Inaction of State Officials

A somewhat different question arises when injury is done to a person's civil rights as a result of official failure to act. Can official inaction be treated as "state action"? *Lynch v. United States* (1951) involved review of the conviction of a Georgia sheriff who had allowed black prisoners in his custody to be kidnapped and beaten by a Ku Klux mob. A Georgia federal court jury found him guilty of having acted under color of law to deprive citizens of their protected rights; and the court of appeals agreed that official inaction, where designed to injure, may be punished. "There was a time when the denial of equal protection of the laws was confined to affirmative acts, but the law now is that culpable official inaction may also constitute a denial of equal protection."

In *Terry v. Adams* (1953), a group of private citizens regularly conducted an unofficial primary prior to the regular Democratic primary to select candidates for office in a Texas county who would then be entered in the regular primary. The theory of this preprimary was that it was private action from which blacks could be constitutionally excluded, but the Supreme Court ruled that the preprimary had become "an integral part" of the election process. Both Justices Black and Frankfurter emphasized that state inaction was the root of the offense. According to Black, the state had permitted "circumvention" to produce the equivalent of a discriminatory election, and Frankfurter referred to the state's "abdication."

Discrimination in Public Accommodations

The *Civil Rights Cases* (1883), as we have seen, held that the Fourteenth Amendment did not prevent discrimination in such privately owned public accommodations as hotels and theaters. Although that decision has never been overruled, the situation of public accommodations has been drastically changed by judicial interpretation and by state and federal statutes.

In the first place, any significant relationship between the state and the enterprise may be interpreted as transferring to the latter the constitutional obligations of the state. The leading case is *Burton v. Wilmington Parking Authority* (1961), involving a parking facility owned and operated by an agency of the state of Delaware. To help finance the building some of the space was leased to commercial operations. This case arose when a restaurant located on the premises refused service to a black. The Supreme Court majority held that its location in, and relationship to, the parking facility had cost the restaurant its "purely private" character. By its inaction in failing to require the restaurant to serve all comers, the state had made itself a party to the refusal of service.

The sit-in cases of the early 1960s furnish additional illustrations of how public accommodations may come under the state action rule. In *Peterson v. Greenville* (1963), restaurant discrimination was held to be state action because a city ordinance required separation of the races. In *Lombard v. Louisiana* (1963), there was no ordinance, but the Court held that city officials had coerced the restaurant manager to operate a segregated facility, which made it state action. *Griffin v. Maryland* (1964) held that an amusement park's exclusion of blacks was state action because, to enforce this policy, the park employed a deputy sheriff who, though working on his off-duty hours, wore his badge and purported to exercise the powers of a deputy sheriff at the park.

However, there must be some link of this kind between the state and the enterprise, however tenuous or indirect, to justify treating the discriminatory action of public accommodations as state action under the Fourteenth Amendment. The Supreme Court has stopped short of a holding that public accommodations are by the very nature of their service public agencies governed by the equal protection clause. This was the position taken by the first Justice Harlan in his dissent to the *Civil Rights Cases,* and it was revived in the sit-in cases by Douglas and Goldberg.[27]

In the Civil Rights Act of 1964, also called the Public Accommodations Act, Congress took over from the Supreme Court the responsibility of determining what rights of access there should be to the most important types of public accommodations. Under the statute full and equal access without discrimination or segregation is guaranteed with respect to hotels and motels, restaurants and catering establishments of all kinds, places of entertainment and sports exhibitions, gasoline stations, and such bars and barber shops as are physically within the premises of a covered establishment. Boarding houses with not more than five rooms for rent are not covered, nor are private clubs or other establishments not in fact open to the public.

This statute invoked the commerce clause as authority for its enactment, and it was on this basis that the Supreme Court promptly upheld the act in *Heart of Atlanta Motel v. United States* (1964). But Congress also relied on the Fourteenth Amendment by defining the applicability of the act to cover discrimination and segregation required by action of the state or carried on "under color of any law" or "any custom or usage required or enforced by officials of the State." In the *Heart of Atlanta* case the Supreme Court found it unnecessary to consider this second basis for congressional action, since the commerce power alone was sufficient for the decision. This ruling relieved the Court from the necessity of reconsidering the *Civil*

---

[27] See *Garner v. Louisiana* (1961) and *Bell v. Maryland* (1964).

Rights Cases of 1883, the decision in which was held here to be "inapposite, and without precedential value."[28]

Private Discrimination and State Action

The state action rule of the Fourteenth Amendment leaves individuals free to discriminate for any reason in their personal relationships, in granting access to their homes, or in the operation of private associations. As Justice Goldberg said in his *Bell* opinion, "Rights pertaining to privacy and private association are themselves constitutionally protected liberties," and courts will safeguard the privilege of every person "to close his home or club to any person . . . on the basis of personal prejudices including race." In *Runyon v. McCrary* (1976), which held that the refusal of private schools to admit black children violated the Civil Rights Act of 1866, the Court's opinion specifically left open the issue of the validity of racially exclusive social clubs and organizations, as well as the legality of schools that limit enrollment to members of one sex or religious faith.

In *Moose Lodge No. 107 v. Irvis* (1972), a black was denied food and beverage service as a guest of a member of a private club. The contention was made—and supported by Douglas, Brennan, and Marshall, in dissent—that by granting the club a liquor license the state had become an "active participant" in its operation. But the majority held that the liquor license did not derogate from the private character of the club. There was here "nothing approaching the symbiotic relationship" between the restaurant and the public parking authority in the *Burton* case.

How far beyond the home or the club does this guarantee of the right to discriminate extend? The principal problems have concerned the buying, selling, and renting of property. "Open occupancy" laws making illegal refusal to sell or to rent to persons because of their race or color have generally met state constitutional tests. The experience of California is instructive. State statutes barred racial discrimination in the sale or rental of any private dwelling of more than four units, and the State Fair Employment Practice Commission was empowered to prevent violations. In 1964 California voters, by a margin of almost two to one, approved an amendment to the state constitution that nullified the effect of these acts and provided that property owners had "absolute discretion" to sell or rent to persons of their choice.

In 1966 the California supreme court in *Mulkey v. Reitman* declared the amendment unconstitutional as state action in violation of the equal protection clause. By adopting the amendment, the court said, the state had become "at least a partner in the . . . act of discrimination," adding that when "the electorate assumes to exercise the law-making function," it is "as

[28] The act was applied in *Daniel v. Paul* (1969).

much a state agency as any of its elected officials." In *Reitman v. Mulkey* (1967) the Supreme Court upheld this position by a vote of five to four, Justice White for the majority ruling that the amendment made the right to discriminate "one of the basic policies of the state." After the amendment was passed, "the right to discriminate, including the right to discriminate on racial grounds, was embodied in the state's basic charter, immune from legislative, executive or judicial regulation at any level of the state government. Those practicing racial discriminations need no longer rely on their personal choice. They could now evoke express constitutional authority." Under this ruling racial discrimination by private persons violates the Fourteenth Amendment if the state takes any action encouraging such discrimination.[29]

In 1968, following the assassination of Martin Luther King, Jr., Congress for the first time passed a civil rights act containing comprehensive open-housing provisions applicable to a broad range of discriminatory practices. A few weeks later, the Supreme Court, in *Jones v. Alfred H. Mayer Co.*, ruled that the provision in the Civil Rights Act of 1866 giving all citizens the same right as white citizens "to inherit, purchase, lease, sell, hold, and convey real and personal property," although never previously so interpreted, was to be given its literal meaning and had made illegal every racially motivated refusal by property owners to rent or sell.[30]

A surprising feature of Justice Stewart's opinion for the Court was his broad reading of the Thirteenth Amendment, which he interpreted to forbid not only slavery but also "the badges and the incidents of slavery." He wrote:

> At the very least, the freedom that Congress is empowered to secure under the Thirteenth Amendment includes the freedom to buy whatever a white man can buy, the right to live wherever a white man can live. If Congress cannot say that being a free man means at least this much, then the Thirteenth Amendment made a promise the Nation cannot keep.

The dissenters, Harlan and White, thought that Stewart's history was "almost surely wrong"[31] and believed that the Court should not have revived an 1866 statute by questionable interpretation when Congress had just adopted a more appropriate fair-housing act.

---

[29] See the extensive discussion by Charles L. Black, Jr., "'State Action,' Equal Protection, and California's Proposition 14," 81 HARVARD LAW REVIEW 69–109 (1967).

[30] The *Jones* decision was followed in *Sullivan v. Little Hunting Park* (1969); also in *Tillman v. Wheaton-Haven Recreation Assn.* (1973), where a swimming pool association was denied status as a private club.

[31] The same conclusion is reached in the extended analysis by Gerhard Casper, "Jones v. Mayer; Clio, Bemused and Confused Muse," in Philip B. Kurland, ed., *The Supreme Court Review: 1968* (Chicago: University of Chicago Press, 1968), pp. 89–132.

FEDERAL PROTECTION OF CIVIL RIGHTS

Since 1957 Congress has adopted at least six major laws providing federal protection for civil rights. The Civil Rights Act of 1957, dealing largely and rather ineffectively with the guarantee of voting rights, also created the Civil Rights Commission, which through its hearings and reports has done much to focus attention on civil rights abuses. The Civil Rights Act of 1960 was also concerned primarily with voting rights. The Civil Rights Act of 1964 was a major statute guaranteeing equal access to public accommodations and barring discrimination in public programs receiving federal financial assistance and in private employment. The Voting Rights Act of 1965, renewed in 1975, finally found a formula for effectively breaking down the barriers to black voting. The Civil Rights Act of 1968 was a fair housing statute. The Equal Employment Opportunities Act of 1972 strengthened Title VII of the 1964 act.

This flurry of legislative activity was comparable to, but much more successful than, the civil rights laws enacted after the Civil War, between 1866 and 1875. In fact, those statutes proved largely valueless. With a hostile Supreme Court and an apathetic public, much of the legislative product of Radical Reconstruction was declared unconstitutional or repealed by later Congresses. What was left was largely ignored and unused by enforcement authorities.

A few provisions of the Reconstruction statutes did survive, however, and have played an important role in recent civil rights litigation. Section 241 of Title 18 of the U.S. Code, which had its origin in the Enforcement Act of 1870, provides a fine of up to $5,000 and imprisonment of up to ten years for a conspiracy by two or more persons to "injure, oppress, threaten, or intimidate any citizen" from exercising, or because he has exercised, any right or privilege "secured" to him by the Constitution or laws of the United States. Section 242, dating from the Civil Rights Act of 1866, provides a fine of $1,000 or one year in prison, or both, for any person who, acting "under color of any law, statute, ordinance, regulation, or custom," willfully deprives any inhabitant of the United States of any of the rights, privileges, or immunities "secured or protected" by the Constitution or laws of the United States. This second section is broader than the conspiracy statute in that its shield covers all "inhabitants," not merely "citizens." Moreover, section 242 refers to substantive acts and not just to conspiracies, and therefore can be used against a single individual who commits unlawful acts providing he is acting "under color of" law.

Another difference between the two sections is that 241 covers "secured" rights, while 242 covers both "secured" and "protected" rights. Initially 241 was given a limited reading as the equivalent of rights of national citizenship, such as the right to vote in national elections or to petition Congress for redress of grievances, and was held not available to enforce Fourteenth Amendment guarantees of equal protection and due process.

The combined use of the two statutes was declared constitutional in the election fraud case of *United States v. Classic* (1941). The Civil Rights Section of the Department of Justice, created by Attorney General Frank Murphy in 1939, relied on section 242 in the police brutality case of *Screws v. United States* (1945). While the statute was held constitutional, the conviction was reversed and a new trial ordered because the judge had not charged the jury that the deprivation of civil rights must be "willful." A conviction under 242 in another police brutality case was upheld in *Williams v. United States* (1951), but the conspiracy conviction under section 241, obtained on the same facts, was reversed by the Court in *United States v. Williams* (1951) because of the narrow interpretation of "secured" rights.

Violence against civil rights workers and blacks in the South during the 1960s led to widespread demands for more effective intervention by the federal government, and the Department of Justice made renewed efforts to use 241 and 242, which were successful in the cases of *United States v. Price* (1966) and *United States v. Guest* (1966).[32] The *Price* case was an aftermath of the murder of three young civil rights workers near Philadelphia, Mississippi, in 1964. A federal indictment against eighteen suspects under 241 was dismissed by the federal district judge in reliance on *United States v. Williams,* but the Supreme Court unanimously overruled the district judge, and in the process broadened the interpretation of 241 to cover not only rights of national citizenship but also Fourteenth Amendment rights. This ruling in the *Price* case made possible the trial of Price and six associates in 1967. Their conviction was the first for a civil rights slaying in Mississippi.

Section 1983

Two statutes generally paralleling the criminal sanctions just discussed allow damage suits against state officers and private persons who violate constitutional rights. The more important is section 1983 of Title 42 of the U.S. Code, which provides for civil suit against any person acting under "color of any statute, ordinance, regulation, custom, or usage" who deprives a citizen of his constitutional rights. This statute can be used in combination with other provisions of the Code to obtain an injunction or declaratory judgment against the enforcement of unconstitutional laws or policies. In this manner the white primary was invalidated, as was segregation in public schools, buses, and parks.[33]

---

[32] The *Guest* decision was important for its construction of the right to travel and also for its holding that section 241 is not limited by a "state action" requirement but authorizes the punishment of "entirely private conspiracies to interfere with the exercise of Fourteenth Amendment rights."

[33] The second statute under which civil suits may be brought is section 1985 of Title 42; it was construed in *Collins v. Hardyman* (1951). See generally Robert K. Carr, *Federal Protection of Civil Rights* (Ithaca, N.Y.: Cornell University Press, 1947).

Section 1983 is also available to secure money damages from officials who exceed legal bounds. In the leading case of *Monroe v. Pape* (1961) the Supreme Court held that police brutality constituted state action within the meaning of the statute. This decision unloosed a flood of private civil rights damage actions in the federal courts, only a few examples of which can be given.

Scheuer v. Rhodes (1974) involved actions of the Ohio National Guardsmen who killed four students at Kent State University in 1970; they were prosecuted under section 242 for depriving the students of their civil rights but were acquitted because of failure to prove "willful" intent. Representatives of the estates of three of the students then brought suit under section 1983 against the governor of Ohio and officers of the National Guard and university. The trial court dismissed the suit on grounds of state immunity, but the Supreme Court held that state officers are not protected by state immunity if in fact they acted under state law in a manner violative of the Constitution. The trial proceedings were then reinstituted, but the jury found in favor of the defendants.

In *Rizzo v. Goode* (1976) a federal district court, having found a "pattern" of police violation of the civil rights of blacks in Philadelphia and "official indifference" to doing anything about it, granted an injunction against the mayor and police officials. By a five to three vote the Supreme Court, narrowly interpreting section 1983, held that "principles of federalism" forbade federal judicial interference in the internal disciplinary affairs of the police department.

Paul v. Davis (1976) ruled against a claimant in a section 1983 damage suit who had been listed by the Louisville police as an "active shoplifter" in a flyer distributed to city merchants. In fact he had been arrested once for shoplifting, but was never tried and the charges were dropped. The Supreme court held that there is no constitutionally guaranteed right to a good reputation, and so no basis for a federal civil rights damage suit, suggesting that the proper remedy was a defamation suit in state court.[34]

Removal of Civil Rights Cases

A statute of 1866, codified as section 1443, Title 28, authorized the removal of civil rights cases under certain circumstances from state to federal courts. Denial of removal petitions was not subject to appeal to the Supreme Court until so provided by the Civil Rights Act of 1964. In *Georgia v. Rachel* (1966) the Court held that the federal district court involved must

---

[34] For a comprehensive analysis of section 1983 cases, see "Developments in the Law—Section 1983 and Federalism," 90 HARVARD LAW REVIEW 1133–1361 (1977). In *Smith v. Wade* (1983) the Court upheld punitive damages against a prison guard who failed to protect a prisoner from rape.

grant a hearing to determine whether defendants under prosecution in state courts for a restaurant sit-in had been ordered to leave the restaurant solely for racial reasons. If so, their rights of free access to public accommodations under the 1964 Civil Rights Act would have been challenged, and they would be entitled to removal of the case to federal court.

However, in another case decided the same day, *City of Greenwood v. Peacock* (1966), the Court by a five to four vote held that removal would not be ordered on allegations that the defendants had been arrested and charged solely because they were blacks or were engaged in helping blacks to assert their civil rights. The majority asserted that the removal statute was not intended "to work a wholesale dislocation of the historic relationship between the state and the federal courts in the administration of the criminal law." If the defendants really were being prosecuted because they were blacks, Justice Stewart said, there were other possible remedies in the federal courts by way of injunction, habeas corpus, and appeal.[35]

Justice Douglas for the dissenters in *Peacock* contended that "the federal regime was designed from the beginning to afford some protection against local passions and prejudices by the important pretrial federal remedy of removal."

While the civil rights revolution originated in the courts, it was subsequently given general support by the other two branches. As of 1983, programs for promotion of racial equality tended to receive continued support from the courts and Congress, but not from the Reagan administration. The most striking event was the rebuff administered by Chief Justice Burger and a near-unanimous Court in the *Bob Jones* case to the Reagan effort to grant tax exemption to racially discriminatory private schools. The extension of the Voting Rights Act, which has proved perhaps the most powerful instrument of racial progress, was only belatedly supported by the administration. The Department of Justice opposed as "quotas" court-designed affirmative action programs. Reagan undertook to replace three members of the Civil Rights Commission, which in 1983 issued two highly critical reports on the administration's enforcement of civil rights. However, racial equal protection rests on a solid foundation of constitutional and statute law and public understanding.

---

[35] The *Peacock* decision was determinative for the Burger Court in *Johnson v. Mississippi* (1975), where a group of blacks in Vicksburg who were conducting a boycott of businesses that were alleged to discriminate in employment were prosecuted for conspiracy and unsuccessfully sought removal of the case to federal court.

11
Property Rights and Substantive Due Process

In the original Constitution, the only specific protection of property rights was the provision forbidding the states to impair the obligation of contracts. The Fifth Amendment forbade the deprivation of property without due process of law or the taking of property without just compensation, both of which were limitations on the federal government. With the Fourteenth Amendment, the pregnant due process formula was extended to the states.

THE PROTECTION OF CONTRACTS

Article I, section 10, forbids any state to "pass any . . . law impairing the obligation of contracts." The fact that this language has comparatively little present-day significance should not be permitted to minimize the outstanding role that it played in an earlier period. In the absence of a due process requirement applicable to the states, the contract clause was invoked against state legislation early and often. As Benjamin F. Wright has noted in his definitive study, up to 1889 the contract clause had been considered by the Court in almost 40 percent of all cases involving the validity of state legislation.[1] During that period it was the constitutional justification for

---

[1] Benjamin F. Wright, *The Contract Clause of the Constitution* (Cambridge, Mass.: Harvard University Press, 1938), p. 95.

seventy-five decisions in which state laws were held unconstitutional, almost half of all those in which legislation was declared invalid by the Supreme Court. But after adoption of the Fourteenth Amendment, there was less and less occasion to invoke the contract clause.

Marshall's contribution to the development of doctrine in this field was preeminent. His four great contract decisions, written between 1810 and 1819—*Fletcher v. Peck* (1810), *New Jersey v. Wilson* (1812), *Sturges v. Crowninshield* (1819), and *Dartmouth College v. Woodward* (1819)—are among the most significant that the Supreme Court has ever handed down. By employing a far broader conception of contract than had prevailed in 1787 and by combining this conception with the principles of eighteenth-century natural law, Marshall was able to make of the contract clause a powerful instrument for the protection of the vested rights of private property.

The original understanding as to the meaning of the contract clause is almost impossible to determine. The general assumption has been that the clause was desired by propertied interests who wanted to protect themselves against the kind of state legislation favoring debtors that had been passed during the hard times of the 1780s—issuance of paper money which was given legal tender status in payment of private debts, granting debtors postponements beyond the contract date for payment of debts, or permitting them to pay debts in installments or in commodities.

Public Contracts

It is almost certainly true that the clause was intended to affect only private contracts—that is, contracts between individuals. Yet in the series of important contract cases decided by the Marshall Court, practically all dealt with public contracts. In the first and most notorious case, *Fletcher v. Peck* (1810), Marshall ruled that a huge land grant secured by bribing the Georgia legislature could not be revoked because the legislative action constituted a contract.[2] Apparently uncertain about the validity of this claim, he also invoked in a rather vague way the ex post facto and bill of attainder provisions, though *Calder v. Bull* (1798) had already held the ex post facto clause to be confined to criminal cases. In addition, and almost in the same breath, he suggested that the limits on the Georgia legislature came not from the Constitution, but from "the nature of society and of government." In his concluding paragraph, he could do no better than say that the rescinding act was invalidated "either by general principles, which are common to our free institutions, or by the particular provisions of the constitution of the United States."

---

[2] See C. Peter Magrath, *Yazoo: The Case of Fletcher v. Peck* (New York: W. W. Norton & Co., Inc., 1967).

This sorry performance inflamed public opinion, which was already antagonistic to the nationalistic trends of the Marshall Court on states' rights grounds. Nevertheless, the doctrine that the contract clause covered public contracts remained firmly established. Marshall himself quickly conquered the doubts he had exhibited in *Fletcher v. Peck,* and in *New Jersey v. Wilson* (1812) applied the contract clause to prevent a state from exercising one of its most fundamental powers, taxation. Tax exemption that had been granted by the colonial New Jersey legislature to an Indian tribe for the land on which they lived was held to be a contract still valid after the Indians had sold the land.

Next came *Dartmouth College v. Woodward* (1819), which held that a charter of incorporation was a contract protected against subsequent legislative infringement.[3] Though this case concerned a college, it was largely business corporations that were to benefit from the decision.

These three decisions raised a truly alarming specter of a venal or unwise legislature giving away the public birthright or even divesting the government of its essential taxing power—actions that would be irremediable under the contract clause. It is hardly surprising that a doctrine so potentially dangerous tended to generate its own correctives, which can be summarized under three headings.

First, the Dartmouth College decision itself recognized that the state may insert as a condition in the corporate charter the right to "amend, alter, and repeal" the same. This reservation is then part of the contract, and exercise of the power does not impair the contractual obligation. Again, the reservation may be not in the contract itself, but in general legislation which has the effect of incorporating the reservation in all charters of subsequent date. Especially after the Dartmouth ruling, such reservations were commonly provided, both by statutory and constitutional provisions.

Second, there is the rule of strict construction of public contracts or grants, which stems from Chief Justice Taney's famous decision in *Charles River Bridge v. Warren Bridge* (1837). The Charles River Bridge, a privately owned toll structure, was incorporated in 1785, and its franchise was extended in 1792. In 1828 Massachusetts incorporated the Warren Bridge and authorized it to build and operate a toll bridge near the other bridge. After a short period the Warren Bridge was to become free and part of the public highway; this would of course be fatal to the toll bridge. Taney, speaking for the Court, ruled that the state had not given the Charles River Bridge an exclusive charter. There was no express language in the contract that another bridge would not be established nearby. Public grants or franchises are to be strictly construed, and nothing passes to the grantee by implication. Taney added: "While the rights of private property are sacredly

---

[3] Francis N. Stites, *Private Interest and Public Gain: The Dartmouth College Case, 1819* (Amherst: University of Massachusetts Press, 1972).

guarded, we must not forget that the community also have rights, and that the happiness and well-being of every citizen depends on their faithful preservation."

Third, contractual grants are subordinate to the power of eminent domain and the police power. In *Stone v. Mississippi* (1880), a lottery franchise had been granted for a definite term of years, but two years later a new constitution was adopted that forbade lotteries. The unanimous Court ruled that "the power of governing is a trust committed by the people to the government, no part of which can be granted away."

Private Contracts

Only about 10 percent of the Supreme Court's contract cases have involved private contracts, but in that number are cases of considerable interest and importance. Again we go back to the Marshall Court for the beginning of the story. *Sturges v. Crowninshield* (1819) involved the validity of a New York bankruptcy act as applied to a contract of debt made *before* the law was passed. Marshall declared the law in violation of the contract clause, which he contended protected all contracts from legislative regulation. The sole exception he was willing to make was for laws abolishing imprisonment for debt.

Although Marshall carried the Court for this extreme view in *Sturges,* he was unable to do so in *Ogden v. Saunders* (1827), where the bankruptcy law being questioned was in force *before* the contract was made. Marshall would have declared this law unconstitutional also, but for the only time in his thirty-four years as Chief Justice he was in the minority on a constitutional issue. The majority held that the *Sturges* decision had to be limited to contracts already made. A statute in effect at the time a contract is entered into is a part of the contract, and therefore cannot be held to impair its obligation. The true meaning of the contract clause, said Justice Johnson, was to protect against "arbitrary and tyrannical legislation over existing right." Bankruptcy legislation was no more in this category than laws regulating usurious contracts or the collection of gaming debts. This view of insolvency laws has been consistently maintained since.

State authority to modify contractual remedies is derived from the police power, and we have already seen that the police power cannot be frustrated by public contracts. Even less should private contracts be permitted to override public policy. Thus a state prohibition act is not invalid because it nullifies contracts for the sale of beer,[4] and contracts of employment may legitimately be modified by later workmen's compensation laws.[5]

---

[4] *Boston Beer Co. v. Massachusetts* (1878).
[5] *New York Central R. Co. v. White* (1917).

As the Supreme Court said in 1905, "Parties by entering into contracts may not estop the legislature from enacting laws intended for the public good."[6]

There may be real difficulty in determining how far a legislature may reasonably go when the "public good" sought under the police power is such a controversial problem as the relief of debtors. The most famous debtor relief case of recent times is *Home Building and Loan Assn. v. Blaisdell* (1934), where the Court by a five to four vote upheld depression legislation passed by Minnesota to prevent the wholesale loss of mortgaged properties by debtors unable to meet their obligations. On application from the mortgagor, state courts could extend the existing one-year period of redemption from foreclosure sales for an additional limited time. During the period while possession was retained, the mortgagor was obliged to apply the income or reasonable rental value to the payment of taxes, interest, insurance, and the mortgage indebtedness.

In upholding the law, Chief Justice Hughes stressed the government's emergency powers. "While emergency does not create power," he said, "emergency may furnish the occasion for the exercise of power." The states have a reserved power to protect the interests of their citizens in time of emergency. They also have an obligation not to impair contracts. These two powers "must be construed in harmony with each other." One must not be used to destroy the other. Certainly "state power exists to give temporary relief from the enforcement of contracts in the presence of disasters due to physical causes such as fire, flood or earthquake." The same power must exist "when the urgent public need demanding such relief is produced by other and economic causes." Hughes concluded: "The question is no longer merely that of one party to a contract as against another, but of the use of reasonable means to safeguard the economic structure upon which the good of all depends. . . . The principle of this development is . . . that the reservation of the reasonable exercise of the protective power of the State is read into all contracts."

Shortly thereafter, less carefully drawn moratorium legislation in two other states was invalidated by the Court,[7] but these decisions do not detract from the authority of the *Blaisdell* opinion. In 1945 Justice Frankfurter for a unanimous Court said that the Hughes opinion had left "hardly any open spaces of controversy concerning the constitutional restrictions of the Contract Clause upon moratory legislation." The *Blaisdell* principle was restated by Frankfurter to say that

> When a widely diffused public interest has become enmeshed in a network of multitudinous private arrangements, the authority of the State "to safeguard the vital interests of its people" . . . is not to be gainsaid by abstracting one such

---

[6] *Manigault v. Springs* (1905); *Energy Reserves Group v. Kansas Power & Light* (1983).

[7] *Worthen Co. v. Thomas* (1934); *Worthen Co. v. Kavanaugh* (1935).

arrangement from its public context and treating it as though it were an isolated private contract constitutionally immune from impairment.[8]

The Contract Clause Redivivus

In 1977, for the first time in almost forty years, the Supreme Court invalidated a state law for violation of the contract clause. A statutory covenant entered into by New York and New Jersey in 1962 had limited the ability of the bistate Port of New York Authority to divert its revenues to subsidization of rail passenger transport. This protection for authority bondholders was repealed in 1974, an action that the Court declared unconstitutional by a four to three vote in *United States Trust Co. v. New Jersey* (1977). Although the Court should defer to legislative judgment where private contracts were involved, Justice Blackmun asserted, heightened scrutiny was necessary when the state was impairing its own obligations. Brennan protested this dusting off of the contract clause and elevating it to the status of regulator of the municipal bond market.

But the next year, in *Allied Structural Steel Co. v. Spannaus* (1978), the Court continued to reinvigorate the clause, this time as applied to private rather than state obligations. A Minnesota pension benefits protection act provided that if employers who had established an employee pension plan terminated it, they were required to pay the state a pension funding charge if their pension funds were insufficient to finance pensions for all employees who had worked for at least ten years. In this case the charge would have been $185,000. By a five to three vote the Court held that this law retroactively modified a pension plan voluntarily assumed by the company, and warned that the contract clause, in spite of its assumed "desuetude," was still part of the Constitution and would be enforced when seriously challenged.

EMINENT DOMAIN

Eminent domain is the power of government to take private property when it is needed for a public purpose. Since such authority is an incident of sovereignty, it requires no explicit constitutional recognition. The Fifth Amendment assumes the existence of this power in the national government when it imposes the requirement of "just compensation." While there is no comparable language in the Fourteenth Amendment, the significant constitutional questions applying to the exercise of eminent domain power by both the states and the federal government are largely the same, namely: What is a public purpose? What is a taking of property? and What is just compensation?

---

[8] *East New York Savings Bank v. Hahn* (1945). The *Blaisdell* opinion was relied on in *City of El Paso v. Simmons* (1965).

Public Purpose

Where a public agency itself proposes to use land for a public building, highway, park, or other facility for general public use, the public character of the taking is obvious. But the taking need not be for a use to which all the public will have access. Condemnation of property for public housing projects, in which only a small percentage of the population can live, is now thoroughly established. The "access" test is not relevant here; rather, public purpose results from the contribution of public housing to slum clearance, reduction of crime and disease, lowering of police and fire costs, and general community improvement.[9]

Eminent domain power is customarily granted to public utility corporations, which have no difficulty in meeting the public use test. Even private corporations or individuals may be considered to qualify under sufficiently pressing circumstances, as in connection with access to water for irrigation in the arid West or the damming of streams for the operation of mills.[10]

The Supreme Court gives great weight to legislative determinations as to what is a public use. In *United States ex rel. TVA v. Welch* (1946) Justice Black said in the opinion for the Court: "We think that it is the function of Congress to decide what type of taking is for a public use." Justice Douglas added, in *Berman v. Parker* (1954): "Subject to specific constitutional limitations, when the legislature has spoken, the public interest has been declared in terms well-nigh conclusive." So far as state cases are concerned, the Supreme Court has tended to follow the decisions of the state courts.

The Taking of Property

Property need not be literally or fully "taken" in order to establish a basis for claiming compensation. An owner may remain in possession of property and still find that by reason of governmental action the use or enjoyment of the property has been seriously eroded.

A classic case is *Pennsylvania Coal Co. v. Mahon* (1922), where Justices Holmes and Brandeis argued this issue. A state law forbade the mining of coal in such a way as to cause the subsidence of residential property. The coal company owned all the subsurface rights under Mahon's land and its mining operations threatened the destruction of his house. On the other hand, the state law destroyed the coal company's property and contract rights. Holmes formulated a pragmatic rule: "that while property may be regulated to a certain extent, if regulation goes too far it will be recognized

---

[9] *City of Cleveland v. United States* (1945).

[10] *Clark v. Nash* (1905), *Otis Co. v. Ludlow Mfg. Co.* (1906). In 1982 a California court ruled that the city of Oakland could invoke eminent domain to purchase the Oakland Raiders professional football team to keep it from being moved to Los Angeles.

as a taking. . . . [A] strong public desire to improve the public condition is not enough to warrant achieving the desire by a shorter cut than the constitutional way of paying for the change." But Brandeis, dissenting, thought that the state had not appropriated property, but merely prevented the owner from making a use which interfered with the paramount rights of the public.

The Brandeis position has been influential in subsequent rulings. A general zoning ordinance restricting the uses to which urban property could be put was upheld in *Euclid v. Ambler Realty Co.* (1926) and more recently in *Agins v. Tiburon* (1980). In *Penn Central Transportation Co. v. New York City* (1978) the city had designated Grand Central Terminal as an historic landmark and denied the railroad company the right to erect a multistory office building on the site. By a six to three vote the Court held this was not a taking. And in *Hodel v. Virginia Surface Mining Assn.* (1981) the Court ruled that the mere enactment of the Surface Mining Act requiring strip-mining operators to restore the land to its original contours after mining did not constitute a taking.[11]

Acts done in the proper exercise of governmental power and not encroaching on private property, though their consequences may impair its use or reduce its value, are not generally regarded as a taking of property. Thus, changes in grade level of a street do not require compensation to owners whose access to their property is impaired, nor does the government have to compensate a riparian owner for cutting off his access to navigable waters by changing the course of a stream to improve navigation. Congress may lower the tariff or cheapen the currency without having to compensate those who suffer losses as a result. Restrictions on use of property in wartime have been held not to constitute a taking of property, even when they extend to a complete ban on its use, as in the *Wartime Prohibition Cases* (1919).

Just Compensation

So far as state takings are concerned, the Supreme Court has pretty well kept out of disputes over the adequacy of compensation. Unless a state court has, by its rulings of law, prevented an owner from receiving substantially any compensation at all, the Court will not intervene. "All that is essential is that in some appropriate way, before some properly constituted tribunal, inquiry shall be made as to the amount of compensation, and when this has been provided there is that due process of law which is required by the Federal Constitution."[12]

---

[11]The California supreme court ruled in *Nestle v. City of Santa Monica* (1972) that, though the property of residents near airports had not been "taken," they could seek damages on grounds of nuisance. See also *Los Angeles v. Greater Westchester* (1980).

[12]*Backus v. Fort Street Union Depot Co.* (1898).

In federal takings, however, the Supreme Court has been more concerned with the standards applied. An owner of land to be condemned is entitled to "market value fairly determined."[13] That value may reflect not only the use to which the property is presently devoted but also that to which it may be readily converted. But a reasonable probability of the land's being devoted to a more profitable purpose must be shown if it is to affect the compensation awarded.[14]

THE INVENTION
OF SUBSTANTIVE DUE PROCESS

Substantive due process is defined by Edward S. Corwin as the judicial doctrine that "every species of State legislation, whether dealing with procedural or substantive rights, [is] subject to the scrutiny of the [Supreme] Court when the question of its essential justice is raised."[15] The transformation of the due process clause from a guarantee of fair procedures into an activist judicial warrant for passing judgment on the substantive policies of legislative regulations must rate as one of the Supreme Court's most significant creative efforts.

Corwin traces the idea to a New York State court decision, *Wynehamer v. New York* (1856), which declared unconstitutional a very drastic prohibition statute making liquor a nuisance that owners must destroy on pain of criminal prosecution. The court concluded that the harsh operation of the statute on liquors lawfully owned at the time the act went into effect amounted to an act of destruction not within the power of government to perform, "even by the forms which belong to 'due process of law.'"

The next year Taney invoked the Fifth Amendment due process clause as a defense of property against substantive legislative power in his *Dred Scott* opinion. In 1870 *Hepburn v. Griswold* set aside the Legal Tender Act of 1862 on the ground, among others, that retroactive application of the law deprived creditors of property without due process of law.

The initial effort to protect property rights under the Fourteenth Amendment was made in the *Slaughterhouse Cases* (1873). Counsel for the New Orleans butchers who were attacking the slaughterhouse monopoly granted by state statute was John A. Campbell, former justice of the Supreme Court. He argued that the Fourteenth Amendment had not been

---

[13] For problems of determining fair value under wartime price ceilings or dislocations of the market, see *United States v. Commodities Training Corp.* (1950), *United States v. Felin & Co.* (1948), and *United States v. Cors* (1949).

[14] See *United States ex rel. TVA v. Powelson* (1943).

[15] Edward S. Corwin, *Liberty against Government: The Rise, Flowering and Decline of a Famous Judicial Concept* (Baton Rouge: Louisiana State University Press, 1948), pp. 135-36.

intended merely to guarantee the rights of the newly freed blacks. This purpose was only incidental to the Amendment's broader goal of protecting "laissez-faire individualism." The colonists who settled this continent were seeking "freedom, free action, free enterprise." A monopolistic charter such as was here involved abridged "privileges and immunities," denied "equal protection of the laws," and was a deprivation of "liberty."

Justice Miller's majority opinion was largely confined to the privileges and immunities point. As for due process and equal protection, Miller observed that they had "not been much pressed" by counsel, and he felt that it was "sufficient to say that under no construction" of the due process clause "that we have ever seen, or any that we deem admissible" could the Louisiana law be held "a deprivation of property." There were four dissenters. Justice Field took his stand primarily on the privileges and immunities clause, but Justice Bradley dissented squarely on due process grounds:

> [The] right to choose one's calling is an essential part of that liberty which it is the object of government to protect; and a calling, when chosen, is a man's property and right. Liberty and property are not protected where these rights are arbitrarily assailed. . . . In my view, a law which prohibits a large class of citizens from adopting a lawful employment, or from following a lawful employment previously adopted, does deprive them of liberty as well as property, without due process of law.

Four years later, in *Munn v. Illinois* (1877), the Court again refused to interfere with a regulatory statute, but by this time all members of the Court had accepted the obligation to appraise the legislation on substantive due process grounds. The state law involved fixed the maximum charges for storage of grain in warehouses and elevators and had been attacked as taking property without due process. Chief Justice Waite for the majority upheld the fixing of rates only after recognizing that a judicial case needed to be made for it on due process grounds. This he did by discovering that grain elevators were in a category of "businesses affected with a public interest" which, like ferries, inns, and gristmills, the common law had recognized as subject to regulation "for the common good." Whether a business fell within this category was primarily for the legislature to determine. Judicial intervention would be permissible only in cases where the Court was able to say of its own knowledge that no "state of facts could exist" which would justify the legislative conclusion. As for the rates and charges fixed by a legislature for businesses affected with a public interest, they were not subject to judicial review. "For protection against abuses by legislatures the people must resort to the polls, not to the courts."

This ruling failed to discourage efforts to involve the courts in reviewing regulatory statutes. In *Davidson v. New Orleans* (1878), Justice Miller was led to comment:

. . . the docket of this court is crowded with cases in which we are asked to hold that State courts and State legislatures have deprived their own citizens of life, liberty, or property without due process of law. There is here abundant evidence that there exists some strange misconception of the scope of this provision as found in the Fourteenth Amendment. In fact, it would seem, from the character of many of the cases before us, and the arguments made in them, that the clause under consideration is looked upon as a means of bringing to the test of the decision of this court the abstract opinions of every unsuccessful litigant in a State court of the justice of the decision against him, and of the merits of the legislation on which such a decision may be founded.

But Miller was no more successful than Canute in holding back the tides. Within a decade the Court was openly considering the "merits" of state legislation. A good statement of the Court's new position was given by Justice Harlan in *Mugler v. Kansas* (1887), where the constitutionality of a state prohibition act was being challenged. The Court had to review the law, Harlan said, because

. . . not . . . every statute enacted ostensibly for the promotion of [the public welfare] is to be accepted as a legitimate exertion of the police powers of the State. There are, of necessity, limits beyond which legislation cannot rightfully go. . . . The courts are not bound by mere forms, nor are they to be misled by mere pretences. They are at liberty—indeed, are under a solemn duty—to look at the substance of things, whenever they enter upon the inquiry whether the legislature has transcended the limits of its authority. If, therefore, a statute purporting to have been enacted to protect the public health, the public morals, or the public safety, has no real or substantial relation to those objects, or is a palpable invasion of rights secured by the fundamental law, it is the duty of the courts to so adjudge, and thereby give effect to the Constitution.

HEALTH, WELFARE, AND MORALS LEGISLATION

Just because judges felt obliged to appraise the "substance" of statutes did not mean, of course, that they were always, or even usually, going to reach unfavorable conclusions as to their validity. Even in the heyday of substantive due process, the great bulk of all regulatory legislation never encountered any problems with judicial review. In spite of the searching inquiry into the "real" purpose of such laws promised by Harlan, the Court's approach tended to be what Corwin calls "presumed validity."[16] Consider the case of *Powell v. Pennsylvania* (1888), where an antioleomargarine statute was accepted as a health measure, in spite of justifiable doubts that this was the major purpose of the enactment. Justice Harlan, in an orgy of double negatives, ruled that the Court

[16]Op. cit., p. 143.

. . . cannot adjudge that the defendants' rights of liberty and property . . . have been infringed by the statute of Pennsylvania, without holding that, although it may have been enacted in good faith for the objects expressed in its title, namely, to protect the public health and to prevent the adulteration of dairy products and fraud in the sale thereof, it has, in fact, no real or substantial relation to those objects. . . . The Court is unable to affirm that this legislation has no real or substantial relation to such objects.

In its subsequent experience the Court generally presumed the validity of statutes enacted for the declared purpose of furthering the public health, welfare, or morals. Regulation of professions or occupations with a close relationship to public health, such as doctors, dentists, druggists,[17] nurses, beauticians, barbers, plumbers, and the like, have been readily accepted. Such regulation, moreover, may extend beyond the basic considerations of health to cover activities only tangentially related. Thus *Semler v. Oregon State Board of Dental Examiners* (1935) upheld a statute that forbade dentists to advertise in any competitive or spectacular manner.

Jacobson v. Massachusetts (1905), upholding a state requirement of vaccination against smallpox, excellently exemplifies the presumption of validity that almost automatically attached to legislation for health purposes. Jacobson offered to prove that vaccination was ineffective or dangerous, but the Court refused to credit his evidence. Justice Harlan was quite willing to believe that there were those, some of them perhaps even doctors, who attached little or no value to vaccination. But

. . . what everybody knows the court must know, and therefore the state court judicially knew, as this court knows, that an opposite theory accords with the common belief and is maintained by high medical authority. We must assume that when the statute in question was passed, the legislature of Massachusetts was not unaware of these opposing theories, and was compelled, of necessity, to choose between them. It was not compelled to commit a matter involving the public health and safety to the final decision of a court or jury. It is no part of the function of a court or a jury to determine which one of two modes was likely to be the most effective for the protection of the public against disease. That was for the legislative department to determine in the light of all the information it had or could obtain.

Similarly, legislation aimed at the prevention and punishment of activities generally regarded in the society as offensive to moral standards is unlikely to generate constitutional objections. But it is only too well known that fanatics often seek on allegedly moral grounds the passage of legislation that amounts to serious invasions of privacy and coercion of individuals with different standards of morality.

[17] One of the few decisions declaring such a statute unconstitutional, *Liggett Co. v. Baldridge* (1926), involving a law requiring all stockholders of a corporation owning drugstores to be licensed pharmacists, was overruled in *North Dakota State Board of Pharmacy v. Snyder's Drug Stores* (1973).

The most striking example was the adoption of prohibition of intoxicating liquor in the United States and in many of the states. Substantive due process was never invoked against prohibition legislation. In *Mugler v. Kansas,* Justice Harlan wrote:

> There is no justification for holding that the State, under the guise merely of police regulation, is here aiming to deprive the citizen of his constitutional rights; for we cannot shut out of view the fact, within the knowledge of all, that the public health, the public morals, and the public safety, may be endangered by the general use of intoxicating drinks; nor the fact, established by statistics accessible to everyone, that the idleness, disorder, pauperism, and crime existing in the country are, in some degree at least, traceable to this evil.

The Supreme Court recognized in the *Mugler* case that the effect of the statute would be to render practically worthless property invested in the liquor business at a time when it was a perfectly legal occupation, but this was not contrary to due process. Moreover, the *Mugler* decision even held it was permissible for the legislature to prohibit individuals from manufacturing intoxicating liquors for their own use, on the ground that such a loophole might cause the prohibitory plan to fail. Along the same line, a subsequent decision held that the mere possession of intoxicating liquor might be prohibited.[18] Indeed, a state might prohibit the sale of *nonintoxicating* malt liquors in order to make effective its prohibition against the sale of intoxicants.[19]

As for federal action, the so-called Wartime Prohibition Act, passed ten days after the Armistice in 1918, was upheld on the basis of the government's war powers in 1919.[20] The adoption of the Eighteenth Amendment of course wrote prohibition into the Constitution.

Long before scientific proof of the dangers of cigarette smoking became available, some states sought to prohibit cigarettes on both health and morals grounds. A Tennessee statute of this sort was sustained by the Supreme Court in *Austin v. Tennessee* (1900). In 1932 a Utah statute that forbade billboard or streetcar advertising of tobacco was upheld by the Supreme Court, Justice Brandeis saying: "The law deals confessedly with a subject within the scope of the police power. No facts are brought to our attention which establish either that the evil aimed at does not exist or that the statutory remedy is inappropriate."[21]

The public welfare that states can promote by use of the police power

---

[18] *Crane v. Campbell* (1917).
[19] *Purity Extract & Tonic Co. v. Lynch* (1912).
[20] *Hamilton v. Kentucky Distilleries and Warehouse Co.* (1919).
[21] *Packer Corp. v. Utah* (1932).

has on occasion been defined in terms broader than the traditional categories of health, morals, and safety. Increasingly the Supreme Court has accepted promotion of public convenience or prosperity, or even aesthetic purposes, as justifying legislative interference with liberty or property.

Euclid v. Ambler Realty Co. (1926), upholding the constitutionality of zoning, was a landmark case in the development of a broader judicial attitude toward police power regulation. Zoning ordinances typically divide a city into various classes of residential, commercial, and manufacturing districts; and buildings and land use within each area must conform to the regulations for this district. Such restrictions of course constitute a serious limitation on freedom of the owner to employ his property as he sees fit, and the Supreme Court held two hearings in the *Euclid* case before it approved the zoning regulations by a six to three vote.

Many of the purposes that zoning seeks to achieve—limits on heights of buildings and billboards, exclusion of offensive trades from residential districts, and so on—had, it is true, already been judically approved.[22] But the exclusion of all businesses and trades, including hotels and apartment houses, from residential districts was a more extreme control than any the Court had approved in the past. To support such restriction, Justice Sutherland rehearsed the findings and the philosophy of the zoning experts as set forth in numerous reports which, he concluded, were "sufficiently cogent to preclude us from saying, as it must be said before an ordinance can be declared unconstitutional, that such provisions are clearly arbitrary and unreasonable, having no substantial relation to the public health, safety, morals, or general welfare."

The *Euclid* decision established the constitutionality of new and far-reaching controls on use of property, but it is significant that Sutherland's defense was based primarily on the old concept of nuisances. It was not until the decision in *Berman v. Parker* (1954), involving the constitutionality under the Fifth Amendment of a slum-clearance and redevelopment program in the District of Columbia, that Justice Douglas for a unanimous Court accepted aesthetics as a proper public purpose in its own right.

> The concept of the public welfare is broad and inclusive. . . . The values it represents are spiritual as well as physical, aesthetic as well as monetary. It is within the power of the legislature to determine that the community should be beautiful as well as healthy, spacious as well as clean, well-balanced as well as carefully patrolled.

[22] See *Welch v. Swasey* (1909), *Cusack v. Chicago* (1917). More recently, some zoning regulations have been attacked as "restrictive" or "exclusionary" under the equal protection clause. See Chapter 12. Regulation of billboards for esthetic and safety reasons was approved in *Metromedia, Inc. v. San Diego* (1981), though there were First Amendment objections to the ordinance.

ECONOMIC REGULATION

It is only when we come to consider legislation regulating economic activities that we see the full potentialities of the doctrine of substantive due process. Judges who were willing to accept state intervention to protect the public health and developed reasons for justifying it tended to be much less ready to accept state intervention in the economy and much more likely to produce rationalizations for striking down state action.[23] As early as 1897, in *Allgeyer v. Louisiana,* the Supreme Court announced the principle that the right to make contracts was a part of the liberty guaranteed by the due process clause, and stated the doctrine of freedom of contract in a most forthright fashion:

> The "liberty" mentioned in [the Fourteenth] Amendment means not only the right of the citizen to be free from the mere physical restraint of his person, as by incarceration, but the term is deemed to embrace the right of the citizen to be free in the enjoyment of all his faculties; to be free to use them in all lawful ways; to live and work where he will; to earn his livelihood by any lawful calling; to pursue any livelihood or avocation, and for that purpose to enter into all contracts which may be proper, necessary and essential to his carrying out to a successful conclusion the purposes above mentioned.

The immediate beneficiaries of this judical antagonism toward economic regulation were customarily business corporations. A word should be said about how corporations came within the protection accorded to "persons" under the due process clause. It is rather anomalous that the Fourteenth Amendment for a half century after its adoption should have been of very little value to the blacks in whose behalf it was primarily adopted, while it should so quickly have been accepted by the Court as a protector of corporate rights. Some have argued that this was not an accident. The "conspiracy theory" of the Fourteenth Amendment presents it as a deliberate Trojan horse which, purporting merely to protect Negro rights, smuggled into the Constitution the principle of judicial review over state legislation affecting corporate property interests. Supporting this contention is the argument made before the Supreme Court in 1885 by Roscoe Conkling, a member of the joint congressional committee which drafted the amendment, that the committee had purposely inserted the term "person" rather than "citizen" in the due process and equal protection clauses in order to cover corporations.[24]

---

[23] *Chicago, M. & St. P. R. Co. v. Minnesota* (1890) was the first case to strike down state economic regulations on substantive due process grounds, holding that the reasonableness of railroad rates was a question for ultimate judicial decision.

[24] *San Mateo County v. Southern Pacific Rr. Co.* (1885). See Howard Jay Graham. "The 'Conspiracy Theory' of the Fourteenth Amendment," 47 YALE LAW JOURNAL 371 (1938), 48 Ibid. 171 (1938).

Actually it requires no such theory, which in any event is now rather thoroughly discredited, to explain the development of judicial concern for corporate rights. A knowledge of the temper of the times is sufficient. In *Santa Clara County v. Southern Pacific Rr. Co.* (1886) the Court was unanimous in asserting that the Fourteenth Amendment covered corporations, Chief Justice Waite saying: "The Court does not wish to hear argument on the question." No dissent was expressed until 1938, when Justice Black sought to repeal a half century of holdings by denying that the amendment had been intended to apply to corporations.[25] Again in 1949 Douglas joined Black in reasserting this view, but at the same time they admitted that "history has gone the other way."[26]

Judicial Acceptance of Economic Regulation

Many types of economic regulation encountered little opposition from the courts. Economic legislation was often presented as based on health considerations, and where courts were convinced that the health rationale was valid they would usually concede constitutionality. This was generally true, for example, of laws regulating hours of work in industrial employment. In *Holden v. Hardy* (1898) the Supreme Court, with only two dissents (Brewer and Peckham), upheld a Utah statute providing for an eight-hour day in mines and smelters. This law was clearly tied in with the protection of life and health. It affected workers in only two occupations which the legislature had judged to be dangerous when too long pursued. Since there were reasonable grounds for holding this conclusion to be true, the Court would not review the legislative decision.

More importantly, the Court went on to challenge the whole freedom of contract idea by pointing out that the workers and owners were not on an equal bargaining basis. Consequently the self-interest of the workers was not a safe guide, and in the interests of the public health the legislature could impose its authority to protect one party to the contract against himself. This case was brought by the employer, who argued solicitously that the law interfered with the right of his employees to contract freely. "The argument," the Court rejoined, "would certainly come with better grace and greater cogency from the latter class."

Muller v. Oregon (1908) unanimously upheld a ten-hour law applying to women in industry. Taking "judicial cognizance" of factors that make women the weaker sex, the Court held that "she is properly placed in a class

---

[25] *Connecticut General Life Ins. Co. v. Johnson* (1938).

[26] *Wheeling Steel Corp. v. Glander* (1949). Considering the importance of groups in a liberal democratic society, it would be a dubious and even illiberal policy to guarantee rights to individuals while denying them to organized groups. See the defense of group rights in *Joint Anti-Facist Refugee Committee v. McGrath* (1951).

by herself, and legislation designed for her protection could be sustained, even when like legislation is not necessary for men and could not be sustained." The Court acknowledged its debt to "the brief filed by Mr. Louis D. Brandeis," which gathered an enormous amount of information on foreign and state laws limiting hours for women, and official reports stressing the dangers to women from long hours of labor. Such laws and opinions "may not be, techically speaking, authorities," the Court said, but "they are significant of a widespread belief that woman's physical structure, and the functions she performs in consequence thereof, justify special legislation restricting or qualifying the conditions under which she should be permitted to toil."

So health considerations provided the Court with police power justification for some hours legislation. For a time it also appeared that health arguments would legitimize regulation of wages, even though the connection with health was more indirect here and the assault on freedom of contract was more painful to employers. An Oregon minimum wage law came up to the Supreme Court in 1917. The Oregon supreme court had upheld the law on the strength of the *Muller* principle, finding it a protection for women's health and also for their morals. In *Stettler v. O'Hara,* the Supreme Court split four to four, with Brandeis abstaining, and thus the state court decision was left in effect. Within the next six years three more state supreme courts upheld minimum wages for women, relying upon the *Stettler* case.

Even the regulation of prices, a still more direct incursion on the principles of laissez faire, was initially approved in the case of *Munn v. Illinois* (1877) where, as already noted, the Court upheld the fixing of rates for Chicago grain elevators on the ground that they fell within a category of businesses recognized by the common law as "affected with a public interest."

In later decisions the Court added such business operations as insurance companies, stockyards, and tobacco warehouses[27] to the category of businesses affected with a public interest and so subject to regulation of rates and charges. The *Munn* principle was also applied in *Davidson v. New Orleans* (1878) to hold that businesses subject to control of rates were not entitled under the due process clause to judicial review of the question of just compensation.

In the early part of the twentieth century, state legislatures began to feel that industrial accidents should be recognized as a cost of production and compensated for by the employer. Laws of various types aiming at this goal were passed. In 1917 the Supreme Court upheld the New York law, saying that although it no doubt limited freedom of contract to some extent,

---

[27] *German Alliance Insurance Co. v. Lewis* (1914), *Cotting v. Godard* (1901), *Townsend v. Yeomans* (1937).

this was a legitimate exercise of the police power for protection of the health, safety, and welfare of an important group of individuals.[28]

Judicial Rejection of Economic Regulation

Although these illustrations of judical acceptance of economic regulation are significant, they are not fully representative of the Supreme Court's position for the first third of the twentieth century. During this period the Court grew steadily more critical of legislative efforts to deal with what were widely regarded as economic abuses or evils and more inflexible in its interpretation of the due process clause.

Lochner v. New York (1905) sounded the Court's call to battle against welfare economics. This case involved a state law that forbade bakery employees to work for more than ten hours a day or sixty hours a week. In spite of the fact that the Court had upheld a ten-hour law for miners in *Holden v. Hardy* (1898), it now declared the New York statute unconstitutional, by a five to four vote.

The law, said Justice Peckham for the majority, could be upheld only as a measure "pertaining to the health of the individual engaged in the occupation of a baker." Did the health of bakers need protection? Peckham did not think so, and he gave two reasons. First, "to the common understanding the trade of a baker has never been regarded as an unhealthy one." Second, statistics regarding trades and occupations show that although "the trade of a baker does not apper to be as healthy as some other trades, [it] is also vastly more healthy than still others." Since there were no special health hazards about baking, then to permit bakers' hours to be regulated would be to permit general legislative control of hours in industry. This was so unthinkable to Peckham that it clinched his argument.

The majority opinion did not bother to hide its distaste for such legislative interference. "Statutes of the nature of that under review, limiting the hours in which grown and intelligent men may labor to earn their living, are mere meddlesome interferences with the rights of the individual." Unless the Court called a halt, we would all be "at the mercy of legislative majorities." The Court must pierce through legislative pretenses when laws purporting to protect the public health or welfare were "in reality, passed from other motives."

There was nothing in Peckham's opinion to suggest that it would come with better grace if employee freedom of contract were defended by employees rather than employers. There was nothing about any inequality of bargaining power on the part of employees. In fact, Peckham inferred that such notions were an insult to red-blooded American workingmen. "There is no contention that bakers as a class are not equal in intelligence

---

[28] *New York Central Ry. Co. v. White* (1917).

and capacity to men in other trades or manual occupations, or that they are not able to assert their rights and care for themselves without the protecting arm of the State, interfering with their independence of judgment and of action. They are in no sense wards of the State."

The Peckham opinion, which has long been a museum piece, called forth some of Justice Holmes's best-known phrases.

> This case is decided upon an economic theory which a large part of the country does not entertain. . . . The Fourteenth Amendment does not enact Mr. Herbert Spencer's *Social Statics*. . . . I think that the word liberty in the Fourteenth Amendment is perverted when it is held to prevent the natural outcome of a dominant opinion, unless it can be said that a rational and fair man necessarily would admit that the statute proposed would infringe fundamental principles as they have been understood by the traditions of our people and our law.

In this instance, Holmes thought that it did not need "research to show that no such sweeping condemnation can be passed upon the statute before us."

Of course Holmes was right in saying that *Lochner* was decided "upon an economic theory." But it is also true that it was decided on a legal theory—that use of the police power was limited to grounds of health, morals, and safety. Holmes concluded that a "reasonable man" might think the New York law "a proper measure on the score of health." But actually it was not a health law. It was, as Peckham charged, a labor law. Holmes knew this, too, and was ready to approve it as a labor law, because "men whom I certainly could not pronounce unreasonable would uphold it is a first instalment of a general regulation of the hours of work." But the Court majority was not willing to follow Holmes's "reasonable man" so far or so fast.

Eighteen years later the *Lochner* ruling was invoked in *Adkins v. Children's Hospital* (1923) to strike down a District of Columbia minimum wage law for women. It had been widely thought that *Lochner* had lost much of its authority, for in the interim the Court had upheld the Oregon ten-hour law for women, and in *Bunting v. Oregon* (1917) it had approved a ten-hour law for both men and women in industry without even mentioning the *Lochner* decision. Consequently, as Chief Justice Taft said in his *Adkins* dissent, there was reason to assume that the *Lochner* case had been "overruled *sub silentio*." But for the five-judge majority in *Adkins, Lochner* was still the law.

The *Adkins* opinion, written by Justice Sutherland, was a paean to freedom of contract in its purest form, with no nonsense about the special needs of women or inequality of bargaining position. The Court saw the statute as

> . . . simply and exclusively a price-fixing law, confined to adult women . . . who are legally as capable of contracting for themselves as men. It forbids two parties having lawful capacity . . . to freely contract with one another in respect of the price for which one shall render service to the other in a purely private employment where both are willing, perhaps anxious, to agree, even though the consequence may be to oblige one to surrender a desirable engagement and the other to dispense with the services of a desirable employee.

Sutherland had two main reasons why this was unconstitutional. First, the standards set up by statute to guide the administering board in fixing minimum wages were too vague and fatally uncertain. The sum necessary to maintain a woman worker in good health and protect her morals is not precise or unvarying. It will depend on her temperament, her habits, her moral standards, her independent resources, and so on. It cannot be determined "by a general formula prescribed by a statutory bureau." Second, the law was invalid because it took account "of the necessities of only one party to the contract," compelling the employer to pay the minimum wage whether or not the employee was worth that much to him.

Chief Justice Taft, dissenting, thought that the *Adkins* case was controlled by the *Muller* decision, and he could see no difference in principle between regulating maximum hours and minimum wages. Holmes agreed.

> The bargain is equally affected whichever half you regulate. *Muller v. Oregon,* I take it, is as good law today as it was in 1908. It will need more than the Nineteenth Amendment to convince me that there are no differences between men and women, or that legislation cannot take those differences into account. I should not hesitate to take them into account if I thought it necessary to sustain this act. . . . But after *Bunting v. Oregon* . . . I had supposed that it was not necessary, and that *Lochner v. New York* . . . would be allowed a deserved repose.

Holmes went on to admit that he personally had doubts about this statute, but they were irrelevant according to his standard of judicial review. "When so many intelligent persons, who have studied the matter more than any of us can, have thought that the means are effective and are worth the price, it seems to me impossible to deny that the belief reasonably may be held by reasonable men."

Following the *Adkins* decision, many states assumed that a minimum wage law which *did* take into account the value-of-service-rendered principle would be constitutional, and passed statutes including such provisions. A New York law of this type came before the Supreme Court in *Morehead v. Tipaldo* (1936), in the midst of the Court's furious battle against the New Deal. The four surviving members of the *Adkins* majority—

Sutherland, Butler, Van Devanter, and McReynolds—joined with Justice Roberts to invalidate the New York law.[29] The value-of-service feature in the New York law was held insufficient to meet the *Adkins* objection, which was dogmatically restated in these words: "The State is without power by any form of legislation to prohibit, change or nullify contracts between employers and adult women workers as to the amount of wages to be paid."

This bland reiteration in 1936 of a conclusion that had had little enough support in the palmy days of 1923 was one of the great mistakes of Supreme Court history, and did more to destroy the country's confidence in the Court as then constituted than some of its more publicized anti-New Deal decisions. The ruling earned the dissent of as distinguished a foursome as ever sat on the high court—Chief Justice Hughes and Justices Brandeis, Cardozo, and Stone. The Chief Justice wrote a long dissent that was a devastating refutation of Butler's majority view, but for present purposes it may be preferable to note Stone's effort to point out to the majority some of the facts of life in 1936.

> In the years which have intervened since the *Adkins* case we have had opportunity to learn that a wage is not always the resultant of free bargaining between employers and employee; that it may be one forced upon employees by their economic necessities and upon employers by the most ruthless of their competitors. We have had opportunity to perceive more clearly that a wage insufficient to support the worker does not visit its consequences upon him alone; that it may affect profoundly the entire economic structure of society and, in any case, that it casts on every taxpayer, and on government itself, the burden of solving the problems of poverty, subsistence, health and morals of large numbers in the community. Because of their nature and extent these are public problems. A generation ago they were for the individual to solve; today they are the burden of the nation.

Here for the first time in an economic regulation case a Supreme Court justice burst out of the traditional health and morals boundaries on state police power and asserted—what was shortly to become axiomatic for the Court—that public power is as broad as is necessary to meet urgent public problems.

During this period the Court also struck out at legislative efforts to protect the organization of labor unions. Congress in 1898 adopted legislation outlawing the so-called "yellow-dog" contract, an agreement not to join a labor union that many employers forced workers to sign as a condition of employment. Discharging an employee of an interstate railroad on grounds of his membership in a labor organization was made a criminal offense against the United States. This statute was declared unconstitutional by the Supreme Court in the 1908 case of *Adair v. United States,* on familiar

---

[29] For an explanation of Justice Roberts's vote, see Felix Frankfurter, "Mr. Justice Roberts," 104 UNIVERSITY OF PENNSYLVANIA LAW REVIEW 311 (1955).

freedom of contract grounds.[30] Reminiscent of Anatole France, who spoke of the majestic equality of the law which forbids both rich and poor to steal bread, beg in the streets, or sleep under bridges, Harlan concluded: "In all such particulars the employer and the employee have equality of right, and any legislation that disturbs that equality is an arbitrary interference with the liberty of contract which no government can legally justify in a free land."

In the area of legislative rate and price fixing, the Court's initial favorable attitude as manifested in *Munn v. Illinois* was reversed by significant decisions in the 1920s. In *Tyson & Brother v. Banton* (1927) a New York law forbidding the resale of theater tickets at more than a fifty-cent markup was declared unconstitutional by a five to four vote. Theaters, said Justice Sutherland, are not public utilities or affected with a public interest.

The following year the Court by a six to three vote in *Ribnik v. McBride* (1928) held unconstitutional New Jersey's effort to regulate the fees charged by employment agencies. Such businesses are "essentially private," and there is no more justification for fixing their rates than for setting the prices for food or housing or fuel.

Legislative efforts at business regulation were not confined to price fixing, of course.[31] In 1920 a Kansas statute declared that food, clothing, fuel, and transportation industries were affected with a public interest, and endeavored to subject them to compulsory arbitration and fixing of wages and working conditions by an industrial relations court. The Supreme Court ruled that a packing company was a "private" concern which could not be constitutionally subjected to such controls.[32] Nebraska in 1921 established maximum weight for loaves of bread, and provided penalties for selling or making bread in other weights. The Court invalidated this measure, which was presented as one to protect consumers from fraud, calling it arbitrary interference with a private business.[33] However, the Court later upheld a statute of the same sort with somewhat modified enforcement standards.[34]

Oklahoma had varying experiences in undertaking to regulate by the licensing power businesses which it conceived to fall within the public interest. In 1929 the Court upheld a state law declaring the business of

---

[30] The Supreme Court struck down a comparable state statute in *Coppage v. Kansas* (1915).

[31] *Adams v. Tanner* (1917) declared invalid a law prohibiting the taking of fees from persons seeking employment.

[32] *Wolff Packing Co. v. Court of Industrial Relations* (1923); see also *Dorchy v. Kansas* (1924).

[33] *Burns Baking Co. v. Bryan* (1924).

[34] *Petersen Baking Co. v. Bryan* (1934).

operating a cotton gin to be one having a public interest, and requiring a showing of public necessity before it could be undertaken.[35] But in the famous case of *New State Ice Co. v. Liebmann* (1932), the Court refused to grant such status to the ice business, holding that it was "as essentially private in its nature as the business of the grocer, the dairyman, the butcher. ... [It] bears no such relation to the public as to warrant its inclusion in the category of businesses charged with a public use."

Finally, the Court's earlier reluctance to undertake judicial review of public utility rate fixing disappeared. *Smyth v. Ames* (1898) held that due process required the courts not merely to review the reasonableness of rates but also to determine whether the rates permitted a fair return on a fair valuation of property devoted to public use. *Smyth v. Ames* opened up over forty years of confusion, as regulatory commissions tried to guess what standards reviewing courts would employ and the methods they would require to be used in determining fair value of utility property.

The Abandonment of Economic Due Process

The structure of substantive due process that the Supreme Court built in these economic cases was probably its most original intellectual achievement during the first third of the twentieth century. Edward S. Corwin referred to substantive due process as "the most important field of American constitutional law."[36] These were the cases for which the Court was best known up to 1933; these were the decisions that primarily gave the Court its reputation as the bastion of conservatism, the protector of property rights, "the sheet anchor of the Republic."[37]

Then, within a few years, the Court completely abandoned economic due process. This striking reversal began with *Nebbia v. New York* (1934), as the Court by a five to four vote accepted the validity of a depression-born law regulating milk prices. A New York State statute had established a milk control board with power to fix minimum and maximum retail prices, and in this case the objective had been to prevent ruinous price cutting by fixing minimum prices. Justice Roberts spoke for the majority, which included also Hughes, Brandeis, Stone, and Cardozo.

Roberts began by admitting that the milk industry had never been regarded as affected with a public interest and had none of the characteristics relied on in the past in attributing such status—no public grant or franchise, no monopoly, no obligation to serve all comers, no devotion of property to a use that the public might itself appropriately undertake. But

---

[35] *Frost v. Corporation Commission* (1929).

[36] Op. cit., p. 64.

[37] See Arthur S. Miller, *The Supreme Court and American Capitalism* (New York: Free Press, 1968).

that made no difference. It was a misconception to think that the power to regulate depended upon holding a franchise or enjoying a monopoly. Munn had no franchise nor anything that could "fairly be called a monopoly." Nor was there any mystical power in the standard, "affected with a public interest." This phrase, rightly understood, "is the equivalent of 'subject to the exercise of the police power' . . . nothing more was intended by the expression." Then came the heart of the *Nebbia* decision.

> It is clear that there is no closed class or category of businesses affected with a public interest, and the function of courts in the application of the Fifth and Fourteenth Amendments is to determine in each case whether circumstances vindicate the challenged regulation as a reasonable exertion of governmental authority or condemn it as arbitrary or discriminatory. . . . The phrase "affected with a public interest" can, in the nature of things, mean no more than that an industry, for adequate reason, is subject to control for the public good.

The *Nebbia* decision was followed by others supporting state and federal price fixing in a variety of fields.[38] However, the contrary decisions of the 1920s had not been specifically overruled, and when a Nebraska statute fixing rates which private employment agencies might charge an applicant for employment came before that state's supreme court in 1940, the court rather unimaginatively declared the law unconstitutional on the authority of *Ribnik v. McBride*. The Supreme Court unanimously reversed the state court in *Olsen v. Nebraska* (1941). "The drift away from *Ribnik v. McBride*," said Justice Douglas, "has been so great that it can no longer be deemed a controlling authority." In *Gold v. DiCarlo* (1965) the Court without opinion upheld a New York law limiting theater-ticket-broker surcharges, in effect overruling the 1927 *Tyson* decision.

In 1937 the Court upheld minimum wage laws for women in *West Coast Hotel Co. v. Parrish*. This case arose under the Washington State minimum wage law which, be it noted, had been passed in 1913 and enforced continuously thereafter, quite irrespective of the *Adkins* ruling. The act, like that of the District of Columbia, contained no value-of-service standard, and so seemed more in defiance of the *Adkins* decision than the New York law had been. But Chief Justice Hughes upheld the Washington law, constructing his majority opinion out of quotations from Taft and Holmes, and asking such questions as "What can be closer to the public interest than the health of women and their protection from unscrupulous and overreaching employers?" More important, he wrote the principles of

---

[38] *Townsend v. Yeomans* (1937), upholding a Georgia statute fixing maximum warehouse charges for the handling and selling of leaf tobacco; *United States v. Rock Royal Co-Operative, Inc.* (1939), upholding the power of Congress to fix minimum prices for milk under the commerce clause; *Sunshine Anthracite Coal Co. v. Adkins* (1940), upholding the price-fixing provisions of the federal Bituminous Coal Act of 1937.

Stone's *Morehead* dissent into the law of the land, thereby finally releasing the police power from dependence on health and morals considerations. The opinion concluded with a direct overruling of the *Adkins* decision. Nothing was said about *Lochner*, but this time we can be sure, with Taft, that it had been overruled *sub silentio*.

In 1941 the Court upheld the minimum wage and maximum hours regulations of the Fair Labor Standards Act, passed in 1938. The validity of this statute under the commerce clause had already been determined in *United States v. Darby Lumber Co.* (1941). Now the due process objections to the statute were disposed of in one short paragraph that cited *Holden*, *Muller*, and *Bunting* on hours, and *West Coast Hotel* on wages. The federal act covered men as well as women, so that *West Coast Hotel* was no precedent at all on minimum wages for men. But the sexual distinction, which as late as 1937 had been absolutely vital in establishing constitutional power, was by 1941 completely unimportant to the Court.

In *Federal Power Commission v. Hope Natural Gas Co.* (1944) the Court definitely repudiated the judicial control over rate making that it had assumed in *Smyth v. Ames*. The *Adair* and *Coppage* doctrine on labor organization was gradually outflanked, but the two decisions were not specifically repudiated until 1949 in *Lincoln Federal Labor Union v. Northwestern Iron & Metal Co.* Involved were a North Carolina statute and a Nebraska constitutional amendment outlawing the closed shop. No person was to be denied an opportunity to work in the two states either because he was or because he was not a member of a labor organization. The Supreme Court unanimously upheld these laws against free speech, equal protection, and due process charges.

It is not the mere reversal of position in these economic due process cases that is surprising. That was bound to happen. The Court could not continue to live in the nineteenth century. But the Court did not merely retreat to the test of reasonableness that it employed in *Jacobson v. Massachusetts*. As Robert McCloskey so well pointed out, the Court appeared to say that it would no longer subject economic legislation to *any* constitutional test.[39] It would abandon any responsibility for reviewing legislative decisions on economic problems and, returning to the spirit of *Munn*, tell plaintiffs to carry their objections to the legislature, not the courts.

Thus in *Olsen v. Nebraska* Justice Douglas for a unanimous Court stated that differences of opinion on the needfulness or appropriateness of a law "suggest a choice which 'should be left where . . . it was left by the Constitution—to the states and to Congress.'" Again, *Day-Brite Lighting v. Missouri* (1952) involved a state law which provided that employees could

[39] "Economic Due Process and the Supreme Court," in Philip B. Kurland, ed., *The Supreme Court Review: 1962* (Chicago: University of Chicago Press, 1962), pp. 34–62.

absent themselves from their jobs for four hours on election days, and forbade employers to deduct wages for their absence. The Court majority admitted that the social policy embodied in the law was debatable, but said: "Our recent decisions make plain that we do not sit as a superlegislature to weigh the wisdom of legislation nor to decide whether the policy it expresses offends the public welfare."[40]

Williamson v. Lee Optical of Oklahoma (1955) asked the Court to review a statute that was the product of an interest group struggle in the Oklahoma legislature, and represented a victory for the ophthalmologists and optometrists of the state over the opticians. It forbade any person not in the first two categories from fitting lenses to the face or duplicating or replacing lenses into frames, except on the prescription of an ophthalmologist or optometrist.

The trial court held that there was no sound health or welfare reason why opticians should not be able to fit old glasses into new frames or to duplicate lenses without a prescription. The Supreme Court agreed that this might be "a needless, wasteful requirement in many cases," but said:

> It is for the legislature, not the courts, to balance the advantages and disadvantages of the new requirement. . . . The day is gone when this Court uses the Due Process Clause of the Fourteenth Amendment to strike down state laws, regulatory of business and industrial conditions, because they may be unwise, improvident, or out of harmony with a particular school of thought.

Finally, in *Ferguson v. Skrupa* (1963) the Court upheld a Kansas statute prohibiting anyone except lawyers from engaging in the business of "debt adjustment," overruling *Adams v. Tanner* (1917) in the process. Black, condemning again the *Lochner-Coppage-Adkins-Burns* line of cases, repeated that "it is up to legislatures, not courts, to decide on the wisdom and utility of legislation." Justice Harlan registered the sole protest against judicial abdication; insisting that the Court could not shirk the responsibility to judge even in this field, he assumed that task and concurred in upholding the statute as bearing "a rational relation to a constitutionally permissible objective."

But McCloskey's question remains a good one. Why is "liberty of economic choice . . . less dispensable to the 'openness' of a society than freedom of expression?" Why should the Court give legislatures unreviewable power in the field of economic legislation, refusing to subject it even to the time-honored test of rationality? Even for a Court convinced that

---

[40] *Dean v. Gadsden Times Publishing Corp.* (1973) upheld a state law requiring employers to compensate employees when absent on jury duty, the Court saying: "If our recent cases mean anything, they leave debatable issues as respects business, economic, and social affairs to legislative decision. We could strike down this law only if we returned to the philosophy of the *Lochner, Coppage,* and *Adkins* cases." See also *New Orleans v. Dukes* (1976).

personal rights are on a higher plane than property rights, how clear is it that these are actually distinguishable categories?

In *Barksy v. Board of Regents* (1954), a New York physician who had organized a committee to aid refugees in the Spanish civil war refused to give his committee's records to the House Committee on Un-American Activities and was convicted of contempt. His license to practice medicine was then revoked because of his criminal record. The Court majority upheld this action as within the state's legitimate power to regulate professions and businesses, but it was too much for Black and Douglas. The latter said: "the right to work, I had assumed, was the most precious liberty that man possesses. Man has indeed as much right to work as he has to live, to be free, to own property." In a 1957 bar-admission case, Black declared for the Court that state-imposed qualifications "must have a rational connection with the applicant's fitness or capacity" to practice the profession.[41]

It is significant that Justice Douglas, having read the Court out of the picture in *Olsen v. Nebraska, Day-Brite Lighting v. Missouri,* and *Williamson v. Lee Optical,* found it necessary to read it at least partially back in again in *Poe v. Ullman* (1961):

> The error of the old Court, as I see it, was not in entertaining inquiries concerning the constitutionality of social legislation but in applying the standards that it did. . . . Social legislation dealing with business and economic matters touches no particularized prohibition of the Constitution, unless it be the provision of the Fifth Amendment that private property should not be taken for public use without just compensation. If it is free of the latter guarantee, it has a wide scope for application. Some go so far as to suggest that whatever the majority in the legislature says goes . . . that there is no other standard of constitutionality. That reduces the legislative power to sheer voting strength and the judicial function to a matter of statistics. . . . While the legislative judgment on economic and business matters is "well-nign conclusive," . . . it is not beyond judicial inquiry.

In the following chapter we shall see how "judicial inquiry" has inevitably led even a "strict constructionist" Court back into the activist tradition of the substantive due process philosophy.[42]

---

[41] *Schware v. New Mexico Board of Bar Examiners* (1957).

[42] See Richard Funston, "The Double Standard of Constitutional Protection in the Era of the Welfare State," 90 POLITICAL SCIENCE QUARTERLY 261 (1975).

12

The New Due Process -
Equal Protection

Due process and equal protection, discussed in the two preceding chapters, rank along with the First Amendment as the most fundamental tenets of the American Constitution. They outrank the First Amendment in breadth and expansive capability. Racial equality is only the most obvious of the demands of the equal protection clause, and freedom of contract, though the first to be discovered by the Supreme Court, is only one of the many substantive meanings that can be read into the due process clause.

The due process and equal protection concepts are closely related. We have already seen that in the District of Columbia school segregation case, *Bolling v. Sharpe*, where the Fifth Amendment rather than the Fourteenth applied, the Court held that due process performed the same function in the District that equal protection did in the states. For Justice Jackson the difference between the two standards was largely a matter of tactics.

> The burden should rest heavily upon one who would persuade us to use the due process clause to strike down a substantive law or ordinance. Even its prudent use . . . frequently disables all government . . . from dealing with the conduct in question . . . leav[ing] ungoverned and ungovernable conduct which many people find objectionable. Invocation of the equal protection clause, on the other hand, does not disable any governmental body from dealing with the subject at hand. It merely means that the prohibition or regulation must have a broader impact. I regard it as a salutory doctrine that cities, states and the Federal Government must exercise their powers so as not to discriminate between their inhabitants, except upon some reasonable differentiation fairly related to the object of regulation. . . . There is no more effective practical

guaranty against arbitrary and unreasonable government than to require that the principles of law which officials would impose upon a minority must be imposed generally.[1]

Following the adoption of the Fourteenth Amendment, it did not take the Supreme Court long to realize the expansionist potentialities in the concepts of equal protection and due process. Justice Miller supposed in the *Slaughterhouse Cases* (1873) that the equal protection clause would never be used except in racial discrimination situations, yet for over half a century it was corporations that were the principal beneficiaries of this standard. The development of the due process clause was even more portentous. As a limit on substantive legislation, it developed into a freewheeling, open-ended doctrine that judges used to "circumscribe legislative choices in the name of newly articulated values that lacked clear support in constitutional text and history."[2]

The bad reputation that substantive due process earned was due to the unwise uses to which this creative judicial urge was put in the first third of the twentieth century. Only the fundamentalist Hugo Black really believed that all the values which American society needed were clearly articulated in the constitutional document. With few exceptions American judges have been convinced that the judicial role is not only interpretation but also extrapolation, not only discovery but also invention. The battle of strict construction was fought and lost in *McCulloch v. Maryland* (1819).

The battle for judicial activism was fought and won even earlier, in *Marbury v. Madison* (1803). Perhaps the best modern defense of the activist role is to be found in Justice Stone's famous *Carolene Products Co.* footnote, quoted in Chapter 2, which defined three situations in which judges should curb their normal deference toward legislatures and subject legislative action to a "more searching judicial inquiry." Those three situations, it will be recalled, were (1) when legislation appears on its face to violate a specific prohibition of the Constitution, such as those of the Bill of Rights; (2) where legislation restricts those political processes that ordinarily can be relied on to prevent undesirable legislation; and (3) where "prejudice against discrete and insular minorities . . . tends seriously to curtail the operation of those political processes ordinarily to be relied upon to protect minorities."

We have already seen how Stone's prescription for judicial positivism fortified the Court for its defense of the First Amendment and the rights of criminal defendants and minorities. But there is lacking in the footnote any suggestion that the Court may need to use its imagination in defense of

---

[1] *Railway Express Agency v. New York* (1949).

[2] Gerald Gunther, "In Search of Evolving Doctrine on a Changing Court: A Model for a Newer Equal Protection, 86 HARVARD LAW REVIEW 1, 8 (1972).

claims newly achieving legitimacy yet lacking support in explicit constitutional language or established constitutional interpretation.

Significantly, Justice Murphy did see this need. When Black was making the literal incorporation argument in his *Adamson* dissent, Murphy, with Rutledge concurring, was careful to reserve the right, not merely to incorporate but, where appropriate, to expand the Bill of Rights. "Occasion may arise where a proceeding falls so far short of conforming to fundamental standards of procedure as to warrant constitutional condemnation in terms of a lack of due process despite the absence of a specific provision in the Bill of Rights," he wrote. In this chapter we deal with significant new personal due process or equal protection rights that the Supreme Court has recognized or is considering for recognition.[3]

FUNDAMENTAL RIGHTS AND TWO-TIER REVIEW

The idea of "fundamental rights" as a justification for protective judicial activism can be traced to *Skinner v. Oklahoma* (1942). The case involved a state habitual-criminal sterilization act, under which persons convicted two or more times of felonies involving moral turpitude could be rendered sexually sterile.

This statute appeared to have constitutional support in *Buck v. Bell* (1927), where the Court with only one dissent had upheld a Virginia statute under which persons affected with hereditary insanity, idiocy, imbecility, feeblemindedness, or epilepsy could be subjected to compulsory sexual sterilization. This operation could be performed only on inmates of state institutions, and adequate provisions were made by the statute for notice, hearing, and judicial review before such operations were performed. In this particular case the law was applied to Carrie Buck, a seventeen-year-old "feeble-minded" female inmate of a state institution whose mother was also a "feeble-minded" inmate of the same institution, and who had given birth to an allegedly mentally defective child just before admission to the institution. The contention was that if she were rendered incapable of childbearing, she could be released from the institution and become self-supporting. In the judicial proceedings held to authorize the operation there was presented, in addition to evidence concerning the mental and social

---

[3] See generally Gunther, supra note 2; Wallace Mendelson, "From Warren to Burger: The Rise and Decline of Substantive Equal Protection," 66 AMERICAN POLITICAL SCIENCE REVIEW 1226 (1972); Laurence H. Tribe, "Toward a Model of Roles in the Due Process of Life and Law," 87 HARVARD LAW REVIEW 1 (1973); Richard Fielding, "Fundamental Personal Rights: Another Approach to Equal Protection," 40 UNIVERSITY OF CHICAGO LAW REVIEW 807 (1973); Henry P. Monaghan, "Foreword: Constitutional Common Law," 89 HARVARD LAW REVIEW 1 (1975); Thomas S. Schrock and Robert C. Welsh, "Reconsidering the Constitutional Common Law," 91 HARVARD LAW REVIEW 1117 (1978).

status of Carrie Buck, testimony in support of the statute by eugenicists to the effect that feeblemindedness was hereditary and incurable.

Justice Holmes's opinion supporting the sterilization order, and accepting without question the scientific justification for the statute, was very brief. This is the heart of it.

> We have seen more than once that the public welfare may call upon the best citizens for their lives. It would be strange if it could not call upon those who already sap the strength of the State for these lesser sacrifices, often not felt to be such by those concerned, in order to prevent our being swamped with incompetence. It is better for all the world, if instead of waiting to execute degenerate offspring for crime, or to let them starve for their imbecility, society can prevent those who are manifestly unfit from continuing their kind. The principle that sustains compulsory vaccination is broad enough to cover cutting the Fallopian tubes. . . . Three generations of imbeciles are enough.

Seldom has so much questionable doctrine been compressed into five sentences of a Supreme Court opinion. The first two sentences state a completely unacceptable standard for measuring legislative action. If it were true that, because the state can demand the supreme sacrifice of life itself, it is thereby justified in demanding any lesser sacrifice, then every constitutional protection could be disregarded at will. Because the government can require a man to lay down his life in battle, it does not follow that he can be deprived of freedom of speech or the right to trial by jury. Moreover, it is a rather perverse view which sees the *Jacobson* decision as a precedent broad enough to cover Carrie Buck. As Walter Berns has said: "It is a broad principle indeed that sustains a needle's prick in the arm and an abdominal incision, if only in terms of the equipment used. It becomes something else again in terms of the results obtained: no smallpox in the one case and no children in the other."[4]

By 1942 the Court had become aware of the moral shortcomings of *Buck v. Bell.* Douglas, writing for the Court in *Skinner,* said: "We are dealing here with legislation which involves one of the basic civil rights of man. Marriage and procreation are fundamental to the very existence and survival of the race." An individual proceeded against under this act "is forever deprived of a basic liberty." Where Douglas invoked equal protection in striking down the act, Stone used due process for the same end. But Jackson more clearly than either based his rejection not on these constitutional provisions but rather on a natural law kind of argument, saying, "There are limits to the extent to which a legislatively represented majority may conduct biological experiments at the expense of the dignity and personality and natural powers of a minority."

---

[4] "Buck v. Bell: Due Process of Law?" 6 WESTERN POLITICAL QUARTERLY 764 (1953).

The doctrine of the *Skinner* case, then, is that when "fundamental rights" are involved, the judicial task is not simply to presume the validity of legislative interference or to apply the minimal rationality test. It is rather to press that "more searching judicial inquiry" of which Stone spoke, even though it requires constitutional extrapolation. In short, protection of fundamental rights requires the rebirth of substantive due process and the invention of substantive equal protection.

EQUAL PROTECTION: THE OLD AND THE NEW

Equal protection, like substantive due process, was originally employed principally in the service of economic claims.[5] Economic equal protection, however, was never carried to the extremes that characterized economic due process, and it produced no such parade of horribles as the *Lochner-Coppage-Adair* line of due process cases that Black inveighed against so often. The old equal protection presumed the validity of challenged legislation and subjected it to only a minimal test of rationality. Seldom is legislation so irrational that it cannot be justified by some state of facts, real or hypothetical.[6]

The Supreme Court generally understood that legislatures, in dealing with the regulation of economic life, must classify and make distinctions based on differences in degree.[7] The decided cases are full of warnings against judicial interference with legislative classifications. The differences between persons or things on which the classification is based need not be scientific or marked, so long as there are some practical distinctions.[8] A classification must be clearly and actually arbitrary to be held invalid, and not merely possibly so.[9] Every presumption as to facts that could conceivably justify the legislative classification will be assumed.[10] The state may do what it can to prevent what it deems an evil, and stop short of those cases in which the harm to the few concerned is thought less important than the harm to the public that would result if the rules laid down were made mathematically exact.[11] Legislative reform may take one step at a time, addressing itself

[5] Robert J. Harris reports that, out of 554 decisions of the Supreme Court up to 1960 in which the equal protection clause was involved, 426 (77 percent) dealt with legislation affecting economic interests, while only 78 (14 percent) concerned state laws alleged to impose racial discrimination or acts of Congress designed to stop it: *The Quest for Equality* (Baton Rouge: Louisiana State University Press, 1960), p. 59.

[6] For an attack on the entire rationality principle, see "Legislative Purpose, Rationality, and Equal Protection," 82 YALE LAW JOURNAL 123 (1972).

[7] *Barbier v. Connolly* (1885).

[8] *Orient Ins. Co. v. Daggs* (1899).

[9] *Bachtel v. Wilson* (1907).

[10] *Crescent Cotton Oil Co. v. Mississippi* (1921).

[11] *Dominion Hotel v. Arizona* (1919).

to the phase of the problem that seems most acute to the legislative mind.[12] The legislature may select one phase of one field and apply a remedy there, neglecting the others.[13]

In spite of the permissive character of the rationality test, economic regulatory statutes were occasionally snagged on the equal protection hook by the pre-New Deal conservative Court.[14] But when the Roosevelt Court took over, equal protection, which Justice Holmes had once referred to as the "usual last refuge of constitutional arguments,"[15] was abandoned almost as completely as substantive due process. No effort was spared to find "rational" justifications for legislative classifications. *Goesaert v. Cleary* (1948) upheld a state statute forbidding women to tend bar unless they were wives or daughters of the proprietor. *Railway Express Agency v. New York* (1949) approved a city traffic regulation forbidding the carrying of display advertising for hire on the sides of the agency's trucks.

Kotch v. Board of River Port Pilot Commissioners (1947) upheld a Louisiana statutory plan of licensing pilots for the port of New Orleans. Members of the licensing board were themselves pilots, and they operated the certification process so that only selected relatives and friends of present pilots could secure licenses. Justice Black ruled that the Court should not interfere with "the right and power of a state to select its own agents and officers." In *Williamson v. Lee Optical of Oklahoma* (1955), legislative regulation of opticians in fitting and replacing lenses completely exempted sellers of "ready-to-wear" glasses from control. The Court was ready with a supporting hypothesis: "For all this record shows, the ready-to-wear branch of the business may not loom large in Oklahoma or may present problems of regulation distinct from the other branches."

On only one occasion after 1937 did the Court fail to defer to the legislature on an economic classification issue, and that was in *Morey v. Doud* (1957), where an Illinois statute had exempted American Express Company money orders from a requirement that any firm issuing money orders in the state must secure a license and submit to state regulation. The state argued that the worldwide operations and unquestioned solvency of this company made the exemption reasonable, but the Court disagreed.

In contrast to the permissiveness of the old equal protection, the new equal protection imposes much more rigorous tests on legislative classifications in those areas where fundamental rights are involved. Rationality is no longer enough. As in the new due process, a compelling state interest must be established by rigid scrutiny to justify a challenged classification

---

[12] *Semler v. Oregon State Board of Dental Examiners* (1935).

[13] *A.F. of L. v. American Sash Co.* (1949).

[14] *Smith v. Cahoon* (1931), *Mayflower Farms v. Ten Eyck* (1936), *Hartford Steam Boiler Inspection and Ins. Co. v. Harrison* (1937).

[15] *Buck v. Bell* (1927).

affecting fundamental rights. Moreover, certain classifications are "suspect" on their face and almost automatically invalid.

Race was the original suspect classification, as we saw in Chapter 10. Voting was accepted as a fundamental right entitled to equal protection in the Reapportionment Cases, and any infringement on the rule of one person, one vote was inherently suspect. The right to travel interstate was confirmed in *Shapiro v. Thompson* (1969) without attributing it to any particular provision.

Alienage has been regarded as a suspect classification, in part because of its racial component. In *Korematsu v. United States* (1944) Justice Black wrote that "all legal restrictions which curtail the civil rights of a single racial group are immediately suspect." And in *Graham v. Richardson* (1971) the Court said that aliens "are a prime example of a 'discrete and insular' minority... for whom ... heightened judicial solicitude is appropriate." *Takahashi v. Fish and Game Commission* (1948) had warned that the power of a state to apply its laws exclusively to its alien inhabitants was confined within narrow limits, and *Graham* ruled that the denial of welfare to lawfully admitted resident aliens was a denial of equal protection. *Plyler v. Doe* (1982) ruled that the minor children of alien immigrants illegally within the United States are nonetheless "within its jurisdiction" and so cannot be denied access to public education by a state.

However, the Court has recently seemed less sure that alienage is a suspect classification. *Cabell v. Chavez-Salido* (1982) upheld a California law requiring "peace officers" to be citizens, *Foley v. Connelie* (1978) approved a New York law limiting service in the state police to citizens, and *Ambach v. Norwick* (1979) ruled that a state may limit public teaching positions to citizens.

Apart from these established suspect classifications, the new equal protection, along with a revived substantive due process, have been challenging old inequalities in several other areas that require more extended comment.

PRIVACY AND THE ABORTION CASES

The foremost example of the new substantive due process was the Court's pronouncement of privacy as a broad constitutional value in *Griswold v. Connecticut* (1965). At issue was a state law forbidding the use of contraceptives or advice as to their use, for violation of which the medical and executive directors of a New Haven planned-parenthood center were convicted. Justice Douglas, speaking for the Court, held that this law interfered with "a right of privacy older than the Bill of Rights." Admittedly this zone of privacy is not specified in the Constitution, but he found it within the "penumbra" of several fundamental constitutional guarantees. There is the right of association in the penumbra of the First Amendment. There is the recognition of the privacy of the home in the Third and Fourth Amendments, as well as the zone of personal privacy derived from the self-incrimination clause of the Fifth Amendment. Finally, there is the Ninth Amendment's warning that the enumeration of certain rights in the Constitution does not mean that there are not others "retained by the people."

Douglas did not go on to the Fourteenth Amendment to invoke the due process clause, presumably because he was sensitive about charges that he would be exhuming substantive due process. Justices Harlan and White, never having rejected substantive due process, had no hesitation in saying that due process was more to the point than vague "penumbras" of the Bill of Rights. For Black also this was substantive due process, and he would have none of it. The Court's reasoning, for him, came straight out of *Lochner* and *Adkins*. This was the same "natural law due process philosophy" which he thought the Court had abandoned and which he charged was "no less dangerous when used to enforce this Court's views about personal rights than those about economic rights." He reiterated his willingness "to hold laws unconstitutional where they are forbidden by the Federal Constitution." But where the Court had no guide as specific as the First Amendment, then he denied that the Court had power "to sit as a supervisory agency over acts of duly constituted legislative bodies and set aside their laws because of the Court's belief that the legislative policies adopted are unreasonable, unwise, arbitrary, capricious or irrational."

Of course Black was right. The Court had created a value out of the whole cloth of the Constitution and used it to superimpose its own views of wise social policy on those of the legislature. It was, as John Hart Ely put it, "Lochnering."[16] But that does not condemn *Griswold*. *Lochner* was bad because it was wrong to conclude that long working hours had no rational relation to health and safety. *Griswold* was right because it struck down a statute that prohibited the use of contraceptives by married couples, a ridiculous law ("uncommonly silly" was Stewart's description) that could have been enforced only by putting policemen in bedrooms. Harlan had condemned the statute four years earlier in his dissent to *Poe v. Ullman* (1961) without ever invoking the test of privacy. He held it repugnant to the old *Palko* test, violative of basic values "implicit in the concept of ordered liberty."[17]

Once enshrined as a constitutional value, privacy demonstrated the

---

[16] "The Wages of Crying Wolf," 82 YALE LAW JOURNAL 920, 944 (1973).

[17] In the *Poe* case, an attack on the constitutionality of the Connecticut statute had been rejected by the Court, five to four, on the ground that the parties bringing the suit lacked standing.

power of an idea whose time has come and was freed from any limitations associated with its origin in *Griswold.* The right asserted there was the privacy of married couples in their bedrooms. *Eisenstadt v. Baird* (1972) brought to the Court a Massachusetts statute that made it illegal for single persons, but not for married persons, to obtain contraceptives in order to prevent pregnancy. The Court held that the statute was neither a health measure nor intended as a deterrent to premarital sexual relations but simply a prohibition on contraception resting on a moral judgment. So considered, it was unnecessary for the Court to invoke due process. It was a violation of equal protection for the state "to legislate that different treatment be accorded to persons placed by a statute into different classes on the basis of criteria wholly unrelated to the objective of the statute." Brennan continued: "If the right of privacy means anything, it is the right of the *individual,* married or single, to be free from unwarranted governmental intrusion into matters so fundamentally affecting a person as the decision whether to bear or beget a child."

Eisenstadt provided the momentum for the abortion decisions in the following year.[18] *Roe v. Wade* (1973) held unconstitutional a strict Texas criminal statute that prohibited abortions at any stage of pregnancy except to save the life of the mother. *Doe v. Bolton* (1973) similarly condemned a Georgia statute that required abortions to be conducted in hospitals, required the interposition of a hospital abortion committee and confirmation by other physicians, and limited abortions to Georgia residents. The opinions in both cases were written by Justice Blackmun, who prior to appointment to the Supreme Court had been a member of the board of the Mayo Clinic, and he prefaced his discussion of the constitutional issues with a "history of abortion, for such insight as that history may afford us."

Blackmun's constitutional position was that the right of privacy, whether a Fourteenth Amendment due process right (as he contended) or a right reserved to the people by the Ninth Amendment, was "broad enough to encompass a woman's decision whether or not to terminate her pregnancy." But this is not an absolute right; Blackmun cited *Jacobson v. Massachusetts* (1905) to reject the position "that one has an unlimited right to do with one's body as one pleases." It is, however, a "fundamental" right, and consequently its regulation can be justified only by a compelling state interest, and through legislation "narrowly drawn to express only the legitimate state interests at stake."

Texas contended that safeguarding the life of the unborn child was

---

[18]For comments and critique, see Harry H. Wellington, "Common Law Rules and Constitutional Double Standards," 83 YALE LAW JOURNAL 221 (1973); Richard A. Epstein, "Substantive Due Process by Any Other Name: The Abortion Cases," in Philip B. Kurland, ed., *The Supreme Court Review: 1973* (Chicago: University of Chicago Press, 1973), pp. 159-86; Ely, supra, note 16.

such a compelling state interest, but Blackmun held that a fetus is not a person whose right to life is guaranteed by the Fourteenth Amendment and that the state, by adopting the position that a fetus is a living person, cannot override the rights of the pregnant woman. He did concede that the state had two legitimate interests justifying intervention—to preserve and protect the health of the pregnant woman and to protect the *potentiality* of human life. Each of these interests "grows in substantiality as the woman approaches term and, at a point during pregnancy, each becomes 'compelling.'"

This stress on time sequence was essential to Blackmun's solution of the constitutional problem of state interest. For the first trimester of pregnancy, during which mortality in abortion is less than mortality in normal childbirth, state interest is minimal, and the abortion decision and its effectuation must be left to the woman and her physician, free from interference by the state. Following the third month, the state may regulate the abortion procedure to the extent reasonably necessary to the preservation and protection of maternal health, including such matters as the qualification and licensing of the person performing the abortion and the facility in which it is performed. Finally, after the fetus becomes viable, roughly at the end of the second trimester, the state interest in protecting life may go so far as to proscribe abortion except when necessary to preserve the life and health of the mother.

Justice Stewart, concurring, wanted it clearly understood that *Roe* was a substantive due process decision, despite the fact that obsequies had been conducted so often for substantive due process, most recently in *Ferguson v. Skrupa* (1963). Justice Rehnquist, dissenting, also wanted it understood that this was substantive due process in the *Lochner* tradition of passing on the wisdom of legislative policies and that breaking up pregnancies into three trimesters with varying permissible restrictions was pure "judicial legislation." White also dissented.

The abortion decisions aroused tremendous opposition, particularly among Catholics, and various "right-to-life" constitutional amendments were proposed in Congress. Many state laws were adopted placing restrictions on abortions, and a constant stream of cases involving these laws came up to the Supreme Court. *Planned Parenthood of Central Missouri v. Danforth* (1976) held that states could not require a married woman to obtain her husband's consent before securing an abortion, and that parents could not exercise an absolute veto over abortions for unmarried daughters under eighteen. *Carey v. Population Services* (1977) ruled that states may not prohibit the sale of contraceptives to minors under sixteen or bar advertising or sale of devices. In *Colautti v. Franklin* (1979) the Court voided as unconstitutionally vague a Pennsylvania law requiring doctors to save the life of a fetus if it "may be" viable.

Bellotti v. Baird (1979) struck down a Massachusetts law requiring unmarried minor females to get permission from their parents or a judge before having an abortion, but *H. L. v. Matheson* (1981) approved a law requiring a doctor to inform the parents of a minor female before performing an abortion on her.

The principal success of the antiabortion forces was in restricting public financing of abortions. In three 1977 decisions, *Beal v. Doe, Maher v. Roe,* and *Poelker v. Doe,* the Court ruled, six to three, that neither the Constitution nor federal law requires states to pay for abortions that are not medically necessary. In particular, *Maher* held that it was not a denial of equal protection for a state to deny Medicaid benefits for abortions while providing them for childbirth.

Successive so-called "Hyde Amendments" to annual congressional appropriation acts went further than *Maher* by denying public funding for certain medically necessary abortions. The Court admitted in *Harris v. McRae* (1980) that this impinged on the constitutional principle recognized in *Roe v. Wade,* but considered that the reasoning in *Maher* still held— namely, that while the government may not place obstacles in the path of a woman's freedom of choice, "it need not remove those not of its own creation. . . . Whether freedom of choice that is constitutionally protected warrants federal subsidization is a question for Congress to answer, not a matter of constitutional entitlement." The Court also disposed in *Harris* of the contention that the Hyde Amendment contravened the establishment clause because its funding restrictions coincided with the religious tenets of the Catholic Church.

In 1983 the Court considered five more abortion cases involving challenges to state laws in Virginia and Missouri and a local ordinance in Akron, Ohio.[19] In general the Court's rulings reaffirmed the constitutional right to abortions and struck down an array of legislative restrictions. In the *Akron* case, a six to three decision, with O'Connor, White, and Rehnquist dissenting, the legislative requirements declared unconstitutional included: a 24-hour waiting period; hospital performance of all abortions after the first three months of pregnancy; and an explanation by doctors to women seeking abortions of the possible adverse physical and emotional consequences. Justice Powell's opinion for the majority stressed that in reaffirming *Roe v. Wade* the Court was honoring the doctrine of stare decisis. Justice O'Connor's dissent attacked the trimester approach as a "completely unworkable" method of reconciling conflicting personal rights and state interests.

Privacy as a constitutional value, of course, extends far beyond the abortion issue, and beyond the possibility of adequate discussion here. Douglas's concurring opinion in *Doe v. Bolton* seemed to equate the right

---

[19] *Simopoulos v. Virginia, Akron v. Akron Center for Reproductive Health, Akron Center for Reproductive Health v. Akron, Planned Parenthood v. Ashcroft,* and *Ashcroft v. Planned Parenthood.*

of privacy with a right of personal autonomy, including "control over the development and expression of one's intellect, interests, tastes, and personality." Some lower courts have interpreted the right of privacy recognized in *Griswold* as extending to any kind of private sexual activity between consenting adults,[20] but the Supreme Court rejected this contention in *Doe v. Commonwealth's Attorney* (1976), by affirming without opinion a lower court ruling upholding a Virginia law prohibiting consensual sodomy.[21]

A principal privacy concern has been the collection of personal information by credit agencies, the police, and various government agencies and its instant availability and potential misuse through storage in computers and data banks.[22] The Fair Credit Reporting Act of 1971 took a first step toward assuring the accuracy and limiting the use of credit reports. The Privacy Act of 1974 permitted individuals to inspect information about themselves contained in government agency files and to challenge or correct the material.

The misnamed Bank Secrecy Act of 1970 actually authorizes the invasion of privacy of bank customers by the government. Enacted because of the difficulty of securing foreign and domestic bank records of customers suspected of illegal activities, the act required banks to make microfilm copies of checks and to report currency transactions over $5,000 into or out of the country. The Court upheld this statute and the administrative regulations issued under it in *California Bankers Assn. v. Shultz* (1974), a case that saw an unusual joinder of bankers and the American Civil Liberties Union in an unsuccessful defense of privacy.

WEALTH AS A SUSPECT CLASSIFICATION

The general rule in capitalist society is that access to goods and services is controlled by the market. Ability to pay, not need, is the criterion. One gets what one can afford to purchase. But even Adam Smith conceded that certain services must be supplied by the community without being rationed through the market, and the modern welfare state has accepted in greater or lesser degree the theory of "just wants"—namely, that certain commodities are so basic that a just society must ensure them to each of its members

---

[20] "The Constitutionality of Laws Forbidding Private Homosexual Conduct," 72 MICHIGAN LAW REVIEW 1616 (1974).

[21] The Court continued to avoid the homosexuality issue, refusing to review in *Gaylord v. Tacoma* (1977) the dismissal of a Washington State school teacher on that ground. *Enslin v. Bean* (1978) let stand a decision permitting North Carolina to prosecute consenting adults for private homosexual acts. See also *Rose v. Locke* (1975).

[22] Arthur R. Miller, *The Assault on Privacy: Computers, Data Banks, and Dossiers* (Ann Arbor: University of Michigan Press, 1971); David M. O'Brien, *Privacy, Law, and Public Policy* (New York: Praeger, 1979). See generally Alan F. Westin, *Privacy and Freedom* (New York: Atheneum, 1967).

regardless of their ability to pay for them. Decisions as to what will be recognized as "just wants" are among the most difficult policy choices on the current political agenda and are essentially legislative. However, the equal protection clause justifies judicial participation in this process.[23]

We have already seen in Chapter 9 what steps the Supreme Court has taken in attempting to ensure that justice will not be denied in the courts for those unable to pay for it. Black's eloquent opinion in *Griffin v. Illinois* (1956) said: "In criminal trials a State can no more discriminate on account of poverty than on account of religion, race, or color." While no one would contend that money has been neutralized so far as court access and representation are concerned, substantial progress has been made through public defenders' offices, public interest law firms, and the federal legal services corporation.[24]

As we shall see in Chapter 13, the Court has endeavored to prevent wealth from being a factor in terms of access to the ballot. In the poll tax case, *Harper v. Virginia State Board of Elections* (1966), Douglas wrote, "Voter qualifications have no relation to wealth nor to paying or not paying this or any other tax." Candidates' filing fees, Burger held in *Bullock v. Carter* (1972), could not be judged on the basis of the old rationality test; under the *Harper* doctrine they must be "closely scrutinized" and sustained only if necessary to accomplish a legitimate state objective.

If access to the courts and to the ballot are fundamental rights, limitations on which are subject to rigid scrutiny and the compelling state interest test, why is not access to equal public education a fundamental right? This issue came to the Court in *San Antonio Independent School District v. Rodriguez* (1973). With the exception of Hawaii, public schools in all states have been financed primarily by the local property tax, though state and federal contributions are increasing. The result is that the level of school finance varies greatly, depending upon the property tax base in the school district. This issue had been taken to the California supreme court in 1971, in the case of *Serrano v. Priest,* and by a vote of six to one that court had ruled that education was a fundamental interest and that discrimination in financing education on the basis of school district wealth was a violation of equal protection.[25]

[23] See Frank I. Michelman, "On Protecting the Poor through the Fourteenth Amendment," 83 HARVARD LAW REVIEW 7 (1969); Ralph K. Winter, Jr., "Poverty, Economic Equality, and the Equal Protection Clause," in Philip B. Kurland, ed., *The Supreme Court Review: 1972* (Chicago: University of Chicago Press, 1972), pp. 41–102; Gayle Binion, "The Disadvantaged Before the Burger Court," 4 *Law and Policy Quarterly* 37 (1982).

[24] See "The New Public Interest Lawyers," 79 YALE LAW JOURNAL 1069 (1970).

[25] The issues are discussed in David A. J. Richards, "Equal Opportunity and School Financing," 41 UNIVERSITY OF CHICAGO LAW REVIEW 32 (1973); Robert L. Graham and Jason H. Kravitt, "The Evolution of Equal Protection—Education, Municipal Services, and Wealth," 7 HARVARD CIVIL RIGHTS–CIVIL LIBERTIES LAW REVIEW 105 (1972); "Educational Financing, Equal Protection of the Laws, and the Supreme Court," 70 MICHIGAN LAW REVIEW 1324 (1972).

The U.S. Supreme Court rejected this reasoning. Justice Powell's opinion held, first, that education, no matter how important, is not a fundamental constitutional right.

> It is not the province of this Court to create substantive constitutional rights in the name of guaranteeing equal protection of the laws. Thus the key to discovering whether education is "fundamental" is not to be found in comparisons of the relative societal significance of education as opposed to subsistence or housing. . . . Rather, the answer lies in assessing whether there is a right to education explicitly or implicitly guaranteed by the Constitution.

The second issue was whether the property tax system of financing public education operated to the disadvantage of some suspect class. Powell held that it did not. There was here no identifiable class of disadvantaged "poor," no "indigents" as in the criminal justice cases. In fact, it was not even evident that the poorest people necessarily clustered in the poorest property districts. Often the poor lived around commercial and industrial areas that provided substantial property tax income for schools. Moreover, any discrimination that there might be against the poor was relative, not absolute. No one was being denied public education: the charge was simply that poor school districts were supplying a poorer quality of education, and Powell did not think that the equal protection clause required "absolute equality or precisely equal advantages."[26]

Rodriguez was a five to four decision, with White, Douglas, Brennan, and Marshall dissenting. White held that the Texas statutory scheme was devoid of a rational basis. Both Brennan and Marshall protested Powell's assertion that the only fundamental rights were those explicitly or implicitly guaranteed in the Constitution. Where, said Marshall, does the Constitution "guarantee the right to procreate . . . or the right to vote in state elections . . . or the right to appeal from a criminal conviction," all of which the Court had previously held to be fundamental rights? Marshall also rejected the defense that mere inequality of education would not deny equal protection so long as there was not complete denial of education.

The reluctance of the Court to order a new basis for school finance is an indication of the limited area within which judges are likely to move in alleviating societal inequalities based on wealth. Substantial reforms in the system of distributive justice are obviously beyond the power of the courts to

---

[26] In *Harris v. McRae* (1980) the Court specifically held that "poverty, standing alone, is not a suspect classification," citing *James v. Valtierra* (1971). In *Board of Education v. Nyquist* (1983) the Court declined to hear a case that would have reopened the issue of equal spending for school districts. *Lassiter v. Department of Social Services* (1981) held that indigent parents do not have an automatic constitutional right to free legal assistance in a court proceeding terminating their legal relationship with their children. But *Little v. Streater* (1981) ruled that Connecticut had violated the due process rights of an indigent prison inmate by requiring him to pay for a blood test that might have aided his effort to defend himself in a paternity suit.

effect. Justice Harlan did not think it was a task for judges even to open up access for indigents to the appeals courts, but his dissent in *Douglas v. California* (1963) did accurately suggest the limits on judicial activism in neutralizing the consequences of poverty.

> Every financial exaction which the State imposes on a uniform basis is more easily satisfied by the well-to-do than by the indigent. . . . The Equal Protection Clause does not impose on the States "an affirmative duty to lift the handicaps flowing from differences in economic circumstances." To so construe it would be to read into the Constitution a philosophy of leveling that would be foreign to many of our basic concepts of the proper relations between government and society. The State may have a moral obligation to eliminate the evils of poverty, but it is not required by the Equal Protection Clause to give to some whatever others can afford.

SEX AS A SUSPECT CLASSIFICATION

The Supreme Court was very slow in recognizing discrimination based on sex as a constitutional problem. In 1873 the Court upheld an Illinois law denying women the right to practice law, and in 1875 it ruled that women had no constitutional right to vote.[27] Even after the adoption of the Nineteenth Amendment in 1920, it took another fifty years to begin to question whether sex might not be a suspect classification. This was one area where Congress was ahead of the Court. The Equal Pay Act of 1963 added to the Fair Labor Standards Act the principle of equal pay for equal work regardless of sex. Title VII of the Civil Rights Act of 1964 prohibited discrimination on the ground of sex by employers, labor organizations, and employment agencies.

The Court finally moved in *Reed v. Reed* (1971), where it declared unconstitutional an Idaho statute which provided that as between persons equally qualified to administer estates, males must be preferred to females. The Chief Justice did not hold sex to be a suspect classification, however. He applied the rationality test, found that the sex criterion was wholly unrelated to the objective of the statute, and so was an arbitrary legislative choice forbidden by the equal protection clause. A similarly based ruling in *Stanton v. Stanton* (1975) held that there was nothing rational in a statute specifying eighteen as the age of majority for females but twenty-one for males.

The issue as to whether sex was a suspect classification was first explicitly discussed in *Frontiero v. Richardson* (1973), which grew out of a federal statute denying to male dependents of female members of the armed forces the allowances and benefits that would be available to female

---

[27] *Bradwell v. State* (1873), *Minor v. Happersett* (1875).

dependents of male soldiers. Brennan wrote the opinion, and he deduced from the unanimous decision in *Reed v. Reed* that the Court had now held that "classifications based on sex, like classifications based upon race, alienage, or national origin, are inherently suspect." But while the Court was unanimous in *Frontiero* in condemning the statute, five justices rejected Brennan's claim that sex was a suspect classification, Powell asserting that it would be "premature" for the Court to take that position while the ratification of the Equal Rights Amendment—which, if adopted, would settle the issue definitively—was pending.[28]

The ERA, failed ratification in 1982, and in the meantime the Supreme Court continued to decide gender discrimination cases, which came up in increasing numbers, on the basis of the old rational means test. Whether sexual distinctions were discriminatory depended on whether they were a rational means to a legitimate end. There was no strict scrutiny. Sex was only a semisuspect classification, and the rationality test was as likely to uphold differential sex treatment as to strike it down.

Treatment of pregnancy is illustrative. Some long-established penalties on pregnant women were challenged. *Cleveland Board of Education v. LaFleur* (1974) held unconstitutional mandatory leave regulations that required pregnant teachers to quit their jobs without pay beginning five months before the expected birth. *Turner v. Department of Employment Security* (1975) struck down a Utah law automatically denying unemployment compensation to pregnant women for twelve weeks before childbirth and six weeks after. *Nashville Gas Co. v. Satty* (1977) ruled that employers could not take away job seniority rights from women workers who go on leave for pregnancy, although those workers need not be granted sick pay.

On the other hand, *Condit v. United Air Lines* (1978) and *Burwell v. Eastern Air Lines* (1981) refused to interfere with airline policies that require stewardesses to take unpaid maternity leave. *General Electric Co. v. Gilbert* (1976) ruled that an employee sickness and accident benefit plan that excluded from its coverage disabilities related to pregnancy did not violate Title VII.

The Court narrowly sustained a long-established gender distinction in *Michael M. v. Superior Court* (1981) when it voted five to four to uphold the California statutory rape law that makes it criminal for a male to have sexual relations with a female under eighteen to whom he is not married, while the female involved is exempt from criminal liability.

---

[28] Brennan again argued unsuccessfully, in *Schlesinger v. Ballard* (1975), that sex was a suspect classification. Here the Court upheld the navy practice of mandatory discharge of male officers not promoted after nine years of active service, whereas female officers were allowed thirteen years because they are barred from combat and most sea duty and so require a longer period to demonstrate their efficiency.

Despite the 1963 equal pay statute, it is well established that pay scales for women are generally lower than for men. But in *County of Washington v. Gunther* (1981) the Court ruled that under the Civil Rights Act women can bring suits claiming they are underpaid in comparison with men, even if they work in jobs (in this case as matrons in a county jail guarding female inmates) that men have never performed. However, advocates of women's rights lost a major battle in *Personnel Administrator of Massachusetts v. Feeney* (1979) where the Court upheld veterans' preference in public employment. Since the great majority of veterans are males, preference to veterans seriously limits opportunities for public employment for women.

Texas Department of Community Affairs v. Burdine (1981) held that Title VII of the 1964 Civil Rights Act, prohibiting discrimination in employment on the grounds of sex, does not obligate an employer to accord preference to women, to restructure employment practices to maximize the number of women hired, or to hire or promote women when their objective qualifications are equal to those of male applicants. The burden of proving intentional discrimination remains at all times with the plaintiff.

A major ruling preserving the gender discrimination was *Rostker v. Goldberg* (1981), which rejected, six to three, the contention that the military draft law was unconstitutional because it applies only to men. The Court thought special deference was owed to Congress in military and national defense issues, and invoked none of the standards used in other equal protection cases.

Widows were required to be treated equally with widowers in several cases,[29] but in *Kahn v. Shevin* (1974) the Court upheld a benign discrimination granting widows, but not widowers, an annual $500 property tax exemption.

Gender-neutral decisions cover a wide range of situations. *Stanton v. Stanton* (1975) invalidated a Utah court ruling that parental support for sons should continue to age twenty-one, but for daughters only until eighteen. *Craig v. Boren* (1976) held unconstitutional an Oklahoma law that, conversely, allowed women to buy beer at age eighteen while males had to wait until twenty-one. *Los Angeles Department of Water and Power v. Manhart* (1978) ruled that women may not be forced to make higher pension contributions than men, even though they live longer and so collect more retirement benefits.

In *Orr v. Orr* (1979) male equality was served by a ruling that state law may not forbid husbands to receive alimony. *Mississippi University for Women v. Hogan* (1982) ordered the last state-financed all-women's college in the country to admit a male to its nursing school. *Dothard v. Rawlinson*

---

[29] *Califano v. Goldfarb* (1977), *Califano v. Silbowitz* (1977), *Wengler v. Druggists Mutual Insurance Co.* (1980).

(1977) held that Title VII does not permit minimum height and weight standards, which few women could meet, for the position of prison guard.

While the record, as we see, is not unmixed, the Court's decisions since 1971 have played a major creative role in the sexual revolution in American law. In fact, Mary Cornelia Porter concludes that "the Court, consciously or not, has been edging toward establishing a 'neutral principle' based on the concept of androgyny, defined . . . as the absolute equality of the sexes as concerns expectations, opportunities, choices, and treatment in private and in public life."[30]

THE FREEDOM OF INTIMATE ASSOCIATION

A cluster of "fundamental rights" relates to what Kenneth L. Karst has called "the freedom of intimate association."[31] The public associational freedoms examined in Chapter 6 were based primarily on the First Amendment. The freedom of intimate conjugal relations upheld in *Griswold v. Connecticut* invoked the First, Third, Fourth, Fifth, and Ninth Amendments, but Douglas deliberately excluded the Fourteenth. Yet the new equal protection-substantive due process has provided the broadest rationale for the freedom of intimate association.

In upholding the right to marry across racial lines in *Loving v. Virginia* (1967) the Court did invoke due process as well as racial discrimination. But the issue was presented more clearly in *Zablocki v. Redhail* (1978), where there was no complicating racial aspect. A Wisconsin statute provided that any divorced resident with minor children not in his custody whom he was obliged by court order to support could not marry without court approval. Marshall's opinion for the Court holding the law unconstitutional asserted that the right to marry was a fundamental right, protected by the rigorous scrutiny-compelling state interest test. But, confronted with the network of restrictions that the states have traditionally fashioned to govern marriage and divorce, he added that he did not mean to challenge "reasonable regulations" that do not significantly interfere with decisions to enter into the marital relationship, such as blood tests. But Powell and Stewart, though concurring in the result, thought that marriage was not a fundamental right but rather, a privilege, limitations on which were subject to due process or equal protection rationality tests.

[30] Androgyny and the Supreme Court," 1 WOMEN AND POLITICS 23 (Winter 1980–81). Confirming this trend, the Court held, five to four, in *Arizona v. Norris* (1983) that Title 7 of the Civil Rights Act was violated when insurance companies paid women lower monthly retirement benefits than males. The justification had been that women on the average live longer than men.

[31] "The Freedom of Intimate Association," 89 YALE LAW JOURNAL 624 (1980).

American law has shown a strong preference for the nuclear family— essentially a couple and its dependent children. But does that justify infringement on personal choice of living arrangements—choices that are increasingly resulting in different living patterns? The Supreme Court did not think so in *United States Department of Agriculture v. Moreno* (1973), where a law aimed at "hippie communes" and limiting food stamps to related people living in one household was invalidated, using traditional equal protection analysis. The extended family was supported in *Moore v. City of East Cleveland* (1977), where a zoning law had been applied to deny "single family" status to a household in which a grandmother had taken in a grandson whose mother had died. But *Village of Belle Terre v. Boraas* (1974) upheld a zoning ordinance drafted to exclude nontraditional families from a Long Island village and applied against a household of six unrelated students, Douglas treating the ordinance as an environmental protection law.

ILLEGITIMACY

In 1968 the Court began to consider whether state laws discriminating against illegitimate children were subject to the constitutional tests of due process and equal protection. Initially no claim was made that newly discovered "fundamental rights" were at stake or that rigid scrutiny of such laws was demanded. *Levy v. Louisiana* (1968) simply applied the old rationality test and concluded that a law denying to illegitimate children the right to recover damages for the wrongful death of their mother, on whom they were dependent, constituted invidious discrimination against them.[32]

Black, Harlan, and Stewart dissented, however, and in the next case, *Labine v. Vincent* (1971), Black had the opportunity to implement his long-standing opposition to use of the "vague generalities" of the due process and equal protection clauses to nullify state legislation. The statute involved barred an illegitimate child from sharing equally with legitimates in the estate of their father, who had publicly acknowledged the child but had died without a will. In a bitter dissent, Brennan charged that the decision upholding this result "cannot even pretend to be a principled decision" and that this statute constituted invidious discrimination, supportable only by "moral prejudice."

Surprisingly, the 1972 Court, with Black and Harlan gone, took a much more sympathetic position. *Weber v. Aetna Casualty Co.* held that

---

[32] Also, in *Glona v. American Guarantee & Liability Insurance Co.* (1968), the Court held that the mother of an illegitimate child could not be denied the right to bring a wrongful death action. Granting this right, said Douglas, could not conceivably further the "sin" of illegitimacy.

workmen's compensation statutes denying equal recovery rights to dependent, unacknowledged, illegitimate children denied equal protection. Powell now conceded that this was an area of "sensitive and fundamental personal rights" requiring "stricter scrutiny." He found that the statute served "no legitimate state interest, compelling or otherwise," and that it was a discriminatory law "relating to status of birth." Visiting society's condemnation of "irresponsible liaisons beyond the bonds of marriage . . . on the head of an infant is illogical and unjust."

Rehnquist, dissenting in *Weber*, was left as the only defender of the Black-Harlan position against expanding the Fourteenth Amendment by the creation of new fundamental rights. To Powell's condemnation of the Louisiana law as "illogical and unjust," he rejoined: "A fair-minded man might regard it as both, but the Equal Protection Clause of the Fourteenth Amendment requires neither that state enactments be 'logical' nor does it require that they be 'just' in the common meaning of those terms."

As it turned out, *Weber* was not the wave of the future. *Mathews v. Lucas* (1976) rejected strict scrutiny and upheld the Social Security Administration requirement that some illegitimate children must prove their dependence upon their divorced father to obtain survivors' benefits, whereas other children were presumed eligible. Stevens, dissenting, was appalled that the government should "add to the burdens that illegitimate children inevitably acquire at birth."

Trimble v. Gordon (1977) struck down as a denial of equal protection an Illinois law allowing children born out of wedlock to inherit by intestate succession only from their mothers, whereas legitimate children could inherit intestate from both mothers and fathers. But this ruling was promptly distinguished in *Lalli v. Lalli* (1978), which went back to *Labine* and *Mathews* for its rationale, holding that two illegitimate children were not entitled to share in their father's estate because during his lifetime he had not obtained a judicial order declaring his paternity. And *Parham v. Hughes* (1979) upheld a Georgia law that precluded a father who had not legitimated a child from suing for the child's wrongful death.[33]

Applying the rationality test to discrimination against illegitimate children has involved the Supreme Court in a quagmire of review of state statutes similar to that in which it floundered with respect to right to counsel from *Powell* to *Gideon*. But, as Karst says, we are probably "still some distance from the day when the Supreme Court will explicitly hold that the status of illegitimacy itself is constitutionally defective."[34]

---

[33] But *Mills v. Habluetzel* (1982) did strike down a Texas law allowing only one year for a paternity suit to identify the natural father of an illegitimate child for support purposes.

[34] Supra, note 31, at p. 682.

THE HANDICAPPED AND RETARDED

"The disabled are as powerless and isolated a minority as any group in American society."[35] However, they have begun to receive federal statutory protection, and their constitutional claims are being pressed in lawsuits, with some success. A landmark case was *Wyatt v. Stickney* (1971), where Judge Frank M. Johnson, Jr., propounded a bill of rights for patients in Alabama's mental institutions. At the Supreme Court level the first substantial decision was *O'Connor v. Donaldson* (1975), which held that a person who is not dangerous cannot be held in an institution by compulsion and without treatment.

The Pennhurst State School and Hospital in Pennsylvania, where conditions were so bad that a district judge had ordered its eventual closing and prohibited new admissions, was responsible for two Supreme Court rulings. The first denied that federal statutes had created any substantive rights for the developmentally disabled.[36] But the second, *Youngberg v. Romeo* (1982), did make the significant ruling that retarded persons committed to state mental institutions have limited constitutional rights to safe conditions, to be free from unnecessary restraints, and to receive enough training to prevent their preexisting self-care skills from deteriorating because of commitment conditions.

The Supreme Court has tended to interpret narrowly congressional legislation for the handicapped. In *Southeastern Community College v. Davis* (1979) a practical nurse was unable to secure admission to the college for clinical work and consequently unable to get a registered nurse's training, because she had a serious hearing loss. The Court held that her exclusion did not violate the federal Rehabilitation Act of 1973. Interpreting the Education for All Handicapped Children Act of 1975, the Court in *Board of Education v. Rowley* (1982) ruled that public schools were not required to provide sign-language interpreters for deaf children. The statute obliged schools to give only enough special help and personal instruction to ensure a minimally adequate education. Similarly, *Community Television of Southern California* (1983) held that the Rehabilitation Act, protecting handicapped individuals from exclusion from the benefits of any program receiving federal financial assistance, did not require public television stations to provide special programming for the hearing-impaired.

[35] Judith A. Baer, "The Burger Court and the Rights of the Handicapped," 35 WESTERN POLITICAL QUARTERLY 339, 357 (1982).

[36] *Pennhurst State School and Hospital v. Halderman* (1981). See also *Schweiker v. Wilson* (1981).

AGE

Classification on the basis of age has been challenged on equal protection grounds, and age discrimination in employment was forbidden by federal statute in 1977. Under that act a fifty-nine-year-old test pilot was restored to his job with back pay in *McDonnell Douglas v. Houghton* (1977). But in a later case, *Vance v. Bradley* (1979), the Court approved a law requiring Foreign Service employees to retire at age sixty, citing the rigors of overseas duty and the need to provide promotions for younger persons. Prior to the 1977 act, *Massachusetts Board of Retirement v. Murgia* (1976) had upheld a requirement that uniformed members of the state police must retire at age fifty, the Court denying that age was a suspect classification.

WELFARE AND MEDICAL CARE
AS FUNDAMENTAL RIGHTS

Welfare and medical care are among the newest claimants for the status of fundamental rights and rigid judicial scrutiny. In *Shapiro v. Thompson*, it was the right to interstate travel, not the right to welfare, that was upheld by the Court. When the welfare issue was presented directly, in *Dandridge v. Williams* (1970), the fundamental right claim was denied. Maryland had placed an absolute limit of $250 per month on the amount of a grant under the Aid-to-Dependent-Children Social Security program, regardless of family size or actual need. For the six-judge majority, Stewart held that this was a "regulation in the social and economic field, not affecting freedoms guaranteed by the Bill of Rights" and consequently subject to review under the old equal protection standard of rationality. He confessed that public welfare assistance, involving "the most basic economic needs of impoverished human beings," was hardly comparable to the regulations of business and industry for which the test of minimal rationality had been developed. But this "dramatically real factual difference" justified no difference in constitutional standards. The Court would not second-guess state views of wise social or economic policy.

Marshall, dissenting along with Douglas and Brennan, vehemently protested this emasculation of equal protection in the area of social welfare administration on the theory that it was economic policy that was involved. "Appellees are not a gas company or an optical dispenser; they are needy dependent children" who are discriminated against by the state "on the wholly arbitrary basis that they happen to be members of large families."

Subsequent decisions confirmed that the Court would apply the old equal protection rule in the welfare field. *Richardson v. Belcher* (1971) upheld, as rationally based and free from invidious discrimination, the federal law which reduced Social Security payments to reflect workmen's compensation awards. In *Jefferson v. Hackney* (1972), Texas, unable to fund all its welfare programs completely, placed a limit of 75 percent of the standard of need on recipients of Aid-to-Dependent-Children grants, who were 87 percent blacks and Chicanos, while funding aid to the aged and the blind, who were predominantly white, at 100 percent and 95 percent. The Court said it would not accept "naked statistical arguments" as proving racial discrimination, and there was no constitutional requirement that each relief category be treated exactly alike.

Medical care received a certain amount of recognition as a constitutional right in *Memorial Hospital v. Maricopa County* (1974). An Arizona statute required one year's residence in a county as a condition to receiving nonemergency hospitalization or medical care at county expense. The Court, invoking the *Shapiro* ruling, held that this durational residency requirement was an invidious classification impinging on the right of interstate travel. Douglas thought the issue was invidious discrimination against the poor, not the right to travel interstate.

HOUSING AND EXCLUSIONARY ZONING

Without a racial component,[37] the Court has found no basis for applying the new equal protection to housing legislation. In *James v. Valtierra* (1971) a California constitutional provision required that low-rent housing projects be approved by majority vote in a community election. The Court accepted this arrangement as conforming with the state's tradition of local participation in expenditure decisions.

Housing as a constitutional right was explicitly rejected in *Lindsey v. Normet* (1972), which upheld Oregon's judicial procedure for eviction of tenants after nonpayment of rent. The appellants argued that the need for decent shelter was a fundamental interest that required the statute to pass the compelling state interest test, but White rejected the contention, saying, "We do not denigrate the importance of decent, safe and sanitary housing. But the Constitution does not provide judicial remedies for every social and economic ill."

The constitutionality of zoning has been accepted ever since *Euclid v. Ambler Realty Co.* was decided in 1926, but more recently it has been subject to attack as an exclusionary device for fencing off the suburbs and excluding low-income families and minorities from access to housing and jobs outside the central city ghettoes. Zoning is exclusionary when it seriously impedes or prevents the construction of lower-cost housing by building codes, and lot size or square footage requirements. The legal argument against exclusion-

[37] See *Reitman v. Mulkey* (1967), *Jones v. Alfred H. Mayer Co.* (1968), *Hunter v. Erickson* (1969), and *Hills v. Gautreaux* (1976).

ary zoning is that, to be a valid use of the police power, zoning must further the general welfare, and that where the effect of zoning laws is to discriminate against a racial minority or the poor, even though the laws may not have been originally discriminatory in motive or purpose, there is a denial of equal protection.[38]

In *Warth v. Seldin* (1975) charges of this kind made against the zoning regulations of a Rochester suburb failed when the Court denied standing to the organizations that brought the suit. Standing was granted in *Village of Arlington Heights v. Metropolitan Housing Development Corporation* (1977), but the Court held that racially discriminatory intent had not been proved as required by *Washington v. Davis.*

INTERPRETIVE VERSUS NONINTERPRETIVE REVIEW

The Supreme Court's ventures into constitutional policy making, outlined in this chapter, have engendered a major debate among practitioners of constitutional theory. One position, ably asserted by Herbert Wechsler,[39] Raoul Berger,[40] Robert Bork,[41] and Justice Rehnquist,[42] holds that Supreme Court policy making is legitimate only when based on value judgments embodied either in some particular provision of the text of the Constitution, or in the overall structure of government ordained by the Constitution. This is the interpretive position, the philosophy of judicial restraint, and it rejects talk about minimal versus strict scrutiny or the calculus of "suspect" classifications.

On the other hand, noninterpretive review justifies making decisions on constitutionality by reference to value judgments other than those constitutionalized by the framers. Activist judges charged with non-interpretivism customarily defend by alleging that they are acting within the spirit and intention, if not the letter, of the Constitution. Non-interpretive review has its defenders among the theorists. Michael J. Perry, though holding that noninterpretive review is contrary to the Constitution as written or as understood by the framers, nevertheless regards expanded review as functionally justified with respect to human rights issues,

[38] "Exclusionary Zoning and Equal Protection," 84 HARVARD LAW REVIEW 1645 (1971).

[39] "Toward Neutral Principles of Constitutional Law," 73 HARVARD LAW REVIEW 1 (1959).

[40] *Government by Judiciary* (Cambridge: Harvard University Press, 1977).

[41] "The Impossibility of Finding Welfare Rights in the Constitution," 1979 *Washington University Law Quarterly* 695.

[42] "The Notion of a Living Constitution," 54 TEXAS LAW REVIEW 693 (1976).

particularly freedom of expression and equal protection.[43] John Hart Ely, while opposed to "substantive" noninterpretive review, approves "participational" review for enforcement of the Ninth Amendment and the privileges and immunities clause as representing value judgments and restraints the framers did not specify.[44] Jesse H. Choper holds that activist judicial review is justified in guarding against governmental infringement on individual libertites, but that separation of powers and federalism issues should be left to the political process.[45]

The Court's history, however, suggests that judicial review and policy making will continue to be judged, not in terms of academic dichotomies, but in the pragmatic perspective so eloquently stated by Justice Holmes in *Missouri v. Holland* (1920):

> When we are dealing with words that also are a constituent act, like the Constitution of the United States, we must realize that they have called into life a being the development of which could not have been foreseen completely by the most gifted of its begetters. It was enough for them to realize or to hope that they had created an organism; it has taken a century and has cost their successors much sweat and blood to prove that they created a nation. The case before us must be considered in the light of our whole experience and not merely in that of what was said a hundred years ago.

[43] *The Constitution, the Courts, and Human Rights* (New Haven: Yale University Press, 1982).

[44] *Democracy and Distrust: A Theory of Judicial Review* (Cambridge: Harvard University Press, 1980).

[45] *Judicial Review and the National Political Process* (Chicago: University of Chicago Press, 1980).

13

Elections
and the Franchise

The framers of the Constitution had to deal with the problem of the franchise only in connection with the selection of members of the House of Representatives, since senators were elected by the state legislatures and presidential electors were appointed in such manner as the state legislatures might direct. Eventually the responsibility for electing the President and members of both houses of Congress devolved upon this same national electorate. Although the states have the major responsibility under the Constitution of determining the standards for voting eligibility, in recent years Congress and the Supreme Court have become increasingly involved in regulating electoral processes.[1]

CONSTITUTIONAL FOUNDATION
OF THE RIGHT TO VOTE

The basic provision in the Constitution governing the right to vote in federal elections is Article I, section 2, which provides that electors for members of the House in the several states "shall have the qualifications requisite for electors of the most numerous branch of the state legislature." By this device the Constitution assured election of the House on a popular

[1] See generally Richard Claude, *The Supreme Court and the Electoral Process* (Baltimore: Johns Hopkins Press, 1970); "Developments in the Law—Elections," 88 HARVARD LAW REVIEW 1111-1339 (1975).

base but avoided creation of a national electorate separate from the state electorates, which were defined by legal provisions varying widely from state to state.

Second, there is the "times, places and manner" clause of Article I, section 4. As already noted, Congress first took action under this authority in 1842, when it required that members of the House should be elected by districts rather than on a general state ticket. An act of 1866 regulated the procedure of state legislatures in choosing senators. The first comprehensive federal statute on elections came in 1870, motivated by the political problems of the Reconstruction period. The Enforcement Act of 1870 and subsequent measures made federal offenses of false registration, bribery, voting without legal right, making false returns of votes cast, interference in any manner with officers of elections, or the neglect by any such officer of any duty required of him by state or federal law.

In addition to these two provisions of Article I, five of the amendments to the Constitution have a bearing on elections and the electorate. The equal protection clause of the Fourteenth Amendment has been applied, as we shall see, to forbid discriminatory practices by state election officials. The Fourteenth Amendment also contains the threat of reduction of representation for denial of the right to vote. When it appeared that this provision would not achieve its purpose of securing the suffrage for blacks, the Fifteenth Amendment was adopted in 1870, specifically guaranteeing that "the right of citizens of the United States to vote shall not be denied or abridged by the United States or by any state on account of race, color, or previous condition of servitude." The Nineteenth Amendment, adopted in 1920, uses the same formula to guarantee women the right to vote. The Fourteenth, Fifteenth, and Nineteenth Amendments all authorize Congress to enforce their provisions by appropriate legislation. The Twenty-fourth Amendment, adopted in 1964, provides that the right to vote in a federal election shall not be denied for failure to pay a poll tax or any other tax, and the Twenty-sixth Amendment extends the franchise to eighteen-year-olds.

In spite of the Fifteenth Amendment's use of the phrase "the right to vote," the Supreme Court was at first reluctant to give effect to such a right. Under Article I, section 2, participation in federal elections depends upon state laws prescribing the electorate, and so it is strictly true, as the Supreme Court held in the early case of *Minor v. Happersett* (1875), that "the Constitution of the United States does not confer the right of suffrage upon anyone." Mrs. Minor had sought to compel election officials in Missouri, where suffrage was limited to male citizens, to accept her vote on the ground that she had a right to vote as a citizen of the United States under the Fourteenth Amendment, but the Court decisively rejected this contention. The following year the Court took a similarly negative attitude toward the Fifteenth Amendment, contending that it did not confer the right to vote on anyone, but merely "invested the citizens of the United States with a new constitutional right which is . . . exemption from discrimination in the exercise of the elective franchise."[2]

Within a decade, however, the Court had reconsidered this doctrine. *Ex parte Yarbrough* (1884) affirmed the conviction of several Klansmen for conspiring to prevent a black, by intimidation, from voting for a member of Congress. They were held to have violated the Enforcement Act of 1870, which provided punishment in cases of conspiracy to injure or intimidate a citizen in the exercise of any federal right. In spite of *Minor v. Happersett*, there was a *right* involved in this case. The earlier decision, explained the Court, merely meant that state law, not the federal Constitution, determined what classes of citizens could exercise the franchise. But once state law had determined who was eligible to vote by statutory provisions covering state elections, then the federal Constitution through Article I, section 2, stepped in to guarantee their *right* to vote for members of Congress.

STATE LIMITATIONS ON THE FRANCHISE

State regulation of the franchise thus proceeds under watchful congressional and constitutional supervision. Of all the state limitations on the franchise, only two have been noncontroversial. All states require that voters be citizens of the United States,[3] and persons who are idiots, insane, or under guardianship are specifically disqualified from voting in almost all states.[4]

Residence

All states require a certain period of residence in the state and locality as a qualification for the franchise. This is understandable for participation in state and local elections, but it is irrelevant in voting for President, and in the Voting Rights Act of 1970 Congress limited voting requirements in presidential elections to a thirty-day registration period.

Extended residence periods to qualify in state and local elections also came into question; in *Dunn v. Blumstein* (1972), the Supreme Court held that such requirements were unconstitutional restrictions on the right to vote and travel. Only bona fide residence and a minimal registration period were permissible residence limitations on the franchise, and Marshall suggested that "30 days appears to be an ample period of time for the State to complete whatever administrative tasks are necessary to prevent fraud." Certainly a year, or even three months, was "too much." But *Marston v. Lewis* (1973) and *Burns v. Fortson* (1973) accepted a fifty-day period.

[2] *United States v. Reese* (1876), *United States v. Cruikshank* (1876).

[3] In the past, however, aliens were permitted to vote in some states. Not until 1928 was there a presidential election in which no alien was eligible to vote.

[4] See "Mental Disability and the Right to Vote," 88 YALE LAW JOURNAL 1644 (1979).

In *Carrington v. Rash* (1965), the Supreme Court ruled that Texas had carried its residence restrictions too far when it provided that members of the armed forces who moved to Texas during the course of their military duty were prohibited from voting in the state so long as they remained in the armed forces. The Court agreed that Texas had a right to require that voters be bona fide residents, but anyone who met that test could not be denied opportunity for equal political representation. "'Fencing out' from the franchise a sector of the population because of the way they may vote is constitutionally impermissible."[5]

Age

In 1943 Georgia broke the traditional voting age barrier of twenty-one, reducing it to eighteen. In the Voting Rights Act of 1970, Congress, influenced by the slogan that if eighteen-year-olds were old enough to be sent to Vietnam they were old enough to vote, set the voting age at eighteen for all federal and state elections. A badly divided Court in *Oregon v. Mitchell* (1970) held that, while Congress could fix the voting age in federal elections, the Constitution guaranteed states the right to set voting "qualifications" for state and local elections. The vote on both issues was five to four, with Justice Black in the majority in each holding. Congress immediately adopted the Twenty-sixth Amendment to reverse the Court's ruling as to state and local elections, and it was promptly ratified.

Imprisonment or Conviction for Crime

Thousands of qualified voters are unable to vote at elections because, though they have not been convicted for crime, they are in prison awaiting trial on nonbailable offenses or because they are unable to post bail. They could, of course, vote by absentee ballot if state law so provided. But in *McDonald v. Board of Election Commissioners of Chicago* (1969), the Supreme Court held that the failure of Illinois to make such provision did not deny the constitutional right to vote.

It subsequently turned out, however, that this decision did not mean what it seemed to say. In *O'Brien v. Skinner* (1974), the Court explained that the *McDonald* decision was based only on deficiencies in the record which had failed to show that appellants were in fact absolutely prohibited from voting by the state. The New York law in *O'Brien* clearly denied absentee ballots or any alternative means of voting to prisoners awaiting trial, and the Court said that this was a denial of equal protection.

State statutes generally deny the right to vote to persons who have been convicted of felonies, this disqualification continuing after they have served

[5]*Evans v. Cornman* (1970) ruled that Maryland could not deny the right to vote in state elections to residents in a federal enclave, the National Institutes of Health.

their sentences. The Supreme Court of California held in 1973 that this lifetime exclusion from the franchise served no compelling state interest; but in *Richardson v. Ramirez* (1974), the Supreme Court found a justification for the disqualification in the almost forgotten section 2 of the Fourteenth Amendment, which impliedly recognizes the right of states to deny the right to vote "for participation in rebellion or other crime." Rehnquist said that if current views about rehabilitating ex-felons stress their return to society in a fully participating role, this must be a legislative, not a judicial, decision.

The Grandfather Clause

A device for racial discrimination in voting was the so-called "grandfather clause," which the Supreme Court declared unconstitutional in *Guinn v. United States* (1915). An Oklahoma law imposed a literacy test for voting but gave exemption for persons whose ancestors had been entitled to vote in 1866. The Court held this provision to be a clear attempt to evade the Fifteenth Amendment. Oklahoma rejoined with a new election registration law that permitted a twelve-day registration period but exempted from the registration requirement those who had voted in the 1914 election under the unconstitutional grandfather clause. The Court held this law also invalid in *Lane v. Wilson* (1939).

Poll Taxes

Poll (or head) taxes were once a familiar source of revenue but gradually fell into disuse. They were revived around 1900 by a number of states and made a condition of the franchise as a deliberate device to reduce the possibility of black voting. In practice the poll tax was a substantial bar to voting by poor whites as well. While the tax was only about two dollars, that was a large sum for many, and there was usually a provision that unpaid back taxes had to be paid if a person wanted to start voting. Moreover, the tax requirement was a source of corruption in elections, taxes often being paid by candidates in return for voting support.

On its face, however, the poll tax was not discriminatory, and in *Breedlove v. Suttles* (1937), the Supreme Court refused to hold that its use constituted a denial of equal protection or a violation of the Fifteenth Amendment. However, it was gradually abandoned, and by 1960 was maintained by only five states—Alabama, Arkansas, Mississippi, Texas, and Virginia.

Efforts in Congress to abolish the poll tax as a voting requirement date back to the early 1940s. Five times between 1942 and 1949, bills to ban the poll tax by statute passed the House but died in the Senate, three times as a result of Southern filibuster.

There was some uncertainty in Congress as to whether it would require a constitutional amendment rather than a statute to outlaw the poll tax. Finally, in 1962, the Senate acquiesced in an amendment banning the poll tax in federal elections, which was ratified in 1964 as the Twenty-fourth Amendment.

Recognizing that a broadened electorate would threaten its long-established power, the Byrd political organization in Virginia immediately put through the state legislature a law requiring voters in federal elections either to pay a poll tax or to file a certificate of residence at least six months prior to each election. The Supreme Court in *Harman v. Forssenius* (1965) held this law unconstitutional as an abridgement of the right to vote, because it imposed a material and burdensome requirement on persons who wished to exercise their constitutional right to vote in federal elections without paying a poll tax.

The poll tax after the Twenty-fourth Amendment remained as a restriction on the franchise in *state* elections in four states, Arkansas having abolished the requirement in 1964. But in 1966 the Supreme Court, in *Harper v. Virginia State Board of Elections,* declared the Virginia poll tax unconstitutional as an "invidious discrimination" and a denial of equal protection. "Voter qualifications have no relation to wealth nor to paying or not paying this or any other tax." The right to vote, the Court added, "is too precious, too fundamental to be so burdened or conditioned." The contrary decision in *Breedlove v. Suttles* was overruled. Justice Black, dissenting, had no doubt that Congress could have abolished the poll tax in state elections by legislation, but he thought that for the Court to take this step itself on the authority of the Fourteenth Amendment was to resort to natural-law reasoning and to usurp the power of amending the Constitution.

Literacy Tests

In 1960 over twenty states had a literacy requirement for voting. Such a test had been upheld by the Supreme Court in *Guinn v. United States* (1915) as so clearly within state power as to require no discussion. The Court unanimously adhered to this view in the North Carolina case of *Lassiter v. Northampton County Board of Elections* (1959), Justice Douglas saying: "Illiterate people may be intelligent voters. Yet in our society where newspapers, periodicals, books, and other printed matter canvass and debate campaign issues, a State might conclude that only those who are literate should exercise the franchise."

Though not charged in this case, the Court in *Lassiter* did recognize that a literacy test, fair on its face, might be used for discriminatory purposes. Since there was overwhelming evidence that the test was in fact used for this purpose in some Southern states, the Civil Rights Commission in its 1961 report on voting recommended that literacy be established by a method which would be objective and not subject to manipulation—

namely, by accepting attainment of the sixth grade in school as fulfilling the literacy requirement. The New York literacy law had this provision.

A special problem was presented in New York, where the requirement of literacy in English excluded from the franchise those members of the large Puerto Rican community who were literate only in Spanish. This issue was raised in *Cardona v. Power* (1966) but was avoided by the Court majority; four justices who did express an opinion on the question were evenly divided as to whether the English requirement was a denial of equal protection to Spanish-speaking citizens.

Interpretation of the Constitution

Particularly in Southern states, literacy tests have been combined with a requirement to understand or interpret provisions of the state or federal constitutions. In *Williams v. Mississippi* (1898) the Supreme Court upheld such a law because on its face it did not discriminate against blacks. But a half century later, in *Davis v. Schnell* (1949), the Court affirmed a lower court ruling that an Alabama "understand and explain" law was invalid on its face because of its legislative setting and the great discretion it vested in the registrar.

This decision had little impact on the continued widespread use of such requirements for achieving disfranchisement on racial grounds. As concern about the denial of black voting rights escalated in the 1950s, it became increasingly clear that the "understanding" test was one of the principal techniques by which Southern registrars excluded blacks from the franchise. In their completely uncontrolled discretion they gave impossibly hard questions to black registrants and refused them registration because of technical or inconsequential errors.

This account of legal barriers to voting does not suggest adequately the fertility of Southern legislatures in devising additional hurdles for would-be black voters, nor of course does it take into account the use of intimidation and violence to prevent black registration or to punish those who voted or participated in voter-registration campaigns. The Civil Rights Commission summarized the situation in its 1961 voting report by pointing out that in at least 129 counties in 10 Southern states less than 10 percent of eligible blacks were registered. In 17 representative "black belt" counties where blacks constituted a majority of the population, only about 3 percent were found to be registered.

THE VOTING RIGHTS ACTS

The Civil Rights Acts of 1957 and 1960 were intended to protect black voting rights, but they were largely ineffective. Both placed the burden of correcting

voting discrimination on Southern federal district judges, who were usually unsympathetic with this goal. It was clear that further and more drastic federal action would be required if the blockade to black voting were to be broken. This action took the form of the Voting Rights Act of 1965, adopted by Congress under the authority granted by section 2 of the Fifteenth Amendment, to enforce by "appropriate" measures its ban on racial discrimination in voting.[6]

This historic act flatly declared that "no voting qualification or prerequisite to voting" was to be imposed to deny or abridge the right of any citizen to vote on account of race or color. The act concentrated on four types of "tests or devices": (1) literacy and understanding tests; (2) educational achievement or knowledge of any particular subject; (3) good moral character; and (4) proof of qualifications by voucher of registered voters. The use of such tests or devices, which had accounted for the great bulk of "legal" discrimination, was prohibited in any state or political subdivision where less than 50 percent of the persons of voting age were registered on November 1, 1964, or had voted in the presidential election of November, 1964.

The 50 percent test was of course a very rough index of voting discrimination. Its use made the statute applicable to six Southern states— Alabama, Georgia, Louisiana, Mississippi, South Carolina, and Virginia— but also to Alaska, twenty-six counties in North Carolina, and a few other scattered counties. It did not apply to Arkansas, Texas, and Florida, where in some sections there were large black populations but few black voters, because those states did not use literacy tests.

In states and counties covered by the act, voting qualifications of the above four types were suspended, and they could be restored only by a suit brought in the district court of the District of Columbia proving that such tests or devices had not been used for purposes of racial discrimination in the preceding five years.[7] Moreover, section 5 placed an affirmative burden on states or local governments to submit changes in electoral laws to the attorney general or the District of Columbia district court for determination whether the electoral change had the purpose or effect of "denying or abridging" the right to vote on account of race. In practice, nearly all submissions under section 5 have been to the attorney general rather than to the District of Columbia court. But most litigation has begun in three-judge federal district courts in the South where either the government or aggrieved voters have sought to force state and local governments to comply with the

---

[6] See Charles V. Hamilton, *The Bench and the Ballot: Southern Federal Judges and Black Voters* (New York: Oxford University Press, 1973).

[7] Alaska won exemption from the 1965 act by this procedure in 1966, but a North Carolina county was denied release in *Gaston County v. United States* (1969).

procedural requirements of section 5. In general, Supreme Court rulings have strictly enforced section 5.[8]

The 1965 statute also provided for appointment by the United States Civil Service Commission of voting examiners in any political subdivision where the attorney general certified that they were needed to enforce the Fifteenth Amendment. These examiners were to register all applicants meeting the voting requirements of state law, insofar as these requirements had not been suspended by the statute. The attorney general acted promptly to place federal examiners in counties with the worst records of discrimination, and within six months the number of blacks registered in Alabama had doubled.

The Supreme Court upheld the constitutionality of the Voting Rights Act in *South Carolina v. Katzenbach* (1966). Admittedly the statute amounted to an unprecedented abridgement of the power to set voting qualifications for the states caught by the 50 percent test. They lost the right to enforce registration laws that could still be enforced in all other states. They had to get the consent of the District of Columbia federal court to resume enforcement of suspended statutes, and permission from the attorney general to adopt new voting-qualification laws.

This was, as the Supreme Court recognized, an "inventive" use of congressional power to enforce the Fifteenth Amendment. But the Court also recognized that the provocation had been great. Congress had tried milder measures, and they had not worked. Now, in the 1965 act, Congress was manifesting a "firm intention" to rid the country of racial discrimination in voting, and the states had only themselves to blame for the drastic remedies adopted.

The Court stated the basic constitutional principle involved in these words: "As against the reserved powers of the States, Congress may use any rational means to effectuate the constitutional prohibition of racial discrimination in voting." The means here employed were rational, the Court held. South Carolina contended that the coverage formula was "awkwardly designed in a number of respects and that it disregards various local conditions which have nothing to do with racial discrimination," but the Court found the formula "rational in both practice and theory." Congress had learned that widespread and persistent discrimination in voting had

[8] See *Allen v. State Board of Elections* (1969), *Perkins v. Matthews* (1971), *Georgia v. United States* (1973), *Connor v. Waller* (1975), *City of Rome v. United States* (1980). But *Richmond v. United States* (1975) and *Beer v. United States* (1976) restricted the discretion of the attorney general. *East Carroll Parish School Board v. Marshall* (1976) held that any voting plan submitted and adopted pursuant to court order was immune from section 5 scrutiny. See Gayle Binion, "The Implementation of Section 5 of the 1965 Voting Rights Act," 32 WESTERN POLITICAL QUARTERLY 154 (1979); Howard Ball, Dale Krane, and Thomas P. Lauth, *Compromised Compliance: Implementation of the 1965 Voting Rights Act* (Westport, Conn.: Greenwood Press, 1982).

typically entailed the misuse of tests and devices, and this was the evil for which the new remedies were specifically designed. The Court was unanimous, except that Justice Black regarded the provisions requiring review of state laws by the District of Columbia court and the attorney general as unconstitutional.

New York was exempt from the effect of the 1965 statute, and consequently its requirement of literacy in English for voting would not have been affected. But at the urging of the state's two senators, Congress inserted a provision prohibiting the states from imposing an English-language literacy test, for the purpose of securing "the rights under the fourteenth amendment of persons educated in American-flag schools in which the predominant classroom language was other than English." Completion of the sixth grade in such a school was to be accepted as meeting the literacy requirement.

While this provision was regarded by many as of dubious constitutionality, the Supreme Court upheld it in *Katzenbach v. Morgan* (1966) as appropriate legislation under section 5 of the Fourteenth Amendment to enforce the equal protection clause. By prohibiting New York from denying the franchise to large segments of its Puerto Rican community, Congress was helping that community gain nondiscriminatory treatment in public services through enhancement of its political power.

The 1965 statute had a dramatic effect. Between 1965 and 1972, black registration in the seven southern states covered by the act increased from 29.3 percent to 56.6 percent, according to the U.S. Civil Rights Commission. The difference between the proportion of white and black voting-age residents registered fell from 44.1 percent to 11.2 percent. There were 1,100 black elected officials in these states by 1974.

The 1965 act had a five-year limitation. It was extended for another five years by the Voting Rights Act of 1970, which made the suspension of literacy tests nationwide[9] and also revised the so-called "triggering" formula to bring more areas under the act's coverage. The statute was again extended in 1975, this time for seven years. The 1975 act made permanent the ban on literacy tests, but its most noteworthy feature was extension to cover areas in twenty-four states where Spanish, Asian languages, and Indian and Alaskan dialects are spoken by large numbers of voters. The act required that bilingual voting information and, in some cases, federal enforcement officers be provided in areas where less than 50 percent of those minorities registered to vote in 1972.

---

[9]The nationwide suspension of literacy tests was upheld in *Oregon v. Mitchell* (1970) on the ground that discriminatory use of literacy tests had been nationwide. The Court mentioned as examples discrimination against Puerto Ricans in New York and against Spanish-Americans in Arizona.

In 1982 the act was again extended, with belated support from the Reagan administration. Section 5, requiring preclearance of changes in electoral procedures, was extended for twenty-five years, but with a "bail-out" procedure for the nine states and portions of thirteen others affected. A showing that the state or district had practiced no discrimination for ten years and had made positive efforts to aid minority participation in the electoral process would free it from the preclearance requirement.

The principal controversy was over section 2, which bars nationwide discriminatory practices such as literacy tests. In *City of Mobile v. Bolden* (1980) the Supreme Court had upheld the Mobile electoral system under which a three-member city commission was elected at large. Though blacks constituted 40 percent of the city's population, no black had ever been elected to the commission. In 1976 a federal district judge ruled that the at-large election system discriminated against blacks and ordered the city to establish a mayor-council form of government. The Supreme Court reversed, six to three, on the ground that since blacks could register and vote without hindrance, their freedom to vote had not been denied or abridged. An electoral system violated the Constitution only if it was "motivated by a racially discriminatory purpose." The equal protection clause, the court said, does not mandate proportional representation or protect any group from electoral defeat.

This decision was attacked by civil rights groups on the ground that purposeful discrimination was difficult to prove, and the House draft of the 1982 bill provided that an election law violation could be proved merely by showing that the procedure "results" in the denial or abridgement of the right to vote. In the Senate, opponents of the bill charged that the "results" test would lead to proportional representation and lawsuits against localities with at-large elections. As finally adopted, the law authorizes judges to consider the "totality of circumstances" surrounding a case, including election results. But plaintiffs would not be allowed to use the act as a basis for establishing racial voting "quotas" or to claim that election results must reflect the minority proportion of the population.

As it turned out, on remand of the *Mobile* decision, the federal district court held the Mobile at-large system discriminatory and unconstitutional. Moreover, *Rogers v. Herman Lodge* (1982) ruled that the at-large electoral system for Burke County, Georgia, was maintained for the invidious purpose of diluting black voting strength. And in *Port Arthur v. United States* (1982) the Court upheld a lower court order requiring a Texas city to hold elections for two city council seats under a plurality rule, rather than a majority vote rule. But *City of Lockhart v. United States* (1983) upheld an election plan on the ground that it was not more unfavorable to minorities' voting strength than the preceding plan. The law required only that there be no retrogression.

THE CONSTITUTIONAL STATUS
OF PRIMARY ELECTIONS

Another device, which was successful for a time in achieving racial discrimination, was to bar blacks from primary elections. The authority of the Constitution and Congress over primaries was thrown into serious doubt by the decision in *Newberry v. United States* (1921). In the Corrupt Practices Act of 1910 Congress had restricted campaign expenditures in securing nomination as well as in the election, and Truman H. Newberry was convicted of violating this statute in his successful campaign for a Michigan senate seat in 1918. The Supreme Court set aside his conviction, five justices holding that when the Constitution referred to election it meant the "final choice of an officer by the duly qualified electors," and that the primary was "in no real sense part of the manner of holding the election."

This ruling was weakened because one of the majority, Justice McKenna, thought that the constitutional situation would be different if Congress had passed the statute in question *after* the adoption of the Seventeenth Amendment providing for the direct election of senators.

In spite of the dubious majority in this case, Congress seemingly accepted this check on its powers and expressly excluded primary elections from the purview of the new Corrupt Practices Act passed in 1925. The Southern states also took the *Newberry* ruling as indicating that no constitutional protections covered primary elections, and so they set about discriminating against black voters in primaries in a perfectly open fashion. In 1923 the Texas legislature flatly prohibited blacks from voting in that state's Democratic primaries. When this statute was tested in *Nixon v. Herndon* (1927), the Supreme Court avoided a reconsideration of the constitutional status of primaries and their relationship to the Fifteenth Amendment. Instead, it invalidated the statute on the ground that it was a "direct and obvious infringement" of the equal protection clause in the Fourteenth Amendment.

The Texas legislature then came back with another law authorizing political parties in the state, through their state executive committees, to prescribe the qualifications for voting in their primaries. The theory of this statute was that what the state could not do directly because of the Fourteenth Amendment, it could authorize political parties to do. The Democratic state executive committee then excluded blacks from primary elections, but in *Nixon v. Condon* (1932) the Court held that the party committee had acted as the agent of the state, which made the action equivalent to that by the state itself, and so unconstitutional as an official denial of equal protection.

In neither of these decisions did the Court question the *Newberry* assertion that party primaries were outside the protection of the Constitution; it was only the fact that state legislation was the basis for party action in these cases which made the Fourteenth Amendment applicable. Taking advantage of this situation, the Texas Democratic party convention, immediately after the *Condon* decision, on its own authority and without any state legislation on the subject, adopted a resolution confining party membership to white citizens. By unanimous vote the Court concluded in *Grovey v. Townsend* (1935) that this action did not infringe the Fourteenth Amendment because it was taken by the party and not by the state.

The Supreme Court thus endorsed the view that political parties are private clubs uncontrolled by constitutional limitations on official action, and that the primaries they hold are constitutionally no part of the election process. Both of these propositions are so directly contrary to the obvious facts of party operation that they were bound to fall sooner or later of their own weight. The occasion for disposing of the *Newberry* doctrine came in 1941. *United States v. Classic* involved a prosecution brought by the Civil Rights Section of the U.S. Department of Justice against election officials in Louisiana who had tampered with the ballots in a primary where candidates for representative in Congress were chosen. The Court pointed out that Louisiana election laws made the primary "an integral part" of the process of electing congressmen, and that in fact the Democratic primary in Louisiana was "the only stage of the election procedure" where the voter's choice was of significance. The Court was thus taking a highly realistic view in its conclusion that the authority given Congress by Article I, section 4, "includes the authority to regulate primary elections when, as in this case, they are a step in the exercise by the people of their choice of representatives in Congress."

The *Classic* opinion did not even mention *Grovey v. Townsend,* but it clearly left the private club theory on very shaky ground. Consequently a new test case from Texas was begun, which resulted in a direct reversal of the *Grovey* decision by the Court in *Smith v. Allwright* (1944). The Court held that after the *Classic* ruling, party primaries could no longer be regarded as private affairs nor the parties conducting them as unaffected with public responsibilities. Noting that parties and party primaries in Texas were in fact regulated at many points by state statutes, the Court reasoned that a party required to follow these directions was "an agency of the State," and if it practiced discrimination against blacks that was "state action within the meaning of the Fifteenth Amendment." [10]

In *Terry v. Adams* (1953) the Court, with only one justice dissenting, applied the principle of *Smith v. Allwright* to invalidate the unofficial primaries conducted in a Texas county by the Jaybird party, a Democratic political organization that excluded blacks. The winners in the Jaybird primaries then entered the regular Democratic party primaries, where over a

[10] See *Rice v. Elmore* (1948) for an unsuccessful attempt to evade this ruling.

sixty-year period they were never defeated for county office. In fact, other candidates seldom filed. The Court ruled that the "Jaybird primary has become an integral part, indeed the only effective part, of the elective process that determines who shall rule and govern in the county," and consequently that the Fifteenth Amendment was applicable and must be observed.

JUDICIAL SUPERVISION OF ELECTIONS

The Supreme Court's initial position was one of great reluctance to get involved in electoral problems other than those raised by racial discrimination. As we have seen, in the *Newberry* case the Court even denied that primaries were part of the election process, and *Colegrove v. Green* warned judges to stay out of the "political thicket" of legislative apportionment.

Party Access to the Ballot

This same attitude governed the Court's reaction in *MacDougall v. Green* (1948). An Illinois statute required that for new political parties to nominate candidates for general election, they must submit petitions signed by at least 25,000 qualified voters, including 200 from each of fifty counties. The Court upheld this law, which obviously handicapped political independents and new parties, as justified by a legislative concern "to assure a proper diffusion of political initiative as between . . . thinly populated counties and those having concentrated masses."

But after *Baker v. Carr, Harper v. Virginia State Board of Elections*, and other decisions of the 1960s, the Court was more willing to accept responsibility for judging the equity of electoral systems. *Moore v. Ogilvie* (1969) held the same Illinois statute unconstitutional and the *MacDougall* decision "out of line with our recent apportionment cases." This statutory discrimination against the populous counties in favor of the rural sections was rejected as "hostile to the one man–one vote basis of our representative government."

Laws with the similar purpose of making it difficult for new parties to get on the ballot were in effect in many other states. In an aftermath of the 1980 Anderson presidential campaign, *Anderson v. Celebrezze* (1983) voided the Ohio early filing deadline for candidates who run without major party support. In 1968 *Williams v. Rhodes* had enabled the George Wallace American Independent Party to get on the Ohio ballot without filing the 433,100 petition signatures required by law. Since established parties were not required to secure any petition signatures, the Court held this was a discriminatory and unequal burden on the right to associate and to vote.

Ohio then revised its election code, one of the new provisions being a requirement that political parties file a loyalty oath. The Court in *Socialist Labor Party v. Gilligan* (1972) dismissed the case on the ground that the minor party involved had not yet suffered any injury, though Douglas, dissenting, thought the statute was "plainly unconstitutional." The Court did reach that conclusion unanimously in *Communist Party of Indiana v. Whitcomb* (1974) in a strong freedom of association defense by Justice Brennan, but the four Nixon appointees concurred only because the two major parties had been certified without filing the oath.

In *American Party of Texas v. White* (1974), the Court upheld requirements that minor parties nominate candidates by convention rather than by primary election and that they gain access to the ballot by submitting up to five hundred petition signatures. However, the Court invalidated the state failure to list minor parties on the absentee ballots.[11]

The Right of Candidacy

It can be contended that the right to be a candidate and the right to vote are two aspects of the same general political right. Although the Court did not explicitly discuss the right to candidacy in *Williams v. Rhodes*, it recognized that the right to vote is functionally dependent upon the ability of candidates to place their names before the electorate. In *Turner v. Fouche* (1970), the Court invalidated a state requirement that all members of a Georgia county school board be freeholders, saying that there is "a federal constitutional right to be considered for public service without a burden of indiviously discriminatory disqualifications."

Exorbitant filing fees were declared an unconstitutional burden on the right to candidacy in *Bullock v. Carter* (1972). Texas law imposed filing fees for local offices that ranged up to a maximum of $8,900, without alternative means of getting on the ballot. Such fees, the Court said, gave the election system a "patently exclusionary character," and other methods must be found of testing the seriousness of candidacies.

The California filing fees in *Lubin v. Panish* (1974) were more reasonable ($701.60 for Los Angeles county commissioner), but again there were no alternative methods of getting on the ballot; even a write-in candidate had to pay fees. The constitutional standard, said Chief Justice Burger, "is that ballot access must be genuinely open to all subject to reasonable requirements." The California system did not meet this test.

Storer v. Brown (1974) upheld a California law that denied a place on the ballot to independent candidates who had been registered members of recognized political parties within seventeen months prior to the election. The law was held to reflect a compelling state interest in protecting the electoral process from splintered parties and unrestrained factionalism.

---

[11]In *Jackson v. Ogilvie* (1971) the Court upheld an Illinois law requiring independent candidates and new parties to obtain more than 25,000 signatures on petitions to get on the ballot for statewide elections. But a quirk in the election laws that would have required more signatures than that for a local election in Chicago was voided in *Illinois State Board of Elections v. Socialist Workers Party* (1979).

The Closed Primary

Many states have a closed system of party primaries, whereby only enrolled members of a political party may vote in that party's primary. A related feature prevents voters from changing parties within specified time periods prior to elections. The New York closed primary system was upheld in *Rosario v. Rockefeller* (1973). The law there required voters to enroll in the party of their choice at least thirty days before the general election in order to vote in the next party primary, a time span of from eight to eleven months. The Court thought that this restriction on changing parties served the legitimate state purpose of avoiding disruptive party raiding. But a more restrictive law was declared unconstitutional in *Kusper v. Pontikes* (1973). Illinois prohibited a person from voting in a primary if he or she had voted in the primary of another political party within the preceding twenty-three months. This unnecessarily burdened a constitutionally protected liberty, Stewart said. The *Rosario* formula showed that a "less drastic means" of achieving the state's purpose was available.

Party Conventions and Campaigns

In the opening stages of the 1972 Democratic national convention, the credentials committee recommended unseating certain delegates from Illinois and California in a contest between pro- and anti-McGovern factions. The losing delegates went to court, and the Court of Appeals for the District of Columbia held the decisions of the credentials committee invalid. The Supreme Court in *O'Brien v. Brown* (1972) promptly reversed the lower court, ruling that a federal court had no authority "to interject itself into the deliberative processes of a national political convention."

A slate of anti-Daley delegates from Illinois was seated at the 1972 Democratic convention, in spite of an injunction issued by an Ilinois judge barring them from acting as delegates. Following the convention, they were held in contempt of the court order; but the Supreme Court in *Cousins v. Wigoda* (1975) held that a national party convention served a "pervasive national interest" superior to that of any state and that the Illinois judge's order had abridged the associational rights of the party and the party's right to determine the composition of its national convention.[12]

Democratic Party v. LaFollette (1981) ruled that the state of Wisconsin could not require the state's delegates to the Democratic national convention

---

[12]*Bode v. National Democratic Party* (1972) let stand a lower court's holding that delegates to the 1972 Democratic national convention need not be divided among the states on a strict basis of one Democrat, one vote. See "One Man, One Vote and Selection of Delegates to National Nominating Conventions," 37 UNIVERSITY OF CHICAGO LAW REVIEW 536 (1970). *Graham v. March Fong Eu* (1976) upheld without opinion the "winner-take-all" primary system used in California to select delegates to the Republican national convention. See also *Ripon Society, Inc. v. National Republican Party* (1976).

to cast their ballots for the winner of the state's presidential primary. The national parties, not the states, set the rules for choosing presidential candidates, and the Wisconsin law violated the party's First Amendment rights of political association.

In December 1979 the three national television networks refused to sell air time to President Carter's reelection committee on the ground that the presidential campaign had not yet begun. The Democrats appealed to the Federal Communications Commission, which ordered the networks to sell the time; and the Supreme Court agreed in *CBS v. FCC* (1981) on the ground that the First Amendment rights of candidates and voters outweighed the constitutional rights of broadcasters.

State Election Problems

In *Fortson v. Morris* (1966), the Court declined by a vote of five to four to extend the one-person, one-vote rationale to the situation of a disputed election for governor in Georgia. The state constitution provided that in case no candidate received a majority in the gubernatorial election, the state legislature should make the choice from between the two highest candidates. This occurred in the 1966 election, and the legislature chose Lester Maddox, though he had fewer votes than his principal opponent. The Court minority thought that legislative election of a governor violated the reasoning of the Georgia county unit case, *Gray v. Sanders,* but Justice Black for the majority ruled that *Gray* was only a "voting case" and had no relation to how a state could elect its governors.

Bond v. Floyd (1966) was a different matter. Julian Bond, a black activist, because of statements he had made in opposition to the war in Vietnam and the draft, was twice denied the seat to which he had been elected in the Georgia legislature. He was prepared to take the required oath to support the federal and state constitutions and he met the other stated qualifications, but the legislature excluded him on the ground that his remarks showed he could not take the oath "in good faith." The Supreme Court, relying primarily on the First Amendment, unanimously held that Bond was entitled to his seat. Warren said, "The manifest function of the First Amendment in a representative government requires that legislators be given the widest latitude to express their views on issues of policy."

In *Baker v. Carr* (1962) Brennan wrote: "Of course the mere fact that [a] suit seeks protection of a political right does not mean it presents a [nonjusticiable] political question." There are "political thickets" that courts will do well to avoid, but access to the franchise and fair election procedures present issues of constitutional rights fundamental to a practicing democracy.

Appendix:
Constitution of the United States

WE THE PEOPLE of the United States, in order to form a more perfect union, establish justice, insure domestic tranquillity, provide for the common defense, promote the general welfare, and secure the blessings of liberty to ourselves and our posterity, do ordain and establish this Constitution for the United States of America.

ARTICLE I

SECTION 1. All legislative powers herein granted shall be vested in a Congress of the United States, which shall consist of a Senate and House of Representatives.

SECTION 2. (1) The House of Representatives shall be composed of members chosen every second year by the people of the several States, and the electors in each State shall have the qualifications requisite for electors of the most numerous branch of the State legislature.

(2) No person shall be a Representative who shall not have attained to the age of twenty-five years, and been seven years a citizen of the United States, and who shall not, when elected, be an inhabitant of that State in which he shall be chosen.

(3) Representatives and direct taxes[1] shall be apportioned among the several States which may be included within this Union, according to their respective numbers, which shall be determined by adding to the whole number of free persons, including those bound to service for a term of years, and excluding Indians not taxed, three fifths of all other persons.[2] The actual enumeration shall be made within three years after the

[1] Modified as to income taxes by the 16th Amendment.
[2] Replaced by the 14th Amendment.

first meeting of the Congress of the United States, and within every subsequent term of ten years, in such manner as they shall by law direct. The number of Representatives shall not exceed one for every thirty thousand, but each State shall have at least one Representative; and until such enumeration shall be made, the State of New Hampshire shall be entitled to choose three, Massachusetts eight, Rhode Island and Providence Plantations one, Connecticut five, New York six, New Jersey four, Pennsylvania eight, Delaware one, Maryland six, Virginia ten, North Carolina five, South Carolina five, and Georgia three.

(4) When vacancies happen in the representation from any State, the executive authority thereof shall issue writs of election to fill such vacancies.

(5) The House of Representatives shall choose their Speaker and other officers; and shall have the sole power of impeachment.

SECTION 3. (1) The Senate of the United States shall be composed of two Senators from each State, chosen by the Legislature thereof,[3] for six years; and each Senator shall have one vote.

(2) Immediately after they shall be assembled in consequence of the first election, they shall be divided as equally as may be into three classes. The seats of the Senators of the first class shall be vacated at the expiration of the second year, of the second class at the expiration of the fourth year, and of the third class at the expiration of the sixth year, so that one third may be chosen every second year; and if vacancies happen by resignation, or otherwise, during the recess of the legislature of any State, the executive thereof may make temporary appointments until the next meeting of the legislature, which (see footnote 3) shall then fill such vacancies.

(3) No person shall be a Senator who shall not have attained to the age of thirty years, and been nine years a citizen of the United States, and who shall not, when elected, be an inhabitant of that State for which he shall be chosen.

(4) The Vice President of the United States shall be president of the Senate, but shall have no vote, unless they be equally divided.

(5) The Senate shall choose their other officers, and also a president pro tempore, in the absence of the Vice President, or when he shall exercise the office of President of the United States.

(6) The Senate shall have the sole power to try all impeachments. When sitting for that purpose, they shall be on oath or affirmation. When the President of the United States is tried, the Chief Justice shall preside: and no person shall be convicted without the concurrence of two thirds of the members present.

(7) Judgment in cases of impeachment shall not extend further than to removal from office, and disqualification to hold and enjoy any office of honor, trust or profit under the United States: but the party convicted shall nevertheless be liable and subject to indictment, trial, judgment and punishment, according to law.

SECTION 4. (1) The times, places and manner of holding elections for Senators and Representatives, shall be prescribed in each State by the legislature thereof; but the Congress may at any time by law make or alter such regulations, except as to the places of choosing Senators.

(2) The Congress shall assemble at least once in every year, and such meeting shall be on the first Monday in December, unless they shall by law appoint a different day.

[3] Modified by the 17th Amendment.

SECTION 5. (1) Each House shall be the judge of the elections, returns and qualifications of its own members, and a majority of each shall constitute a quorum to do business; but a smaller number may adjourn from day to day, and may be authorized to compel the attendance of absent members, in such manner, and under such penalties as each House may provide.

(2) Each House may determine the rules of its proceedings, punish its members for disorderly behavior, and, with the concurrence of two thirds, expel a member.

(3) Each House shall keep a journal of its proceedings, and from time to time publish the same, excepting such parts as may in their judgment require secrecy; and the yeas and nays of the members of either House on any question shall, at the desire of one fifth of those present, be entered on the journal.

(4) Neither House, during the session of Congress, shall, without the consent of the other, adjourn for more than three days, nor to any other place than that in which the two Houses shall be sitting.

SECTION 6. (1) The Senators and Representatives shall receive a compensation for their services, to be ascertained by law, and paid out of the Treasury of the United States. They shall in all cases, except treason, felony and breach of the peace, be privileged from arrest during their attendance at the session of their respective Houses, and in going to and returning from the same; and for any speech or debate in either House, they shall not be questioned in any other place.

(2) No Senator or Representative shall, during the time for which he was elected, be appointed to any civil office under the authority of the United States, which shall have been created, or the emoluments whereof shall have been increased during such time; and no person holding any office under the United States, shall be a member of either House during his continuance in office.

SECTION 7. (1) All bills for raising revenue shall originate in the House of Representatives; but the Senate may propose or concur with amendments as on other bills.

(2) Every bill which shall have passed the House of Representatives and the Senate, shall, before it become a law, be presented to the President of the United States; if he approve he shall sign it, but if not he shall return it, with his objections to that House in which it shall have originated, who shall enter the objections at large on their journal, and proceed to reconsider it. If after such reconsideration two thirds of that House shall agree to pass the bill, it shall be sent, together with the objections, to the other House, by which it shall likewise be reconsidered, and if approved by two thirds of that House, it shall become a law. But in all such cases the votes of both Houses shall be determined by yeas and nays, and the names of the persons voting for and against the bill shall be entered on the journal of each House respectively. If any bill shall not be returned by the President within ten days (Sundays excepted) after it shall have been presented to him, the same shall be a law, in like manner as if he had signed it, unless the Congress by their adjournment prevent its return, in which case it shall not be a law.

(3) Every order, resolution, or vote to which the concurrence of the Senate and House of Representatives may be necessary (except on a question of adjournment) shall be presented to the President of the United States; and before the same shall take effect, shall be approved by him, or being disapproved by him, shall be repassed by two thirds

of the Senate and House of Representatives, according to the rules and limitations prescribed in the case of a bill.

SECTION 8. (1) The Congress shall have power to lay and collect taxes, duties, imposts and excises, to pay the debts and provide for the common defense and general welfare of the United States; but all duties, imposts and excises shall be uniform throughout the United States;

(2) To borrow money on the credit of the United States;

(3) To regulate commerce with foreign nations, and among the several States, and with the Indian tribes;

(4) To establish an uniform rule of naturalization, and uniform laws on the subject of bankruptcies throughout the United States;

(5) To coin money, regulate the value thereof, and of foreign coin, and fix the standard of weights and measures;

(6) To provide for the punishment of counterfeiting the securities and current coin of the United States;

(7) To establish post offices and post roads;

(8) To promote the progress of science and useful arts, by securing for limited times to authors and inventors the exclusive right to their respective writings and discoveries;

(9) To constitute tribunals inferior to the Supreme Court;

(10) To define and punish piracies and felonies committed on the high seas, and offenses against the law of nations;

(11) To declare war, grant letters of marque and reprisal, and make rules concerning captures on land and water;

(12) To raise and support armies, but no appropriation of money to that use shall be for a longer term than two years;

(13) To provide and maintain a navy;

(14) To make rules for the government and regulation of the land and naval forces;

(15) To provide for calling forth the militia to execute the laws of the Union, suppress insurrections and repel invasions;

(16) To provide for organizing, arming, and disciplining the militia, and for governing such part of them as may be employed in the service of the United States, reserving to the States respectively, the appointment of the officers, and the authority of training the militia according to the discipline prescribed by Congress;

(17) To exercise exclusive legislation in all cases whatsoever, over such district (not exceeding ten miles square) as may, by cession of particular States, and the acceptance of Congress, become the seat of the government of the United States,[4] and to exercise like authority over all places purchased by the consent of the legislature of the State in which the same shall be, for the erection of forts, magazines, arsenals, dockyards, and other needful buildings; and

(18) To make all laws which shall be necessary and proper for carrying into execution the foregoing powers, and all other powers vested by this Constitution in the government of the United States, or in any department or officer thereof.

[4] Modified by the 23rd Amendment.

SECTION 9. (1) The migration or importation of such persons as any of the States now existing shall think proper to admit, shall not be prohibited by the Congress prior to the year one thousand eight hundred and eight, but a tax or duty may be imposed on such importation, not exceeding ten dollars for each person.

(2) The privilege of the writ of habeas corpus shall not be suspended, unless when in cases of rebellion or invasion the public safety may require it.

(3) No bill of attainder or ex post facto law shall be passed.

(4) No capitation, or other direct, tax shall be laid, unless in proportion to the census or enumeration herein before directed to be taken.[5]

(5) No tax or duty shall be laid on articles exported from any State.

(6) No preference shall be given by any regulation of commerce or revenue to the ports of one State over those of another: nor shall vessels bound to, or from, one State, be obliged to enter, clear, or pay duties in another.

(7) No money shall be drawn from the Treasury, but in consequence of appropriations made by law; and a regular statement and account of the receipts and expenditures of all public money shall be published from time to time.

(8) No title of nobility shall be granted by the United States: and no person holding any office of profit or trust under them, shall, without the consent of the Congress, accept of any present, emolument, office, or title, of any kind whatever, from any king, prince, or foreign State.

SECTION 10. (1) No State shall enter into any treaty, alliance, or confederation; grant letters of marque and reprisal; coin money; emit bills of credit; make anything but gold and silver coin a tender in payment of debts; pass any bill of attainder, ex post facto law, or law impairing the obligation of contracts, or grant any title of nobility.

(2) No State shall, without the consent of the Congress, lay any imposts or duties on imports or exports, except what may be absolutely necessary for executing its inspection laws; and the net produce of all duties and imposts, laid by any State on imports or exports, shall be for the use of the Treasury of the United States; and all such laws shall be subject to the revision and control of the Congress.

(3) No State shall, without the consent of Congress, lay any duty of tonnage, keep troops, or ships of war in time of peace, enter into any agreement or compact with another State, or with a foreign power, or engage in war, unless actually invaded, or in such imminent danger as will not admit of delay.

ARTICLE II

SECTION 1. (1) The executive power shall be vested in a President of the United States of America. He shall hold his office during the term of four years,[6] and, together with the Vice President, chosen for the same term, be elected, as follows:

(2) Each State shall appoint, in such manner as the legislature thereof may direct, a number of electors, equal to the whole number of Senators and Representatives to which the State may be entitled in the Congress: but no Senator or Representative, or person

[5] Modified by the 16th Amendment.
[6] Modified by the 22nd Amendment.

holding an office of trust or profit under the United States, shall be appointed an elector.

The electors[7] shall meet in their respective States, and vote by ballot for two persons, of whom one at least shall not be an inhabitant of the same State with themselves. And they shall make a list of all the persons voted for, and of the number of votes for each; which list they shall sign and certify, and transmit sealed to the seat of the government of the United States, directed to the president of the Senate. The president of the Senate shall, in the presence of the Senate and House of Representatives, open all the certificates, and the votes shall then be counted. The person having the greatest number of votes shall be the President, if such number be a majority of the whole number of electors appointed; and if there be more than one who have such majority, and have an equal number of votes, then the House of Representatives shall immediately choose by ballot one of them for President; and if no person have a majority, then from the five highest on the list the said House shall in like manner choose the President. But in choosing the President, the votes shall be taken by States, the representation from each State having one vote; a quorum for this purpose shall consist of a member or members from two thirds of the States, and a majority of all the States shall be necessary to a choice. In every case, after the choice of the President, the person having the greatest number of votes of the electors shall be the Vice President. But if there should remain two or more who have equal votes, the Senate shall choose from them by ballot the Vice President.

(3) The Congress may determine the time of choosing the electors, and the day on which they shall give their votes; which day shall be the same throughout the United States.

(4) No person except a natural born citizen, or a citizen of the United States, at the time of the adoption of this Constitution, shall be eligible to the office of President; neither shall any person be eligible to that office who shall not have attained to the age of thirty five years, and been fourteen years a resident within the United States.

(5) In the case of the removal of the President from office, or of his death, resignation, or inability to discharge the powers and duties of the said office, the same shall devolve on the Vice President, and the Congress may by law provide for the case of removal, death, resignation, or inability, both of the President and Vice President, declaring what officer shall then act as President, and such officer shall act accordingly, until the disability be removed, or a President shall be elected.[8]

(6) The President shall, at stated times, receive for his services, a compensation, which shall neither be increased nor diminished during the period for which he shall have been elected, and he shall not receive within that period any other emolument from the United States, or any of them.

(7) Before he enter on the execution of his office, he shall take the following oath or affirmation:—"I do solemnly swear (or affirm) that I will faithfully execute the office of President of the United States and will to the best of my ability, preserve, protect and defend the Constitution of the United States."

SECTION 2. (1) The President shall be commander in chief of the army and navy of the United States, and of the militia of the several States, when called into the actual

---

[7] This paragraph was replaced in 1804 by the 12th Amendment.
[8] Replaced by the 25th Amendment.

service of the United States; he may require the opinion, in writing, of the principal officer in each of the executive departments, upon any subject relating to the duties of their respective offices, and he shall have power to grant reprieves and pardons for offenses against the United States, except in cases of impeachment.

(2) He shall have power, by and with the advice and consent of the Senate, to make treaties, provided two thirds of the Senators present concur; and he shall nominate, and by and with the advice and consent of the Senate, shall appoint ambassadors, other public ministers and consuls, judges of the Supreme Court, and all other officers of the United States, whose appointments are not herein otherwise provided for, and which shall be established by law: but the Congress may by law vest the appointment of such inferior officers, as they think proper, in the President alone, in the courts of law, or in the heads of departments.

(3) The President shall have power to fill up all vacancies that may happen during the recess of the Senate, by granting commissions which shall expire at the end of their next session.

SECTION 3. He shall from time to time give to the Congress information of the state of the Union, and recommend to their consideration such measures as he shall judge necessary and expedient; he may, on extraordinary occasions, convene both houses, or either of them, and in case of disagreement between them, with respect to the time of adjournment, he may adjourn them to such time as he shall think proper; he shall receive ambassadors and other public ministers; he shall take care that the laws be faithfully executed, and shall commission all the officers of the United States.

SECTION 4. The President, Vice President and all civil officers of the United States, shall be removed from office on impeachment for, and conviction of, treason, bribery, or other high crimes and misdemeanors.

ARTICLE III

SECTION 1. The judicial power of the United States, shall be vested in one Supreme Court, and in such inferior courts as the Congress may from time to time ordain and establish. The judges, both of the Supreme and inferior courts, shall hold their offices during good behavior, and shall, at stated times, receive for their services, a compensation, which shall not be diminished during their continuance in office.

SECTION 2. (1) The judicial power shall extend to all cases, in law and equity, arising under this Constitution, the laws of the United States, and treaties made, or which shall be made, under their authority;—to all cases affecting ambassadors, other public ministers and consuls;—to all cases of admiralty and maritime jurisdiction;—to controversies to which the United States shall be a party;—to controversies between two or more States;—between a State and citizens of another State;[9]—between citizens of different States;—between citizens of the same State claiming lands under grants of different States, and between a State, or the citizens thereof, and foreign States, citizens or subjects.

(2) In all cases affecting ambassadors, other public ministers and consuls, and those in which a State shall be party, the Supreme Court shall have original jurisdiction. In all

[9] Restricted by the 11th Amendment.

the other cases before mentioned, the Supreme Court shall have appellate jurisdiction, both as to law and fact, with such exceptions, and under such regulations as the Congress shall make.

(3) The trial of all crimes, except in cases of impeachment, shall be by jury; and such trial shall be held in the State where the said crimes shall have been committed: but when not committed within any State, the trial shall be at such place or places as the Congress may by law have directed.

SECTION 3. (1) Treason against the United States, shall consist only in levying war against them, or in adhering to their enemies, giving them aid and comfort. No person shall be convicted of treason unless on the testimony of two witnesses to the same overt act, or on confession in open court.

(2) The Congress shall have power to declare the punishment of treason, but no attainder of treason shall work corruption of blood, or forfeiture except during the life of the person attainted.

ARTICLE IV

SECTION 1. Full faith and credit shall be given in each State to the public acts, records, and judicial proceedings of every other State. And the Congress may by general laws prescribe the manner in which such acts, records and procedings shall be proved, and the effect thereof.

SECTION 2. (1) The citizens of each State shall be entitled to all privileges and immunities of citizens in the several States.

(2) A person charged in any State with treason, felony, or other crime, who shall flee from justice, and be found in another State, shall on demand of the executive authority of the State from which he fled, be delivered up, to be removed to the State having jurisdiction of the crime.

(3) No person held to service or labor in one State, under the laws thereof, escaping into another, shall, in consequence of any law or regulation therein, be discharged from such service or labor, but shall be delivered up on claim of the party to whom such service or labor may be due.

SECTION 3. (1) New States may be admitted by the Congress into this Union; but no new State shall be formed or erected within the jurisdiction of any other State; nor any State be formed by the junction of two or more States, or parts of States, without the consent of the legislatures of the States concerned as well as of the Congress.

(2) The Congress shall have power to dispose of and make all needful rules and regulations respecting the territory or other property belonging to the United States; and nothing in this Constitution shall be so construed as to prejudice any claims of the United States, or of any particular State.

SECTION 4. The United States shall guarantee to every State in this Union a republican form of government, and shall protect each of them against invasion; and on application of the legislature, or of the executive (when the legislature cannot be convened) against domestic violence.

ARTICLE V

The Congress, whenever two thirds of both Houses shall deem it necessary, shall propose amendments to this Constitution, or, on the application of the legislatures of two thirds of the several States, shall call a convention for proposing amendments, which, in either case, shall be valid to all intents and purposes, as part of this Constitution, when ratified by the legislatures of three fourths of the several States, or by conventions in three fourths thereof, as the one or the other mode of ratification may be proposed by the Congress; Provided that no amendment which may be made prior to the year one thousand eight hundred and eight shall in any manner affect the first and fourth clauses in the ninth section of the first article; and that no State, without its consent, shall be deprived of its equal suffrage in the Senate.

ARTICLE VI

SECTION 1. All debts contracted and engagements entered into, before the adoption of this Constitution, shall be as valid against the United States under this Constitution, as under the Confederation.

SECTION 2. This Constitution, and the laws of the United States which shall be made in pursuance thereof; and all treaties made, or which shall be made, under the authority of the United States, shall be the supreme law of the land; and the judges in every State shall be bound thereby, anything in the constitution or laws of any State to the contrary notwithstanding.

SECTION 3. The Senators and Representatives before mentioned, and the members of the several State legislatures, and all executive and judicial officers, both of the United States and of the several States, shall be bound by oath or affirmation to support this Constitution; but no religious test shall ever be required as a qualification to any office or public trust under the United States.

ARTICLE VII

The ratification of the conventions of nine States, shall be sufficient for the establishment of this Constitution between the States so ratifying the same.

done in Convention by the unanimous consent of the States present the seventeenth day of September in the year of our Lord one thousand seven hundred and eighty-seven, and of the independence of the United States of America the twelfth. In witness whereof we have hereunto subscribed our names.

Go Washington—
Presidt. and Deputy from Virginia

Articles in addition to and amendment of the Constitution of the United States of America, proposed by Congress, and ratified by the legislatures of the several States, pursuant to the fifth article of the original Constitution.

ARTICLE I[10]

Congress shall make no law respecting an establishment of religion, or prohibiting the free exercise thereof; or abridging the freedom of speech, or of the press; or the right of the people peaceably to assemble, and to petition the government for a redress of grievances.

ARTICLE II

A well regulated militia, being necessary to the security of a free State, the right of the people to keep and bear arms, shall not be infringed.

ARTICLE III

No soldier shall, in time of peace be quartered in any house, without the consent of the owner, nor in time of war, but in a manner to be prescribed by law.

ARTICLE IV

The right of the people to be secure in their persons, houses, papers, and effects, against unreasonable searches and seizures, shall not be violated, and no warrants shall issue, but upon probable cause, supported by oath or affirmation, and particularly describing the place to be searched, and the persons or things to be seized.

ARTICLE V

No person shall be held to answer for a capital, or otherwise infamous crime, unless on a presentment or indictment of a grand jury, except in cases arising in the land or naval forces, or in the militia, when in actual service in time of war or public danger; nor shall any person be subject for the same offense to be twice put in jeopardy of life or limb; nor shall be compelled in any criminal case to be a witness against himself, nor be deprived of life, liberty, or property, without due process of law; nor shall private property be taken for public use, without just compensation.

ARTICLE VI

In all criminal prosecutions the accused shall enjoy the right to a speedy and public trial, by an impartial jury of the State and district wherein the crime shall have been committed, which district shall have been previously ascertained by law, and to be informed of the nature and cause of the accusation; to be confronted with the witnesses

[10] The first ten Amendments were adopted in 1791.

against him; to have compulsory process for obtaining witnesses in his favor, and to have the assistance of counsel for his defense.

ARTICLE VII

In suits at common law, where the value in controversy shall exceed twenty dollars, the right of trial by jury shall be preserved, and no fact tried by a jury shall be otherwise reexamined in any court of the United States, than according to the rules of the common law.

ARTICLE VIII

Excessive bail shall not be required, nor excessive fines imposed, nor cruel and unusual punishments inflicted.

ARTICLE IX

The enumeration in the Constitution, of certain rights, shall not be construed to deny or disparage others retained by the people.

ARTICLE X

The powers not delegated to the United States by the Constitution, nor prohibited by it to the States, are reserved to the States respectively, or to the people.

ARTICLE XI[11]

The judicial power of the United States shall not be construed to extend to any suit in law or equity, commenced or prosecuted against one of the United States by citizens of another State, or by citizens or subjects of any foreign State.

ARTICLE XII[12]

The electors shall meet in their respective States and vote by ballot for President and Vice-President, one of whom, at least, shall not be an inhabitant of the same State with themselves; they shall name in their ballots the person voted for as President, and in distinct ballots the person voted for as Vice-President, and they shall make

[11] Ratified in 1795; proclaimed in 1798.
[12] Adopted in 1804.

distinct lists of all persons voted for as President, and of all persons voted for as Vice-President, and of the number of votes for each, which lists they shall sign and certify, and transmit sealed to the seat of the government of the United States, directed to the president of the Senate;—The president of the Senate shall, in the presence of the Senate and House of Representatives, open all the certificates and the votes shall then be counted;—The person having the greatest number of votes for President, shall be the President, if such number be a majority of the whole number of electors appointed; and if no person have such majority, then from the persons having the highest numbers not exceeding three on the list of those voted for as President, the House of Representatives shall choose immediately, by ballot, the President. But in choosing the President, the votes shall be taken by States, the representation from each State having one vote; a quorum for this purpose shall consist of a member or members from two thirds of the States, and a majority of all the States shall be necessary to a choice. And if the House of Representatives shall not choose a President whenever the right of choice shall devolve upon them, before the fourth day of March next following, then the Vice-President shall act as President, as in the case of the death or other constitutional disability of the President.—The person having the greatest number of votes as Vice-President, shall be the Vice-President, if such number be a majority of the whole number of electors appointed, and if no person have a majority, then from the two highest numbers on the list, the Senate shall choose the Vice-President; a quorum for the purpose shall consist of two thirds of the whole number of Senators, and a majority of the whole number shall be necessary to a choice. But no person constitutionally ineligible to the office of President shall be eligible to that of Vice-President of the United States.

ARTICLE XIII[13]

SECTION 1. Neither slavery nor involuntary servitude, except as a punishment for crime whereof the party shall have been duly convicted, shall exist within the United States, or any place subject to their jurisdiction.

SECTION 2. Congress shall have power to enforce this article by appropriate legislation.

ARTICLE XIV[14]

SECTION 1. All persons born or naturalized in the United States, and subject to the jurisdiction thereof, are citizens of the United States and of the State wherein they reside. No State shall make or enforce any law which shall abridge the privileges or immunities of citizens of the United States; nor shall any State deprive any person of life, liberty, or property, without due process of law; now deny to any person within its jurisdiction the equal protection of the laws.

SECTION 2. Representatives shall be apportioned among the several States according to their respective numbers, counting the whole number of persons in each

[13] Adopted in 1865.
[14] Adopted in 1868.

State, excluding Indians not taxed. But when the right to vote at any election for the choice of electors for President and Vice President of the United States, Representatives in Congress, the executive and judicial offices of a State, or the members of the legislature thereof, is denied to any of the male inhabitants of such State, being twenty-one years of age, and citizens of the United States, or in any way abridged, except for participation in rebellion, or other crime, the basis of representation therein shall be reduced in the proportion which the number of such male citizens shall bear to the whole number of male citizens twenty-one years of age in such State.

SECTION 3. No person shall be a Senator or Representative in Congress, or elector of President and Vice President, or hold any office, civil or military, under the United States, or under any State, who, having previously taken an oath, as a member of Congress, or as an officer of the United States, or as a member of any State legislature, or as an executive or judicial officer of any State, to support the Constitution of the United States, shall have engaged in insurrection or rebellion against the same, or given aid or comfort to the enemies thereof. But Congress may by a vote of two thirds of each House, remove such disability.

SECTION 4. The validity of the public debt of the United States, authorized by law, including debts incurred for payment of pensions and bounties for services in suppressing insurrection or rebellion, shall not be questioned. But neither the United States nor any State shall assume or pay any debt or obligation incurred in aid of insurrection or rebellion against the United States, or any claim for the loss or emancipation of any slave; but all such debts, obligations and claims shall be held illegal and void.

SECTION 5. The Congress shall have power to enforce, by appropriate legislation, the provisions of this article.

ARTICLE XV[15]

SECTION 1. The right of citizens of the United States to vote shall not be denied or abridged by the United States or by any State on account of race, color, or previous condition of servitude.

SECTION 2. The Congress shall have power to enforce this article by appropriate legislation.

ARTICLE XVI[16]

The Congress shall have power to lay and collect taxes on incomes, from whatever source derived, without apportionment among the several States, and without regard to any census or enumeration.

[15] Adopted in 1870.
[16] Adopted in 1913.

ARTICLE XVII

The Senate of the United States shall be composed of two Senators from each State, elected by the people thereof, for six years; and each Senator shall have one vote. The electors in each State shall have the qualifications requisite for electors of the most numerous branch of the State legislatures.

When vacancies happen in the representation of the State in the Senate, the executive authority of such State shall issue writs of election to fill such vacancies: *Provided,* That the legislature of any State may empower the executive thereof to make temporary appointments until the people fill the vacancies by election as the legislature may direct.

This amendment shall not be so construed as to affect the election or term of any Senator chosen before it becomes valid as part of the Constitution.

ARTICLE XVIII[17]

SECTION 1. After one year from the ratification of this article the manufacture, sale, or transportation of intoxicating liquors within, the importation thereof into, or the exportation thereof from the United States and all territory subject to the jurisdiction thereof for beverage purposes is hereby prohibited.

SECTION 2. The Congress and the several States shall have concurrent power to enforce this article by appropriate legislation.

SECTION 3. This article shall be inoperative unless it shall have been ratified as an amendment to the Constitution by the legislatures of the several States, as provided in the Constitution, within seven years from the date of the submission hereof to the States by the Congress.

ARTICLE XIX[18]

The right of citizens of the United States to vote shall not be denied or abridged by the United States or by any State on account of sex.

The Congress shall have power to enforce this article by appropriate legislation.

ARTICLE XX[19]

SECTION 1. The terms of the President and Vice President shall end at noon on the 20th day of January, and the terms of Senators and Representatives at noon on the 3rd day of January, of the years in which such terms would have ended if this article had not been ratified; and the terms of their successors shall then begin.

---

[17] Adopted in 1919. Repealed by Article XXI.
[18] Adopted in 1920.
[19] Adopted in 1933.

SECTION 2. The Congress shall assemble at least once in every year, and such meeting shall begin at noon on the 3rd day of January, unless they shall by law appoint a different day.

SECTION 3. If, at the time fixed for the beginning of the term of the President, the President elect shall have died, the Vice President elect shall become President. If a President shall not have been chosen before the time fixed for the beginning of his term, or if the President elect shall have failed to qualify, then the Vice President elect shall act as President until a President shall have qualified, and the Congress may by law provide for the case wherein neither a President elect nor a Vice President elect shall have qualified, declaring who shall then act as President, or the manner in which one who is to act shall be selected, and such person shall act accordingly until a President or Vice President shall have qualified.

SECTION 4. The Congress may by law provide for the case of the death of any of the persons from whom the House of Representatives may choose a President whenever the right of choice shall have devolved upon them, and for the case of the death of any of the persons from whom the Senate may choose a Vice President whenever the right of choice shall have devolved upon them.

SECTION 5. Sections 1 and 2 shall take effect on the 15th day of October following the ratification of this article.

SECTION 6. This article shall be inoperative unless it shall have been ratified as an amendment to the Constitution by the legislatures of three-fourths of the several States within seven years from the date of its submission.

ARTICLE XXI[20]

SECTION 1. The eighteenth article of amendment to the Constitution of the United States is hereby repealed.

SECTION 2. The transportation or importation into any State, Territory or Possession of the United States for delivery or use therein of intoxicating liquors in violation of the laws thereof is hereby prohibited.

SECTION 3. This article shall be inoperative unless it shall have been ratified as an amendment to the Constitution by conventions in the several States, as provided in the Constitution, within seven years from the date of submission hereof to the States by the Congress.

ARTICLE XXII[21]

SECTION 1. No person shall be elected to the office of the President more than twice, and no person who has held the office of President, or acted as President for more than two years of a term to which some other person was elected President shall be elected to the office of the President more than once. But this Article shall not apply to any person holding the office of President when this Article was proposed by the

[20] Adopted in 1933.
[21] Adopted in 1951.

Congress, and shall not prevent any person who may be holding the office of President, or acting as President, during the term within which this Article becomes operative from holding the office of President or acting as President during the remainder of such term.

SECTION 2. This Article shall be inoperative unless it shall have been ratified as an amendment to the Constitution by the legislatures of three-fourths of the several States within seven years from the date of its submission to the States by the Congress.

ARTICLE XXIII[22]

SECTION 1. The District constituting the seat of Government of the United States shall appoint in such manner as the Congress may direct:

A number of electors of President and Vice-President equal to the whole number of Senators and Representatives in Congress to which the district would be entitled if it were a State, but in no event more than the least populous state; they shall be in addition to those appointed by the states, but they shall be considered, for the purposes of the election of President and Vice-President, to be electors appointed by a state; and they shall meet in the District and perform such duties as provided by the twelfth article of amendment.

SECTION 2. The Congress shall have power to enforce this article by appropriate legislation.

ARTICLE XXIV[23]

SECTION 1. The right of citizens of the United States to vote in any primary or other election for President or Vice-President, for electors for President or Vice-President, or for Senator or Representative in Congress, shall not be denied or abridged by the United States or any state by reason of failure to pay any poll tax or other tax.

SECTION 2. The Congress shall have power to enforce this article by appropriate legislation.

ARTICLE XXV[24]

SECTION 1. In case of the removal of the President from office or his death or resignation, the Vice President shall become President.

SECTION 2. Whenever there is a vacancy in the office of the Vice President, the President shall nominate a Vice President who shall take the office upon confirmation by a majority vote of both houses of Congress.

[22] Adopted in 1961.
[23] Adopted in 1964.
[24] Adopted in 1967.

SECTION 3. Whenever the President transmits to the President pro tempore of the Senate and the Speaker of the House of Representatives his written declaration that he is unable to discharge the powers and duties of his office, and until he transmits to them a written declaration to the contrary, such powers and duties shall be discharged by the Vice President as Acting President.

SECTION 4. Whenever the Vice President and a majority of either the principal officers of the executive departments, or of such other body as Congress may by law provide, transmit to the President pro tempore of the Senate and the Speaker of the House of Representatives their written declaration that the President is unable to discharge the powers and duties of his office, the Vice President shall immediately assume the powers and duties of the office as Acting President.

Thereafter, when the President transmits to the President pro tempore of the Senate and the Speaker of the House of Representatives his written declaration that no inability exists, he shall resume the powers and duties of his office unless the Vice President and a majority of either the principal officers of the executive department, or of such other body as Congress may by law provide, transmit within four days to the President pro tempore of the Senate and the Speaker of the House of Representatives their written declaration that the President is unable to discharge the powers and duties of his office. Thereupon Congress shall decide the issue, assembling within 48 hours for that purpose if not in session. If the Congress, within 21 days after receipt of the latter written declaration, or, if Congress is not in session, within 21 days after Congress is required to assemble, determines by two-thirds vote of both houses that the President is unable to discharge the powers and duties of his office, the Vice President shall continue to discharge the same as Acting President; otherwise, the President shall resume the powers and duties of his office.

ARTICLE XXVI[25]

SECTION 1. The right of citizens of the United States, who are eighteen years of age, or older, to vote shall not be denied or abridged by the United States or by any state on account of age.

SECTION 2. The Congress shall have the power to enforce this article by appropriate legislation.

PROPOSED AMENDMENTS

Representation of the District of Columbia in the Congress

SECTION 1. For purposes of representation in the Congress, election of the President and Vice-President, and Article V of this Constitution, the District constituting the seat of government of the United States shall be treated as though it were a State.

[25] Adopted in 1971.

SECTION 2. The exercise of the rights and powers conferred under this article shall be by the people of the District constituting the seat of government, and as shall be provided by the Congress.

SECTION 3. The twenty-third article of amendment to the Constitution of the United States is hereby repealed.

SECTION 4. This article shall be inoperative, unless it shall have been ratified as an amendment to the Constitution by the legislatures of three-fourths of the several States within seven years from the date of its submission. [Proposed by Congress on August 22, 1978.]

Equal Rights Amendment

Proposed by Congress on March 22, 1972 with a seven-year period for ratification specified in the resolution proposing the amendment. When it appeared that three-fourths of the state legislatures would not ratify by March 22, 1979, Congress extended the period for ratification to June 30, 1982, but efforts to secure sufficient additional ratifications were unsuccessful and the amendment lapsed.]

SECTION 1. Equality of rights under the law shall not be denied or abridged by the United States or by any state on account of sex.

SECTION 2. The Congress shall have the power to enforce, by appropriate legislation, the provisions of this article.

SECTION 3. This amendment shall take effect two years after the date of ratification.

Index of Cases

Name and Subject Index